C000062122

Style, Wit and Word-Play

To Mark & Diane

Love from

Tao Tao

Chang Tsin

27 July, 2012

Style, Wit and Word-Play:
Essays in Translation Studies
in Memory of David Hawkes

Edited by

Tao Tao Liu, Laurence K. P. Wong
and Chan Sin-wai

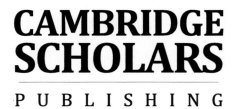

**CAMBRIDGE
SCHOLARS**

P U B L I S H I N G

Style, Wit and Word-Play:
Essays in Translation Studies in Memory of David Hawkes,
Edited by Tao Tao Liu, Laurence K. P. Wong and Chan Sin-wai

This book first published 2012

Cambridge Scholars Publishing

12 Back Chapman Street, Newcastle upon Tyne, NE6 2XX, UK

British Library Cataloguing in Publication Data
A catalogue record for this book is available from the British Library

Copyright © 2012 by Tao Tao Liu, Laurence K. P. Wong and Chan Sin-wai and contributors

All rights for this book reserved. No part of this book may be reproduced, stored in a retrieval system,
or transmitted, in any form or by any means, electronic, mechanical, photocopying, recording or
otherwise, without the prior permission of the copyright owner.

ISBN (10): 1-4438-3571-4, ISBN (13): 978-1-4438-3571-8

TABLE OF CONTENTS

PREFACE

When we think of the translation of Chinese literature into English, many of us will call to mind certain outstanding practitioners in this art. David Hawkes (1923-2009) was one of them, a distinguished translator and interpreter of classical Chinese literature. To translate a literary work the translator must do more than understand the original work and its nuances; he or she must also be able to turn the original into what is virtually a new work in a different language, a new work that engages with a new set of readers within the culture and expectations of a different world. Few translators have been able to do this convincingly. David Hawkes was one of the few. He was steeped in the Chinese language and in Chinese culture, and was especially familiar with the texts of the Chinese classics. At the same time he was a widely read humanist, at home in the literatures and cultures of Europe.

There is a growing interest in translated literature in the English-speaking world. When The Chinese University of Hong Kong decided to organize a conference on the translation of Chinese literature into English, we hoped that David Hawkes, who was then living in Oxford, might be able to join us in person. Regrettably, although he supported the idea and was tempted to come, he was already in poor health. He died before the conference actually took place. The conference which forms the basis of the articles in this book was dedicated to his memory.

David was educated at the University of Oxford and was the Oxford Professor of Chinese from 1960 to 1971. He taught and supervised many students, some of whom went on to teach all over the world. When he himself resigned from the Chair in order to devote himself to translating the *Hongloumeng*, he was made a Senior Research Fellow at All Souls College. In subsequent years he and his wife Jean retired to the hills of Wales. His outlook was tempered in the Oxford tradition of humanities. It was therefore natural that we should gather together for the conference several participants with an Oxford background. These included his collaborator in the *Hongloumeng* enterprise, friend and son-in-law, John Minford, who graduated from Oxford and has since moved on to other pastures; Mark Elvin, who was once his colleague; Allan Barr and Chloë Starr, both of whom completed their doctorates at Oxford; and Tao Tao Liu, who was David's pupil, colleague and friend. These and others formed the nucleus. To them were added a number of other scholars in the field, such as Laurence Wong and Fan Shengyu. Their first part of the book consists of articles on Hawkes' translations, with especial attention being paid to *The Story of the Stone*, his superb translation of *Hongloumeng*. The rest of the book contains articles on various other aspects of literary translation from the Chinese by John C. Y. Wang, Chan Sin-wai and Kuo-ch'ing Tu.

It is fitting that the publication of this book should coincide with the establishment of the new Translation Archive at The Chinese University of Hong Kong. David's own papers, his correspondence and working notes, will be deposited in the new Archive, which will be an important resource for all those interested in translation studies.

We are grateful to the Cambridge Scholars Press for publishing this volume. We owe a special debt of thanks to Professor John Minford for going over the entire proof and making many valuable suggestions. We would also thank Rosaline Chan Miu Fong, Florence Li Wing Yee and other colleagues at The Chinese University who helped organize the conference and especially Miranda Lui Wing Man for her great efforts in the production of the manuscript for publication through all its stages.

—Tao Tao Liu, Laurence K. P. Wong and Chan Sin-wai

INTRODUCTION
"STYLE, WIT AND WORD-PLAY" – REMEMBERING DAVID HAWKES (1923-2009)

TAO TAO LIU
INSTITUTE FOR CHINESE STUDIES
OXFORD UNIVERSITY

We remember David Hawkes as an outstanding scholar of Chinese literature and the translator of one of its classics, the *Hongloumeng*《紅樓夢》, the novel that he named as *The Story of the Stone* in English, a translation in five volumes that he completed with John Minford. David Hawkes was not only a translator but an interpreter of Chinese literature. As a scholar, his career included being professor of Chinese at Oxford until he resigned to devote himself to the task of translating *The Story of the Stone*. The appearance of his translation of Cao Xueqin's novel sealed his reputation.[1] Much praise has been already heaped on this work, and studies have already been written about it. More appears in this book, so there is no need for me to repeat what has been said already. He was a highly cultured person, and his works show an understanding of Chinese poetry and the arts that was based on a deep knowledge of his own European culture. As one of the editors of this volume, and a former pupil and friend of David Hawkes, I now offer an introduction to him as a translator.

Even before the publication of the *Stone*, Hawkes had shown interest in the translation of Chinese literature into English. Several of his essays, articles and book reviews, collected and edited as *Classical, Modern and Humane* by John Minford and another of his pupils, Wong Siu-kit, discuss the subject.[2] They show that he had throughout his career thought deeply about translating Chinese literature into English, thoughts often expressed with wit and style. Two main ideas stand out, one is the eternal conflict between the production of "beautiful" translations by poets and that of

---

[1] The first three volumes were translated by David Hawkes (Harmondsworth: Penguin Classics, Vol. 1, 1973; Vol. 2, 1977; Vol. 3, 1980).

[2] Hong Kong: The Chinese University Press, 1989.

philologists who know the language but may turn the beautiful original into "dross."[3] Hawkes' own experience of thinking about and working on translations meant that he understood this quandary, and difficulties facing translators of literature. The other great challenge is how to convey in the translation of poetry some idea of the original prosody. He was always acutely aware of the importance of prosody to Chinese poetry, and how Chinese poets employed different prosodic forms and used them for different purposes. He was under no illusion about the efforts of many to translate Chinese poetry into rhymed English poetry. But at the same time he was saddened that many readers who knew nothing about Chinese had the impression that Chinese poets wrote in versions of *vers libre* whilst the richness and the skill of dealing with complex prosody passed them by. He felt that although *vers libre* is the default position for most translators of Chinese poetry, yet a good translation into rhymed English poetry, rare as that might be, takes the prize. His admiration for Arthur Waley was heightened by one of the few poems that Waley successfully translated into rhymed English poetry. He wished there were more.[4]

Hawkes not only translated the *Hongloumeng* from the Chinese, but had also published other translations: the ancient Chinese poem, the *Chuci* 《楚辭》 (1959);[5] poems of Du Fu, *A Little Primer of Tu Fu* (1967);[6] and a Yuan Dynasty drama, the *Liu Yi and the Dragon Princess* (2003).[7] Although his publications in book form were not numerous, it is the quality rather than the quantity of his work that counts. The complete translation of the *Chuci* was the first in English, and formed part of his doctoral dissertation completed in 1956 and published three years later. On the re-publication of the book in 1985, he made few changes to the translation, although he re-wrote the introduction incorporating new

---

[3] "Translating from the Chinese," reprinted in *Chinese: Classical, Modern and Humane* (1989), 231-36.

[4] "Translating from the Chinese," 243.

[5] *Ch'u Tz'u – The Songs of the South: An Ancient Chinese Anthology* (Oxford at the Clarendon Press, 1959), revised edition, *The Songs of the South: An Ancient Chinese Anthology of Poems Qu Yuan and Other Poets* (Harmondsworth: Penguin Classics, 1985).

[6] *A Little Primer of Du Fu* (Oxford at the Clarendon Press, 1967), revised edition *A Little Primer of Du Fu* (Hong Kong: Research Centre for Translation, The Chinese University of Hong Kong, 1987).

[7] *Liu Yi and the Dragon Princess: A Thirteenth-Century Zaju Play by Shang Zhongxian* (Hong Kong: The Chinese University Press, 2003).

scholarship and his more mature thoughts on the subject in the intervening twenty years. He said in the preface to the new edition that the translation was the work of his more youthful self, almost a different person, which he felt reluctant to touch, a wise decision given the freshness and spontaneity of the translation, especially with the first two, "On encountering sorrow" (*Lisao*) and "The Nine Songs" (*Jiuge*). These translations are works of poetry, at the same time as keeping scrupulously to the original text in a scholarly interpretation of the original poems with all their textual problems. In *A Birthday Book for Brother Stone*, one contributor tells how he was touched by the poetic nature of the *Songs of the South* in English and inspired by the translation of the *Chuci* to set some poems to music.[8]

A Little Primer of Tu Fu (1967) was ground-breaking in format, offering an entire scholarly exegesis and word-by-word translation of the original as well as a fluent prose rendering of thirty-five poems by Du Fu taken from the easily accessible anthology *Three Hundred T'ang Poems* 《唐詩三百首》. The format is one that he had offered his students for the B.A. course in Chinese at Oxford, now available in book form for anyone with a modicum of knowledge of Chinese. It de-mystifies the reading of Chinese poetry for a much larger audience, and it enables them to understand how to approach Chinese poetry, offering many of Du Fu's best loved poems, giving an insight to the poet. It was not surprising that he privately called it "Teach yourself Du Fu";[9] it was a format that others followed for translating and interpreting Chinese poetry.

When he came to translate *The Story of the Stone* (volume one in 1973, followed by volumes published in 1977 and 1980), Hawkes was determined to bring out the richness of the original novel in full, both the prose parts and the poems, in what amounts to a re-creation of the original in English. This is what makes the translation so unique. *The Story of the Stone* is an English novel that can be read for its own sake with pleasure. In fact the *Hongloumeng* in Chinese and the *Stone* in English can both be

---

[8] Colin Huehns, "Six Settings of the *Nine Songs* by Qu Yuan," in *A Birthday Book for Brother Stone for David Hawkes at Eighty*, edited by Rachel May and John Minford (Hong Kong: The Chinese University Press and the Hong Kong Translation Society, 2003), 148-60. This volume in celebration of his 80th birthday contains more than forty tributes from his friends and admirers in the form of personal notes, poems, calligraphy, articles and translations, which shows how much he was liked and valued.

[9] According to Glen Dudbridge, the *University College Gazette* (Oxford, 2010).

read separately or in tandem by readers of Chinese, enjoyed partly for their own sakes and partly for the delight in seeing how the translator(s) have commuted the original into English with wit and imagination, including all the poetry parts. John Minford acknowledges that he was the junior partner in this enterprise in age as well as experience. It was Hawkes who convinced Penguins to publish the novel in English. He set the pattern for the manner in which the translation should be presented. He translated the first three volumes, comprising the eighty chapters that are generally agreed to be the undisputed text by Cao Xueqin, whilst the final forty chapters mainly followed the first full text published in 1791 edited by Gao E. As an interpreter and expert (or "Redologist," translating "紅學" the Chinese name for the Cao Xueqin industry, taking its cue from the "red" in the first published title), Hawkes scrutinized all the versions of the novel that are extant, along with the huge secondary literature on the subject. His determination to interpret the novel as he thought the author intended meant that he was selective with the different readings, taking them from different extant versions. In effect the English translation was also a critical edition of the Chinese text.

The glory of this translation lies in his deep understanding of Chinese literature and culture, seldom seen in a non-Chinese, although I often think of Hawkes as someone very like a traditional Chinese scholar, with his wide interest in all aspects of Chinese culture. At the same time, this knowledge and love of Chinese culture was one that was based on an equally deep and broad knowledge of the English and European culture which facilitated the relationship between the English text and an English-speaking readership.

Liu Yi and the Dragon Princess, a Yuan *zaju* 雜劇 published in 2003 after the appearance of the *Stone*, was in an even more innovative format. Actually Hawkes' interest in Yuan drama goes back to the late 60s when he held a seminar for graduate students and colleagues at the Oriental Institute in Oxford in reading and discussing Yuan drama. Instead of being a straightforward translation of a Yuan Dynasty play, the texts of which are in any case full of difficulties even for Chinese scholars let alone for a translator, *Liu Yi and the Dragon Princess* is an adaptation and re-interpretation of the original that tries to offer the English-speaker the same experience that the original audience might have had and put in a form that could be performed on the stage. We have very little knowledge about the staging of *zaju*. We know even less than we know about the Shakespearean stage. Yuan Dynasty drama was a popular genre, and as with all popular genres the surviving texts are fraught with difficulties.

Music seems to have formed the most important part of the audience experience to the extent that talented (and proud) poets at the time were willing to produce libretti for the arias, which were often in high-flown and enigmatic language, hard to decipher now. In any case, except for the arias which shine out, the spoken lines are rather garbled in the texts such as we have them, possibly because they were actors' improvisations, and much of the dialogue is often full of contradictions that get in the way of a coherent storyline.

Here he offers a version of one early play, *Liu Yi chuan shu*《柳毅傳書》, in which he cleans up the discrepancies in the dialogue and re-arranges them, adding a narrator based on such a character that appears in other plays, but keeping the supremacy of the lyrics of the arias. Along with the desire to present Yuan drama to a present-day audience as a coherent dramatic experience, the translations of the lyrics are made into English rhymed verse, which as Hawkes says meant greater freedom textually from the original and also freer interpretation. In comparing them with the original, it is clear that he leaves nothing out of the original text, but he changes the order, and alters the function of words, such as nouns to verbs, and verbs to adverbs; these are not translations that students can use as cribs. Some of the liberties he takes can be seen as a matter of interpretation in a difficult medium with rules no longer very obvious to us. He re-creates these arias as English poems with rhyme, much as he had dealt with the poetic passages in *The Story of the Stone*. As for the prose parts in the translation, they are similar to his approach to the colloquial dialogues for his translation of the *The Story of the Stone*.

In fact this book is much more than a translation: taking up more pages than either of the other two sections——the introduction and the translation——is what is modestly called an "appendix." It is devoted to a scholarly and minute examination of how the lyrics of the sung arias obeyed the patterns of prosody of the *qu* 曲, and how the extra-metrical or "padding words" worked. It is accepted that prosodic patterns for the *qu* followed a syllabic count much as the *shi* 詩 had done earlier, except that they contained irregular lines as opposed to the regular syllabic line of the *shi*, which was composed in a classical language that was generally mono-syllabic. Here Hawkes suggests that the writers of the *qu* were having to cope with a more evolved version of the Chinese language, one that contained more multi-syllables units, leading to a more stressed language, somewhat as modern Chinese is now. Therefore their adherence to the *qu* patterns was more complicated than simply obeying a syllabic count. They followed the dictates of sense, rhythm and music, adhering to the metrical prosody more freely, adding extra-metrical "padding words" to clarify the sense or to fit the music. What Hawkes does in this appendix is to investigate the use of a more colloquial register of language in Chinese poetry, for the purpose of the drama that rose to prominence in the Yuan Dynasty, long after the traditional prosodic rules for poetry had already been formulated several centuries earlier in the Tang. These ideas about poetic prosody can only be speculative since no one knows what the reality was like during performance. It is a great pity that Hawkes did not investigate further the prosodic nature of Chinese poetry through the ages, as the Chinese language evolved.

His examination of the lyrics also shows a concern with music and musical form, elements which are now mainly lost. The method and ambition in the production of this translation shows a large degree of innovation; this time again, Hawkes was not merely in the business of translation. He was also re-interpreting and presenting to an English-speaking audience what the original experience might have been like in the Yuan Dynasty.

Hawkes' life illustrates his devotion to literature, so I will narrate some events to put his translations in context. He started his undergraduate degree at Christ Church, Oxford, in Classical studies, the study of ancient Greek and Roman. The degree course was interrupted by service in the war, when he learnt and used Japanese in a team of code breakers, which must have introduced him to East Asia. He returned to Oxford in 1945 to switch to Chinese. He took the recently instituted degree in Chinese, and since the course had been devised to look as much as possible like an East Asian version of the Classics course in ancient Greek and Latin, he had no training in modern colloquial Chinese. So he went to China in 1948, determined to improve his language skills in modern Chinese, and succeeded in pursuing graduate studies at Peking University, with the help of William Empson, who happened to be teaching there. Empson was at that time writing the *Seven Types of Ambiguities,* and David said he watched him typing it out, when he made his frequent calls in their the old Chinese house. Hawkes stoically learnt modern and colloquial Chinese whilst the civil war between the Nationalists and Communists was raging around him. He and his wife Jean (also a literary translator, from the French), who had joined him in Beijing, only returned to England when it was made clear to them by the British authorities that they had to leave.

After a spell as a lecturer in Chinese at Oxford, he became the Professor. In his inaugural lecture in 1961 we can find most of the aspects that were dear to his heart about Chinese studies. He himself is an illustration of his insistence that the scholar of Chinese needs to command both classical and modern languages. In the lecture he talks of a contemporary ballad, *Wang Gui yu Li Xiangxiang*《王貴與李香香》by Li Ji 李季.[10] He draws attention to the presence of a metaphor for marriage, dolls representing husband and wife, each made from a piece of clay that is kneaded together and re-made. It is a metaphor found much earlier, and alluded to in a commentary in learned classical Chinese written in the seventeenth century, itself referring to a poem written in fourteenth century colloquial Chinese. Hawkes uses all this to illustrate how in Chinese studies, a scholar must be capable of reading both classical and modern Chinese and all its permutations through time and different registers, in order to understand the literature. In fact in 2009, barely half a year before he died, he published an article remembering William Empson which focused on this same ballad and its literary antecedents.[11] This time he was able to enjoy the video (courtesy of You-Tube) of contemporary renderings of traditional ballads, the *shuntianyou* 順天游, the genre imitated in 1948 by *Wang Gui yu Li Xiangxiang*. He retained this lively curiosity and keen appreciation in all aspects of Chinese literature and arts throughout his life.

Hawkes resigned his professorship at Oxford in 1970, one reason being his commission by Penguins to translate the *Hongloumeng* which he published over the next ten years, appearing in 1973, 1977 and 1980. He was never the standard academic, and he frequently found academe frustrating. So it was not always easy for him and his family at this juncture. Had he been able to, he might well have followed the steps of his friend and mentor Arthur Waley (to whom Hawkes had become literary executor in 1961) who after resigning from an assistantship in the British Museum print room, never held a job, least of all an academic one, whilst he lived an intensive life studying and publishing on Chinese literature and history.[12] However, All Souls College at Oxford did offer Hawkes a Fellowship until his retirement. Then he went to a remote farm house in

---

[10] *An Inaugural Lecture before the University of Oxford on 25 May 1961* (Oxford: Oxford University Press, 1961).

[11] "Mix Them Grain by Grain," *Times Literary Supplement* (13 February 2009), 13-15.

[12] "[T]he best translations of all are by the philologist-poets like Arthur Waley; but such people are rare, and we cannot wait for them to be born," in "Translating from the Chinese," reprinted in *Chinese: Classical, Modern and Humane* (1989), 231-36.

Wales for many years, from where he returned to Oxford in 2000, where his wife still lives.

Hawkes was a scholar with high literary sensibility and creativity, but we should not underestimate his linguistic talents. Just as he was rigorous about the interpretation of the content of any given work, he was equally concerned with the language. His school education gave him a base in ancient Greek and Latin for his first course at Oxford to study Classics. He built on this through the rest of his life for. Prior to learning Chinese, he had learnt Japanese for war service. He was capable in several European languages such as French and Italian, and later in life he learnt Welsh. Needless to say he read and spoke Chinese fluently. This linguistic talent coupled with his ability to manipulate language worked magic in his translations. He was equally sensitive to the use of language in the work of others; in a review of the translation of a novel by Ch'ien Chung-shu (aka Qian Zhongshu, 錢鍾書 1910-1998), *Fortress Besieged*《圍城》(1947),[13] originally printed in the *Times Literary Supplement*, 27 June 1980,[14] he says that the "style, wit and word-plays of the original make it the sort of text that only luck and an unlimited amount of time (more than most translators can afford) could do justice to."[15] At the cost of doing violence to this quotation by putting it in a different context, I would say that "style, wit and word-play" are what Hawkes himself excelled in as a translator and as a wordsmith of the English language.

When I talked over the production of this volume with David's wife, Jean, and daughter, Verity, in Oxford, they brought him back to life vividly by imagining his reaction to it, an embarrassment that "such a fuss" was being made. It brings to my mind his modesty about his scholarship, and his determination to learn more about literature, rather than dwell on the immense quantity and depth that he already knew.

---

[13] Translated by Jeanne Kelly and Nathan K. Mao (Bloomington: Indiana University Press, 1979).

[14] "Smiling at Grief," reprinted in *Chinese: Classical, Modern and Humane* (1989), 280-85.

[15] "Smiling at Grief," 284.

A Tribute to Brother Stone

John Minford
School of Culture, History and Language
College of Asia and The Pacific
Australian National University

Department of Translation
The Chinese University of Hong Kong

It is quite unusual to dedicate an academic conference to the memory of an individual. It was an inspired decision to dedicate this meeting to the memory of David Hawkes, who sadly passed away in Oxford at the age of eighty-six, on the morning of 31 July last year. I am greatly honoured to have been asked to pay tribute to David today, and at the same time profoundly aware that whatever I may say will fall far short of his true stature and achievement, and that I can never really hope to succeed in conveying more than a fraction of the admiration and affection I feel for him, as a man and a scholar, as a literary translator and teacher. I should add in passing that David himself would surely have protested at all of this, having throughout his life refused honours, adulation and fuss of any kind. He was never comfortable with life in academia, and declined to accept several honorary degrees.

Rather than proceed in an academic fashion, therefore, I wish to do two quite modest things: to tell his story briefly, and to illustrate that story with a simple sequence of eight pictures, accompanied with an informal commentary, mostly consisting of David's own words. I believe that these images, even though some of them are of less than perfect quality technically, can evoke better than words something of the unique flavour of his life and times, of his personality and of his world. The commentary was provided by David for his daughter Rachel, to explain a much longer series of family photos. In one case (the May 1950 wedding photo) I have reproduced his commentary almost in its entirety, as it is such an extraordinary record of a moment in time, and brings together such a fascinating group of people.

[I] Life and Times

David Hawkes was one of the greatest translators from the Chinese of the past century. He will be best and longest remembered for two major works: the first and earliest, his superb version of the hauntingly lyrical (and extremely difficult) early anthology of shamanistic poetry, *The Songs of the South*《楚辭》; the second, his extraordinarily rich, versatile and loving re-creation of the first three volumes of the great eighteenth century novel *The Story of the Stone*《紅樓夢》. This last, a supreme example of the translator's art, was, when it first appeared, hailed in the *Times Higher Education Supplement* as "one of the best translations into English of our time," and has since been the subject of numerous critical studies. It set entirely new standards for the translation of Chinese fiction. "David of all people," wrote his contemporary and friend Cyril Birch, "had the learning, the wit, and the command of the aristocratic culture to meet the challenge."[1] The *Stone* was his crowning achievement, his own favourite project.[2] Into it he poured all of his scholarship and creative passion and invention. He had dreamed of working on it ever since his student days in Peking in 1948, when he learned "modern" Peking Chinese from a retired Manchu official by reading the novel from the beginning. His identification with the work and its author was so complete that, when in 1970 he finally decided to translate it in full, he gave up his Chair at Oxford, in order to dedicate himself totally to the task. He himself wrote that this was a novel "written and rewritten by a great artist with his very lifeblood."[3] The same can be said of the translation itself. David brought to bear such a wide range of rhetorical skills, such penetrating insight into character, such finely honed dialogue, such superbly crafted versification; but more than anything, such a profound sense of humanity, such fun and exhilaration, such melancholy and wisdom. In it he succeeds in grasping to the full, and yet at the same time transcending, the sheer Chineseness of

---

[1] From Cyril Birch's "Tribute to David," in *A Birthday Book for Brother Stone*, eds. Rachel May and John Minford (Hong Kong: The Chinese University Press and The Hong Kong Translation Society), 8.

[2] A detailed account of the manner in which David entered upon this project can be found in my essay "Truth and Fiction in the Translation of *The Story of the Stone*," included in the forthcoming volume entitled *Approaches to Teaching The Story of the Stone*, edited by Andrew Schonebaum and Tina Lu, to be published shortly by the Modern Languages Association in New York.

[3] Introduction to *The Golden Days*, volume one of *The Story of the Stone* (Harmondsworth: Penguin Books, 1973), 46.

the work, making it into a real novel for the English reader, revealing it as a masterpiece of world literature. He did this out of sheer love of the book. "If I can convey to the reader even a fraction of the pleasure this Chinese novel has given me," he wrote in 1973, in his Introduction to the first volume of the translation, "I shall not have lived in vain."[4] His love of the book stayed with him all his life, although he never had much time for the so-called "discipline" of *hongxue* 紅學. In his last months he embarked on an ambitious new *Stone*-project, the editing of a complete bilingual edition of the translation for publication in Shanghai.

David Hawkes was born on 6 July 1923, and grew up in East London. In 1942 he went up to Christchurch College, Oxford, for a year initially, to study the abbreviated Classical Mods syllabus, and then spent the remaining war years first studying Japanese, and then teaching it, to code-breakers at the Bedford Inter-Services Intelligence Centre. After the war he returned to Oxford to study, transferring to the newly established Honours School of Chinese, under the former missionary E. R. Hughes. At that time the Oxford Chinese syllabus was exclusively classical, and he spent many hours with Hughes studying the *Ritual Classic* 《禮記》, the *History Classic* 《尚書》, the *Poetry Classic* 《詩經》, the *Four Books* 《四書》, and other parts of the Chinese canon. In 1948 began what was certainly the most influential period in his life, when (on his own initiative) he travelled out to Peking (then in the last throes of the civil war) and began studying as a postgraduate student at Peking University, attending classes by such legendary older scholars as Yu Pingbo 俞平伯 (1899-1990), Luo Changpei 羅常培 (1899-1958), Tang Lan 唐蘭 (1900-1979) and Lin Geng 林庚 (1910-2006).[5] In Peking he also became part of the circle of the poet William Empson and his South African sculptor wife, Hetta Crouse. Empson's intellectual and poetic genius made a lasting impression, and the couple's bohemian lifestyle (some found it outrageous) attracted him.[6] On 5 May 1950, in newly liberated Peking he married his wife Jean, who had travelled out on her own by ship to join him. They finally left Peking in 1951. David never went back to Peking, or to China. But he remembered every last detail of the old city, and himself

---

[4] *The Golden Days*, 46.

[5] David wrote the entry for Yu Pingbo in Boorman and Howard's *Biographical Dictionary of Republican China* (New York, 1970).

[6] Much of this is chronicled in John Haffenden's two-volume biography of Empson.

remarked more than once that he could find his way around every *hutong* in his dreams.

On his return to Oxford, David completed his doctoral dissertation on *The Songs of the South* 《楚辭》. His distinguished work attracted the attention of the pre-eminent British sinologist and translator of the time, Arthur Waley (1889-1966), who went on to become his mentor and friend, and at the end of his life named him as his literary executor. Elected to the Chair of Chinese in 1959, David spent a dozen years building up a fine department, where literary and classical studies flourished, but where modern China was by no means ignored. He rapidly acquired an enormous international reputation, as a scholar rigorous in his methods, encyclopedic in his reading, and humane in his mode of expression. He was an inspiring teacher, giving scholarly but entertaining lectures that betrayed his early love of the theatre. He resigned from the Oxford Chair in 1971, and after a brief interval, was made a Research Fellow of All Souls, a position which enabled him to complete his three volumes of the *Stone* (published from 1973 to 1980).

David and Jean retired to the Welsh hills in 1984. David now thought he might give up Chinese altogether, and generously donated his fine collection of Chinese books to the National Library of Wales at Aberystwyth, where it was catalogued (as part of his librarianship training) by Wu Jianzhong 吳建中, now head librarian of the Shanghai Library. He still found time to revise his *Songs of the South* for Penguin Classics (published in 1985 with a greatly expanded commentary), and otherwise began to concentrate on the study of the Welsh language. He also read widely in the history of religion, on which subject he wrote a brilliant series of essays in the form of letters to a grandchild, *Letters from a Godless Grandfather* (published privately in Hong Kong in 2004). He was a biting (and often hilariously funny) critic of the sheer nonsense that so often passes for religion. He was also to the end a passionate opponent of American and British military involvement in the Middle East, raging against the Iraq war and against Israel's brutal treatment of the Palestinians, and joining in more than one protest march.

His life and his work were both inspired and overshadowed by a strongly melancholic streak. He was a true genius, a towering figure in his profession. What he wrote in 1966 in his obituary of Arthur Waley is equally true of himself. "Greatness in men is a rare but unmistakable quality. In our small profession it is unlikely we shall see a man of such magnitude again."[7]

[II] Eight Photographs, with a commentary largely based on David's own notes

(1)   Ancestors

This is an ancestral photograph, from about 1885. David's great-grandfather George Thomas Hammond (1828-1897) is seated at the far left. David used to own his cello. (The *Zephyr* which he is holding is not a newspaper but a piece of music.) The couple standing and sitting below the Chinese embroidery, he holding a newspaper, she holding a teacup, are David's Grandpa and Grandma Hawkes – Jesse Hawkes (1855-1945) and Mary Ann Elizabeth Hammond (1859-1935). A great promoter of the Co-

---

[7] The obituary of Arthur Waley appeared in the scholarly journal *Asia Major*, New Series, Vol. XII (1967). It was reprinted in the collection of Hawkes' essays, *Classical, Modern and Humane* (Hong Kong: The Chinese University Press, 1989), 253-58. The above section, "Life and Times," is loosely based on the obituary I myself wrote for David, which appeared in the *London Times* of 28 August 2009.

operative Movement, Jesse Hawkes was at one time Secretary of the first
Co-operative Steam Laundry in England, and later, in about 1921, helped
David's father to start a machine laundry in Leyton.

(2)   The schoolboy

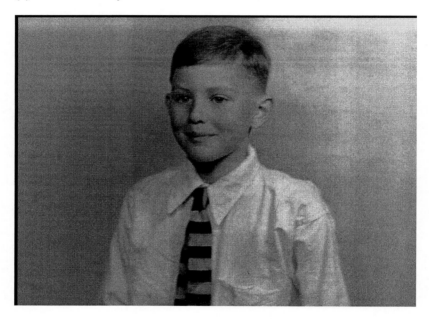

Taken in 1931, this shows David as a school-boy, wearing his school tie,
and the uniform of St Joseph's Convent School, which was opposite the
family home in Cambridge Park, Wanstead E. 11, London. He had been
sent there because a rough boy had broken his front tooth at the previous
school, and in this photo he is "smiling in a way designed to hide the
damage."

(3) The young man in Peking

David writes: "This was taken in the grounds at the back of the Research Students' Hostel in Dongchang hutong, one of the hostels of the National Peking University ('Beida') in Peking (or 'Beiping' as it was when I went there) in the summer of 1949. The hostel had been built by the Japanese as a prison for the Chinese officers during the Occupation. It was rather a grim place, but some of the undergraduate hostels were worse. I think the photo was taken by an Indian student called Murti. Most of the students were Chinese but there was a group of Indians there as well who kept pretty much to themselves."

(4) David and Jean's wedding reception, in the British Legation, May 1950

David writes that this photograph was "taken on the 5th May 1950, after a Service of Blessing conducted by Bishop Scott of North China in the Bryans' house in the old British Embassy Compound. We have just come out of the house to be photographed. Bishop Scott (in his cap) can be seen at the back, to the left of my head. Starting from the left, with a hand in his side pocket, is Grauer (or Grauers), the Swedish Consul... The smiling plump-faced woman next to him is Lentje van der Hoeven from the Dutch Embassy. Bearded and rather darkling at the back is our dear friend Max Bickerton, who knew Rewi Alley as a boy in New Zealand and who ended his days as a tenant of the Empsons in Studio House, Hampstead. Hetta Empson is standing beside him, peeping over the top of the heads in front of her. The stocky man with glasses, with hands clasped over his abdomen, is a missionary called John Stewart. His wife, Jean, is the dark-haired woman beside him wearing a dark jacket and floral blouse. They were missionaries belonging to one of the Free Churches. I think their mission was called the Sunshine Mission. Hetta, Max and I got to know them when we were cycling round Peking in 1949 soliciting signatures for a telegram to be sent to the British Government urging them to recognize the newly established People's Republic. Standing behind them and in front of Hetta Empson is Mrs Graham, the British Consul's wife. Behind Jean Stewart and to the right of her is Adele Rickett, wife of Alleyn Rickett. They were an American couple studying at one of the universities outside the city – I think it was Tsing Hua. A little over a year after this they were arrested on a charge of espionage and held in prison until released under an agreement made between China and France when De Gaulle recognized the People's Republic two or three years later. Between Adele and the Bishop, with gleaming spectacles and taller than both, is the British Consul, Mr Graham, who registered our marriage. Later that evening he was assaulted at our wedding party by a British Communist called Michael Shapiro… To the right of the Bishop and above my head is Theo Peters, one of the Secretaries… He sang Lieder for the edification of selected Brits. To his right, at the end of that row, is Derek Bryan, the Senior Secretary and occupant of No. 6, outside which we are standing. The Chinese woman standing behind my right shoulder wearing the white wedding favours, is his wife, Liang Hongying, a Fukienese Quaker and fanatical lifelong supporter of the Chinese Communists, which is possibly why Derek, who was extremely competent and fluent in Chinese, was forced to leave the Service not long after we left China… Between my face and Hongying's is the beaming face of the American Walter Brown who lived with the Empsons until they left Peking in 1952 (when he went back to the US)… Between my head and Jean's is Robert Ruhlmann. He was actually taller than me, but I think must have been asked to flex his knees to make the people behind visible. William Empson is standing next to Jean, a little behind her… Peeping from the back behind William's shoulder and Mum's is Alleyn Rickett. I. A. Richards is the balding bespectacled gent beside William. Pamela Fitt, later Pamela Youde, is looking at something interesting to the right, outside the picture, and Harriet Mills, arrested and imprisoned when the Ricketts were, is holding a drink and also looking at whatever it was outside the picture. I wonder what it was."

(5) With Professor Homer Dubs and Wu Shichang, Oxford, mid-late 1950s

At the time, the three of them were colleagues in the Oxford Chinese department.

(6) At work on *The Story of the Stone*, in his study, 59 Bedford Street, Oxford, c. 1980

(7) At our French home, Fontmarty, c. 2006

(8) Among the flowers, Charleston, Sussex, 2009

I took this photograph in early July last year (2009), when we visited
Charleston, the Sussex country haunt of the Bloomsbury set (whom David
so much admired). I have chosen to end with this partly because it is one
of my personal favourites, but also because it captures something of the

deep love of nature that was inseparable from David's deep love of literature. It was David who wrote of the third and fourth of the Nine Songs that they constituted "the most hauntingly beautiful part of the Nine Songs, a shaman's love song as he pursues, through rivers, lakes and wooded islands, a brooding presence which he senses and sometimes believes he can hear, but never, or only in faint, fleeting glimpses, ever sees..." The smile on his face in this photograph captures something of the sense of wonder that enabled him to travel in his mind to a far-away world, a present-day shaman-translator, to recreate that "ancient time in which men loved, even more than they feared, the mysterious world of nature that surrounded them."[8]

We owe such a debt of gratitude to this great man. Many of us here today have been the recipients of his teaching, of his friendship, kindness and generosity over the years. Every year more and more readers across the world will continue to discover the marvels of his re-creations of China's literary heritage. May his work continue to bring us all pleasure, and his total dedication to his craft inspire us all, in our calling as translators.

---

[8] *The Songs of the South: An Anthology of Ancient Chinese Poems* (London, 1985), 106-107.

What is the Point of Making Translations into English of Chinese Literature: Re-examining Arthur Waley and David Hawkes

Tao Tao Liu
Institute for Chinese Studies
Oxford University

We all understand why a translation is made for utilitarian purposes, which can serve practical ends and result in commercial gain. It is a different matter with the translation of a work of literature, which generally has no direct utilitarian purpose, and seldom results in financial gain. These are usually made out of the determination, or even a sense of mission, of the translator, who has to work long and hard to convince people of the value of a work that they have selected from a foreign culture and language. In societies like the English-speaking ones, that prize originality above all else in literature, translations can be perceived as somehow second-hand, and do not garner the same praise that original creations or research material generate. Yet this does not seem to put people off: translations are constantly made, and are even growing in number at present. Some have attributed this to greater globalization; more readers have widened their horizons beyond their own language. Some attribute the rise to new academic disciplines, such as feminism and translation studies itself, that rely on foreign sources that need to be made known more widely. They all contribute to the proliferation of translations, but at the end of the day it is the wishes and the circumstances of the translators that most count, which is what I aim to examine in this paper.

However, history is not always kind to translations in that they have a short life span: translations made only a few decades ago are already often forgotten. This can be attributable to changes in literary fashions, a drop in interest in the original work or type of work, or to the fact that the style of a translation seems no longer in tune with the times so that new translations of the same work are produced to suit changing taste. In other words, the fate of a translation seems to be much the same as that of any creative work of literature, poetry or fiction, in pleasing a fickle readership; success or popularity is not necessarily a guide to long lasting value. So translations seem to be assessed by the same criteria that creative works usually are.

In the past not all successful translations were made directly from the original source language into the target language. Quite a number were made via another language, by translating a work already popular in another European language: the very first translation from the Chinese into English was rendered by Bishop Percy (who is generally known for the work he produced on English and Scottish ballads).[1] The rendering was done from a Portuguese translation of a Chinese fictional work, and was published in 1761.[2] Two of the most popular Chinese works of fiction in English were first translated from the German by Franz Kuhn and then turned into English in 1939 and 1958.[3] This was not thought of as unusual. For instance in sixteenth century England, which was a time of huge interest in translation, translations had a great influence on original works. Where would Shakespeare's *Antony and Cleopatra* be without his borrowings from North's translation of Plutarch, which was translated via the French version by Amyot (1579)? This is true in particular if the language is perceived to be difficult and not easily acquired, such as Latin in the case of Plutarch above, and Chinese for our purpose here.

Actually the most influential translator of English fiction into Chinese over the last century or so was Lin Qinnan (1852-1924). He did not know English himself. Knowing European languages was still rare in his day at the end of the nineteenth century. Instead he used the services of young men who had learnt these languages whilst studying other subjects abroad, and turned their oral translations into Chinese. Nevertheless, the effect of

---

[1] Thomas Percy (1729-1811), *Percy's Reliques of Ancient English Poetry*, 1765, (reprinted London: J.M. Dent, 1906).

[2] Kai-chong Cheung, "The *Haoqiu zhuan,* the First Chinese Novel Translated in Europe: With Special Reference to Percy's and Davis's Renditions," in *One into Many: Translation and Dissemination of Classical Chinese Literature*, ed. Leo Tak-hung Chan (Amsterdam and New York: Rodopi, 2003), 29-38.

[3] *Hongloumeng*, English translation, by Florence and Isabel McHugh as *Dream of the Red Chamber* (London: Routledge & Kegan Paul, 1958) and *Chin p'ing mei* with an introduction by Arthur Waley (London: Bodley Head, 1939), English translation by Bernard Miall from the abridged version by Franz Kuhn (Leipzig: Insel-verlag, 1930).

his translations on the readership was an unprecedented opening of their horizons. His translations were as instrumental in making the middle class understand foreign ways and the foreign mindset as were the philosophical and scientific translations becoming available to the Chinese then. Translated literature is cultural interaction.

In earlier days when knowledge of the Chinese language was minuscule in the West, most translations were targeted at people who knew no Chinese. This puts translations into English of Chinese literature into a slightly different class from those from languages and societies (such as those of Europe) familiar to the English-speaking reader. Nowadays there are far more people who already know Chinese, not counting those who are native Chinese speakers but who read English, so translators have to direct their works at two constituencies: one that does not know Chinese, and one that does. Translations via an intermediary translation in a third language are deemed not acceptable today, which may provide another reason why earlier translations do not attract readers any more.

My interest is not mainly in the quality of a translation as regards its fidelity to or betrayal of the original text, which has been well dealt with in studies in the theories of translation. I am more interested in the effects of a translation on the target readership as cultural interactions between the source and target cultures. I would like to examine again the works of Arthur Waley (1889-1966), this pioneer of translators into English, mainly from Chinese poetry, to see if one can cast light on what made him do translations, and what made him so important a translator of Chinese literature in the English-speaking world before the Second World War. I will also say a few words about David Hawkes (1923-2009), who was more recent as a translator, to whose memory this volume is dedicated, and who was also appointed literary executor by Waley.

The post-colonial critic Tejaswini Niranjana writes that translation into English appropriates the cultural products of another race to make them suitable for consumption by the English.[4] These translations are perceived as inferior to works in English. An example of this was the English translations of William Jones in the eighteenth century who turned material on the Hindu laws into English mainly for the benefit of colonial administrators. I do not believe that this is true for translations of Chinese literature which is not for utilitarian purposes. It is nevertheless worth considering translations in context, relating them to their specific time and

---

[4] *Siting Translation: History, Post-Structuralism and the Colonial Context* (Berkeley and Oxford: University of California Press, 1992), 10-16.

place in history, in order to understand fully their effects and reception. In this regard, firstly we have to say that literary translations from the Chinese cannot be easily fitted into the colonial pigeonhole. Secondly, my experience in English literature tells me that the most valued translations from a foreign language do not place these works in an inferior position to original works in English.

In past English history China has been so marginal to its perception of the world order, that when it appears in a translation into English, it has to leap quite a credibility gap in the English reader. The stereotype of China in the eighteenth and nineteenth centuries alternated between a kingdom of philosophers as it appeared to someone like Voltaire, and a society envisioned by the *Farther Adventures of Robinson Crusoe* (1719), a degenerate form of "Oriental Despotism" that was better left at the other end of the world.[5] Thank heavens the English did not have to rule them on the scale of India and the Middle East, especially after the Opium Wars in the mid-nineteenth century! Culturally Chinese did not appeal to the taste of the Europeans. It had far less appeal than the Middle East and India. As far as the visual arts was concerned, it appealed rather less than the Japanese arts. The *Rubaiyat of Omar Khayyam* was first published in English translation in 1859, became a huge success, and according to the 1988 edition of the *Oxford Companion to English Literature* contains "amongst the most frequently quoted lines in English poetry."[6] Nothing from the Chinese is on this level in English. The Chinese language was known to be very difficult, and Chinese culture seemed very remote to the English, even at the end of the nineteenth century, when the English people were avidly reading the accounts of all kinds of explorers and travelers going to far flung places.

When translations of Chinese poetry into English first saw the light of day at the beginning of the twentieth century, we need to be aware that there were massive changes taking place in English poetry at the time. English poetry had had a long and successful run since the Romantics at the beginning of the nineteenth century, but there were negative factors emerging, such as the dominance of the iambic rhymed couplet, the gradual descent into sentimentality, and the rise of a tendency to wordiness and ornamentation. In other words poetry had developed bad habits. Against this background new movements were emerging, such as that of the Imagist poets in America, who were experimenting with plain

---

[5] Printed for W. Taylor at the *Ship* in *Pater-Noster-Row*. MDCCXIX.
[6] "Omar Khayyam" entry. Editor Margaret Drabble (Oxford: Oxford University Press, reprinted 1988), 716.

language.[7] "Imagism" was a term invented by Ezra Pound. It was a creed to which he adhered (at first, until he turned to other ways of thinking), and was espoused by Amy Lowell, its leading poet, who incidentally also greatly admired Chinese poetry. Arthur Waley was involved at the beginning of this movement; he personally knew many literary figures in London, and was friendly with Ezra Pound and T. S. Eliot during their time in London. In an interview with Roy Fuller in 1963, he described how he regularly met with them at dinner on Monday evenings at a restaurant in Frith Street, London.[8] He read Pound's renderings from the Chinese before they were published, but he denied that they had any influence on him. Eliot was to say in 1962, with reference to the idea that "every literature may influence every other," that "the poetical translations from the Chinese made by Ezra Pound, and those made by Arthur Waley have probably been read by every poet writing in English."[9]

Most people would consider the renderings by Ezra Pound of Chinese poems into English, *Cathay* (1915), as the beginning of modernist English poetry.[10] Pound was wildly enthusiastic about things Chinese, taking up Confucianism later in ways that were, as it was pointed out to him by Achilles Fang at Harvard, not at all what the original was about.[11] Pound was in any case convinced that translations were important to literary life; one of Pound's main "tenets at that time was that English literature is nourished by translation and that the great ages of English literature are great ages of translation."[12] *Cathay* is accounted one of Pound's best poetic inspirations.

---

[7] Amy Lowell said "What sets the poets of today apart from those of the Victorian era is an entirely different outlook," *Tendencies in Modern American Poetry* (New York: Macmillan Company, 1917), vii. The tenets of the Imagist poets were expounded on pages 235-49.

[8] "Arthur Waley in Conversation: BBC Interview with Roy Fuller," reprinted in *Madly Singing in the Mountains: An Appreciation and Anthology of Arthur Waley*, ed. Ivan Morris (London: George Allen and Unwin, 1970), 140-42.

[9] In his appendix on "The Unity of English Culture," in *Notes Towards the Definition of Culture* (London: Faber and Faber, 1962), 113.

[10] *Cathay. Translations by Ezra Pound. For the Most Part from the Chinese of Rihaku, from the Notes of the Late Ernest Fenollosa, and the Decipherings of the Professors Mori and Ariga* (London: Elkin Mathews, 1915).

[11] Mary Paterson Cheadle, *Ezra Pound's Confucian Translation* (Ann Arbor: University of Michigan, 1997), 50-51. I am indebted to Professor Robert Young of the Department of English, New York University, for this reference.

[12] Morris, *Madly Singing in the Mountains* (1970), 141.

We know how Pound arrived at his translations from the Chinese, which was from the notes of another American, Ernest Fenollosa (1853-1908), who had been in Japan, and read Chinese poetry through the Japanese with a Japanese tutor. Pound was given Fenollosa's notebooks on the Chinese poems in 1913 by Fenellosa's widow. The notebooks contained verbatim notes from his tutorials, often word for word exegesis of Chinese poems (not always totally accurately recorded, such is the nature of tutorial notes), which Pound put into English in his own way. What Pound did with his renderings in English verse was to create a new way of poetic expression that laid the groundwork for the rise of a new form of English poetry. The majority of people who admire *Cathay* see it as a milestone in English poetry, regardless of its origins.

Actually 1915 was not the first date of published translations of Chinese poetry. In the 1910s there was a crop of translations and renderings into English from Chinese poetry. The earliest and most highly respected translation from the Chinese was in missionary efforts in the nineteenth century. Translating the core texts of Chinese religion and ethics was amongst the first duties of a missionary like James Legge, who was familiar with the hermeneutics of biblical texts. He gave word for word prose translation of these texts, which included the *Book of Odes* in between 1861 and 1872.[13] This translation was instrumental in setting off interest in Classical Chinese poetry. What Legge did initially was to put the poems into plain prose. It was a good strategy: translating poetry is notoriously difficult. Once the decision has been taken to turn it into prose in the target language, the reader is usually left with a piece that is manifestly more than just plain prose in English. The importance of the plain translation of the poetry by Legge lay in achieving a text that was crying out for a better form.[14]

Legge's prose renderings did spark interest in the mind of Helen Waddell, who made her first foray into publication in 1913, *Lyrics from the Chinese*, a little book of twenty-five poems. In the preface she acknowledged her debt to the prose translation of the *Odes* by James Legge. Waddell later achieved great renown as a mediaeval Latin scholar. Her publishers, Constables of London, put out thirteen editions of *Lyrics*

---

[13] *The Chinese Classics, with a Translation, Critical and Exegetical Notes, Prolegomena, and Copious Indexes by James Legge* (London: Trübner, 1861-1872, reprinted Hong Kong: Hong Kong University Press, 1960). Legge did a later partial translation for the *The Sacred Books of the East Vol. III.*
[14] Legge himself produced his verse rendering of what he termed"*The She King or The Book of Ancient Poetry*" in 1876 (Oxford: Clarendon Press, 1879).

between 1913 and 1947; it was reprinted in 1987 by the Malvern Press.[15] The number of printings probably meant that it was never out of print even during the years of restrictions on paper during the Second World War. She wrote how thrilled she was when she found out that nine hundred and four copies had been sold within a few weeks of publication.[16] In her translations she took liberties with Legge's prose renderings. Her poems (and they should be acknowledged as "hers") were cleverly crafted in stanzas, they had the rhythm of what people expected of poetry, as well as the appeal of the exotic. Moreover, they had a brevity and precise imagery that was fresh, chiming in with the rising movement of modernity. Its use of rhyme was done in such a way as to give shape to the poems and promote a rhythm that flowed, rather than the end-stopped "race to the end" style of rhyming couplets that people had come to expect from traditional versification at that time. But their popularity was as English poetry; it is doubtful how much her readership were necessarily interested in China, or even wanted the genuine Chinese article, and almost none would have known Chinese, or were even familiar with Legge's prose translation. Rather, they were convinced by her ability to bring out what they assumed (as she was the daughter of an Irish Presbyterian pastor reading the missionary Legge) to be the best of the Chinese.

In 1910 Clifford Bax published twenty poems from the Chinese.[17] In the preface, Bax tells us how he had travelled to Japan and met with a Buddhist monk who knew several European languages, and translated many poems extempore to him from Chinese sources, which Bax took down and later worked into English and published; a process not unlike what Pound did with Fenellosa's notes. Bax in a final note to his book referred to several more works as suggestions for further reading. These

---

[15] *Lyrics from the Chinese*, 1st ed. (London: Constable and Co, 1913). Again I am indebted to Professor Robert Young.

[16] Monica Blackett, *Mark of the Maker, a Portrait of Helen Waddell* (London: Constable, 1973), 27.

[17] *Twenty Chinese Poems* was published by W. Budd, Orpheus Press, in 1910. A later anthology appeared in 1920: *Twenty-five Chinese Poems*, paraphrased by Clifford Bax (London: Hendersons, 1st ed. 1920, 2nd ed. revised and enlarged 1921). John Walter de Gruchy in *Orienting Arthur Waley, Japonism, Orientalism, and the Creation of Japanese Literature in English* (Honolulu: Hawaii University Press, 2003), 167, note 3, quotes from an unpublished source, a doctorate dissertation by Ruth Pelmutter, "Arthur Waley and His Place in the Modern Movement Between the Wars," University of Pennsylvania 1971, that in an undated letter written after 1913 to Clifford Bax, Waley had told Bax that it was Bax's translations that inspired him to study ancient languages.

included the *Wisdom of the East* series published by John Murray in London. Two titles were written by Launcelot Cranmer-Byng, one of the editors of the *Wisdom of the East* series, who rendered his poems via the translations of Herbert Giles, Professor of Chinese at Cambridge. His two collections were *The Lute of Jade* in 1909 (2nd edition 1911) and *The Feast of Lanterns* in 1916. There were various other published collections printed later.[18]

Surveying these works and their dates together, we can see a trend around the early decades of the twentieth century of renderings of Chinese poetry into English by highly literate and creative people, who (for want of a better word) dabbled in adaptation from all kinds of sources to create new poems in English. This was probably their aim, they did not consider them in a separate category as "translations." As Hugh Kenner said with reference to Pound's initiating of the modernist movement in English poetry, "Composition *à la mode chinoise* was one of the directions of the *vers libre* movement."[19] Kenner felt that although Pound's translation from the Chinese abandoned rhyme and fixed prosody, yet "his real achievement… was to rethink the nature of an English poem."[20]

Cathay has been much chewed over by critics. Whilst I agree with George Steiner's praise of Pound's *Cathay*, I disagree with what he said about the other translators of the time, including Arthur Waley, whom he consigned to the rubbish bin because they were too alike, "an ensemble of peculiar coherence."[21] It is because of the very existence of a whole body

---

[18] Amongst them *Plucking the Rushes* which was not published until 1968, edited by David Holbrook (London: Heinemann Educational, 1968), who put together the translations of Waley, Waddell, Pound and a few others, and saw these poems not as translations, but as English poetry of their era. "We can enjoy the poetry, and feel its relevance to our essential problems of the inward life."

[19] *The Pound Era* (New York and London: University of California Press, Berkeley, 1971), 196.

[20] *The Pound Era*, 199.

[21] George Steiner, *After Babel: Aspects of Language and Translation* (New York and London: Oxford University Press, 1975, reprinted 1977), 358-59. Whilst preference for one version over another is a matter of personal taste, it is often the case that the renderings of the Pounds and Waddells of this world, who knew no Chinese original, may appeal more to the individual taste as poetry in English to those who know no Chinese. The preference for individual versions has to be a matter of personal taste. George Steiner's preference for Pound's version of "The Songs of Ch'ang-an" (*Changgan xing*) over Arthur Waley's is similarly a personal choice; the reasons that he gives, derived from the critiques of other scholars as to the fidelity of Pound's version to the essence of the original, do not agree with my personal taste for Waley's version.

of adaptations from something very different from English poetry that shaped the "coherence": it was a trend, all pushing in the same direction which made for swifter acceptance of modernist poetry in English. It is a process similar to the acceptance of new artistic trends in painting that the post-Impressionists made in France; they were influenced by Japanese art, and frequently inserted Japanese themes into their paintings. In this way they familiarized certain Japanese elements and made them their own.

Some may say that it was Pound who set Waley an example with his *Cathay*, and that Waley followed him.[22] Yet Waley himself tells how he was not indebted to anyone. We can assume that he was part of a creative process that was taking place amongst poets and poetry lovers in London at that time.[23] The emergence of the new poetry was in the air, and poets each composed in their own way.

Waley published his first book, *170 Chinese Poems*, in 1918. Itwas very well received, with twelve impressions of the first edition, and six impressions of his second edition.[24] In his preface to the 1962 edition of this book, he mentions how in 1940 he was asked by the typing girls in the government office where he worked during the war, to sign his book.[25] He said that they liked his translations of poetry "that mainly deals with the concrete and particular, with things that one can touch and see…and not with abstract conceptions such as Beauty and Love." This anecdote shows the popularity of the book amongst the wider reading public, and its particular attraction. Incidentally it also reminds us how different reading habits were in those days—if "typing girls" existed now, they would be most unlikely to be reading poetry. Taste in reading changes, but Waley appears to have been writing at a time when poetry in English was something read by the many, not just an activity for the few that it is now. His account of why his poems were liked also highlights the emphasis on the realistic approach that Waley sought from the Chinese, that chimed in with the need for new approaches to poetry in English.

Pound and Eliot were the poets who were to go on to develop modernist English poetry into a far more elitist activity than Waley's; the

---

[22] Hugh Kenner, *The Pound Era* (1971), 206-207.

[23] Morris, *Madly Singing in the Mountains* (1970), 144-45.

[24] Francis A. Johns, *A Bibliography of Arthur Waley* (New Brunswick, N.J: Rutgers State University, 1968, 2nd ed., London and Atlantic Highlands: Athlone Press, 1988), 6-14, gives all the printings from the first in 1918 (London: Constable and Co.) and details of the poems set to music.

[25] "Introduction to *A Hundred and Seventy Chinese Poems* (*1962 edition*)," reprinted in Morris, *Madly Singing in the Mountains* (1970), 135.

later *Cantos* by Pound are a flight in which few people could follow. As John Walter de Gruchy said (with reference to Japanese literature, and we must not forget that Waley was active in Japanese literature as well), "Waley set himself against the elitist modernism of Yeats and Pound, who were consciously creating an unpopular literature for the chosen few."[26] In terms of diction, he made use of the conventional language of poetry in English, he did not follow Pound and the modernists into the later manifestation of modernism that was inaccessible to most people. He retained the traditional language of poetry but excised the stereotypical, so that he was more accessible to the ordinary reader.

Waley invented a form of prosody for his own use which he was to call later a kind of "sprung rhythm," which he was to explain as similar to that Gerard Manley Hopkins made famous. Waley said in his interview with Roy Fuller that he had seen the manuscript of Gerard Manley Hopkins when it was in the possession of Robert Bridges' wife before publication in 1918.[27] He had invented his own version by using as many stresses in the English line as there were in the original Chinese line (not entirely strict, if one counted the stresses of each line, much as the prosody of Regulated Verse in the Tang Dynasty was more honored in the breach than in the observing). Hugh Kenner may congratulate us for having Pound as the first "translator" of Chinese poetry, and he quoted T.S. Eliot who wrote in 1928 that Pound invented China for England at that time establishing a benchmark for Chinese poetry in English.[28] But we have Waley to thank for blazing a trail for translators.

Perhaps Waley did not feel the need to make a wholesale change in the language of English poetry since he was grappling with new languages already. Waley was at the time working at the British Museum Japanese and Chinese print room, and learning these languages from scratch, ostensibly so that he could do his job properly. But he was a gifted linguist, and a natural scholar, which enabled him to delve into the scholarship of the Chinese and explore Chinese literature through its own utterances. Waley was not content with the amateurish approach then fashionable, whereby Chinese poetry was rendered with emphasis on the end result for the eyes of those who neither knew nor cared about the provenance. He was the first professional translator of Chinese literature, always "fully

---

[26] Walter de Gruchy, *Orienting Arthur Waley* (Honolulu: University of Hawaii Press, 2003), 12.

[27] Morris, *Madly Singing in the Mountains* (1970), 144.

[28] Steiner quotes Hugh Kenner from "The Invention of China" in *Spectrum* IX (1967): 359.

armed with the heavy scholarly paraphernalia" of Chinese studies.[29] He may have been a captive of the state of scholarly knowledge in his time, and he made mistakes, but he understood—and always tried to understand—the real Chinese world and its culture behind the poetry he was translating, and more importantly valued Chinese scholarship. We may disagree about the degree of his "fidelity or betrayal" of the original, but he always understood and admired the original culture. Unlike the study of France or Germany at that time, Chinese studies in England was almost non-existent apart from missionary efforts. The English universities almost totally ignored China and the "Far" East. Waley was pioneering in his study of classical Chinese culture and literature through reading its own sources. His approach was the opposite of colonial top-down aestheticism decried by post-colonial scholars like Niranjana.

Waley never managed the oral side of learning Chinese, but he probably felt no great need for it, for there was very little, if any, opportunity for speaking in Chinese to people about the things he was interested in. He has been castigated for not visiting China, but his work never focused on anything later than the China of several centuries ago, and more often than not he was dealing with the China of a thousand years ago, in the Tang Dynasty. China as a place, like any place, has changed greatly. Moreover, he was working on written texts, which the Chinese have always been superbly good at preserving and propagating; he probably would not have obtained much from a visit to China for his studies in those difficult pre- and post-war days, especially since the archaeological finds that make such a difference to the present-day study of ancient texts were only at a preliminary stage in his lifetime.

Classical Chinese texts constitute a realm of literature to itself; not only are they often difficult, requiring a life time's knowledge and experience to understand their background and tradition, but the scholarly paraphernalia are daunting. Waley was not afraid to enter this realm, and by doing so set out the parameters by which foreign scholars of Chinese literature to come participated in the studying of Chinese texts: translations become clearly seen as another method by which interpretations of literary texts are conveyed. Waley can be said to be the first scholar-translator of Chinese texts into English, a path that he blazed for many to follow.

This did not mean that he despised those without his learning. Waley was also canny in another way: he chose poems to translate into English

---

[29] "Arthur Waley," in *An Encyclopedia of Translation, Chinese-English, English-Chinese*, eds. Chan Sin-wai and David Pollard (Hong Kong: The Chinese University Press, 1995), 425.

that are easily comprehensible without the need for massive footnotes. A large part of the *170 Chinese Poems* was written by Bo Juyi, who was a poet well known for writing lucid poems in simple language, and was consequently rather despised by the erudite for not being learned or allusive. This of course is a positive reason for being put into a different language, where the readers could not be expected to have the same cultural education or the background that the original readers had. Andre Lefevere shows how incomprehensible translations can be by analysing six translations of a poem by Su Dongpo (on the *Chibi fu*).[30] It happens that Su Dongpo is one of the more dense and most erudite poets in Chinese history, who assumed that an equal knowledge of Chinese history and tradition existed in his readers, and was therefore free with his use of allusions. The difficulties encountered by his translators in poems such as this one, and their individual and differing solutions to such problems, can create confusion in the less knowing reader. The conclusion that Lefevere draws, whilst not offering any solutions, is that for a translation to be acceptable, readers of the translation must be able to engage with, or "receive," the product in order for the poem in English to enter the readers' own "culture." Waley appears to have avoided the problems of background knowledge by choosing poems like those by Bo Juyi.

Waley went on to publish many books not only on the poems that he translated, but also on other aspects of Chinese literary history. It is hard to fault him for his instinctive understanding of Chinese literary culture, even if his knowledge showed the limitations of his time. In the tribute paid to him by the art historian Michael Sullivan, Sullivan shows that although Waley only had access to a rather poor collection of paintings in the British Museum at that time, his *Introduction to the Study of Chinese Painting* (1923), "[a]ppearing when it did, was a very original book. Other Western writers had drawn upon Chinese sources before Waley, but he used them much more critically, separating the sense from the nonsense with great skill and wit. In some ways it was just the sort of book that a Chinese scholar might have written."[31] Or we can say that Waley for all his limitations engaged with Chinese culture, and succeeded in cultivating a real understanding.

---

[30] "Translation as the Creation of Images or 'Excuse me, Is This the Same Poem?'" in *Translating Literature,* ed. Susan Bassnett for the English Association (Cambridge: Woodbridge, 1997), 79.
[31] "Reaching out" in Morris, *Madly Singing in the Mountains* (1970), 108-13.

History has not been that kind to Waley; he died saddened by the little notice taken of his last work *Ballads and Songs from the Tunhuang*.[32] Interest in China had moved on to contemporary social studies, and ancient Chinese culture was now a minority taste. English literature had long gone beyond the Pound era. He was no longer at the cutting edge of Chinese studies, or a performer on the stage that is English literature. Many scholars in the West and in China, that is those who read English, were not impressed with Waley's work and often in conversation decried his works or consigned them to the annals of history. Whilst Waley did not exclude a wider reading public, he was perhaps writing for a constituency that often knew no Chinese, and one which possibly was more interested in English literature, or in literature of a kind that emerged from a different source than the usual range of the English literary heritage, who still greatly valued his contribution. In any case, the translations that Waley did before the war remain classics. Although many more translations have been made of the *Book of Odes*, I am not aware that his translations of Bo Juyi, that form part of his original *170 Chinese Poems,* have been superseded.

Even as his star waned, he was handing on the baton to younger scholars, in particular to David Hawkes, whom he made his literary executor in 1962.[33] Waley died in 1966. In many ways Hawkes shared many of the same characteristics that had made Waley so distinguished; the grounding in English and Chinese cultures; the rigorous scholarship and the approach to Chinese literature that was understanding and had an instinctive empathy.[34]

Hawkes had to do more as he worked in a different time and different world: he became a fluent speaker of Chinese; he had to hold an academic post down (Professorship of Chinese at the University of Oxford) with all its responsibilities; he travelled the world (including China) to engage with other scholars; and he covered a much larger range extending to contemporary Chinese literature. Like Waley, Hawkes was also grounded in the Classical tradition of the west, that is the study of ancient Greek and Roman literature, which underlie European culture; both were men of culture in every sense of the word as understood in English.

---

[32] London: George Allen and Unwin Ltd., 1960.

[33] Alison Waley, *A Half of Two Lives* (London: Weidenfeld and Nicholson, 1982), 239.

[34] I here have to declare my interest in that David Hawkes was my supervisor and a family friend; my husband and I became close to David and Jean in the latter years of his life when he lived in Oxford.

Hawkes began his studies in ancient Classical Chinese literature, working on the *Chuci,* the *Songs* of *the South,* for which he published not only learned articles but also a full translation of a difficult text.[35] What he is known best for outside the circle of Chinese scholars, is his translation with John Minford of the great novel *Hongloumeng* by Cao Xueqin (c.1715-63). This giant of a novel had previously only been incarnated and abridged in English as *The Dream of the Red Chamber,* but Hawkes preferred to call his complete translation by an alternate name, that of *The Story of a Stone.* He chose to publish it in Penguin Classics to ensure a wider public. This translation joins the ranks of the outstanding fiction in English of the late twentieth century. I will not be commenting on this work as a translation since other chapters will do so, except to say that it reads as though it were a novel originally written in English intended for an English-speaking readership. It was well received by those in the wider reading public who did not know any Chinese or anything about Chinese culture. Like Waley he did not exclude a wider readership.

The *Story of the Stone* was not a straightforward piece of translation, since there are multiple contemporary, or near contemporary, copies of the work. The author Cao Xueqin died before he could finish the novel, so exactly how much he wrote is still open to doubt. It is a story that wholly engages its readers; the text has many unresolved editorial confusions, and there are contemporary comments which survive in manuscript. All of this gives the novel an air of mystery, which has given rise to a whole academic industry in China called *hongxue* (紅學) "Redology," after the best known title which contains the word "red." What Hawkes did was to immerse himself in these studies, and to put together out of the numerous readings a composite and consistent text that that he believed would have been what the author wanted. It is an interpretative critical edition, only it was in English.

His appendices to volume 3 show his careful consideration of editorial minutiae.[36] Apart from the translation itself, the introduction to the first

---

[35] *Ch'u Tz'u, Songs of the South, an Ancient Chinese Anthology* (Oxford: Clarendon Press, 1959).

[36] A few weeks before David Hawkes' death, he happened to tell me that a publisher in Shanghai wanted to bring out a bilingual text using his translation. He seemed to be in something of a panic, as he told me that because he had put together a composite text, there was really no single text his translation could follow in bilingual form. He had generously given away his entire library, and he did not even have the editions on which he had based his work. I offered to take him some of the editions that I happened to have, inherited from my mother, to

volume shows a depth of rigorous knowledge and understanding of Chinese culture that is superior to any in the West, together with a familiarity and love of European culture that formed the backbone of his scholarship, much as it had Arthur Waley's who had been a pioneer.

Poetry was the dominant and rising medium of early twentieth century English literature, when Waley was in the company of Pound and Eliot. By the end of the century, in the mainstream of English literature, interest and creativity moved further towards prose in English, in particular to fiction. One prize-winning novel in English, *A Suitable Boy* by Vikram Seth, released in 1993, provides an interesting take. Seth started an interest in Chinese when he was an undergraduate at Oxford. His novel is about four families in India at the time of the partition, with a cast of characters almost to rival that in the *Story of the Stone*. Seth acknowledged the influence of the *Stone* on his novel: the way it reflected not just the individual characters but society at large; a love story at its heart which does not dominate; and the length of the novel as well as its breadth. In form, he cast the titles of the chapters in rhyming couplets much as Hawkes had done with his translation of Cao Xueqin's rhyming titles to chapters.

A Suitable Boy is part of the sea change that had come over English fiction in the late twentieth century. As with many other art forms in the late capitalist societies of the west, fiction has fragmented. One particular rising trend in novels was represented by those set not in the heartland of metropolitan England or east coast America, the traditional place of English fiction since the early nineteenth century, but in its ex-colonies such as India and Australia. India in particular produced many, such as *Midnight's Children* by Salman Rushdie in 1981. It was part of the rise of the "english" novel, with a small "e," by writers who would not have been part of the recognized literary establishment, and who were not necessarily born native English-speaking.[37] This kind of fiction was buttressed by what became known as postcolonial literary theory, an elastic term as acknowledged by its proponents. Postcolonial literature has by definition nothing to do with Chinese literature, since China was technically never a colony of the West. Even less can it be applied to an earlier China before the rise of imperialist West. Even less does post-colonial literary theory

---

whom David had dedicated his first volume, so I packed up the books ready to take to him. But he had to go to hospital before I managed to get them to him. For further details of the bilingual edition, see the article by Fan Shengyu. *Eds.*

[37] Bill Ashcroft, Gareth Griffiths and Helen Tiffin, *The Empire Writes Back: Theory and Practice in Post-colonial Literatures* (London: Routledge, 1989).

have to do with the majority of the readers of these novels in English. Nevertheless, the interest generated by writers of the ex-colonies who wanted to re-examine their former identities, to reject the supremacy of the west, and to lift their eyes away from the metropolitan Western culture, opened horizons. Interest in the "Far" East was already growing. Readers were receptive to the translation of a Chinese novel, from a land that is more marginalized than India in the Western consciousness, moreover a novel that was written in the past from a period in Chinese history that still felt itself unthreatened by the west, thereby promising the "real" Chinese culture.

Contemporaneous with this rise of fiction in English has been the rise of economic and corporate globalization. Economic power appears to be declining from its previously secure position in the West. There is much greater interest in the non-west, and therefore greater interest in its cultural products. Fiction has always been acknowledged to be a good source of understanding a culture, one of the ways of cultural interaction, and many translations have been done on that premise. Actually we have to admit that translated material does not hold its own as well as material specifically written for the readership in its own language. *Wild Swans* by Chang Jung (1991), written in English for an English-speaking readership, outsells any translation. This book, and many others like it, form part of the English fictional world, even whilst wearing the clothes of a foreign culture. As China opened up after Maoist isolation, this volume, along with other biographies such as *Life and Death in Shanghai* by Nien Cheng (1987), formed a new trend, if not a literary industry, in biography and fictionalized biographies of the twentieth century. All of this fed an interest in the west on the society of twentieth century China, rather than its culture.

Foreign culture appeals to a different set of people from those interested in the social sciences of foreign societies, even though the latter may approach cultural products for information. Contemporary China as an economic powerhouse has started to generate an interest that had never been accorded its culture. David Hawkes' translation was produced before the Western public's interest in the economic rise of China. Chinese culture at that time was marginal in the cultural landscape of Europe. But *Stone* was well received as a literary phenomenon, not just as part of a "China fever" based on its economic rise.

So I believe that the translation of *The Story of the Stone* will ensure a special place for David Hawkes in the pantheon of English literature, much as the translation of *170 Chinese Poems* has for Arthur Waley. They both achieved renown in the English literature of their time; they can be said to have participated in its creation. *The Story of the Stone* cannot be said yet to have the same number of reprints as *170 Chinese Poems* or possibly to have had the same impact on the reading public. But from anecdotal evidence for the novel in English, and the many printings that the poems had many decades ago, it is not only those engaged in Chinese studies in the West that read these works.

Translations share the same reception as works of literature created in the same language, mainly because the target readership, whether they know the original language or not, have the same expectations; what they read must be outstanding, not just merely readable, in English. In my attempt to understand what is the point of making translations into English from Chinese literature and why people do it, by examining the paths of Arthur Waley and David Hawkes in turning classical Chinese literature into English, it seems to me that the point is to write outstanding works in English, based on a full understanding and rigorous exploration of the cultures of both the Chinese and the English, and to effect a cultural interaction that otherwise would not exist. Both Arthur Waley and David Hawkes in making their translations into English from the Chinese were contributing to new contemporary literary trends in English literature. Successful translators not only produce works that are outstanding in their own right, they make elements of a foreign culture available to their readers in such a way that they can engage with it as part of their own culture.

SURPRISING THE MUSES:
DAVID HAWKES'
A LITTLE PRIMER OF TU FU

LAURENCE K. P. WONG
DEPARTMENT OF TRANSLATION
THE CHINESE UNIVERSITY OF HONG KONG

David Hawkes' *A Little Primer of Tu Fu*, published by Oxford University Press in 1967, is a primer and more than a primer if we go by the second definition of the word given by *The Oxford English Dictionary* (hereafter referred to as *OED*):

> 2. a. An elementary school-book for teaching children to read; formerly, 'a little book, which children are first taught to read and to pray by' [...]; 'a small prayer-book in which children are taught to read' [...].[1]
> b. By extension, a small introductory book on any subject.[2]

In the sense that it teaches beginners elementary Chinese grammar, Chinese prosody, and basic historical facts about the poet Du Fu, it is a primer.[3] In the sense that it is the product of meticulous research and rigorous scholarship, containing fine prose translations of Du Fu's poems, it is more than a primer. In this paper, I shall discuss Hawkes' prose

---

[1] *The Oxford English Dictionary*, first ed. James A. Murray, Henry Bradley, W. A. Craigie, combined with A Supplement to *The Oxford English Dictionary*, ed. R. W. Burchfield, 2nd ed. prepared by J. A. Simpson and E. S. C. Weiner (Oxford: Clarendon Press, 1989), XII, 480.

[2] *OED*, XII, 481.

[3] The romanization in the Wade-Giles system for 杜甫 is "Tu Fu"; in the *Pinyin* 拼音 system, the name of the poet is romanized as "Du Fu." Throughout this paper, I shall be using the *Pinyin* system except in cases where I am quoting names already romanized in the Wade-Giles system. In indicating aspirates, sinologists and translators have used different signs: the apostrophe ("'"), the inverted apostrophe ("'"), and the single initial quotation mark ("'"). To avoid confusion, I have consistently used the apostrophe ("'") throughout this paper.

translations, and show to what extent the translator has succeeded in preserving many of the qualities of the originals in poetic terms despite the inherent limitations of prose as a medium for poetry translation.[4] Whenever necessary, I shall examine Hawkes' translations alongside those by other translators, closely analysing them, so that we can see more clearly the merits of Hawkes' versions relative to those of other versions, and draw conclusions which are more objective.

When a translator opts for prose instead of verse as his medium, there are qualities or stylistic effects he has to sacrifice, among them music and rhythmic variety, which verse, with its many prosodic resources, such as metre, rhyme, and phonological devices, is best equipped to reproduce. In Act I, scene i, ll. 141-49 of Shakespeare's *A Midsummer Night's Dream*, for example, in which Lysander contends that "The course of true love never did run smooth," we can see the resources of verse being skilfully tapped by the poet:[5]

---

[4] In the Author's Introduction, Hawkes says, "I have written this book in order to give some idea of what Chinese poetry is really like and how it works to people who either know no Chinese at all or know only a little. To write it I have taken all the poems by Tu Fu contained in a well-known Chinese anthology, *Three Hundred T'ang Poems*, arranged them chronologically, transliterated them, explained their form and historical background, expounded their meaning, and lastly translated them into English prose. The translations are intended as cribs. They are not meant to be beautiful or pleasing. It is my ardent hope that a reader who is patient enough to work his way through to the end of the book will, by the time he reaches it, have learned something about the Chinese language, something about Chinese poetry, and something about the poet Tu Fu" (David Hawkes, *A Little Primer of Tu Fu* (Oxford: Clarendon Press, 1967), ix). The statement is modest, likely to give one the impression that the book is nothing more than a primer. On close scrutiny, however, one will see that it is more than a primer, with "beautiful" and "pleasing" prose translations of Du Fu's poems, which only a master hand can produce. Throughout the book, Hawkes' learning, including his understanding of Chinese prosody, of Tang history in general and of Du Fu's life in particular, of Chinese culture, of the Chinese language, and of Chinese and English literature, is impressive without being intrusive. Judging by the lucid presentation of his wealth of knowledge, Hawkes' "ardent hope" is totally realizable with any "patient enough" reader. As a thorough discussion of Hawkes' learning and scholarship is a topic for another paper, I shall concentrate only on his translations.

[5] William Shakespeare, *The Arden Shakespeare: Complete Works*, eds. Richard Proudfoot, Ann Thompson, David Scott Kastan, and H. R. Woudhuysen, consultant editor, Harold Jenkins (London: Cengage Learning, 1998), 892.

Or, if there were a sympathy in choice,
War, death, or sickness did lay siege to it,
Making it momentany as a sound,
Swift as a shadow, short as any dream,
Brief as the lightning in the collied night,
That, in a spleen, unfolds both heaven and earth,
And, ere a man hath power to say 'Behold!',
The jaws of darkness do devour it up:
So quick bright things come to confusion.[6]

The parallelism and the series of similes in lines 3-5 emphasize the brevity of love. The deployment of three similes in the same syntactic pattern creates a piling-up effect, so that the speaker's point is relentlessly driven home. At the same time, rhythmic variety that reinforces semantic meaning is created through the manipulation of syntax and pauses. Thus line 3, with five feet running on without an internal pause, contrasts with line 2, which has two internal pauses (one after "war," the other after "death"); line 4, with an internal pause after "shadow," contrasts with line 3, and slows down the rhythm, which picks up in line 5 because of the absence of an internal pause. Having swept across the page in line 5, the speech is briefly checked by "That" and "in a spleen" in line 6, only to be followed by the onslaught of "unfolds both heaven and earth." Then, the speech is slightly held back in line 7 by a subordinate clause ("ere a man hath power to say 'Behold!'") after "And," which makes the climax ("The jaws of darkness do devour it up") all the more overwhelming. Coming as it does after the climax, the last line, in the form of a comment ("So quick bright things come to confusion."), again without an internal pause, brings the whole passage to a satisfying close. In just nine lines, Shakespeare has, by exploiting the possibilities of verse to the full, succeeded in accelerating and decelerating his language in sync with the message he wants to convey to his audience, thereby staging a mini-drama in auditory terms, in which the speaker's train of thought rises and falls, going through exciting twists and turns and gripping the audience's attention from beginning to end.

Discussing, in his famous essay entitled "Poetry and Drama," the function of Shakespeare's dramatic poetry, which is in blank verse, Eliot has convincingly argued that certain qualities or feelings can only be expressed by poetry, which are beyond the reach of prose:

---

[6] Shakespeare, 892.

There are great prose dramatists—such as Ibsen and Chekhov—who have at times done things of which I would not otherwise have supposed prose to be capable, but who seem to me, in spite of their success, to have been hampered in expression by writing in prose. This peculiar range of sensibility can be expressed by dramatic poetry, at its moments of greatest intensity. At such moments, we touch the border of those feelings which only music can express. We can never emulate music, because to arrive at the condition of music would be the annihilation of poetry, and especially of dramatic poetry. Nevertheless, I have before my eyes a kind of mirage of the perfection of verse drama, which would be a design of human action and of words, such as to present at once the two aspects of dramatic and of musical order.[7]

In commenting in the same essay on the following line spoken by Othello,

Keep up your bright swords, for the dew will rust them,

Eliot says, "The line of Othello expresses irony, dignity, and fearlessness; and incidentally reminds us of the time of night in which the scene takes place. Only poetry could do this."[8] Opting to translate Du Fu's poetry into prose, therefore, Hawkes has to forgo the opportunity to "touch the border of those feelings which only music can express."

Similar qualities created through verse can be found in Eliot's "The Love Song of J. Alfred Prufrock":

The yellow fog that rubs its back upon the window-panes,
The yellow smoke that rubs its muzzle on the window-panes,
Licked its tongue into the corners of the evening,
Lingered upon the pools that stand in drains,
Let fall upon its back the soot that falls from chimneys,
Slipped by the terrace, made a sudden leap,
And seeing that it was a soft October night,
Curled once about the house, and fell asleep.[9]

---

[7] T. S. Eliot, *On Poetry and Poets* (London: Faber and Faber Limited, 1957), 86-87.
[8] Eliot, *On Poetry and Poets*, 83.
[9] T. S. Eliot, *Collected Poems 1909-1962* (London: Faber and Faber Limited, 1963), 13.

In describing "the smoke that blew across the Mississippi from the factories of his home-town of St Louis, Missouri,"[10] Eliot exploits rhythm, pauses, repetition to personify the "yellow fog," so that, in the rhythmic movement of the lines, the image reminds one of a cat that lingers,[11] then rouses from sloth and executes a series of quick actions suggested by the stressed first syllable at the beginning of lines 3, 4, 5, and 6 ("Licked," "Lingered," "Let fall," "Slipped"). Following this series of quick actions, Eliot further turns the rhythm to account: after the stressed "Slipped," he introduces two unstressed syllables ("by/the"), then a stressed one followed by an unstressed one ("'ter/race"), then a clause in which three stressed syllables suggest effort ("'made a 'sudden 'leap") and the actual leaping of a cat; after the stressed "leap" in line 6, the rhythm slows down ("And seeing that it was a soft October night"), and relaxes, suggesting a cat that, after so much activity, eventually falls asleep ("Curled once about the house, and fell asleep"), an image further reinforced by the neat rhyme "leap-asleep." As one reads on, one can feel the rhythm tightening and relaxing in accordance with the semantic meaning,[12] so that the lines are functional not only semantically and phonologically, but also kinaesthetically.[13]

Choosing to translate Du Fu's poems into prose, which is not capable of the subtleties of Shakespeare's or Eliot's verse, Hawkes has settled for something less ambitious. Yet, despite the limitations of his medium, he has succeeded in reproducing or re-creating many of the poetic effects found in the originals, excelling all other translators, including those who use verse as their medium.[14]

---

[10] B. C. Southam, *A Student's Guide to the Selected Poems of T. S. Eliot* 6th ed. (London: Faber and Faber Limited, 1994), 50. 1st ed. 1968.

[11] This is suggested by two seven-foot lines which are in iambic metre ("The yellow fog that rubs its back upon the window-panes, / The yellow smoke that rubs its muzzle on the window-panes") and are structurally similar ("The yellow [...] that rubs its [...] the window-panes") with a slight variation (with "fog," "back," and "upon" replaced respectively by "smoke," "muzzle," and "on"), thereby preserving similarity while preventing monotony.

[12] The meaning of a poem generally consists of two levels: the semantic and the non-semantic. The latter consists, in turn, among other things, of the phonological and syntactic levels.

[13] For a detailed discussion of the music of Eliot's poetry, see Helen Gardner, *The Art of T. S. Eliot* (London: The Cresset Press, 1949), especially chapters 2 and 3, entitled "Auditory Imagination" and "The Music of *Four Quartets*" respectively.

[14] It must be admitted, though, that there are qualities in Du Fu's poetry which can never be adequately translated into another language no matter whether the translator uses prose or verse as his medium, and no matter who the translator is.

As "China's Greatest Poet,"[15] Du Fu has inherited and created almost all the qualities that typify the finest of traditional Chinese poetry, one of which is the ability to re-create natural scenery in words, as can be seen in the following lines of "*Lü ye shu huai*"〈旅夜書懷〉("Thoughts Written While Travelling at Night"):[16]

細草微風岸
危檣獨夜舟
星垂平野闊

These qualities include those which are strictly language-bound, such as qualities dependent on the paratactic nature of Chinese, on the symmetry and antithetical structure of the Chinese couplet, on Chinese phonology, including the interplay of level-tone 平聲 and oblique-tone 仄聲 words, and on the often indeterminate grammatical relationship between words in a line. Thus the famous couplet "萬里悲秋常作客，百年多病獨登台" in "*Deng gao*"〈登高〉("From a Height") loses its pleasing semantic symmetry as well as the interplay between its level- and oblique-tone words when translated as "Through a thousand miles of autumn's melancholy, a constant traveller racked with a century's diseases, alone I have dragged myself up to this high terrace" (Hawkes, 205). The English translation has a beauty of its own, but that beauty is the beauty of English poetry, not the beauty peculiar to the antithetical structure of the Chinese couplet. As a matter of fact, Hawkes himself was aware of what could not be translated, particularly in the case of Du Fu. Thus in commenting on the form of "*Chun wang*"〈春望〉, he made the following perceptive remark: "This is a formally perfect example of a pentasyllabic poem in Regulated Verse. Not only the middle couplets, but the first couplet, too, contain verbal parallelism. It is amazing that Tu Fu is able to use so immensely stylized a form in so natural a manner. The tremendous spring-like compression which is achieved by using very simple language with very complicated forms manipulated in so skilful a manner that they don't show is characteristic of Regulated Verse at its best. Its perfection of form lends it a classical grace which unfortunately cannot be communicated in translation. That is the reason why Tu Fu, one of the great masters of this form, makes so comparatively poor a showing in foreign languages" (Hawkes, 46-47). But, as Du Fu's untranslatability, or the untranslatability of classical Chinese poetry, for that matter, is a topic for another full-length paper, I shall not go into further details here.

[15] This is the subtitle of William Hung's book on Du Fu, which expresses a view likely to be shared by the majority of discerning critics of classical Chinese poetry. See William Hung, *Tu Fu: China's Greatest Poet* (Cambridge: Harvard University Press, 1952).

[16] In quoting Du Fu's poems, I use *Pinyin* in romanizing the original titles; the English translations of the titles, with *Pinyin* replacing Wade-Giles romanization, are Hawkes' unless indicated otherwise.

月湧大江流 [.]¹⁷

The lines present a quiet scene in which there is a boat by the river bank, with the waters flowing under the moon and the stars hanging down over a vast expanse of land. There is peace as well as motion.

In Hawkes' translation, a similar scene is re-created with equally vivid details:

> By the bank where the fine grass bends in a gentle wind, my boat's tall mast stands in the solitary night. The stars hang down over the great emptiness of the level plain, and the moon bobs on the running waters of the Great River.[18]

With strokes as delicate as those in the original, the translation first paints a quiet scene which is near the narrator's point of observation, and then, with a panning shot, lets the reader see "the stars" hanging down "over the great emptiness of the level plain," together with the bobbing moon, and "the running waters of the Great River." The movement from what is close by to what is panoramic is controlled with great precision.

In his version, "Thoughts While Travelling at Night," Hung describes the boat as moving:

> Between two shores of tender grass, in the slight breeze, Glides this lonely high-masted boat. The stars seem to reach down to the fields, flat and wide; The moon seems to be swimming as the Great River flows [.][19]

In so doing, he has destroyed the functional ambiguity of the original, which, not indicating whether the boat is moving or moored by the river bank, allows the reader's imagination free play. At the same time, because of the fluidity of Chinese syntax, "獨" in the phrase "獨夜舟" can be applied to "夜," creating a kind of pathetic fallacy, an effect which Hawkes has accurately conveyed to the English reader.[20] In Hung's

---

¹⁷ Hawkes, 200.
¹⁸ Hawkes, 202.
¹⁹ Hung, 256.
²⁰ Pathetic fallacy is "the poetic convention whereby natural phenomena which cannot feel as humans do are described as if they could: thus rain-clouds may 'weep', or flowers may be 'joyful' in sympathy with the poet's (or imagined speaker's) mood. The pathetic fallacy normally involves the use of some metaphor which falls short of full-scale personification in its treatment of the natural world. [...] The rather odd term was coined by [...] Ruskin in the third volume of his *Modern Painters* (1856). Ruskin's strict views about the accurate representation of

version, not only has this suggestiveness disappeared, but the word "夜" is left untranslated; when the translator wishes to convey the original's imagery, he can, either because of his insufficient sensitivity to the source text or because of his inadequate command of the target language, turn a dynamic image ("月湧") into one which is feeble and comical: "The moon seems to be swimming."

In comparison with Hawkes' version, the versions of two other translators of the poem, namely, Hamill and Waley, also pale:[21]

> Thin grass bends on the breezy shore,
> and the tall mast seems lonely in my boat.
>
> Stars ride low across the wide plain,
> and the moon is tossed by the Yangtze.
> ("Night Thoughts While Travelling")[22]

Fine grasses	ruffled by breeze
Tall mast	lone boat moored by the bank.
Stars overhang	the unending plain
Moon bobs	in water's moving mass.

("Written at Night when Travelling")[23]

In Hamill's version, the richly suggestive "獨夜舟" is nowhere to be found, and the word "tossed" in the last line evokes associations with coins or quoits, thereby detracting from the dignity of the image ("月湧大江流") and giving it an undesirable touch of levity.[24] In Waley's version, which has pared down connective words, apparently to achieve concision,

---

nature led him to distinguish great poets like Shakespeare, who use the device sparingly, from lesser poets like Wordsworth and Shelley, whose habitual use of it becomes 'morbid'. Later critics, however, employ the term in a neutral sense" (Chris Baldick, *The Concise Oxford Dictionary of Literary Terms* (Oxford: Oxford University Press, 1990), 163).

[21] This Waley (Jonathan Waley) should not be confused with the more famous translator Arthur Waley.

[22] Sam Hamill, trans., *Facing the Snow: Visions of Tu Fu*, with calligraphy by Yim Yse (New York: White Pine Press, 1988), 95.

[23] Jonathan Waley, trans., *Du Fu: Spring in the Ruined City: Selected Poems* (Exeter: Shearsman Books, 2008), 88.

[24] In everyday English, it is, of course, idiomatic to say something like "the boat is tossed by the waves," but here, "the moon" should not be collocated with "tossed," a verb that triggers associations not warranted by the context.

the suggestiveness of "獨夜舟" is also missing, showing that the translator, like Hamill, either cannot appreciate Du Fu's craftsmanship or lacks the ability to reproduce the same stylistic effect. His "water's moving mass," evoking associations with physics rather than describing a natural scene, also shows that he cannot even handle a relatively easy phrase with precision.

Watson's translation, "A Traveler at Night Writes His Thoughts," is, generally speaking, a sensitive rendering:

> Delicate grasses, faint wind on the bank;
> stark mast, a lone night boat:
> stars hang down, over broad fields sweeping;
> the moon boils up, on the great river flowing.[25]

In dispensing with connectives so as to re-create in English the paratactic structure of the Chinese language, Watson has achieved considerable concision and produced imagistic lines; however, as English is largely hypotactic, this technique makes the poem sound un-English against the background of English poetry, which is very rarely pared down to this extent. Moreover, whereas the absence of connectives in Chinese poetry does not destroy the implied linkage between words, which is automatically supplied by native speakers of Chinese when they are reading, the artificial deletion of connectives in English not only makes the lines sound unnatural, but also takes away the linkage, so that the words or phrases function almost as disparate lexical items. Watson's choice of words, too, is not altogether felicitous. On the one hand, the words "Delicate" and "faint" tend to evoke associations with weakliness. On the other, though presenting a sharp, even startling, image of the mast, "stark," being unnecessarily forbidding, evokes associations with bareness, desolation, stiffness, rigidity, the unpleasant, and the negative, failing to harmonize with the peaceful atmosphere described in the original. The same can be said of "lone," which is at odds with the tranquillity of the scene and the poet's feeling of contentment, which are implied by Hawkes' "solitary." [26]

---

[25] Burton Watson, trans., *The Selected Poems of Du Fu* (New York: Columbia University, 2002), 118.

[26] It must be admitted, though, that, because of its special syntactic structure, the line "星垂平野闊," which is not the same thing as "星垂闊平野," already borders on the untranslatable. Of all the versions quoted, Hawkes' comes closest to the original; still, it is more a version of "星垂闊平野" than of "星垂平野闊." The latter, because of the ambiguous relationship between "闊" and the rest of the line

Alley's rendering, "Night Thoughts of a Traveller," is a mixed performance:

> Thin reeds, and from the land
> A soft breeze; our mast stands
> Tall and stark in the night
> And I am alone; stars hang
> Over the great plain, and
> The moon moves with the flowing river [...][27]

"A soft breeze," a close equivalent of "微風," is as sensitive as Hawkes' "a gentle wind." However, "reeds" is not the same thing as "草"; "stark" is, as in Watson's version, at odds with the tranquillity depicted by Du Fu. In taking the adjective "獨" in "獨夜舟" to describe the narrator ("And I am alone") instead of the night or the night boat, Alley has either miscomprehended the original or deliberately avoided tackling the poet's bold and evocative phrase, which can describe the night, the boat, or the night boat as solitary at the same time. In the last line ("The moon moves

---

and between "闊" and "平野," has more than one layer of meaning. While sharing exactly the same lexical items with "星垂闊平野," it can also have the following meaning: "As the stars hang down [the level plain], the level plain expands in dimension (or increases in vastness)," in which "闊," primarily a static adjective, has taken on verbal force and become dynamic. In European languages, an adjective can also come after a noun, as in *consul general* in English, or *la Maison Blanche* in French, or *la Casa Bianca* in Italian, but the postposition of the adjective in these phrases does not normally add any new layer of meaning to the collocation as does its counterpart in Chinese. Watson's translation (118), "stars hang down, over broad fields sweeping; / the moon boils up, on the great river flowing," shows that the translator is aware of the original's syntactic fluidity, and tries to reproduce the same effect in English. However, because of the syntactic limitations of the English language, despite their postposition ("fields sweeping," "river flowing"), the two keywords ("sweeping" and "flowing") have only become participial; because of this, they still fail to convey the functional ambiguity of the original, which adds an additional layer of meaning to the line. In his exegesis of lines 5 and 6 ("三顧頻煩天下計[;]兩朝開濟老臣心") of "*Shu xiang*" 〈蜀相〉 ("The Chancellor of Shu"), Hawkes (107) shows that he is aware of this peculiarity of Chinese syntax: "The grammar of these two lines may seem more than a little puzzling. They are examples of the sort of 'pregnant construction' which is fairly common in Chinese syntax, where predication includes a much wider range of relationships than it does in European languages.[...]"

[27] Rewi Alley, trans., *Tu Fu: Selected Poems*, compiled by Feng Chih (Peking: Foreign Languages Press, 1962), 135.

with the flowing river"), too, the verb "moves," lacking specificity, has reduced the dynamic scene ("月湧"), which makes a powerful impact on the reader, to something general and vapid.

In McCraw's version, "Expressing My Feelings, on a Night of Travel,"

A fine grassy, light breezy bank;
A tall masted, lonesome night boat.
The stars droop, as flat wilds widen;
The moon bobs, in great Jiang's flow [,][28]

the functional ambiguity arising from the fluidity of Chinese syntax, which allows the reader's imagination plenty of freedom, is destroyed because of an ill-chosen translation strategy: using the subordinate endocentric construction to translate the first and second lines, in which "bank" ("岸") is the head word of "A fine grassy, light breezy bank" and "boat" ("舟") is the head word of "A tall masted, lonesome night boat," the translator has failed to bring about a free interplay between words, which is a prominent feature of the original. The choice of words, too, is less than felicitous. Whereas "獨" in the original is neutral, "lonesome" in the translation carries negative connotations. The word "droop" in the third line, suggesting weakness and lifelessness, is not equivalent to "垂" in "星垂平野闊," either, for the Chinese word suggests no weakness or lifelessness; it is a less accurate rendering than Hawkes' "hang" in "The stars hang down over the great emptiness of the level plain." Finally, romanizing "江" as "Jiang," the translator is more likely to bewilder the reader than to help him enter the world of the original.

Bynner's version, entitled "A Night Abroad," is largely a deviation:

A light wind is rippling at the grassy shore....
Through the night, to my motionless tall mast,
The stars lean down from open space,
And the moon comes running up the river.[29]

Even where the interpretation is generally correct, the translator's handling of the imagery lacks the sensitivity expected of translators of poetry. For

---

[28] David R. McCraw, *Du Fu's Laments from the South* (Honolulu: University of Hawaii Press, 1992), 63.

[29] Witter Bynner, trans., *The Jade Mountain: A Chinese Anthology, Being Three Hundred Poems of the T'ang Dynasty 618-906*, from the texts of Kiang Kang-hu (New York: Alfred A. Knopf, 1929), 152.

example, translating "月湧大江流" as "the moon comes running up the river," Bynner has rendered the scene not only unpoetic, but comical, intrusively evoking the image of a runner.[30]

Kenneth Rexroth, a poet himself, adopts a totally different approach, an approach similar to Pound's when the latter translated Chinese poetry into English: taking the original as a point of departure so as to write his own poem. The result is what one would call a piece of "transwriting," entitled "Night Thoughts While Travelling":

> A light breeze rustles the reeds
> Along the river banks. The
> Mast of my lonely boat soars
> Into the night. Stars blossom
> Over the vast desert of
> Waters. Moonlight flows on the
> Surging river.[31]

A fine poem in its own right, the "translation" cannot bear scrutiny alongside the original if one tries to identify corresponding sense-units in

---

[30] In his Introduction, Bynner has made the following remark about Chinese poetry:

> Because of the absence of tenses, of personal pronouns and of connectives generally, the translator of Chinese poetry, like the Chinese reader himself, has considerable leeway as to interpretation. If even in English, so much more definite a language, there may be varying interpretations of a given poem, it is no wonder that critics and annotators have differed as to the meaning of poems in Chinese. There have been frequent instances in this volume where Dr. Kiang and I have discussed several possible meanings of a poem and have chosen for translation into the more definite language the meaning we preferred. (Bynner, xviii)

It is true that, because of the characteristics of Chinese poetry enumerated by Bynner, the translator "has considerable leeway as to interpretation"; however, the meanings of lines 1-3 and 5-6 in the original are so clear and unambiguous that they leave no "leeway as to interpretation" in this instance. The deviation from the meaning of the original can only be explained by two possible factors: either Bynner, "a westerner [...] without a knowledge of the Chinese tongue" (Bynner, xiii), has not been able to re-present the correct interpretation made by Kiang Kang-hu, Bynner's collaborator, or Kiang himself has misinterpreted the original. As, judging by his Introduction, Bynner appears to be trying to translate in accordance with his and Kiang's interpretation, one should not attribute his deviation to a deliberate attempt at "rewriting."

[31] Kenneth Rexroth, trans., *One Hundred Poems from the Chinese* (New York: New Directions, 1971), 33.

both.[32] For example, nowhere in the original does Du Fu say that "The /
Mast of my lonely boat *soars* / Into the night."[33] It is worth noting, too,
that, ending lines 2 and 6 with the definite article "the," Rexroth tends to
lead the reader to conclude that his poem is prose printed in lines separated
at random. Upon closer examination, though, one may say that, in so
doing, Rexroth is trying to highlight "Mast" in line 3 and "Surging" in line
7.[34]

From the above discussion, it is clear that, though "*Lü ye shu huai*" "is
one of Du Fu's dearest-loved, most-translated, and best-analyzed poems in
English,"[35] it does not seem to have benefited from the passage of time or
from the large number of attempts by various translators; to date, no
translation has yet succeeded in equalling, much less surpassing, Hawkes'.

While the scene in "*Lü ye shu huai*" is relatively quiet and tranquil,
moving from what is close by to what is far from the point of observation,
the following scene, from "*Deng gao*" 〈登高〉 ("From a Height"), is one
of large-scale motion, a panorama from the very beginning:

風急天高猿嘯哀
渚清沙白鳥飛迴
無邊落木蕭蕭下
不盡長江滾滾來 [.][36]

---

[32] Rexroth is to Hawkes very much as Pound is to Arthur Waley. As poets, Rexroth
and Pound freely exploited Chinese poems for the purpose of re-creation, while
Waley and Hawkes conscientiously and meticulously translated Chinese poems
into English. In other words, Rexroth and Pound are not translators in the strict
sense of the word, while Waley and Hawkes are. A distinction must be drawn
between Rexroth and Pound, though: while Rexroth does follow certain parameters
set by his "source text," Pound does not seem to have considered himself under
any obligation to follow any parameters; he is interested only in "rewriting" or
"writing" his own poems. At times, though, Rexroth comes very close to Pound in
his "rewriting" project. Thus he can, in "To Wei Pa, a Retired Scholar," translate
"人生不相見" as "The lives of many men are / Shorter than the years since we
have / Seen each other" (Rexroth, 11), lines which are no longer recognizable as
"translation."

[33] My italics.

[34] Used too often, as is the case in Rexroth's volume, this "technique" can cease to
be effective and become irksome to the reader.

[35] McCraw, 64.

[36] Hawkes, 203.

In Hawkes' translation, the scene is characterized by an equally grand sweep:

> The wind is keen, the sky is high; apes wail mournfully. The island looks fresh; the white sand gleams; birds fly circling. An infinity of trees bleakly divest themselves, their leaves falling, falling. Along the endless expanse of river the billows come rolling, rolling.[37]

In both the original and the translation, the reader is greeted by a scene of sound and motion set in a vast expanse of space; with the wind blowing, the apes wailing, the birds circling, and the "infinity of trees bleakly divest[ing] themselves" above the fresh island and the gleaming sand, autumn is heard, seen, and felt through the senses.

Watson's translation, "Climbing to a High Place," again dispensing with connectives, is remarkable by virtue of its concision:

> Wind shrill in the tall sky, gibbons wailing dolefully;
> beaches clean, sands white, overhead the circling birds:
> leaves fall, no end to them, rustling, rustling down;
> ceaselessly the long river rushes, rushes on.[38]

In the four lines quoted above, only the essentials of the original poem are presented; the "spare parts" required by the hypotaxis of English are omitted, resulting, as pointed out earlier, in a loss in naturalness. The choice of words and the rhythm are not flawless, either. First, one does not know why Watson has preferred "tall" to "high" in his translation of "天高." Second, the word "dolefully" tends towards the funereal and the gloomy, which is much stronger than "哀." To describe the grief-evoking wail of an ape or a gibbon, "mournfully" is a more appropriate word. Third, the word "beach," likely to trigger associations with swimmers, sun-tanning, beach volleyball, beachheads, etc., is too modern for the scene. Fourth, though "白" normally has a pat equivalent in "white," its appearance in the collocation "沙白" has taken on a more specific shade of meaning, which is conveyed with precision by Hawkes' "white [...] gleams" in "the white sand gleams."

In re-presenting the scene, Watson is also less meticulous. His "overhead the circling birds," though similar to Hawkes' "birds fly circling" at first glance, suffers in comparison. In the original, Du Fu has

---

[37] Hawkes, 205.
[38] Watson, 146.

not indicated whether or not the birds are overhead. As is clear from the title of the source text, the poet is observing the river, the "infinity of trees," and the birds from a vantage point higher than the river, at times perhaps even higher than the birds; judging from the description in line 1 ("風急天高"), he must be looking at the islets (or sand-banks) and the birds from quite a distance; even if the birds may fly overhead at times, coming closer to the poet, they should not be constantly "overhead," for they are circling, at one moment nearer the islets in the distance, at another nearer the observer. With "circling" put before "birds," too, the dynamic scene in the original, rendered with great precision by Hawkes ("birds fly circling"), is reduced to something static, reminding the reader of the difference between "星垂闊平野" and "星垂平野闊" discussed in footnote 26.

Furthermore, any gain in concision resulting from the omission of connectives in line 3 is outweighed by the harm done to the rhythm. In the original, "無邊落木蕭蕭下" is, in terms of rhythm, a continuous sweep, which is captured by Hawkes' "An infinity of trees divest themselves, their leaves falling, falling," in which the main clause, with a string of seemingly endless syllables, suggests the sweep, and the nominative absolute ("their leaves falling, falling"), loosely attached to the main clause, parallels the fluidity and flexibility of paratactic Chinese both rhythmically and syntactically; in Watson's translation, the omission of connectives, with three pauses separating four units of almost equal length, gives the poem an abrupt rhythm, which bears little resemblance to the continuous music of the original. The phrase "rustling, rustling down," though reproducing the onomatopoeic effect of "蕭蕭," cannot adequately present the grand, panoramic scene of "無邊落木蕭蕭下." Unlike Hawkes' phrase "falling, falling," which is made up of two trochaic feet, both ending in an unstressed syllable, Watson's rendering, with the line ending in a stressed syllable ("down"), is unduly emphatic, so that the feeling of something petering out as conveyed by "蕭蕭下" in the original fails to come through.

By virtue of its twelve syllables running on uninterrupted before coming to a halt, thereby suggesting the endless rolling of the waves, line 4 is rhythmically closer to the original. Nevertheless, it is not without flaws: "rushes, rushes on" is, in both rhythmic and semantic terms, too hasty; the large number of sibilants ("ceaselessly the long river rushes, rushes on")[39] in the form of /s/ or /ʃ/, too, is not in keeping with the

---

[39] My italics.

majestic rolling of billows.

   In Young's translation, entitled "From a Height,"

> Vast sky, sharp wind,
> and the gibbons wailing sadly
>
> the white sand on the island looks fresh
> birds are wheeling above it
>
> everywhere the trees
> are silently shedding leaves
>
> and the long river, ceaselessly
> comes churning and rushing on [,][40]

line 1 of the first stanza dispenses with the definite article *the*, apparently to achieve concision and paratactic effects. Line 2 of the second stanza conveys the same vivid motion of birds flying above the island. However, the word "sadly," being a general word, lacks the narrower and more specific semantic field of "哀," and "silently" fails to capture the meaning of "蕭蕭," which, being onomatopoeic, suggests the sound of the wind or of the leaves falling. In translating "蕭蕭" as "bleakly [...] falling, falling," Hawkes has succeeded in conveying the onomatopoeic effect, first with a word ("bleakly") that describes the mood of autumn, which is associated with the falling of leaves, then with a reduplication ("falling, falling"), which matches the reduplication of the original, and in which the alliteration in "*f*alling, *f*alling"[41] approximates to the repeated initial consonant of "蕭蕭" (*x*iao *x*iao).[42] In Young's version, there is no evidence that the translator has paid such meticulous attention to the original's subtle phonological effects.

   The same can be said of Young's rendering of "滾滾." As a reduplication, the Chinese collocation not only describes the billows of the Changjiang (Yangtze) River rolling forward, but also conveys through onomatopoeia the sound of the surging billows. Whereas Hawkes' "rolling, rolling" has re-created this effect, Young's "churning and rushing on" suggests little of the original onomatopoeia; worse still, the word "churning," in most everyday contexts taken to mean "To agitate, stir, and

---

[40] David Young, trans., *Du Fu: A Life in Poetry* (New York: Alfred A. Knopf, 2008), 198.
[41] My italics.
[42] My italics.

intermix any liquid, or mixture of liquid and solid matter; to produce froth, etc. by this process,"[43] tends to pull the reader towards its other common meaning: "To agitate *milk* or *cream* in a churn so as to make butter; to produce *butter* thus,"[44] reminding him more of a churner or a ship's motor than of nature.

In terms of diction and comprehension of the original, Young is also less competent than Hawkes. Whereas Hawkes' "mournfully" conveys the same plaintive quality as "哀," Young's "sadly," describing a generic feeling rather than a more specific one as the original does, fails to convey the precise emotive shade of the gibbons' wailing. His "the white sand on the island looks fresh," on the other hand, is an unwarranted telescoping of two ideas ("渚清" and "沙白") into one, thereby "short-changing" the reader by presenting him with only part of the scene depicted by Du Fu. Worse still, in the telescoping, the translator has distorted the meaning of the original, which unequivocally says it is the "渚" which is "清"; in Young's version, "清" has been mistakenly made to qualify "沙."

Bynner, perhaps because of his need to rely on his collaborator for the interpretation of the original, comes up in his version, entitled "A Long Climb," with images not found in the original:

In a sharp gale from the wide sky apes are whimpering,
Birds are flying homeward over the clear lake and white sand,
Leaves are dropping down like the spray of a waterfall,
While I watch the long river always rolling on.[45]

The birds that "fly circling"[46] in the original have been made to fly "homeward"; the image of "the spray of a waterfall" has been read into "無邊落木蕭蕭下," to say nothing of the word "dropping," which, normally suggesting a quick, short, and, very often, isolated movement and referring to objects heavier than leaves, such as a coin, fails to describe the more gentle but large-scale falling of the leaves of the "infinity of trees"[47] described by Du Fu.

Highly sensitive to Du Fu's techniques, Hawkes is able to go imagistic in the same way as the poet does whenever the original calls upon him to do so, as can be seen in his translation of the following lines in "*Yong huai*

---

[43] *OED*, III, 208.
[44] *OED*, III, 208.
[45] Bynner, 155.
[46] Hawkes, 205.
[47] Hawkes, 205.

guji" 〈詠懷古迹〉 (2) ("Thoughts on an Ancient Site" (2)):

諸葛大名垂宇宙
宗臣遺像肅清高
三分割據紆籌策
萬古雲霄一羽毛 [.][48]

Chu-ko Liang's great fame resounds through the ages. The likeness of this
revered statesman still impresses with its sublime expression. The tripartite
division of empire hampered his great designs; yet he soars through all the
ages, a single feather floating high among the clouds.[49]

The first three lines both in the original and in the translation roam through
time and history, like a camera panning up and down, enabling the reader
to experience the vast sweep of Du Fu's imagination; in the fourth line, the
camera first pans through aeons, then emerges from time into space, going
up with a wide sweep, and, finally, zooms in on "a single feather," driving
home the poet's point: that Zhuge Liang ("Chu-ko Liang" in Hawkes'
translation) is way above all other statesmen or strategists. The fourth line,
juxtaposing "a single feather" with "the clouds" on high, is imagistic in
that the whole argument is clinched by one sharp image.

   In Davis' translation of the same lines in his "Feelings on Ancient
Sites" (V),

Chu-ko's great fame has been handed down to the world;
The honored minister's surviving portrait is austere and lofty.
Confined to a third of the empire, he contrived his plans;
Over all antiquity, a solitary bird in the clouds [,][50]

not only is the phrase "垂宇宙" turned into a prosaic phrase with a less
concrete action-verb, "handed down to the world,"[51] the cinematographic

---

[48] Hawkes, 178. "遺像" in the line "宗臣遺像肅清高" is the reading of Du Fu 杜
甫, *Dushi xiangzhu*《杜詩詳註》, annotated by Qiu Zhao'ao 仇兆鰲, 5 Vols.
(Beijing: Zhonghua Shuju 中華書局, 1979), Vol. 4, 1506. Hawkes' (178) reading is
"遺象," which must be either a misprint or a variant reading of the Chinese edition
used by Hawkes.
[49] Hawkes, 180.
[50] A. R. Davis, *Tu Fu*, Twayne's World Authors Series: A Survey of the World's
Literature, general editor Sylvia E. Bowman, editors Howard S. Levy and William
R. Schultz (New York: Twayne Publishers, Inc., 1971), 115.
[51] Though the first line in Hawkes' version, "Chu-ko Liang's great fame resounds

effect resulting from the juxtaposition of the grand with the tiny in the fourth line is also destroyed by the substitution of "a solitary bird" for "a single feather."

Lost in the fluidity of Chinese syntax, Bynner, in his translation of the same poem, entitled "Thoughts of Old Time" (II), appears to have difficulty even in making out the relationships between the lexical items as well as in comprehending the original as a whole:

> Chu-kê's prestige transcends the earth;
> There is only reverence for his face;
> Yet his will, among the Three Kingdoms at war,
> Was only as one feather against a flaming sky.[52]

In line 1, the image of "垂宇宙" is missing; in line 2, only one lexical item in the original line ("像") is translated; the third and fourth lines, because of the translator's inability to comprehend the corresponding lines in the original, which are independent of each other, have been forcibly yoked together by a grammatical relationship of the translator's invention. As a result, even though the feather image is preserved, the dramatic effect of the feather image in contrast to the vast space is missing, to say nothing of the puzzling phrase "flaming sky," in which "flaming" arises out of nothing. At best, Bynner's "translation" can qualify only as a grossly curtailed, grossly distorted paraphrase of the original.

If Du Fu in *Deng gao* ("From a Height") is using what cinematographers would call panning in describing the wind, the sky, the islets, the birds that fly circling, and the trees shedding their leaves, the last two lines in "*Su fu*"〈宿府〉("A Night at Headquarters") are what they would call zooming in:

清秋幕府井梧寒
獨宿江城蠟炬殘
永夜角聲悲自語
中天月色好誰看
風塵荏苒音書絕
關塞蕭條行路難
已忍伶俜十年事

---

through the ages" is more forceful than Davis' corresponding line, it must be pointed out that the original "垂宇宙" has the sense of a paragon, a shining example hanging down from high to be looked up to as a model for all ages and for all posterity, in which "垂" is more static than Hawkes' dynamic "resounds."

[52] Bynner, 157.

強移棲息一枝安 [.][53]

In the clear autumn air, the *wu-t'ung* trees beside the well in the courtyard of the Governor's headquarters have a chilly look. I am staying alone here in the River City. The wax candle is burning low. Through the long night distant bugles talk mournfully to themselves, and there is no one to watch the lovely moon riding in the midst of the sky. Protracted turmoils have cut us off from letters, and travelling is difficult through the desolate frontier passes. Having endured ten years of vexatious trials, I have perforce moved here to roost awhile on this single peaceful bough.[54]

The first six lines are about the here and now, commenting on the present state of affairs; the last two lines sum up Du Fu's eight-and-a-half-year experience "since the outbreak of the An Lu-shan rebellion" and describes his feelings about life as Yan Wu's 嚴武 subordinate.[55] In lines 1-7, the camera moves on the literal plane, sweeping over the "*wu-t'ung* trees," the "distant bugles," and "the lovely moon," then shifts from specific objects and scenes to the general state of affairs ("風塵荏苒音書絕[;]關塞蕭條行路難"), and to a looking back upon the past ten years, and, finally, rising to the metaphorical plane in line 8 and leaving behind the general, zooms in on the very specific: "強移棲息一枝安." In Hawkes' translation, the camera follows the same path, ending with an equally effective zooming in: "I have perforce moved here to roost awhile on this single peaceful bough."

In Davis' translation, "Spending the Night at Headquarters,"

At the general's headquarters in clear autumn the *wu-t'ungs* by the well are cold;
As I pass the night alone in the river city, the candles burn low,
While, the long night, horn notes wail, I mutter to myself;
The beauty of the moon in the sky, who else watches?
The wind and dust continue; news is cut off;
The frontier is lonely; the roads are difficult.
I have endured a state of distress for ten years;
Now I am forced into the ease of "resting on a single branch [,]"[56]

the last line is also a zooming in, but the progression from the cosmic to the last shot is interrupted by the clause "I mutter to myself" in line 3,

---

[53] Hawkes, 129.
[54] Hawkes, 131-32.
[55] Hawkes, 131.
[56] Davis, 90.

which, apart from being a mistranslation,[57] focuses on the narrator "I" prematurely.

In McCraw's translation, "Lodging at Staff Bureau,"

> Limpid Fall at the staff bureau, wellside paulonias chill;
> Lonely lodging in River Citadel, waxen candles gutter.
> Bugle notes thru an endless night make doleful monologue;
> Moonlight in the middle heavens: charming, but who sees it?
> Windblown dust interminable, news and letters curtailed;
> Border barriers so desolate, a hard road to travel.
> I have endured roaming alone through ten years of ado,
> & barely reached a restful roost, a single branch of repose [,][58]

the camera follows the movement of the original and ends with a zooming in. However, the truncated syntax resulting from the omission of connectives gives the movement a staccato effect, which is not found in the original. Nor is the choice of words felicitous. "[C]itadel," meaning "The fortress commanding a city, which it serves both to protect and to keep in subjection" or "[a] strong fortress, a stronghold,"[59] is not the same thing as "江城" in the original, which is just a city by the river, as is accurately rendered by Hawkes. At the same time, it should be pointed out that, even in a short translation, McCraw is unable to remain consistent in his spelling, a flaw which can only be put down to sloppiness: using "thru" in line 3 but "through" in line 7, the former being the "informal, simplified spelling" of the latter;[60] using "and" in line 5 but using "&" in line 8.

The German version by von Zach, entitled "Nacht im Hauptquartier," is semantically accurate:

> Der kühle Herbst ist im Hauptquartier eingezogen; es frösteln die Sterculia-Baüme am Brunnen.
> Allein verbringe ich die Nacht in der Stadt am Strome (Ch'engtufu), das Wachslicht geht seinem Ende entgegen.
> Die lange Nacht hindurch ertönen die Klänge der Hörner, während ich traurig Monologe halte.

---

[57] In the original line, "永夜角聲悲自語," the subject of "悲自語" is "角聲," not the narrator. For this reason, Hawkes' "Through the long night distant bugles talk mournfully to themselves" is correct, and Davis' "While, the long night, horn notes wail, I mutter to myself" is wrong.

[58] McCraw, 39.

[59] *OED*, III, 248.

[60] Flexner et al., *The Random House Dictionary of the English Language* (New York: Random House, 1987), 1978.

Mitten am Himmel glänzt der Mond, um von wem gesehen zu werden? (d.
   h. ich allein ergötze mich daran).
Ununterbrochen herrscht (in China) wildes Kriegsgetümmel, und aus der
   Heimat kommen keine Nachrichten mehr.
Die Grenzpässe sind verlassen, die Wege gefährlich zu begehen.
Schon zehn Jahre lang ertrage ich diese Einsamkeit (fern von der Heimat).
Geswungen bin ich hierher (ins Hauptquartier) übersiedelt, um wie ein
   Vogel Ruhe zu finden auf einem Ast.[61]

However, in rendering the images, von Zach is less sensitive to the
original than Hawkes. In line 3 of the original, for example, it is the
"distant bugles" ("角聲") that "talk mournfully to themselves" ("悲自語").[62]
Von Zach has mistaken "I" ("ich") for the subject ("distant bugles"):
"während ich traurig Monologe halte" (literally "while I am holding a sad
monologue," that is, "talking to myself mournfully"). With the
introduction of a simile ("wie ein Vogel," meaning "like a bird"), the last
line, literally in English, reads: "I have perforce, like a bird, moved to the
headquarters to find rest on a branch." Because of the simile, the direct
and forceful metaphor in the original is diluted.

In his translation, entitled "Staying at the General's Headquarters,"
Bynner is able to capture the original's general drift, but its finer shades
have escaped his grasp:

I hear the lonely notes of a bugle sounding through the dark.
....
My messengers are scattered by whirls of rain and sand.
....
Yet, I who have borne ten years of pitiable existence,
Find here a perch, a little branch, and am safe for this one night.[63]

In the first line, "自" is left untranslated. In the second, the translator has
read "My messengers are scattered by whirls of rain" into the source text.
The last line is semantically correct, but, with "Find here a perch, a little
branch" put before "and am safe for this one night," the cinematographic
progression of the original is disrupted, or, more precisely, reversed, so that
the version fails to end in a zoom-in climax, which is a distinctive feature

---

[61] Erwin, von Zach, übersetzt von, *Tu Fu's Gedichte*, Vol. 1., Harvard-Yenching
Institute Studies VIII, edited with an introduction by James Robert Hightower
(Cambridge, Massachusetts: Harvard University Press, 1952), 405-406.
[62] Hawkes, 131-32.
[63] Bynner, 156.

of the original and of Hawkes' translation.

In his version entitled "I Pass the Night at General Headquarters," Rexroth freely adapts the original for creative purposes, translating "永夜角聲悲自語" as "All night long bugle / Calls disturb my thoughts,"[64] which is hardly recognizable as a version of the original. In his last two lines, "I perch here like a bird on a / Twig, thankful for a moment's peace," the climax of the original is replaced by an anticlimax.[65] Had he been sensitive to the original, he would have ended his poem with the phrase "on a / Twig."[66]

In *"Li ren xing"*〈麗人行〉 ("Ballad of Lovely Women"), Du Fu makes use of the zoom-in technique again to show how sated "the great ladies of the court" are with the delicacies set before them:[67]

犀筯厭飫久未下
鸞刀縷切空紛綸 [.][68]

But the choptsticks of rhinoceros-horn, sated with delicacies, are slow to begin their work, and the belled carving-knife which cuts those threadlike slices wastes its busy labours.[69]

To emphasize the sumptuousness of the banquet, the poet focuses on the expensive chopsticks and the carving-knife instead of the people. In translating the two lines, Hawkes keeps the same focus, zooming in on the chopsticks and the carving-knife.

Watson's version,

but ivory chopsticks, sated, dip down no more,
and phoenix knives in vain hasten to cut and serve [,][70]

---

64 Rexroth, 25.
65 Rexroth, 25.
66 One does not know whether Rexroth could read Chinese. If he could not, it would not be fair to Du Fu to tinker with or transmogrify his poems in this way and palm the products off as "translations" of Du Fu's work on readers who are not able to read Chinese, for, in so doing, the "translator" could mislead the readers, doing Du Fu a disservice rather than a service. The same can be said of translators like Bynner, who, having only a collaborator or collaborators to guide them, mess up Du Fu's poems beyond recognition and pass them off as Du Fu's work.
67 Hawkes, 21.
68 Hawkes, 19.
69 Hawkes, 27.
70 Watson, 17.

though retaining the chopsticks and the knives as the focus, has moved towards generalization: whereas Hawkes' "slow to begin their work" succeeds in reproducing the hesitancy conveyed by the original "久未下," and the phrase "those threadlike slices" reinforces the focusing effect of "the belled carving-knife," Watson's "dip down no more" describes a forthright motion that suggests no hesitancy.

Davis' rendering,

> The rhinoceros-horn chopsticks, through satiety, long are unused;
> Morsels, fine-shredded by the phoenix knife, lie vainly heaped [,][71]

is problematic for two reasons. First, "through satiety, long are unused" does not indicate that the lovely women have had so much of the delicacies that they just do not have any more appetite to pick up more food, so that their chopsticks are held in the air, no longer eager to descend on the dishes, as it were. Second, "long are unused" can lead the reader to think that the chopsticks, having been stowed away, have remained unused for a long time. Third, the shifting of the focus from the carving-knife ("phoenix knife" in Davis' version) to the "Morsels" ("Morsels [...] lie vainly heaped") in the second line is also undesirable, since the focus of the original is unequivocally on the carving-knife ("鸞刀縷切空紛綸"), just as the focus of the preceding line is on the "rhinoceros-horn chopsticks," that is, on the cutlery rather than on the food.

With the imagery blurred through generalization, Bynner's version, entitled "A Song of Fair Women," is more like prose than poetry:

> Though their food-sticks of unicorn-horn are lifted languidly
> And the finely wrought phoenix carving-knife is very little used [...][72]

In the first line, the idea of "厭飫" is missing. In the second, a concrete phrase, "空紛綸," is turned into an abstract generalization: "is very little used."

From the above examples, we can see how sensitive Hawkes is to the poetic qualities of Du Fu's originals. Sometimes, even the handling of a common expression can show his superiority over other translators. For example, in translating the following lines of *"Danqingyin: Zeng Cao Jiangjun Ba"* 〈丹青引：贈曹將軍霸〉("A Song of Painting. To General Ts'ao Pa"),

---

[71] Davis, 37.
[72] Bynner, 171.

良相頭上進賢冠
猛將腰間大羽箭
褒公鄂公毛髮動
英姿颯爽來酣戰 [,]73

which describe the portraits of two great soldiers "distinguished for their services towards the founding of the [Tang] dynasty,"74 Hawkes has succeeded first in re-presenting equally vivid portraits of two great soldiers, then in capturing their spirit by preserving the freshness of the image "酣戰," on which the liveliness of the portraits depends:

> On the heads of good ministers you painted 'Promotion of the Worthy' hats; at the belts of fierce generals you painted 'Big Feather' arrows. The Duke of Pao and the Duke of O,75 their beards and hair bristling, appeared, from their heroic and forbidding expressions, to be drunk with many battles.76

With their garments, armour, and expressions painted in memorable strokes, the characters stand out conspicuously, and are enlivened further by the finishing touch: "to be drunk with many battles," which is a sensitive rendering of "酣戰." In the eyes of an uninspired translator, "酣戰" may simply be regarded as a stock phrase, meaning, in abstraction and with no figurative force, "to fight fiercely" or "fierce battle," and conveyed in the target language as such.77

In William Hung's translation, neither the physical description nor the spirit of the characters is comparable to Hawkes' in terms of vividness:

> You can recognize the state ministers by their high hats. You know the great generals by the huge plumed arrows hanging from their belts. The hair of Marshals Tuan Chih-yüan and Yü-ch'ih Ching-tê shimmers; Their

---

73 Hawkes, 134.
74 Hawkes, 140.
75 The "Duke of O" refers to Yuchi Jingde 尉遲敬德. As a one-character surname, "尉" is pronounced "Wei" and romanized as such; as a two-character surname, or compound surname, "尉" is romanized as "Yu" ("Yü" in the Wade-Giles system); Hawkes' Wei-ch'ih Ching-te, should, therefore, read "Yü-ch'ih Ching-te [strictly speaking, Ching-tê in the Wade-Giles system]." As a matter of fact, Yü-ch'ih Ching-tê's name is Yü-ch'ih Kung ["Yuchi Gong" in the *Pinyin* system] 尉遲恭; Ching- tê is Yü-chih Kung's *zi* 字(style).
76 Hawkes, 144.
77 As we shall see, this is exactly what Hung did.

brave faces express thoughts of fierce battle.[78]

On the one hand, "huge plumed arrows," with its Latin origin in "plumed," is less striking than "'Big Feather' arrows," in which "Feather," being of Anglo-Saxon origin, is bolder and more forceful; on the other, the word "shimmers," though attractive in itself by virtue of its light image, is a deviation, for there is no light image in the original. What makes Hung's version inferior to Hawkes' version, in particular, is the line "Their brave faces express thoughts of fierce battle," which lacks the boldness and concreteness of Hawkes' version, "appeared, from their heroic and forbidding expressions, to be drunk with many battles," a rendering that has preserved the "intoxication" image of the original "酣."[79]

Davis' rendering, entitled "Song of Painting: Presented to General Ts'ao Pa," conveys much of the original's spirit:

> On the heads of noble ministers were "Promoted Worthy" hats;
> At the waists of fierce Generals, great-feathered arrows.
> The hair of the Dukes of Pao and O bristled;
> Their heroic aspect was alive with love of battle.[80]

The first three lines are generally comparable to Hawkes' corresponding lines; however, when it comes to the translation of "酣戰," it is Hawkes' bold image that excels: compared with "drunk with many battles," Davis' "love of battle," like Hung's "thoughts of fierce battle," appears abstract

---

[78] Hung, 212.

[79] Whether because of sloppiness, or because of incompetence, Hamill (101), in rendering the same poem (of 40 lines), has taken only lines 5-8 as his source text: "學書初學衛夫人[,]但恨無過王右軍[.]丹青不知老將至[,]富貴於我如浮雲." Even in rendering these much less challenging lines, on which his target text, "Homage to the Painter General Ts'ao," is supposed to be based, the translator is unable to come up with an accurate version: "As Lady Wei's star pupil, your calligraphy / was compared to General Wang's. / Impervious to old age, when you painted, / prosperity slipped past you like clouds." The original does not say that Ts'ao Pa was "Lady Wei's star pupil," nor does it say Ts'ao's "calligraphy / was compared to General Wang's," nor does it say as a fact that "prosperity slipped past [Ts'ao Pa] like clouds." The rendering appears particularly amateurish when compared with Hawkes' much more accurate translation: "In calligraphy you first studied under the Lady Wei, your only regret being that you could not excel Wang Hsi-chih. Painting, you forget the advance of old age: to you wealth and rank are as insubstantial as floating clouds" (Hawkes, 143-44). Like Rexroth and Bynner, Hamill is also doing Du Fu an injustice.

[80] Davis, 134.

and vague.

With almost all the specific details missing, Bynner's drastically generalized version, entitled "A Song of a Painting: To General Ts'ao," also fails to evoke the original image:

> You crowned all the premiers with coronets of office;
> You fitted all commanders with arrows at their girdles;
> You made the founders of this dynasty, with every hair alive,
> Seem to be just back from the fierceness of a battle.[81]

With "進賢冠" and "大羽箭" respectively generalized as "coronets" and "arrows," with "褒公" and "鄂公" rendered as "the founders of this dynasty," and with "來酣戰" mistranslated as "just back from the fierceness of a battle," in which the image "酣" has disappeared in the process of generalization, the version is much less vivid than both the original and Hawkes' translation.

Speaking in English for Du Fu, as it were, Hawkes can match the poet in his ability to convey, in just a couple of lines, startling sense impressions which work in mysterious ways. Take "*Ji Han Jianyi Zhu*" 〈寄韓諫議注〉 ("For the Admonisher, Han Chu"), for example, in which two lines condense a good deal of the visual:

鴻飛冥冥日月白
青楓葉赤天雨霜 [.][82]

In rendering these two lines, Hawkes is able to convey to readers of the target text a scene which, in terms of visual qualities, is equally evocative:

> A wild swan flies in the dark depths of heaven; the sun is moon-white;
> frost descends on the reddening leaves of the green maples.[83]

The colours of the original are reproduced, which is a relatively easy task for the translator; what makes the translation remarkable is not the substitution of one English colour-word for another; rather, it is the translator's capturing of the elusive, the uncanny, and the ineffable that makes his version stand out. The word "冥" in "冥冥" in the first line has a pat equivalent in Chinese-English dictionaries. It is translated, for

---

[81] Bynner, 164.
[82] Hawkes, 165.
[83] Hawkes, 173.

example, by "dark" or "obscure" in the *Pinyin Chinese-English Dictionary*.[84] But in the Chinese line quoted above, because of the interaction or, to use a metaphor, inter-induction, between the semantic units ("鴻飛," "冥冥," "日月白"), "冥冥" appears to the reader to have shed its normal dictionary meaning, and taken on a layer of meaning which cannot be immediately pinned down: while still retaining a trace of its original meaning, it has come to suggest something other-worldly, something mystical, made much more so by the preceding line ("濯足洞庭望八荒").[85] By rendering it as "dark depths," Hawkes has succeeded in conveying this suggestive and mystical quality, which is reinforced by "the sun is moon-white," just as the suggestive and mystical quality in the original is reinforced by "日月白."[86] In the second line, not only is the original visual impact reproduced ("the reddening leaves of the green maples"), but the subtle and intricate turn of phrase is closely attended to. In the Chinese expression "葉赤," because of the quasi-verbal nature of the collocation, there is a fluid and dynamic relationship between "葉" and "赤," which is different from the relationship between "赤" and "葉" in the more common collocation "赤葉." In "赤葉," with an adjective qualifying a noun, the relationship

---

[84] Wu Jingrong et al., comp., *The Pinyin Chinese-English Dictionary*《漢英詞典》(New York: John Wiley and Sons, Inc., 1983), 477.

[85] As a matter of fact, because of this inter-induction between semantic units, which cannot be completely analysed or explained, the whole line "鴻飛冥冥日月白" is permeated by a sense of the mystical. Of all Chinese poets, Du Fu is the greatest master in creating this kind of magic, magic which the reader can feel, but which he can hardly dissect, analyse, or explain because of the subtle and elusive suggestiveness released as a result of various semantic units working upon one another, units which, when standing separately by themselves, are just common lexical items. Another example which is equally difficult to analyse and explain but which has the same kind of magic and casts a similar spell on the reader with its complex and inexplicably fugitive connotations is the line "山空鳥鼠秋" from no. 1 of the poet's *"Qinzhou zashi"*〈秦州雜詩〉("Poems Written on Various Occasions in Qinzhou") series, which consists of 21 poems. For a detailed discussion of this and other lines which share the same quality, see Huang Guobin 黃國彬 [Laurence Wong], *Zhongguo san da shiren xinlun*《中國三大詩人新論》(Taipei: Crown Press 皇冠出版社, 1984), 48-50. For Du Fu's *"Qinzhou zashi"*〈秦州雜詩〉("Poems Written on Various Occasions in Qinzhou") series, see Du Fu 杜甫, *Dushi xiangzhu*《杜詩詳註》, annotated by Qiu Zhao'ao 仇兆鰲.

[86] It must be admitted, though, that "日月白" is open to other interpretations. For example, the adjective "白" can be taken to qualify both "日" and "月," that is, both the sun and the moon are white.

between the two words is static. Sensitive to this subtle difference, Hawkes makes a point of also using a verbal adjective ("reddening") to translate "赤." Had the phrase "red leaves" or the clause "the leaves are red" been used, the dynamic scene in the original would have been destroyed. Having tapped the associative potentiality of the quasi-verbal "赤," Du Fu intensifies the sensuous appeal of the line by using the expression "天雨霜," which contains a tactile and, again, dynamic image. Rising to the challenge once again, Hawkes has succeeded in coming up with an equally sensuous image: "frost descends."

Translating the same lines into verse, Jenyns has not, in his version entitled "Sending a letter to Mr. Han, the Censor," benefited from the medium he employs:

A Wild swan flew into the distance white as the sun or moon.
The leaves of the green maple turn red,
The sky is like to drop hoar frost [....][87]

Both "flew into the distance" and "white as the sun or moon" are much less startling than the original images. The second and third lines, which are the equivalent of only one line in the original, also suffer in terms of verbal economy as a result of the restructuring.

Again taking liberties with the source text, Bynner, in his version entitled "A Letter to Censor Han," has left much of the original imagery untranslated:

Wildgeese flying high, sun and moon both white,
Green maples changing to red in the frosty sky [....][88]

The original "冥冥" is nowhere to be found; and the forceful "天雨霜," in which there is a verb "雨" adding to the drama, is reduced to a plain, static description: "in the frosty sky."

If the lines discussed above are a formidable challenge to translators, lines in which Du Fu conjures up the dreamlike and the phantasmagoric are much more so. A case in point is "*Meng Li Bo*" 〈夢李白〉 (1)[89]

---

[87] Soame Jenyns, trans., *A Further Selection from the Three Hundred Poems of the T'ang Dynasty*, the Wisdom of the East Series, ed. J. L. Cranmer-Byng (London: John Murray, 1944), 36.

[88] Bynner, 165.

[89] Traditionally read "Li Bo," the poet's name is read "Li Bai" in modern spoken Chinese.

("Dreaming of Li Po" (1)), in which he describes how the great poet Li Bo, who is 11 years his senior, comes and goes in his dream:

魂來楓林青
魂返關塞黑
落月滿屋梁
猶疑照顏色 [.]⁹⁰

The ingenious deployment of colour-words ("魂來楓林青[;]魂返關塞黑") creates a surreal atmosphere marked by a feeling which is poignant yet elusive and, again, hard to pin down, reinforced by a sense of wistfulness and loss in the two lines that follow, "落月滿屋梁[,]猶疑照顏色," lines which are equally surreal, but which, in contrast to what is depicted in the first two lines, describe a scene that belongs to the real world.

Hawkes' translation conveys the same atmosphere with equally evocative visual images:

> When your soul left, the maple woods were green: on its return the passes were black with night. Lying now enmeshed in the net of the law, how did you find wings with which to fly here? The light of the sinking moon illumines every beam and rafter of my chamber, and I half expect it to light up your face.⁹¹

As visually sharp as the original, the description of Li Bo's soul travelling to where Du Fu is and of his return home is etched into the reader's mind; the lines describing the moment Du Fu wakes up realistically present the feelings and mood of one still in a dreamy state, not knowing whether he is awake or still dreaming.

In Watson's translation,

> His spirit came from where maple groves are green,
> then went back, left me in borderland darkness.
> Now you're caught in the meshes of the law;

---

⁹⁰ Hawkes, 88.

⁹¹ Hawkes, 92. The sentence, "Lying now enmeshed in the net of the law, how did you find wings with which to fly here?" is the English translation of two lines ("君今在羅網[,]何以有羽翼?") preceding the Chinese quotation. The whole poem in Chinese reads: "死別已吞聲[,]生別常惻惻[.]江南瘴癘地[,]逐客無消息[.]故人入我夢[,]明我長相憶[.]君今在羅網[,]何以有羽翼[?]恐非平生魂[,]路遠不可測[.]魂來楓林青[,]魂返關塞黑[.]落月滿屋梁[,]猶疑照顏色[.]水深波浪闊[,]無使蛟龍得" (Hawkes, 87-88).

> how could you have wings to fly with?
> The sinking moon floods the rafters of my room
> and still I seem to see it lighting your face [,][92]

the waking moment is a closer rendering of the original than Hawkes' in that "seem" conveys the poet's uncertainty more accurately than "half expect," for it suggests more realistically the trance-like state of one having just woken up, whereas "half expect" expresses a state of mind closer to that of one who is able to exercise his volition. Watson's "floods," describing the moon when the poet wakes from his dream, is also preferable to Hawkes' "illumines," though the latter, in isolation, is the normal equivalent of "照." This is because when one wakes up on a moonlit night, with one's eyes having grown used to the absence of light, one normally finds the moonlight dazzling. For this reason, "floods" is a more realistic description of the light the poet sees on waking up than "illumines," which suggests a less intense, less overwhelming optical image. However, in rendering the two lines which are visually most evocative ("魂來楓林青[;]魂返關塞黑"), Watson has deviated from the original and offered an interpretation different from Hawkes': Li Bo's soul resides where there are maple groves; Du Fu is an inhabitant of the borderland. This, however, is not what the original says. In the original, the two lines "魂來楓林青[,]魂返關塞黑" actually contrast two moments in time: the moment Li Bo's soul comes to visit Du Fu in the latter's dream and the moment he leaves Du Fu and makes his way "home"—that is, if a soul has a "home"; they do not indicate or suggest that Li Bo lives in a place "where maple groves are green" or that Du Fu is "in borderland darkness." Moreover, though "黑" can be translated by either "dark" or "black," the context of the original favours Hawkes' "black," which is visually sharp, evocative, and even startling. Hawkes' superiority can also be seen in his use of the second person ("When your soul left, the maple woods were green") in comparison with Watson's use of the third person ("His spirit came from where maple groves are green"): Hawkes' second person, tallying with the second person in the original, as is made clear by the line, "君今在羅網[,]何以有羽翼" ("Lying now enmeshed in the net of the law, how did you find wings with which to fly here?"), gives the translation the same kind of immediacy as the original does, whereas

---

[92] Watson, 77. Like Hawkes, Watson has, in his translation, also reversed the order of the original's lines. The two lines, "Now you're caught in the meshes of the law; / how could you have wings to fly with?", are the translation of the Chinese lines "君今在羅網[,]何以有羽翼?"

Watson's third person has a distancing effect, detracting from the friendship between Li Bo and Du Fu.

In rendering the same lines, Davis, in his version entitled "Dreaming of Li Po," has similar difficulties:

> Your soul came from the green of maple forests;
> Your soul returns from the darkness of the passes.
> Just now you lie in the net's meshes;
> How could you find wings?
> The sinking moon fills my house beams;
> I think it lights up your face.[93]

In reading the translation, one misses the surreal atmosphere of the original; the temporal relationship between "魂來楓林青[;]魂返關塞黑," expressed in Chinese without any connectives, disappears in the English version; perhaps not quite sure about this relationship and wanting to play safe, Davis has rendered the original lines as separate independent units. Equally unsatisfactory is the line "The sinking moon fills my house beams": "fill," often applied to vessels, such as a cup, and to liquids, such as water, fails to re-present accurately the scene depicted by the line "落月滿屋梁." Even with as simple a word as "疑," Davis' imprecision is obvious: being too unequivocal, the word "think" in "I think it lights up your face" lacks the uncertainty denoted by "疑," which is more accurately translated by either Hawkes' "half expect" and, in particular, Watson's "seem to see."

Hamill's version, also entitled "Dreaming of Li Po," shows that the translator has difficulty comprehending the original:

> Your spirit is in the heart of green maple,
> your spirit returns to the dark frontier.
>
> Tangled in nets of law, tell me,
> how can the spirit soar?
>
> Moonlight fills my room. Your poor face
> shines, reflected in the rafters.[94]

The original does not say that Li Bo's "spirit is in the heart of green maple," nor does it say that "your spirit returns to the dark frontier."

---

[93] Davis, 147.
[94] Hamill, 49.

Reproducing—or, to be more precise, producing—a piece of writing in English that bears only a tangential relationship with the original, Hamill cannot be expected to come anywhere close to Hawkes or, for that matter, to Watson or Davis. In sloppily translating the original into two unrelated lines, he has, as is to be expected, overlooked the temporal relationship between "魂來楓林青" and "魂返關塞黑," which Hawkes has accurately preserved. Judging by the first two lines, it is also clear that the translator is unaware of the difference between "楓林青" and "青楓林" as well as between "關塞黑" and "黑關塞." Coming after a noun, the adjectives "青" and "黑" have each an opening-up effect, and take on some verbal force, whereas, when put before the nouns "楓林" and "關塞" respectively, they will become restricted, capable of qualifying only the nouns. In the fourth line ("how can the spirit soar?"), the concrete image of "羽翼" in the original is reduced to a generalizing "soar." In the last two lines, a visually specific image in the original ("落月滿屋梁") is watered down, becoming a general description: "Moonlight fills my room"; "顏色" is distorted, to be forcibly equated with "Your poor face"; and "照顏色" is mistranslated as "reflected in the rafters."

Bynner's version, "Seeing Li Po in a Dream" (I), is equally problematic:

> You came to me through the green of a forest,
> You disappeared by a shadowy fortress...
> ....
> ...I woke, and the low moon's glimmer on a rafter
> Seemed to be your face, still floating in the air.[95]

In the first two lines, "楓林" is reduced to a generalized phrase ("a forest"), and a place or region ("關塞") is changed to a single building ("fortress"). The third and fourth lines are surreal, even phantasmagoric, by themselves; however, grossly distorting the original, they can only be regarded as "rewriting."

Von Zach's German version has, on the whole, retained the sense-units of the original:

> Seine Seele kam aus dem Lande der grünen Ahornwälder und kehrte wieder dahin zurück aus der hiesigen dunklen Wüste der Grenzgegenden.

---

[95] Bynner, 160-61.

Du bist doch jetzt als Verbannter gewissermassen in einem Netz verstrickt, wie konntest Du da Deine Flügel gebrauchen?
Die Strahlen des sinkenden Mondes füllen das Innere meiner Kammer; noch kommt es mir vor, dass sie Deine Gesichtszüge bescheinen.[96]

However, the relationship between "魂來" and "楓林青" on the one hand and between "魂返" and "關塞黑" on the other is misinterpreted; before "魂來" and "魂返," a conjunction or a conjunctive phrase like "when" or "at the moment when," is to be understood, which Hawkes' version has brought out in English by amplification. Apparently unable to detect this temporal relationship, von Zach has supplied only two adverbial phrases of place: "aus dem Lande der grünen Ahornwälder" (out of the land of green maple groves), "aus der hiesigen dunklen Wüste der Grenzgegenden" (out of the dark wilderness of the frontier region here); the result is, again as to be expected, a mistranslation. In comparison, the last line appears less problematic, but even so, it has retained only part of the surreal quality of the original, for, in the first half, "Die Strahlen des sinkenden Mondes füllen das Innere meiner Kammer" (the rays of the sinking moon fill the interior of my room) has reduced the concrete "屋梁" to a general phrase, "das Innere meiner Kammer" (the interior of my room) instead of Hawkes' much more vivid and more concrete rendering, "The light of the sinking moon illumines every beam and rafter of my chamber," which has reproduced the stark details of the original line.

In the poem just discussed, what stands out in the imagery is the visual quality; in *"Yueye yi shedi"*〈月夜憶舍弟〉 ("Thinking of My Brothers on a Moonlit Night"), it is the auditory effect that arrests the reader's attention—and at the very beginning of the poem:

戍鼓斷人行
邊秋一雁聲
露從今夜白
月是故鄉明
有弟皆分散
無家問死生
寄書長不達
況乃未休兵 [.][97]

---

[96]   von Zach, 185.
[97]   Hawkes, 73.

In the first two lines, the silence, remoteness, and solitariness of the far-off setting are suggested by "斷人行" and "邊秋," then reinforced by "戍鼓" and "一雁聲." In rendering these lines, Hawkes has paid meticulous attention to the auditory imagery, conveying the same kind of night-scene:

> Travel is interrupted by the war-drums of the garrisons. The sound of a solitary wild goose announces the coming of autumn to the frontier.[98]

In translating the second line, though, because of the non-paratactic nature of English, Hawkes has specified the relationship between "邊秋" and "一雁聲," whereas in the original, the two phrases are just juxtaposed, meaning something like "frontier autumn, the sound of a wild goose," so that the reader's imagination is given total freedom to come up with various relationships between the two phrases. Though unable to retain the original's functional ambiguity and imposing certain parameters on the reader's imagination, Hawkes' rendering gains in sharpness, concision, and dramatic immediacy, with "announces" working as the fulcrum of the second line, forcefully drawing the reader's attention to the transition between seasons, so much so that the line can almost be appreciated independently as an Imagist poem.[99]

In the corresponding lines in Watson's version, entitled "On a Moonlit Night Thinking of My Younger Brothers,"

> Martial drums cut off all human concourse;
> borderland autumn, cry of a lone wild goose [...][100]

parataxis allows the reader's imagination free play, but "concourse," being an unduly formal word in the given context, fails to chime in with the general style of the translation; the word "borderland," too, is less sharp, less precise than Hawkes' "frontier" in suggesting the remoteness and solitariness of "邊秋."

In Davis' version, "Thinking of My Brothers on a Moonlit Night,"

> The guard tower drum puts an end to men's passing;
> In the frontier autumn—a single wild goose's cry [,][101]

---

[98] Hawkes, 77.

[99] One could, of course, argue that these qualities are achieved at the expense of semantic accuracy.

[100] Watson, 64.

[101] Davis, 73.

"puts an end to men's passing," being in the same register as "斷人行," is more in keeping with the original than Watson's "cut off all human concourse" and even Hawkes' "Travel is interrupted," since the original line describes the now and here, whereas "Travel" is a more fitting description of a general state of affairs. By using a dash, Davis has ingeniously preserved the Chinese parataxis of the original without making his English version sound unnatural or obtrusive.[102]

In his translation, entitled "Under the Evening Moon Thinking of my Younger Brother," Jenyns sets up no grammatical relationship between "邊秋" and "一雁聲," thereby coming closer to the functional fluidity of the original; in rendering the first line, though, he has taken the phrase "斷 人行" as an observation about a general state of affairs rather than a comment on what is happening at a particular moment during the night:

> The throb of drums from (distant) garrisons holds up all communications,
> On the frontiers in autumn one goose is calling.[103]

Taking liberties with the original, Bynner's version, entitled "Remembering My Brothers on a Moonlight Night," cannot be regarded as translation in the strict sense of the word:

> A wanderer hears drums portending battle.
> By the first call of autumn from a wildgoose at the border,
> He knows that the dews tonight will be frost.
> …How much brighter the moonlight is at home!
> O my brothers, lost and scattered,

---

[102] It should also be pointed out that both Davis' "Worse still there's no end to the war!" (73) and Watson's "much less now, with hostilities unceasing!" (64) are more accurate renderings of the original "況乃未休兵" than Hawkes' "and it will be worse now that we are at war once more [,]" for the original means that the war has not yet ended. Hawkes, of course, knows what "未休兵" means, as can be seen in his exegesis of the line "況乃未休兵": "Especially as not-yet end fighting" (Hawkes, 76), but he has chosen to interpret it differently, a strategy reflected even from his rendering of the first line: "Travel is interrupted by the war-drums of the garrisons" (Hawkes, 77). In other words, he has taken "戍鼓斷人行" as a description of the general state of affairs in time of war, not the description of a particular moment. Appearing alongside "邊秋一雁聲," however, the first line is clearly a description of the here and now, that is, of a particular moment at night, to be followed by the poet's reflections on the general: "露從今夜白[;]月是故鄉明."
[103] Jenyns, 59. One does not know, though, why he has translated "雁" as "goose" instead of "wild goose."

What is life to me without you?
Yet if missives in time of peace go wrong—
What can I hope for during war?[104]

Lines 1-3 and 5-6, except for certain similar lexical items, bear little resemblance to the original lines.

The foregoing paragraphs, concentrating on the visual and the auditory, may lead one to think that Du Fu's imagery tends to appeal to one sense at a time; the fact is otherwise: very often, the poet's imagery can appeal to several senses at the same time, as can be seen in the following lines from "*Bingju xing*" 〈兵車行〉 ("Ballad of the Army Carts"):

君不見青海頭
古來白骨無人收
新鬼煩冤舊鬼哭
天陰雨溼聲啾啾 [.][105]

In these lines, visual ("白骨," "天陰"), auditory ("新鬼煩冤舊鬼哭," "聲啾啾"), and tactile images ("雨溼") combine to drive home the horrors of war.

In Hawkes' version, "Ballad of the Army Carts," the horrors of war are conveyed in equally evocative images:

"Why look, sir, on the shores of the Kokonor the bleached bones have lain for many a long year, but no one has ever gathered them up. The new ghosts complain and the old ghosts weep, and under the grey and dripping sky the air is full of their baleful twitterings."[106]

---

[104] Bynner, 150.

[105] Hawkes, 8. In Hawkes' version, "煩冤" in the line "新鬼煩冤舊鬼哭" reads "煩怨." See Du Fu, *Dushi xiangzhu*《杜詩詳註》, Vol. 1, 116. Possibly, "怨" is a misprint. In reading *A Little Primer of Tu Fu*, one is impressed by Hawkes' meticulous and rigorous scholarship and unsurpassed translations. However, one also notices quite a number of errors in respect of *pinyin* and Chinese characters. Given the learning and calibre of the author-cum-translator, the errors must have been due to factors beyond his control. This hypothesis is, to a large extent, confirmed by the edition under discussion, in which the errata were corrected by having the correct characters in Chinese or *pinyin* script pasted on the page. In the 1987 reprint (Hong Kong: Renditions Paperbacks), most of these errors were corrected by the editors, who included the late Professor D.C. Lau.

[106] Hawkes, 17.

"[B]leached bones" and "grey [...] sky" are visual; "the old ghosts weep" and "baleful twitterings" are auditory, and "dripping sky" is tactile, with "twitterings" and "dripping" being onomatopoeic. Working together, all the images present concrete details of the battlefield on which the soldiers died.

In comparison with Hawkes' version, Hung's "The Song of War Chariots" appears rather uninspired:

> "Do you not know that in the region near Kokonor Since ancient times human bones have been left to bleach in the sun? New ghosts murmur while the old ones weep, You can always hear them when night or rain comes."[107]

Whether in visual or auditory terms, it is less vivid and concrete than Hawkes' version: while "left to bleach in the sun" is an idiomatic way to suggest that no one gathers the bones up, the original, "古來白骨無人收," being so emphatic, calls for something more specific, as is supplied by Hawkes' version. "[M]urmur," which can be used of both favourable and unfavourable ways of expressing one's feelings, is not an adequate rendering of "煩冤"; "night," coming from a Du Fu expert like Hung, is an unexpected misinterpretation of "天陰"; the last line, "You can always hear them when night or rain comes [,]" is the most unsatisfactory: it has reduced to a vague generalization an auditory image that drives home the eeriness of the scene.[108]

In Watson's version, "Ballad of the War Wagons,"

> "You've never seen what it's like in Koko Nor?
> Years now, white bones no one gathers up,
> new ghosts cursing fate, old ghosts wailing,

---

107 Hung, 65.

108 In the Introduction to his *A Little Primer of Tu Fu*, Hawkes has paid tribute to Hung: "I make no apology for the inadequacy of this briefing, because I want the reader to meet Tu Fu straight away and to become acquainted with him through his poems. If, after reading them, he is still desirous of more information about Tu Fu's life and work, he cannot do better than turn to Dr. William Hung's excellent *Tu Fu* (Harvard, 1952), which contains a full biography of the poet and translations of many more of his poems than are contained in this little book" (Hawkes, xi-xii). Coming from a great translator like Hawkes, this is a compliment Hung could well have been proud of. But, judging by this translation and others in Hung's book, one would tend to think that the above tribute must have been partly prompted by the generosity of a magnanimous fellow practitioner.

skies dark, drizzly rain, the whimpering, whimpering voices [,]"[109]

the scene is also made vivid and concrete through the use of visual ("white bones"), auditory ("wailing," "whimpering, whimpering voices"), and tactile ("drizzly rain") images. However, judging by his choice of words, Watson's ability to suggest the nuances of the original is not comparable to Hawkes': while "white" is the normal dictionary equivalent of "白" in "白骨," it does not fit in with the context as aptly as Hawkes' "bleached," which suggests the effect of wind and rain on the bones over the years, and which is what the context requires; "drizzly rain," indicating fine rain as it does, is somewhat too poetic for a scene where so many soldiers have died in vain and where their spirits still mourn their futile deaths; finally, "whimpering," though onomatopoeic like Hawkes' "twitterings," is more suitable for describing "a child about to burst into tears,"[110] since its first meaning in the *OED* is "[t]o utter a feeble, whining, broken cry, as a child about to burst into tears; to make a low complaining sound";[111] in other words, it is less related to ghosts complaining under an overcast, dripping sky. As a result, it fails to suggest the eeriness of the scene as effectively as "twitterings" does.[112] Apparently determined to adhere to parataxis at all costs, Watson has made his character, who is talking about history, speak unnatural and truncated English.

In Davis' version, "Song of the War Carts,"

"Sir, have you not seen, near Kokonor,
The white bones from olden times, no one collects?
New ghosts complain, old ghosts lament;
At night or in the rain, their voices moan [,"][113]

apart from the mistranslation "At night" (for "天陰") and the generalized "rain" (for the more specific "雨溼"), "moan" fails to re-present the auditory eeriness of "啾啾."

In his translation, entitled "Song of the War Carts," Young, paying scant attention to the original, has deviated from its sense-units or simply

---

[109] Watson, 9.

[110] *OED*, XX, 235.

[111] *OED*, XX, 235.

[112] To be sure, the word "whimper" has other meanings too: "To complain pulingly; to 'whine': esp. *for, after,* [...] *to* something" (*OED*, XX, 235); "[t]o utter or express in a whimper"; "[o]f an animal, esp. a dog: To utter a feeble querulous cry" (*OED*, XX, 236).

[113] Davis, 36.

omitted them:

> "Have you seen how the bones from the past
> lie bleached and uncollected near Black Lake?
> the new ghosts moan, the old ghosts moan—
> we hear them at night, hear them in rain."[114]

The reader is first struck by the translator's amazing "boldness" in substituting "Black" for "青," which is normally translated by "blue."[115] In the last but one line, the translator does not even care to distinguish between "煩冤" and "哭." Even more unbelievable is his blatant disregard for the setting of the poem: whereas "天陰" in the original clearly indicates that the drama takes place in the daytime, the translator has substituted "night" for day. Given this "free" approach on the part of the translator, the reader can no longer expect to see him conscientiously coming to grips with "天陰," "雨溼," or "聲啾啾"; these important sense-units, which Hawkes and Watson have painstakingly tackled, are simply omitted—the "easiest" way to surmount difficulties in translation.

In Wu Juntao's version, "The Chariots Rattle On,"

> "Don't you see, far away at the Lake of Chinhai,
> "E'er since the ancient times skulls're spread under the sky?
> "The new ghosts are resentful while the old ones cry,
> "In the gloomy wet days they sadly wail and sigh [,]"[116]

partly because of the translator's attempt at rhyming and partly because of his shaky command of the target language, the original has undergone a good deal of distortion or, to put it more mildly, refraction. First, "skulls" has unnecessarily narrowed down the meaning of "白骨," which does not exclusively refer to "skulls." Second, "無人收," a specific and concrete detail, is generalized as "spread under the sky." Third, "wail and sigh," being generic, is, in auditory terms, less memorable than either Watson's "whimpering, whimpering" or Hawkes' "twitterings." Fourth, the word "sigh," which is not the same thing as "煩冤," is introduced apparently because of the need to find a rhyme-word for "[...]hai," "sky," and "cry." Leaving the finer shades of meaning in the original unattended to, the

---

[114] Young, 44.

[115] "青絲," referring to hair, especially a woman's hair, is an exception, in which "青" normally means "black."

[116] Wu, 50.

version conveys much less of the original's meaning than either Watson's or Hawkes' version has done.[117]

In Alley's translation, "Ballad of the War Chariots," the line "君不見青海頭" is omitted; the remaining three lines are simply joined to those preceding "君不見青海頭":

> Now, we peasants have learnt one thing:
> To have a son is not so good as having
> A daughter who can marry a neighbour
> And still be near us, while a son
> Will be taken away to die in some
> Wild place, his bones joining those
> That lie bleached white on the shores
> Of Lake Kokonor, where voices of new spirits
> Join with the old, heard sadly through
> The murmur of falling rain.[118]

The translation is not translation in the true sense of the word; it is, again, what translation theorists would call "rewriting," in which little or no attention need be paid to the actual sense-units, images, or nuances of the original; the "translator" is free to perform whatever operations he wishes to perform on the source text.

It is worth noting, too, that Alley's "translation," though printed as separate lines in the same way English verse is printed, is, strictly speaking, only prose divided into lines at random or in accordance with the constraints of space on the page; being printed as separate lines, it has the semblance of verse, but it is not verse in prosodic or artistic terms.

Equally problematic is Alley's English style: whereas the original lines are lively and, at the time Du Fu wrote the poem, colloquial, with short units that characterize spoken language, the English version is one lengthy complex sentence with four subordinate clauses ("who can marry a neighbour / And still be near us"; "while a son / Will be taken away to die in some / Wild place"; "That lie bleached white on the shores / Of Lake Kokonor"; "where voices of new spirits / Join with the old"), together with a nominative absolute ("his bones joining those [...]") and a past participial phrase ("heard sadly through / The murmur of falling rain"),

---

[117] It should also be pointed out that the romanization "Chinhai" for "青海" belongs neither to the Wade-Giles system nor to the *Pinyin* system of romanization. In the Wade-Giles system, "青海" is romanized as "Ch'ing-hai"; in the *Pinyin* system, it is romanized as "Qinghai."
[118] Alley, 13.

which are well thought out and well organized, with a syntactic sophistication found more often in written English than in spoken English. In contrast to Alley, Hawkes has used a much less complex syntax, dividing the three lines in the original into two English sentences, each of which is a compound sentence with the clauses joined by "but" or "and." As compound sentences are more common than complex sentences in English conversations, in which speakers frequently tag one clause to another, using such conjunctions as "and" and "but," Hawkes' version is a much more realistic re-presentation of the original.

Deviating widely—especially in the last few lines—from the source text, Bynner's version, "A Song of War-Chariots," is, again, an exercise in rewriting:

> …Go to the Blue Sea, look along the shore
> At all the old white bones forsaken—
> New ghosts are wailing there now with the old,
> Loudest in the dark sky of a stormy day.[119]

Two action-verbs in the original, "煩冤" and "哭," are merged into one, becoming "wailing." In the last line, apart from the more general word "dark," an inaccurate translation of "陰," which subtly distinguishes the sky in the original from any other sky, the translator has read "a stormy day" into the poem.

Von Zach's German version, "Die Erzählung von den Kriegswagen," is on the whole a competent rendering. However, its concluding lines are less concrete, less vivid than Hawkes':

> Hast Du nicht gehört, wie an den Ufern des Kukunors seit den ältesten Zeiten gebleichte Knochen (chinesischer Soldaten) umherliegen, ohne dass sie begraben wurden?
> Die Geister der frisch Gefallenen sind von Unmut erfüllt, während jene der früher Getöteten weinen.
> Wenn der Himmel bewölkt ist und ein feiner Regen niedergeht, erheben sich dort traurige Stimmen."[120]

"[G]ebleichte Knochen" (bleached bones) and "Wenn der Himmel bewölkt ist" (when the sky is overcast) are visually concrete renderings, but "erheben sich dort traurige Stimmen" (there arise doleful voices) fails to translate the eerie and onomatopoeic image of the original "啾啾," which

---

[119] Bynner, 170.
[120] von Zach, 27.

Hawkes' "baleful twitterings" has so vividly presented in English.

In discussing "*Lüye shu huai*"〈旅夜書懷〉 ("Thoughts Written While Travelling at Night"), I have shown how the poem's natural scenery contributes to the tranquil mood. In the second half of the poem, which has not been quoted, the tranquil mood gives place to the poet's personal reflections about himself. In other poems by Du Fu, natural scenery can give rise to reflections not about the poet himself, but about his wife and children. A case in point is "*Yueye*"〈月夜〉 ("Moonlit Night"):

今夜鄜州月
閨中只獨看
遙憐小兒女
未解憶長安
香霧雲鬟溼
清輝玉臂寒
何時倚虛幌
雙照淚痕乾 [.][121]

Tender and moving, the poem begins with the moon, which the poet and his wife, though far apart, can see in different places; then it describes the poet's affectionate thoughts about his children and wife, finally ending on a poignant note: "何時倚虛幌[,] 雙照淚痕乾[?]"

Successfully tuned in to the original's wavelength, Hawkes' version, "Moonlit Night," captures the same kind of tenderness with the same lightness of touch:

> Tonight in Fu-chou my wife will be watching this moon alone. I think with tenderness of my far-away little ones, too young to understand about their father in Ch' ang-an. My wife's soft hair must be wet from the scented night-mist, and her white arms chilled by the cold moonlight. When shall we lean on the open casement together and gaze at the moon until the tears on our cheeks are dry?[122]

The simplicity of language, just as simplicity of language in the original does, matches the musings of a person away from home thinking of his family. The second sentence, putting the poet in his children's consciousness, is as full of tenderness as the original; particularly effective is the phrase "my [...] little ones," which, like "小兒女," conveys with a realistic touch the father's affection for his children. The third sentence,

---

[121] Hawkes, 28.
[122] Hawkes, 32.

making use of images as visual and tactile as those in the original, presents, in equally vivid terms, the poet's imagined reunion with his wife, and ends on an equally poignant note.

As the original is relatively short, it will be especially revealing to compare Hawkes' translation with the full versions by other translators, namely, Hung's "Moonlight Night," Watson's "Moonlight Night," Davis' "Moonlit Night," Alley's "Moonlight Night," Young's "Moonlight Night," and Bynner's "On a Moonlight Night":

> The same moon is above Fu-chou tonight; From the open window she will be watching it alone, The poor children are too little To be able to remember Ch'ang-an. Her perfumed hair will be dampened by the dew, The air may be too chilly on her delicate arms. When can we both lean by the wind-blown curtains And see the tears dry on each other's face? (Hung, 101)

> From her room in Fuzhou tonight,
> all alone she watches the moon.
> Far away, I grieve that her children
> can't understand why she thinks of Chang'an.
> Fragrant mist in her cloud hair damp,
> clear lucence on her jade arms cold—
> when will we lean by chamber curtains
> and let it light the two of us, our tear stains dried? (Watson, 28)

> Tonight the Fu-chou moon,
> In her chamber alone she watches.
> From afar I pity my little children
> Who know not enough to remember Ch'ang-an.
> With fragrant mist her cloud-hair-knots are damp;
> In the chill moonlight her jade arms are cold.
> When shall we lie within the empty curtains
> And it shine on both, our tear-traces dry? (Davis, 50)

> This night at Fuchow there will be
> Moonlight, and there she will be
> Gazing into it, with the children
> Already gone to sleep, not even in
> Their dreams and innocence thinking
> Of their father at Changan;
> Her black hair must be wet with the dew
> Of this autumn night, and her white
> Jade arms, chilly with the cold; when,

Oh when, shall we be together again
Standing side by side at the window,
Looking at the moonlight with dried eyes. (Alley, 31)

Tonight
in this same moonlight

my wife is alone at her window
in Fuzhou

I can hardly bear
to think of my children

too young to understand
why I can't come to them

her hair
must be damp from the mist

her arms
cold jade in the moonlight

when will we stand together
by those slack curtains

while the moonlight dries
the tear-streaks on our faces? (Young, 69)

Far off in Fu-chou she is watching the moonlight,
Watching it alone from the window of her chamber—
For our boy and girl, poor little babes,
Are too young to know where the Capital is.
Her cloudy hair is sweet with mist,
Her jade-white shoulder is cold in the moon.
...When shall we lie again, with no more tears,
Watching this bright light on our screen? (Bynner, 148)

Hung's translation is a generally accurate rendering of the poem. There
are three lines, though, which do not quite match the original. First, the
phrase "The poor little children" fails to convey the poet's tender affection,
for "poor" has a different meaning from "憐," which in classical Chinese
poetry often means "to love," "to treat with tender affection," of which
Hawkes' "think with tenderness" is the more accurate translation. Second,

"香霧雲鬟溼" does not say that the poet's wife has perfumed hair; Hung's "perfumed hair" is the result of his reading too much into the original. Third, in the original, the line "清輝玉臂寒" conveys a husband's love and tenderness through the juxtaposition of "清輝" and "玉臂"; with "清輝" omitted in Hung's version, "The air may be too chilly on her delicate arms," the same effect is nowhere to be found.

Compared with Hung's version, Watson's is more sensitive. As usual, his paratactic rendering is characterized by concision; "fragrant mist in her cloud hair damp" has retained the functional ambiguity of the original, conveying the same tender note. The last line, too, is a closer rendering of the original than Hawkes' corresponding sentence, in that "light the two of us" treats the moon as the subject as does the original, whereas Hawkes' "gaze at the moon" has turned the original's subject into the object of the sentence; being in verse handled with precision, the translation also has a rhythm that is in keeping with the rise and fall of the mood.

Overall, though, Watson's version is not without flaws. First, the tone of "children," in terms of register, cannot convey the father's tender affection in the original as effectively as Hawkes' "little ones." Second, "her children" creates an undesirable distancing effect between father and children, deviating from the immediacy of "遙憐小兒女," which is translated accurately by Hawkes' "I think with tenderness of my far-away little ones." Third, "lucence," an unduly formal word derived from the Latin *lucere*, meaning "to be bright, shine, glitter," is off-key; as a result, it detracts from the tender affection suggested by the original.[123]

In Davis' version, the phrase "fragrant mist" and the line "In the chill moonlight her jade arms are cold" have a lightness of touch in keeping with the original. Nevertheless, there are a number of lines and phrases that hamper the communication in English of the poet's tender affection. First, though lines 1 and 2 in the original are an inversion in form, they are natural by the standards of idiomatic Chinese; expressed as an inversion in English, the two corresponding lines sound artificial. Second, "pity" in line 2 is not the true sense of "憐"; nor does it connote fatherly affection as the original does. Third, "When shall we lie within the empty curtains?" is a serious distortion of the original, carrying as it does associations that border on the risqué and suggesting that the translator, instead of choosing the wrong word in the target language, may have misinterpreted "倚."

---

[123] D. P. Simpson, comp., *Cassell's Latin Dictionary: Latin-English: English Latin*, 5th ed. (New York: Macmillan, 1968), 351.

Alley's version is largely a piece of rewriting, with a lot of meanings read into the original: "Gazing into it [the moon], with the children / Already gone to sleep, not even in / Their dreams and innocence," "Her black hair." Because of this major flaw, the version is not redeemed by the last four lines, which, apart from the unnecessary repetition ("when, / Oh when") and the unwarranted substitution of "the window" for "虛幌," are tender and touching.

Freely omitting the original sense-units and appearing to be writing a poem of his own, Young is on a par with Alley. In the first two stanzas, the idea of the poet's wife watching the moon alone in Fuzhou is replaced by a drastically abridged version, even though one could argue that the act of moon-watching in the original is implied in the translation. With the exception of "children" and, to a lesser extent, "young," the third and fourth stanzas have little in common with lines 3 and 4 of the original, which the English version is supposed to translate. Then, in stanza 6, apparently because of the paratactic nature of Chinese, the translator does not seem to have been able to know what to make of the two corresponding lines in the original, in which "清輝," "玉臂," and "寒" are juxtaposed with no connectives indicating how they are related to one another, so that he can do nothing but mechanically enumerate the same items in English, misplacing "cold" in the process, and coming up with a line which, though poetic in itself, bears no resemblance whatsoever to the original.

By using the present tense ("she is watching the moonlight") instead of the future in translating the first line, as Hawkes does ("will be watching this moon alone"), Bynner has changed the original's conjectural tone to an affirmative statement. The phrase "are too young to know where the capital is" also misses the point of the original, which is translated with precision by Hawkes: that the poet's "far-away little ones [are] too young to understand about their father in Ch'ang-an." [124] Furthermore, in rendering "倚" as "lie," the translator slips in the same way as Davis has done, evoking undesirable connotations that border on the erotic: "When shall we lie again [...]" Finally, in rendering "淚痕乾" as "with no more tears," the translator has failed to convey the tender touch suggested by "淚痕," which is more subtly differentiated than the phrase "with no more tears."

If Hawkes' superiority in translating "Yueye"〈月夜〉 ("Moonlit Night") is seen in his handling of the tender lyricism of the original, his mastery in

---

[124] Hawkes, 32.

translating "*Ai wangsun*" 〈哀王孫〉 ("The Unfortunate Prince") is unmistakable in his treatment of the dramatic:

長安城頭頭白鳥
夜飛延秋門上呼
又向人家啄大屋
屋底達官走避胡
金邊斷折九馬死
骨肉不得同馳驅
....
高帝子孫盡隆準
龍種自與常人殊
豺狼在邑龍在野
王孫善保千金軀
不敢長語臨交衢
且爲王孫立斯須
....
愼勿出口他人狙
哀哉王孫愼勿疏
五陵佳氣無時無 [.][125]

The poem describes the narrator's "encounter in a Ch'ang-an street with a terrified young prince" during the An Lu-shan rebellion, in which "the families of princes, officials, and high-ranking officers who had accompanied the Emperor in his flight were hunted down and massacred, down to the smallest infant."[126] The opening of the poem and the advice given by the narrator to the terrified young prince are presented in dramatic terms, the description of the setting is vivid, and the narrator's words moving, objectively reflecting the poet's loyalty to the imperial family.[127]

---

[125] Hawkes, 33-35.

[126] Hawkes, 36.

[127] My interpretation of Du Fu's role in the poem is different from Hawkes': "In order to enhance the pathos of the prince's predicament, Tu Fu assigns himself a very unflattering role in this poetic record of his encounter. He appears first of all as rather pleased with himself for having spotted, from the T'ang equivalent of the 'Hapsburg lip', a member of the imperial family; then rather proud to be talking to a real prince; then scared for his own safety; then garrulously retailing the rumours, which in an enemy-occupied city must pass for news; and then apparently abandoning him, after a lot of completely valueless admonitions, to fend for himself. There is no evidence in the poem that the assistance of which the unfortunate prince was so manifestly in need was forthcoming" (Hawkes, 37). I

In translating the poem, Hawkes once again excels the other translators:

> Hooded crows from the battlements of Ch'ang-an flew cawing by night over the Gate of Autumn and thence to the homes of men, pecking at the great roofs, warning the high ministers who dwelt beneath to flee from the barbarian. Golden whips were flailed until they snapped and royal horses sank dead with exhaustion beneath them; but many of the Emperor's own close kin were unable to gallop with him.
>   ....
>   ...but descendants of the August Emperor all have the imperial nose; the Seed of the Dragon are not as other men are.
>   Wolves and jackals now occupy the city; the dragons are out in the wilds: Your Highness must take care of his precious person! I dare not talk very long with you here beside the crossroads, but I will stand with Your Highness just a little while.
>   ....
>   ...But we must mind what we say, with so many spies about. Alas, poor prince! Be on your guard! May the protecting power that emanates from the Imperial Tombs go always with you![128]

The imminent danger depicted in the original is suggested with an equally strong ominous sense and the fleeing of the imperial family is presented in equally violent terms. After the scene is properly set, the dialogue begins, in which the reader sees the narrator coming to life the moment he begins to speak.

---

believe the poem is a true record of what actually happened. Given the helplessness of an old man in Ch'ang-an, where a horrifying massacre was taking place, Du Fu's reaction and behaviour are understandable and pardonable. In his speech, we can feel his loyalty to the imperial family. Though he cannot give really useful assistance, he has, considering his own predicament, done his best to console the prince. Lines 13-14 reveal the poet's reverence for and pride in the characteristic lineaments of the members of the imperial family. Line 15 is the utmost limit the speech of a loyal subject could go in his denouncing of An Lu-shan's treason. At the same time, lines 23-24 express his unflagging allegiance to the Emperor, line 27 conveys genuine sympathy and concern, and line 28 is cogent evidence of his faith in the imperial family's final victory. To readers brought up in democratic societies and unused to the general submissiveness of the people prevalent in China from ancient times to this day, Du Fu's trying to "fend for himself" *is* obnoxious. But I would take this as an example that shows how cultural or societal differences can affect readers' responses to a text.

[128] Hawkes, 43-44.

In Watson's translation, "Pitying the Prince," the scene is set with the same kind of suspense as the original:

> Over Chang'an city walls white-headed crows
> fly by night, crying above Greeting Autumn Gate.
> Then they turn to homes of the populace, pecking at great mansions,
> mansions where high officials scramble to flee the barbarians.
> Golden whips broken, royal steeds dropping dead,
> even flesh and blood of the ruler can't all get away in time.[129]

In terms of diction, Hawkes' "Hooded crows," "cawing," "snapped," "sank dead," and "gallop," being more vivid and specific, are respectively preferable to Watson's "white-headed crows," "crying," "broken," "dropping dead," and "get away in time." Being prose, though, Hawkes' translation is, at times, less compressed, particularly because of the presence of intratextual glosses: "warning the high ministers," "were flailed until," "with exhaustion beneath them." Hawkes' "flee from the barbarian" is also a less vivid description of the royal family running away helter-skelter than Watson's "scramble to flee the barbarians," in which the amplification "scramble" conveys what in the original is understood and need not be expressed. However, when it comes to translating the description of the Emperor's descendants in the poet's address to "himself or the reader,"[130]

> Sons and grandsons of the founder all have high-arched noses;
> heirs of the Dragon line naturally differ from plain people [,][131]

Watson's "Sons and grandsons" (for "子孫"), "the founder" (for "高帝"), "high-arched noses" (for "隆準"), and "heirs of the Dragon line" (for "龍種") lack the royal aura respectively of Hawkes' "descendants," "the August Emperor," "the imperial nose," and "the Seed of the Dragon," which are in keeping with the overall register of the speech in the original. At the same time, while "隆準" in Chinese, because of its long association with the first emperor of the Han Dynasty, Liu Bang 劉邦, is a respectable and formal collocation, Watson's "high-arched noses" is too colloquial and somewhat comical, likely to trigger associations with modern plastic surgery, especially with the "nose job."

---

[129] Watson, 26.
[130] Hawkes, 40.
[131] Watson, 26.

When it comes to the poet's speech, Watson's version—the concluding lines in particular—tends to sound somewhat curt because of the translator's strategy of compressing meaning by making English as paratactic as possible:

"Wild cats and wolves in the city, dragons in the wilds,
prince, take care of this body worth a thousand in gold!
I dare not talk for long, here at the crossroads,
but for your sake, prince, I stay a moment longer.
....
Take care, say nothing of this—others wait in ambush!
I pity you, my prince—take care, do nothing rash!
Auspicious signs over the five imperial graves never for a moment cease."[132]

The limitations of Watson's translation strategy are especially obvious when the above lines are read alongside Hawkes': whereas Hawkes' version reflects a loyal, empathic subject really caring about the prince's person, Watson's sounds like a string of blunt, unfeeling orders, bordering, in the case of "I pity you," on the patronizing. In terms of accuracy and style, Watson's translation also has room for improvement: the phrase "Wild cats and wolves" has translated only "狼," but not "豺," which has a close equivalent in Hawkes' "jackals"; a word-for-word rendering of "千金軀," "this body worth a thousand in gold," too, goes against idiomatic English, and sounds too wordy for conversational purposes. Lastly, "哀哉" is an interjection expressing pity or sympathy; it is not the same thing as "I pity you"; a much more accurate rendering than Watson's, Hawkes' "Alas, poor prince!" conveys with greater precision what the original is intended to convey.

Read alongside the original and Hawkes' translation, Davis' is very much a watered-down version of the high drama presented in the original:

A white-headed crow from Ch'ang-an's city wall,
Flying by night, croaked over Staying-Autumn Gate,
And going to men's houses, pecked at the mansions,
Whence great officials fled to escape the Tartars.
The golden whip was broken, the nine-horse team died;
The family did not wait to gallop away together.[133]

---

[132] Watson, 26-27.
[133] Davis, 50.

This is because "white-headed," "croaked," and "pecked at the mansions" are not, respectively, as specific as the corresponding source texts or as Hawkes' "hooded," "cawing ," and "pecking at the great roofs," of which "cawing" is especially evocative of the ominous as well as of the imminent disaster suggested by the original lines. At the same time, "the nine-horse team died" is a less violent description of the death of the royal horses than either Watson's "dropping dead" or Hawkes' "sank dead with exhaustion," even though Watson's "dropping dead" is in the wrong register, sounding as it does comical rather than disturbing.

In describing the facial features of the members of the royal family, Davis' version,

The founder's descendants all have prominent noses;
The dragon seed is naturally unlike ordinary men [,][134]

is more accurate than Watson's in terms of register: "descendants" is more formal than "Sons and grandsons," which, though a word-for-word translation of the original "子孫," does not have its broader sense ("descendants"), and is less formal, less suitable for the context of the poem. Davis' "prominent noses," too, is preferable to Watson's literal rendering ("high-arched noses"), since it is favourable and does not evoke undesirable associations as "high-arched noses" does. Nevertheless, it still falls short of Hawkes' "the imperial nose," which, used generically, best describes the physiognomy common to all the members of the royal family. Like Hawkes' "the Seed of the Dragon," Davis' "The dragon seed" also more readily evokes the aura associated with royalty than Watson's "heirs of the Dragon line." However, though his "naturally unlike ordinary men" expresses the tone of the original more precisely than Hawkes' "are not as other men are," the singular "is" after "The dragon seed" is less apt than Hawkes' plural "are," since "龍種" in the original is used collectively, and refers to all the descendants of the "August Emperor," not just one member of the royal family in isolation.

Compared with Waton's version, Davis' concluding lines are less curt:

"Take care not to say a word! Others are spies!
Oh! my prince, be not careless!
From the Five Tombs the auspicious aura is never absent!"[135]

---

[134] Davis, 50.
[135] Davis, 51.

"Take care not to say a word" and "Oh! my prince, be not careless" come closer to Hawkes' version, though they do not convey the same degree of empathy as Hawkes' "we" in "But we must mind what we say, with so many spies about." Overall, Hawkes' rendering of the conversation is more finely tuned to the original than either Watson's or Davis' version.

In respect of the dramatic, Hawkes' mastery is most unmistakably shown in his translation of "*Bingju xing*" 〈兵車行〉 ("Ballad of the Army Carts"). Though the whole poem is a piece of high drama from beginning to end, space will allow me to concentrate only on the most salient points. First, let us look at the opening lines:

車轔轔
馬蕭蕭
行人弓箭各在腰
爺孃妻子走相送
塵埃不見咸陽橋
牽衣頓足攔道哭
哭聲直上干雲霄 [.][136]

> The carts squeak and trundle, the horses whinny, the conscripts go by, each with a bow and arrows at his waist. Their fathers, mothers, wives, and children run along beside them to see them off. The Hsien-yang Bridge cannot be seen for dust. They pluck at the men's clothes, stamp their feet, or stand in the way weeping. The sound of their weeping seems to mount up to the blue sky above.[137]

Both the original and Hawkes' translation present the actors ("the conscripts," "their fathers, mothers, wives, and children"), the sounds ("The carts squeak and trundle"), the actions ("run along beside them to see them off," "pluck at the men's clothes, stamp their feet, or stand in the way weeping"), the confusion, and the setting ("The Hsien-yang Bridge" that "cannot be seen for dust") in great detail, which are concrete and vivid, so that an unforgettable picture of war-time Chang'an is etched into the reader's memory. As one reads the original and the translation aloud, one can feel a sense of urgency and immediacy conveyed by the rhythm, which is in keeping with the dramatic tension created on the semantic level.

---

[136] Hawkes, 6. In the line "爺孃妻子走相送," "爺" reads "耶" in Du Fu, Vol. 1, 113. Both characters mean "father."
[137] Hawkes, 17.

As a translation of the same poem, Hung's "The Song of War Chariots" is also dramatic, but it does not convey the same kind of urgency and immediacy:

> Chariots rumble, horses neigh, Men are marching with bows and arrows. Parents, wives, and children rush to bid them farewell; The rising dust obscures the Hsien-yang Bridge. They clutch at the soldiers' clothes, stumble, and bar the road; Their cries pierce the clouds.[138]

In terms of onomatopoeic effect, the line "Chariots rumble, horses neigh" is also evocative, but semantically "Chariots" is off-key, for the vehicles referred to in the original are unlikely to be chariots, since the poem only describes conscripts leaving their families, not a battle in action. The word "marching," too, paints too heroic a picture of the conscripts, who are unlikely to want to leave their parents, wives, and children. The original phrase "爺孃妻子," enumerated in Hawkes' version one by one ("Their fathers, mothers, wives, and children"), has a crowding effect, which increases the tempo and intensity of the drama; with "爺孃" summed up in one word ("Parents"), the drama is turned into something less gripping. The phrase "rush to bid them farewell," too, is visually less effective than Hawkes' "run along beside them to see them off," since the fathers, mothers, wives, and children in the original are already running beside the conscripts, as is indicated by "走相送," not "rush[ing] to bid them farewell"; the phrase "bid them farewell," being unnecessarily formal, is inferior to Hawkes' colloquial "see them off," which closely matches the register of the original. Though a forceful action-verb in itself, Hung's "clutch," meaning "[t]o seize with claws or clutches; to seize convulsively or eagerly"[139] or "[t]o make a clutch *at*, to make an eager effort to seize"[140], tends to suggest someone desperate, such as a drowning man, trying, out of fear, to grasp something for support; in the context of the poem, Hawkes' "pluck at" describes the action with more precision. Furthermore, Hung's "stumble, and bar the road" (for "牽衣頓足") are both semantically and stylistically inaccurate; "stumble," being disyllabic, impedes the rhythm, thereby reducing the intensity of the drama. Hawkes' "pluck [...] stamp [...], or stand in the way," apart from being semantically and stylistically accurate, are rhythmically more effective because of the use of forceful monosyllables. Finally, Hung's "pierce the

---

[138] Hung, 64.
[139] *OED*, III, 375.
[140] *OED*, III, 376.

clouds," being unnecessarily violent, is, both semantically and stylistically, less accurate than Hawkes' corresponding rendering.

Compared with Hung's version, Watson's "Ballad of the War Wagons" is sensitive and readable:

Rumble-rumble of wagons,
horses whinnying,
war-bound, bow and arrows at each man's waist,
fathers, mothers, wives, children running alongside,
dust so thick you can't see Xianyang Bridge,
snatching at clothes, stumbling, blocking the road, wailing,
wailing voices that rise straight up to the clouds.[141]

The onomatopoeia of "Rumble-rumble" makes the war wagons audible, though "兵車" in the original is something more humble than "war wagons," and has been more precisely translated by Hawkes' "army carts." While "snatching at" is not quite the same thing as "牽" in "牽衣," which is more precisely translated by Hawkes' "pluck at," it is stylistically preferable to Hung's "clutching at." Like Hung, though, Watson has chosen "stumbling," which suggests the action of nearly falling over, whereas "頓足" only describes someone desperate putting his feet one after the other down either in protest or in desperation, an action which is accurately described by Hawkes' "stamp their feet." Watson's last line, "wailing voices that rise straight up to the clouds," translating "直上" with precision, is more forceful even than Hawkes' corresponding version, which has not attended to "直" in "直上." Nevertheless, because of the staccato effect resulting from parataxis, as well as of the use of many disyallabic participles ("running," "snatching," "stumbling," "blocking"), all of which are trochaic and have a rise-fall intonation, the rhythm is less sinewy and lacks the vigour and force of Hawkes' monosyllables ("run," "pluck," "stamp," "stand"), which contribute in no small measure to the intensity of the drama. Further reducing the dramatic effect, there is the undesirable pause resulting from the passive voice expressed by the past participle "war-bound" in line 3 as well as from a whole line ("dust so thick you can't see Xianyang Bridge") separating line 4 and line 6: the pause impedes the rhythm and the whole line separating line 4 and line 6 takes away the momentum built up by lines 1-4. Hawkes' keener sensitivity to the original drama and rhythm is unmistakably reflected in his sentence pattern and in his use of verbs in the first paragraph: apart

---

[141] Watson, 8.

from the third sentence, which is not key to the action, all the sentences, in the active voice, have the subject-verb pattern; with the exception of the present participle "weeping," which modifies the main action-verb "stand," all the other verbs are in the simple present tense, with no rhythm-weakening trochaic present participles; as a result, an irresistible on-gong thrust is created, thereby intensifying the drama.

With the masterly re-creation of the dialogue that follows, the drama, just as gripping as what has gone before, takes a new turn in the form of a speech delivered on the stage. To illustrate my point, I need only quote the following lines from the original and Hawkes' as well as other translators' versions:

長者雖有問
役夫敢申恨
且如今年冬
未休關西卒
縣官急索租
租稅從何出 [.][142]

"Though you are good enough to ask us, sir, it's not for the likes of us to complain. But take this winter, now. The Kuan-hsi troops are not being demobilized. The District Officers press for the land-tax, but where is it to come from? " (Hawkes, 17)

"You are indeed kind to ask about our troubles; How dare we to air our grievances? Let us just take the present winter: You know the Kuan-hsi troops have not yet returned, The government is ruthlessly collecting taxes […]" (Hung, 65)

"You, sir, ask these questions,
but recruits like us hardly dare grumble out loud.
Still, in winter this year,
troops from here, West of the Pass, not yet disbanded,
officials started pressing for taxes—
tax payments—where would they come from?" (Watson, 9)

In Hung's translation, the tone is more like that of written English than of spoken: not using contractions, saying "You are indeed kind" instead of "You're indeed kind" and "Let us take" instead of "Let's take," the conscripts have been made to speak a language remote from colloquial

---

[142] Hawkes, 7.

English. Nor is the register appropriate: "air our grievances" does not sound like a phrase used by an apparently uneducated conscript; "ruthlessly" (for "急"), on the other hand, is semantically inaccurate; and "ruthlessly collecting taxes" (for "急索租") is both imprecise and weak when compared with Hawkes' "press for land-tax." Grammatically, too, Hung's "How dare we to air our grievances?" should be replaced by "How dare we air our grievances?"

Watson's translation comes closer to the register of spoken English than Hung's. The staccato effect, again resulting from parataxis, is less objectionable here, since it is in keeping with the tone of someone speaking breathlessly.[143] The phrase "pressing for taxes," like Hawkes' corresponding version, conveys the same nuance as "急索租," though "grumble out loud" (for "申恨") is over-emphatic, missing the subtle nuance of the original.[144]

Closely following Du Fu, Hawkes can move effortlessly from high drama to "story-telling." Thus, in translating "*Liren xing*"〈麗人行〉 ("Ballad of Lovely Women"), he is as masterly as Du Fu in recounting events, capturing beauty and re-presenting pomp and majesty before the eyes of his readers:

三月三日天氣新
長安水邊多麗人
態濃意軟淑且真
肌理細膩骨肉勻
繡羅衣裳照暮春
蹙金孔雀銀麒麟
....
背後何所見
珠壓腰衱穩稱身 [.][145]

---

[143] It is arguable, though, whether such an impression is intended by Du Fu in view of the fact that the original lines are well-turned phrases in continuous syntax.
[144] Perhaps because of the paratactic nature of Chinese, a grammatical link between "未休關西卒" and "縣官急索租," which is understood in idiomatic Chinese, has escaped the notice of all the translators under discussion. With the link supplied, a minor amplification called for by idiomatic English, the two lines would be something like: "Before the Guanxi ("Kuan-hsi" in the Wade-Giles system) troops were demobilized, the District Officers were already pressing for the land-tax."
[145] Hawkes, 18-19.

On the day of the Spring Festival, under a new, fresh sky, by the lakeside in Ch'ang-an are many lovely women. Their breeding and refinement can be seen in their elegant deportment and proud aloofness. All have the same delicate complexions and exquisitely proportioned figures. In the late spring air the peacocks in *passement* of gold thread and unicorns of silver thread glow on their dresses of embroidered silk. [...] And what do we see at their backs? Overskirts of pearl net, clinging to their graceful bodies.[146]

Though Hawkes confesses that "[i]t is virtually impossible to get much idea of the clothing and jewellery described in the last few lines,"[147] what he has achieved is remarkable, in that the details of the original are reproduced with highly realistic touches, depicting the festive spring scene by the lakeside, which can be visualized by the reader through the translation.

In choosing to translate Du Fu's poetry into prose, Hawkes has, as I have pointed out at the beginning of this paper, given up the opportunity of tapping the resources of verse. Yet, being a sensitive translator able to use the target language with a skill and craftsmanship which many translators using verse cannot hope to aspire to, he can, very often, create effects which, normally, can only be created in verse. In discussing his translation of "*Deng gao*" 〈登高〉 ("From a Height"), I have pointed out how, in terms of rhythm, his version ("An infinity of trees bleakly divest themselves, their leaves falling, falling. Along the endless expanse of river the billows come rolling, rolling.") has captured the rhythm of the original "無邊落木蕭蕭下，不盡長江滾滾來，" and surpassed even verse translations. In the following translation of "*Wen guanjun shou Henan Hebei*" 〈聞官軍收河南河北〉 ("On Learning of the Recovery of Honan and Hopei by the Imperial Army"), he succeeds in exploiting rhythm on an even larger scale, so that the message communicated on the semantic level is powerfully reinforced by the rhythm:

劍外忽傳收薊北
初聞涕淚滿衣裳
卻看妻子愁何在
漫卷詩書喜欲狂
白日放歌須縱酒
青春作伴好還鄉
即從巴峽穿巫峽

---

[146] Hawkes, 26.
[147] Hawkes, 23.

便下襄陽向洛陽 [.][148]

To the land south of Chien-ko news is suddenly brought of the recovery of Chi-pei. When I first hear it, my gown is all wet with tears. I turn and look round at my wife and children, and have not a sorrow in the world. Carelessly I roll together the volumes of verse I have been reading, almost delirious with joy. There must be singing out loud in full daylight: we must drink and drink! I must go back home: the green spring shall be my companion. I shall go at once, by way of the Pa Gorge, through the Wu Gorge, then to Hsiang-yang, and so, from there, on towards Loyang![149]

The poem sings of the exultation brought about by the victory of an army standing for righteousness and royalty. Joy and the surging of emotions resonate throughout the poem. The opening is forceful and direct, gripping the reader's attention from the very first line, to be followed by a series of actions mirroring the poet's state of mind, finally culminating in two lines that hurtle along to the end at breath-taking speed. In Hawkes' translation, this rhythmic effect is accurately reproduced; the onward thrust is an effect only poets practised in their craft can create: "I shall go at once, by way of the Pa Gorge, through the Wu Gorge, then to Hsiang-yang, and so, from there, on towards Loyang!" As one reads this sentence, one is hurled forward, wave after wave, as though shooting through the Three Gorges in a swift boat, until it culminates in the final thrust: "on towards Loyang." One major difference between prose and verse is that, with the former, the writer is harder put to create various kinds of rhythmic effect; yet in the last sentence of Hawkes' translation, a kinaesthetic image is created by the skilful manipulation of the syntax, reminding the reader very much of Eliot's meticulous control of rhythm in the lines from "The Love Song of J. Alfred Prufrock" quoted at the beginning of this paper.

Besides Hawkes' superb performance, Davis' version, entitled "Hearing that the Imperial Armies Have Recovered Ho-nan and Ho-pei," suffers considerably in comparison:

Beyond the Sword Pass suddenly is reported the recovery of Chi-pei;
When I first hear of it, tears fill my robe.
I turn to look at my wife and children; where is their grief now?
Carelessly I roll up the *Songs* and *Documents*; my joy is almost mad.
In broad daylight I start to sing; I must indulge in wine.

---

[148] Hawkes, 117.
[149] Hawkes, 120.

With green spring for company, joyfully we'll go home.
At once from the Pa Gorges we'll go through the Wu gorges,
Then down to Hsiang-yang and on to Lo-yang.[150]

The opening is as direct as that of Hawkes' version; however, the joy of
the narrator is less dramatic, less impressive, suggesting much less of the
original "喜欲狂." At the same time, "I start to sing," apart from being a
misinterpretation of the original,[151] which describes only the narrator's
thoughts, not action, is a far cry from Hawkes' "There must be singing out
loud." "I must indulge in wine," too, is a distortion of the original: while
"須縱酒" refers to the here and now, "I must indulge in wine" can refer to
the narrator's resolution, something he makes up his mind to do over a
longer span of time in the future. Added to these infelicities are the
undesirably large number of pauses and the repetitive "subject-verb"
pattern in lines 5-6, as a result of which the rhythm, instead of being
emotionally stirring like that of the original and of Hawkes' corresponding
lines, sounds monotonous and lethargic. Finally, in sharp contrast to
Hawkes' version, the last two lines are rhythmically too unvaried, too
predictable, so that they just grind wearily to a halt, in which the reader
can no longer feel the poet's wild joy. Not so with Hawkes' version, in
which there is acceleration as well as deceleration in the speed of language,
made possible by the translator's skilful manipulation of the pauses and of
the length of the units between them.

McCraw's version, "On Hearing Imperial Forces Have Recovered the
Northeast," is marred by misinterpretations, ill-chosen words, and
unwarranted generalizations:

Beyond Swords, we suddenly learn they regained North Thorn!
When first I heard, falling tears flooded down my robes.
Turning to see my wife & children—where is there any woe!
Wildly roll up my verses & books—nearly crazed with joy.
In broad daylight sing out loud, indulge yourself with wine!
Green springtime will escort us, just right for going home.
Once through the Ophid Gorge, we'll thread Witch Gorge,
Then straight down to Xiangyang, and on toward Loyang![152]

---

[150] Davis, 86.

[151] Davis' "tears fill my robe" for "涕淚滿衣裳" is also a misinterpretation; by
using "fill" for "滿," the translator has turned "衣裳" into a vessel which one can
fill with liquid; Hawkes' translation, "my gown is all wet with tears," is a more
accurate version based on the correct interpretation of the original.

[152] McCraw, 153.

Without a subject, "Wildly roll up my verses & books" reads like a personal reference to the general; like Davis' "tears fill my robe," "falling tears flooded down my robes" has distorted the meaning of "滿衣裳"; the word "flooded," in particular, is grossly off-key because of its undesirable associations with torrential rains preceding a natural disaster. With pauses that impede the rhythm, the last two lines also lack the onward thrust of Hawkes' version.

Young's version, "Good News about the War," is, generally speaking, a vivid description of the poet's joy:

> Here in Sichuan we get word
> of the full recovery of the Central Plains
>
> I blubber so much at the news
> I soak the clothes I'm wearing
>
> I turn to my wife and children
> all our cares are gone!
>
> and like a maniac I start
> packing, rolling up all my poems
>
> now we can sing and dance
> right here in broad daylight
>
> drink some wine
> and then some more
>
> delirious, I want to start for home
> the green spring my companion
> I'll go out through the great
> Yangzi River gorges
>
> on to Xiangyang and finally
> be back home in Luoyang!¹⁵³

However, the choice of words is imprecise. First, "Here in Sichuan" does not suggest the remoteness of "劍外." Second, "blubber" reminds the reader of a child "weep[ing] nosily without restraint" or of a child "say[ing]

---

¹⁵³ Young, 153.

[something], esp[ecially] incoherently while weeping,"[154] something Du Fu, though overjoyed, would not have done. Third, "rolling up all my poems" is problematic, since poems, not being a material, cannot, strictly speaking, be rolled up; to make "poems" "roll-uppable," one would have to collocate the word with a more concrete noun, as Hawkes has done: "roll together the volumes of verse." Fourth, "drink some wine / and then some more" is a feeble rendering even when judged by the standards of prose, especially in comparison with Hawkes' "we must drink and drink." Finally, the last four lines, which are supposed to translate the climax of the whole poem, are even less satisfactory: though arranged as verse, that is, in separate lines, they are basically prose: limp, feeble, with the rhythm remaining untuned to the sense. By reading the translation, one cannot visualize the narrator being wild with joy, imagining himself to be going on a precipitous journey down the Changjiang River "by way of the Pa Gorge, through the Wu Gorge, then to Hsiang-yang, and so, from there, on towards Luoyang."[155]

Unable to reproduce the sweep of the original's language and rhythm, Hung's version, "Hearing of the Recovery of Ho-nan and Ho-pei by the Imperial Forces," shares the same flaw:

> Let us sail at once through the Gorges of Pa and the Gorges of Wu-shan,
> Let us thence turn toward Hsiang-yang on our way to Lo-yang.[156]

The repetition of the pattern "Let us" and the end-stopping of the first line make it impossible to suggest through rhythm the precipitous and sweeping movement of the original.

Also in verse but even less inspired is Bynner's version, entitled "Both Sides of the Yellow River Recaptured by the Imperial Army":

> Back from this mountain, past another mountain,
> Up from the south, north again—to my own town![157]

With the lines chopped up into almost equal portions, resulting in a staccato effect, the translation is a far cry from the hurtling sweep of both

---

[154] Flexner et al., 227. The *OED* definition is equally uncomplimentary: "To weep effusively; to weep and sob unrestrainedly and noisily. (Generally used contemptuously and in ridicule for 'weep'" (*OED*, II, 322).
[155] Hawkes, 120.
[156] Hung, 193.
[157] Bynner, 154.

the original and Hawkes' translation.[158]

Generally considered to be the poet with the widest stylistic range in classical Chinese poetry, Du Fu has, in stylistic terms, probably written the largest number of poems that tax translators' resources to the utmost. In the following paragraphs, I shall show how Hawkes' stylistic range matches Du Fu's much more closely than does the stylistic range of any other translator examined in this paper.

To begin with, let us see how he renders the homely, of which "*Ke zhi*" 〈客至〉 ("The Guest") is an example known by most Chinese readers:

舍南舍北皆春水
但見群鷗日日來
花徑不曾緣客掃
蓬門今始爲君開
盤飧市遠無兼味
樽酒家貧只舊醅
肯與鄰翁相對飲
隔籬呼取盡餘杯 [.][159]

The waters of springtime flow north and south of my dwelling. Only the flocks of gulls come daily to call on me. I have not swept my flower-strewn path for a visitor, and my wicker-gate opens the first time today for you. Because the market is far away, the dishes I serve you offer little variety; and because this is a poor household, the only wine in my jars comes from an old brewing. If you are willing to sit and drink with my old neighbour, I shall call to him over the fence to come and finish off the remaining cupfuls with us.[160]

In both the original and the translation, the language is plain and simple, and the tone intimate and conversational, perfectly suited to the purpose: to describe a friendship that reveals itself through the scenery, the objects, and the tone of the narrator's speech.

In comparison, Watson's version, "A Guest Arrives," is less precise in terms of style, register, and comprehension:

North of my lodge, south of my lodge, everywhere spring rivers;
day by day all I see are flocks of gulls converging.

---

[158] It should be noted, too, that, with the specific place names replaced by common nouns, Bynner's version is another piece of "rewriting."
[159] Hawkes, 109.
[160] Hawkes, 111-12.

Flower paths never before swept for a guest,
my thatch gate, opening for you, opens for the first time.
For food—the market's far—no wealth of flavors;
for wine—my house is poor—only old muddy brew.
If you don't mind drinking with the old man next door,
I'll call across the hedge, and we'll finish off what's left.[161]

In the first place, the phrase "North of my lodge, south of my lodge," though a close imitation of "舍南舍北" in structural terms, is monotonously repetitive. Without carefully comparing it with the original, one may argue that, since they are structurally equivalent, their stylistic effects should also be equivalent. On close scrutiny, however, one will see that they are stylistically different even though they are structurally similar. The reason is not far to seek: whereas the original places "舍" at the beginning of the first and the second half of the Chinese phrase, Watson's English version puts the equivalent of "舍" ("of my lodge") at the end of the two halves; as a result, in the Chinese original, because of the similarity ("舍") between the first and the second half in respect of their initial units and because of the dissimilarity between them in respect of their final units ("南," "北"), an aesthetic tension between similarity and dissimilarity as well as an antithetical relationship between "南" and "北" is set up, thereby giving the four-syllable phrase an aesthetically pleasing quality not present in Watson's translation. To solve Watson's problem, one would have to change the bipartite phrase to something like "my lodge's north, my lodge's south."[162]

Less difficult to detect is the second flaw of the version, which is the result of misinterpretations: "皆春水" does not mean "everywhere spring rivers"; instead, the phrase only means that there is water both north and south of the poet's "dwelling," as is the case in Hawkes' version; nor does it say whether there is one river or two rivers, much less "everywhere spring rivers." By specifying the exact number of rivers, which is not warranted by the original, Watson has destroyed the poem's functional ambiguity.

Third, being a much more formal word than the Chinese "來," "converging" is, in terms of register, off-key, reminding us of the translator's use of the unduly formal expression "human concourse" in "Martial drums cut off all human concourse" for "戍鼓斷人行," which

---

[161] Watson, 84.
[162] Though stylistically desirable, this restructuring is not, of course, allowed by the normal English idiom.

has already been discussed.

Fourth, it is interesting to note that Watson's liberal use of contracted forms ("market's far," "don't mind," "I'll call," "we'll finish off," "what's left") has not helped him capture Du Fu's homely style; instead, it has, together with the truncation of sentences throughout the poem, given the reader the impression of someone talking incoherently. In contrast, and curiously enough, Hawkes' version, though using uncontracted instead of contracted forms ("If you are willing," "I shall call to him"), is closer to the homely style of the original. Upon analysis, one will discover that the success of Hawkes' version lies in the translator's use of the right register, not in contractions and broken syntax, which are extraneous and easier to master. In other words, here, contracted forms and unorganized speech are not the stylistic features required to re-present the original's homely style and familiar tone.

In *"Zeng Wei Ba Chushi"* 〈贈衛八處士〉, the style is also homely, but the stage is set for more characters:

人生不相見
動如參與商
今夕復何夕
共此燈燭光
少壯能幾時
鬢髮各已蒼
訪舊半爲鬼
驚呼熱中腸
焉知二十載
重上君子堂
昔別君未婚
兒女忽成行
怡然敬父執
問我來何方
問答乃未已
驅兒羅酒漿
夜雨剪春韭
新炊間黃粱
主稱會面難
一舉累十觴
十觴亦不醉
感子故意長
明日隔山岳

世事兩茫茫 [.]¹⁶³

Often in this life of ours we resemble, in our failure to meet, the Shen and
Shang constellations, one of which rises as the other one sets. What lucky
chance is it, then, that brings us together this evening under the light of this
same lamp? Youth and vigour last but a little time.—Each of us now has
greying temples. Half of the friends we ask each other about are dead, and
our shocked cries sear the heart. Who could have guessed that it would be
twenty years before I sat once more beneath your roof? Last time we
parted you were still unmarried, but now here suddenly is a row of boys
and girls who smilingly pay their respects to their father's old friend. They
ask me where I have come from; but before I have finished dealing with
their questions, the children are hurried off to fetch us wine. Spring chives
are cut in the rainy dark, and there is freshly steamed rice mixed with
yellow millet. 'Come, we don't meet often!' you hospitably urge, pouring
out ten cupfuls in rapid succession. That I am still not drunk after ten cups
of wine is due to the strength of the emotion which your unchanging
friendship inspires. Tomorrow the Peak will lie between us, and each will
be lost to the other, swallowed up in the world's affairs.¹⁶⁴

Whether in the original or in translation, the poem is like a mini-drama, in
which the characters, because of the precision with which the poet and the
translator handle the register, all appear before the reader's eyes like real
persons; the language in the original and in the translation is unadorned,
just appropriate for the occasion; there is action that befits the scene, in
which two old friends meet after a lapse of many years, during which a lot
of changes have taken place ("Last time we parted you were still
unmarried, but now here suddenly is a row of boys and girls who
smilingly pay their respects to their father's old friend"). Images ranging
from the visual ("Spring chives," "dark," "yellow millet") to the olfactory
("freshly steamed rice") to the synaesthetic ("rainy dark") in the
translation appeal to the senses as much as those in the original. Ending on
a note that is slightly melancholy and wistful, both the original and the
translation show how a poem about friendship can be moving and life-like
through the use of homely images and unadorned language.

    Jenyns' translation, "A Presentation to Wei Pa, a retired Scholar,"¹⁶⁵
has conveyed the original in outline, but is unsatisfactory for a number of
reasons. First, line 1, translated as "Friendship are made only to be

---

¹⁶³ Hawkes, 67-68.
¹⁶⁴ Hawkes, 72.
¹⁶⁵ Jenyns, 18.

broken," is a misinterpretation; the line, "In life friends cannot often meet,"[166] offered in a footnote as an alternative rendering, is stylistically prosaic and semantically inaccurate.[167] Second, "But now I meet you my heart is warmed" (for "驚呼熱中腸") lacks the startling, dramatic quality of the original image. Third, the "行" image in "兒女忽成行" is generalized as "family" in "Now all of a sudden I find you with a family of sons and daughters." Fourth, the lively and vivid description of the meeting between two friends in the original is reduced to a blurred sketch in the translation:

> Politely and with looks of pleasure they wait on their father's old friend
> Asking me from where I come.
> We have not yet come to the end of our questions and answers,
> (When) you bid the youngsters bring wine and set it before us.[168]

The line "驅兒羅酒漿," translated by Hawkes as "the children are hurried off to fetch us wine," in which "hurried" closely matches the original "驅," is reduced to a generalized "you bid the youngsters bring wine and set it before us." Fifthly, "夜雨," which is synaesthetic, and which is rendered with precision as "rainy dark" by Hawkes, has been changed to a matter-of-fact phrase: "evening rain." Finally, a homely and simple line, "主稱會面難," translated into an equally homely and simple line by Hawkes, has been shifted to an unduly formal register: "The host discourses of how difficult it is to bring about a meeting."[169]

---

[166] Jenyns, 18.

[167] It is interesting to note that the original line ("人生不相見") and Hawkes' translation ("Often in this life of ours [...] in our failure to meet"), though also using simple language, do not give one the same impression as Jenyns' line does. This is because in Du Fu's and Hawkes' line, the speaker gives one the impression that he has a large vocabulary from which he can choose the appropriate words to suit the occasion or the context, whereas in Jenyns' version, the speaker, very much like a child, has only a limited vocabulary, so that, when he speaks, he has no choice but to use simple words, words which, though simple, cannot convey with precision the simplicity of language required by the context. In other words, whereas the simplicity of language in Du Fu's original and in Hawkes' translation is deliberate and intended to create the right kind of stylistic effect—which it has created, the "simplicity of language" in Jenyns' version is involuntary and fails to suit the occasion.

[168] Jenyns, 18.

[169] Jenyns, 18.

Examined alongside Hawkes' version, Bynner's "To My Retired Friend Wêi," also suffers:

> We little guessed it would be twenty years
> Before I could visit you again.
> When I went away, you were still unmarried;
> But now these boys and girls in a row
> Are very kind to their father's old friend.
> They ask me where I have been on my journey;
> And then, when we have talked awhile,
> They bring and show me wines and dishes,
> Spring chives cut in the night-rain
> And brown rice cooked freshly a special way.[170]

Though the register in general chimes in with that of the original, the line "Are very kind to their father's old friend" is vague and prosaic, preserving little of the original line "怡然敬父執," which enables the reader to visualize the scene. This is because the words "怡然敬" are sharper, more concrete, more specific than the words "are very kind to." The original "驅兒羅酒漿," with the evocative verb "驅" left untranslated, is, again, reduced to something general and unspecific: "They bring and show me wines and dishes." In the last but one line, "night-rain" lacks the synaesthetic compression of the original, which Hawkes' "rainy dark" has succeeded in capturing. In the last line, the original "黃粱," which contributes so much to the visual appeal of the poem, is left untranslated.

Intimate and familiar, Rexroth's translation, "To Wei Pa, a Retired Scholar," is in the right register. The following lines, for example, depict a homely scene in terms as realistic as those in the original:

> When we parted years ago,
> You were unmarried. Now you have
> A row of boys and girls, who smile
> And ask me about my travels.
> How have I reached this time and place?
> Before I can come to the end
> Of an endless tale, the children
> Have brought out the wine. We go
> Out in the night and cut young
> Onions in the rainy darkness.
> We eat them with hot, steaming,

---

[170] Bynner, 158-59.

Yellow millet.[171]

However, there is too much rewriting in the "translation": "問答乃未已" is paraphrased as "Before I can come to the end / Of an endless tale"; "驅" in "驅兒羅酒漿" is omitted, so that the action described in the original is simplified: "the children / Have brought out the wine." Of all the translators discussed in this paper, though, Rexroth is the only one after Hawkes to have accurately rendered the synaesthetic image "夜雨": "rainy darkness."[172]

Written in a diametrically opposite style, the following description of pomp and pageantry is illustrative of another level to which Du Fu's style can freely move:

憶昔霓旌下南苑
苑中萬物生顏色
昭陽殿裏第一人
同輦隨君侍君側
輦前才人帶弓箭
白馬嚼齧黃金勒 [.][173]

In rendering these lines from "*Ai jiangtou*" 〈哀江頭〉 ("By the Lake"), Hawkes is able to re-create a scene of equal grandeur, painting an equally evocative picture in visual terms:

I remember how formerly, when the Emperor's rainbow banner made its way into the South Park, everything in the park seemed to bloom with a brighter colour. The First Lady of the Chao-yang Palace rode in the same carriage as her lord in attendance at his side, while before the carriage rode

---

[171] Rexroth, 11.

[172] It is not possible to decide whether Rexroth has been influenced by Hawkes or has, because of his sensitivity as a poet, been more capable than other translators of re-creating this synaesthetic image. Given the fact that his volume was published in 1971, that is, four years after *A Little Primer of Tu Fu* came out, he may well have read Hawkes' translation before he produced his own, substituting "rainy darkness" for "rainy dark" during the process of "translation." In going through his volume, *One Hundred Poems from the Chinese*, one cannot find conclusive evidence that Rexroth could read Du Fu in the original, for nowhere does he appear to have produced his "versions" with direct reference to Du Fu's Chinese text. Against this background, therefore, he may well have written poems based on translations of Du Fu's work, including Hawkes' *A Little Primer of Tu Fu*, without having been able to read Chinese.

[173] Hawkes, 49-50.

maids of honour equipped with bows and arrows, their white horses champing at golden bits.[174]

Though reproducing largely the same sense-units, Hung's rendering, "Lamentation by the River," lacks the majestic sweep of the original as well as of Hawkes' version, which befits the scene of splendour described by the poet:

When the rainbow banners used to descend upon the South Park, The whole park burst into color. The first lady from the Chao-yang Palace Accompanied His Majesty in his carriage. Before it rode lady courtiers, each with bow and arrows, On white horses champing restlessly at golden bits.[175]

This is because the large number of pauses arising from end-stopped lines have a clogging effect, hampering the onward thrust of the rhythm.[176]

---

[174] Hawkes, 55.

[175] Hung, 106.

[176] At this point, it may be asked why the original, with every one of its lines being end-stopped, does not share the same flaw as Hung's translation. The answer lies in the difference between classical Chinese verse and Hung's translation: while Du Fu's end-stopped lines are regular, giving the poem a continuous movement that is characteristic of blank verse, particularly the blank verse of Milton, Hung's end-stopped lines have the effect of chopping up the sense-flow. Much more sensitive to language than all the translators examined in this paper, Hawkes uses a prose here which, if printed as separate lines, would be very much like blank verse even if the metre may not be regular. In the following paragraphs, I shall compare Hawkes' language with Milton's. As a matter fact, Hung's inferiority to Hawkes in using English can be seen even at the very beginning of his version. In translating "少陵野老吞聲哭，春日潛行曲江曲" as "I am an old rustic from Shao-ling who cries hard but not loud, For I want to attract no attention as I stroll by the Meandering River in the spring sun" (Hung, 106), he has turned two highly vivid and concrete lines of poetry into prose: "cries hard but not loud" (for "吞聲哭") and "For I want to attract no attention as I stroll" (for "潛行") are wordy and clumsy, which is evidence either of the translator's limited vocabulary or of his inability to hit on the *mot juste* when called upon to do so. This fumbling for the right word or right phrase, characteristic of translators who are not able to use the target language competently, becomes immediately obvious the moment Hung's lines are put alongside Hawkes': "The old fellow from Shao-ling weeps with stifled sobs as he walks furtively by the bends of the Serpentine on a day in spring" (Hawkes, 55). Like the original "吞聲哭," how much more economical and precise than Hung's "cries hard but not loud" Hawkes' "weeps with stifled sobs" is! And Hawkes' "walks furtively" (for "潛行") is far superior to Hung's "For I want to

Along with his exceptional ability to render scenes of grandeur,
Hawkes' language can rise even to the epical, soaring together with Du Fu
to heights which only epic poets are capable of reaching. Take Du Fu's
description of horses in "*Wei Feng Lushi zhai guan Cao Jiangjun
huamatu*" 〈韋諷錄事宅觀曹將軍畫馬圖〉 ("On Seeing a Horse-painting
by Ts'ao Pa in the House of the Recorder Wei Feng") and Hawkes'
translation:

曾貌先帝照夜白
龍池十日飛霹靂 [.][177]

On one occasion, when he painted our late Imperial Majesty's grey, Night
Shiner, thunders rolled for ten days over the face of the Dragon Pool.[178]

此皆騎戰一敵萬
縞素漠漠開風沙
其餘七匹亦殊絕
迥若寒空雜霞雪
霜蹄蹴踏長楸間 [.][179]

[…] both of them, a match for ten thousand in mounted combat. The white
silk ground behind them seems to open out into a vast expanse of
wind-blown sand.
    The other seven horses in the painting are also magnificent specimens.
Remote above them, sunset and snow commingle in a wintry sky. Their

---

attract no attention as I stroll[.]" In reading Hung's translation, one has the
impression of a missile hitting only the periphery instead of homing in on the
target. Perhaps, like all the translators whose first language is not English (for
example, Wu Juntao), Hung has only a limited command of the target language;
for this reason, instead of saying "weeps with stifled sobs" and "walks furtively,"
both of which are beyond his linguistic competence and resources, he has to make
do with a limited vocabulary and express the "same ideas" circuitously,
involuntarily resorting to circumlocution, as it were. This is basically what
beginners are taught to do in English courses with subtitles like "Saying whatever
you want to say in 1,000 words." This does not mean, of course, that native
speakers are, ipso facto, competent users of their mother tongue; as my discussion
in the foregoing paragraphs has shown, native speakers of English can also bungle
miserably. Needless to say, in making this observation, I assume that, apart from
Hung and Wu, all the other translators studied in this paper are native speakers of
English.

[177] Hawkes, 144.
[178] Hawkes, 154.
[179] Hawkes, 146-47.

frosty hooves paw and trample a road lined with tall catalpa trees.[180]

In both the original and the translation, the horses are presented in magnificent terms, a stylistic feature which is the hall-mark of all great epics in Western literature.

In rendering the same lines in his version, "A Drawing of a Horse by General Ts'ao at Secretary Wêi Fêng's House," Bynner shows less sensitivity in his choice of words:

> He painted the late Emperor's luminous white horse.
> For ten days the thunder flew over Dragon Lake [...]
> ....
> They are war-horses. Either could face ten thousand.
> They make the white silk stretch away into a vast desert.
> And the seven others with them are almost as noble....
> Mist and snow are moving across a cold sky,
> And hoofs are cleaving snow-drifts under great trees—[181]

The lines are either "rewritten" or generalized, differing widely from the original. Unable to tackle with sufficient competence the visually evocative image "照夜白," Bynner can only come up with an uninspired version, "luminous white horse," which pales in comparison with Hawkes' highly accurate, highly evocative "[our late Imperial Majesty's] grey, Night Shiner." Because of the vague "flew" and of the glib flow of the rhyhm, particularly in the relatively loose phrase "flew over Dragon Lake," the line "For ten days the thunder flew over Dragon Lake" lacks the majesty and ponderousness of Hawkes' version in terms of both diction and rhythm: "thunders rolled for ten days over the face of the Dragon Pool." In Hawkes' version, the action-verb "rolled" (/'rəʊld/), because of its long diphthong /əʊ/ and its consonants /l/ and /d/, all of which help to prolong its utterance, forcefully grips the reader's attention, thereby suggesting a more awesome movement of the "thunders." With the phrase "for ten days" put after "rolled," the duration of the movement is further lengthened before it comes to an end, so that the rolling of the "thunders" is emphasized. Perhaps less sensitive to the qualities of phonetic sounds or less adept at using the target language, Bynner is not able to give his translation the same kind of suggestiveness: his "flew," apart from being a less specific, less apt word than Hawkes' "rolled,"

---

[180] Hawkes, 155.
[181] Bynner, 162.

suffers because of the smoother vowel /uː/ in /fluː/, which takes less effort and time to pronounce, and is therefore less effective in suggesting the ponderous rolling of thunders over the Dragon Pool. Even in his deployment of the same words, Bynner's auditory sensitivity is unimpressive: by putting "For ten days" before "flew," the action-verb on which the awesomeness and majesty of the rolling thunder hinge, the translator has given a shorter duration to the thunder's "flight," so that it comes to an end immediately after the phrase "over Dragon Lake."

Upon closer analysis, one will see that even between Bynner's "Dragon Lake" and Hawkes' "Dragon Pool," there is a significant difference in terms of stylistic effect. Though Bynner's "lake," pronounced /leɪk/, has a diphthong (/eɪ/), which takes more time to pronounce than a short vowel, its final consonant is a velar plosive /k/, which tends to shorten the whole sound /leɪk/ in the process of pronunciation. Hawkes' "Pool," pronounced /puːl/, is, in terms of sound value, phonologically preferable to "Lake": its long vowel /uː/ prolongs the duration of the pronunciation, and is then reinforced by /l/, which, when read aloud, can lengthen the whole line in temporal terms, thereby suggesting more effectively the majestic rolling of the thunder over "the Dragon Pool."[182] Semantically, in rendering "騎戰" as "war-horses," Bynner has failed to convey the real meaning of the original, which Hawkes has accurately translated: "in mounted combat." His rendering of the line "縞素漠漠開風沙" ("They make the white silk stretch away into a vast desert.") is pedestrian when compared with Hawkes' corresponding line ("The white silk ground behind them seems to open out into a vast expanse of wind-blown sand."): the two series of three stressed syllables in a row ("white silk ground," "wind-blown sand") powerfully reinforce, by phonological means, a scene of epic proportions. Bynner's "vast" is effective by virtue of the labio-dental fricative /v/ and the long vowel /ɑː/, both of which require much effort to pronounce properly, thereby kinaesthetically suggesting the space unfolding before the reader's eyes. However, "desert" (/ˈdez.ət/, being a trochee ending in an unstressed syllable (/ət/), which is made up of a short vowel (/ə/) and an alveolar plosive consonant (/t/), is anticlimactic. In the last but one line, "雜" is left untranslated, and "霞" is mistranslated as "mist."

In "*Guan Gongsun Daniang dizi wu jianqi xing*" 〈觀公孫大娘弟子舞

---

[182] When one appreciates a poem, even if one does not read it aloud, one still tends silently to vocalize the syllables, or, to personify the reading process, the poem still reads itself aloud to one's "mind's ear."

劍器行〉 ("On Seeing a Pupil of Kung-sun Dance the *Ch'ien-ch'i*—A Ballad"), Du Fu's language and style come very close to the works written by such epic poets as Homer, Virgil, and Milton:

昔有佳人公孫氏
一舞劍器動四方
觀者如山色沮喪
天地爲之久低昂
㸌如羿射九日落
矯如群帝驂龍翔
來如雷霆收震怒
罷如江海凝清光 [.][183]

In time past there was a lovely woman called Kung-sun, whose *chien-ch'i* astonished the whole world. Audiences numerous as the hills watched awestruck as she danced, and, to their reeling senses, the world seemed to go on rising and falling, long after she had finished dancing. Her flashing swoop was like the nine suns falling, transfixed by the Mighty Archer's arrows; her soaring flight like the lords of the sky driving their dragon teams aloft; her advance like the thunder gathering up its dreadful rage; her stoppings like seas and rivers locked in the cold glint of ice.[184]

Let us first look at Book VIII, lines 7-17 of Homer's *Iliad*, in which Zeus addresses "a gathering of the gods upon the topmost peak of many-ridged Olympus" asserting his supremacy and omnipotence:[185]

"μήτε τις οὖν θήλεια θεὸς τό γε μήτε τις ἄρσην
πειράτω διακέρσαι ἐμὸν ἔπος,   ἀλλ' ἅμα πάντες
αἰνεῖτ', ὄφρα τάχιστα τελευτήσω τάδε ἔργα.
ὃν δ' ἂν ἐγὼν ἀπάνευθε θεῶν ἐθέλοντα νοήσω
ἐλθόντ' ἢ Τρώεσσιν ἀρηγέμεν ἢ Δαναοῖσι,
πληγεὶς οὐ κατὰ κόσμον ἐλεύσεται Οὔλυμπόνδε·
ἤ μιν ἑλὼν ῥίψω ἐς Τάρταρον ἠερόεντα,
τῆλε μάλ', ἧχι βάθιστον ὑπὸ χθονός ἐστι βέρεθρον,
ἔνθα σιδήρειαί τε πύλαι καὶ χάλκεος οὐδός,
τόσσον ἔνερθ' 'Αΐδεω ὅσον οὐρανός ἐστ' ἀπὸ γαίης·

---

[183] Hawkes, 189-90.
[184] Hawkes, 199.
[185] Homer [Ομηρος], *The Iliad*, with an English translation by A. T. Murray, Vol. I, the Loeb Classical Library, 170, ed. G. P. Goold (Cambridge, Massachusetts: Harvard University Press, 1988), 339.

γνώσετ᾽ ἔπειθ᾽ ὅσον εἰμὶ θεῶν κάρτιστος ἁπάντων."[186]

Let not any goddess nor yet any god essay this thing, to thwart my word, but do ye all alike assent thereto, that with all speed I may bring these deeds to pass. Whomsoever I shall mark minded apart from the gods to go and bear aid either to Trojans or Danaans, smitten in no seemly wise shall he come back to Olympus, or I shall take and hurl him into murky Tartarus, far, far away, where is the deepest gulf beneath the earth, the gates whereof are of iron and the threshold of bronze, as far beneath Hades as heaven is above earth: then shall ye know how far the mightiest am I of all gods.[187]

In the following lines (Book VIII, lines 75-77), also from the *Iliad*, Homer describes how Zeus decides the fates of the Achaeans during their combat with the Trojans:

αὐτὸς δ᾽ ἐξ" Ιδης μεγάλ᾽ ἔκτυπε, δαιόμενον δὲ
ἧκε σέλας μετὰ λαὸν᾽ Αχαιῶν· οἱ δὲ ἰδόντες
θάμβησαν, καὶ πάντας ὑπὸ χλωρὸν δέος εἷλεν.[188]

Then himself he thundered aloud from Ida, and sent a blazing flash amid the host of the Achaeans; and at sight thereof they were seized with wonder, and pale fear gat hold of all.[189]

In the first passage, the imagined action of Zeus hurling the gods from heaven down to Tartarus involves vast spaces, just as the action in Du Fu's description as well as in Hawkes' version does. In the second passage, the language used by Homer to describe Zeus "thunder[ing] aloud from Ida" and the "blazing flash" he "sent" "amid the host of the Achaeans" bears a close resemblance to Du Fu's Chinese and Hawkes' English. Hawkes' translation, also in a European language,

Her flashing swoop was like the nine suns falling, transfixed by the Mighty Archer's arrows [...] her advance like the thunder gathering up its dreadful rage [,]

is especially Homeric. Indeed, without the sources indicated, the reader might well be led to think that the translation of Du Fu's lines by Hawkes is quoted from the *Iliad*.

---

[186] Homer, 338.
[187] Homer, 339.
[188] Homer, 342.
[189] Homer, 343.

The same kind of illusion may be evoked after one has read Book II, lines 692-98 of Virgil's *Aeneid*, in which the hero of the poem, Aeneas, describes how an omen was sent from heaven as his father Anchises was praying to Jupiter:

> "Vix ea fatus erat senior, subitoque fragore
> intonuit laevum, et de caelo lapsa per umbras
> stella facem ducens multa cum luce cucurrit.
> illam, summa super labentem culmina tecti,
> cernimus Idaea claram se condere silva
> signantemque vias; tum longo limite sulcus
> dat lucem, et late circum loca sulpure fumant."[190]

> "Scarcely had the aged man thus spoken, when with sudden crash there was thunder on the left and a star shot from heaven, gliding through the darkness, and drawing a fiery trail amid a flood of light. We watch it glide over the palace roof and bury in Ida's forest the splendour that marked its path; then the long-drawn furrow shines, and far and wide all about reeks with sulphur."[191]

The crash of thunder and the shooting star conjure up a scene as awesome as that in Du Fu's description in Chinese and in Hawkes' English translation quoted above.

When the reader looks at Book I, lines 44-49 and Book VI, lines 749-53 of Milton's *Paradise Lost*, in particular, he may be even more likely to be misled in his effort to identify the author, easily mistaking them for Hawkes' translation of Du Fu's poem and vice versa:

> Him the Almighty Power
> Hurled headlong flaming from th' ethereal sky
> With hideous ruin and combustion down
> To bottomless perdition, there to dwell
> In adamantine chains and penal fire,
> Who durst defy th' Omnipotent to arms.[192]

---

[190] Virgil [Publius Vergilius Maro], *Eclogues. Georgics. Aeneid I-VI*, with an English translation by H. Rushton Fairclough, revised by G. P. Goold, the Loeb Classical Library, edited by G. P. Goold, LCL 63 (Cambridge, Massachusetts: Harvard University Press, 1999), 362.

[191] Virgil, 363.

[192] John Milton, *Poetical Works*, ed. Douglas Bush (London: Oxford University Press, 1966), 213.

> Forth rushed with whirlwind sound
> The chariot of Paternal Deity,
> Flashing thick flames, wheel within wheel, undrawn,
> Itself instinct with spirit, but convoyed
> By four Cherubic shapes.[193]

The above lines are characterized by a grand sweep, a large-scale movement, and a ferocious onslaught suggested by the rhythm, all of which share a close affinity with Du Fu's poem and Hawkes' translation. Depicting scenes or forces of cosmic proportions, the images and the language inspire awe and trigger associations with the sublime, bearing the hallmark of what Christopher Ricks calls "the Grand Style" in his famous book, *Milton's Grand Style*.[194]

Returning to Du Fu's original and Hawkes' translation and reading them aloud, we will see that the source and target texts are similar in more respects than one: a majestic rise and fall like the flowing and ebbing of the sea; a symmetry in the movement of the rhythm, especially in the third and fourth couplets, in which Hawkes' English ("Her flashing swoop was like the nine suns falling, transfixed by the Mighty Archer's arrows; her soaring flight like the lords of the sky driving their dragon teams aloft; her advance like the thunder gathering up its dreadful rage; her stoppings like seas and rivers locked in the cold glint of ice.") dances in sync with Du Fu's Chinese.

---

[193] Milton, 336.

[194] Christopher Ricks, *Milton's Grand Style* (Oxford: Clarendon Press, 1963). Ricks begins chapter 2, entitled "The Grand Style," by quoting, first, Arnold, "He is our great artist in style, our one first-rate master in the grand style," and, then, Johnson, "The characteristick quality of his poem is sublimity. He sometimes descends to the elegant, but his element is the great. He can occasionally invest himself with grace; but his natural port is gigantick loftiness. He can please when pleasure is required; but it is his peculiar power to astonish" (Ricks, 22); afterwards he proceeds to discuss "four important Miltonic topics: rhythm or music, syntax, metaphor, and word-play" (Ricks, 23). The following words used by Ricks in discussing Belial's reply to Moloch in Book II of *Paradise Lost*, particularly lines 170-86 ("What if the breath that kindl'd ["kindled" in Bush's edition] those grim fires / [...] Ages of hopeless end; this would be worse"), are, to a large extent, also applicable to Du Fu's poem and Hawkes' translation: "He drives relentlessly through 'what if...or...what if...', and then sweeps to his annihilating climax, foreseen and deliberately held back [...] When a sentence surges forward like that, the end of it seems less a destination than a destiny" (Ricks, 30). "It is this ability to harness the thrust of his syntax which sustains Milton's great argument [...]" (Ricks, 31).

In rendering the same lines, Hung has failed to rise to the same epic grandeur:

> In former days, there was a beautiful woman, Madame Kung-sun, Whose performance of the Sword Pantomime Dance was everywhere applauded. Spectators, massed mountain-high, all bore a breathless countenance, For they felt as if heaven struggled against earth. She bent back: you saw nine falling suns shot down by the fabulous I; She leaped: you beheld gods astride flying dragons in the clouds. She advanced: you awaited the thunder and lightning from a gathering storm of anger and fury; She stopped: you contemplated the mellowed light over a vast sea.[195]

The register ("was everywhere applauded," "bent back," "leaped"), this time unduly colloquial, is not in tune with the language of epics. Nor is the translator's comprehension of the original satisfactory: "bore a breathless countenance" is not the same thing as "色沮喪"; "as if heaven struggled against earth" has distorted "天地爲之久低昂." In the line "來如雷霆收震怒," "雷霆" is the subject, "收" the transitive verb, and "震怒" the object; though enumerating the same lexical items in his translation, Hung does not seem to have been able to make out their grammatical relationships, so that Du Fu's real message gets lost in the translation: "She advanced: you awaited the thunder and lightning from a gathering storm of anger and fury."

Bynner, though using verse as his medium, turns out something closer to prose than to poetry—and with a large number of mistranslations:

> There lived years ago the beautiful Kung-sun,
> Who, dancing with her dagger, drew from all four quarters
> An audience like mountains lost among themselves.
> Heaven and earth moved back and forth, following her motions,
> Which were bright as when the Archer shot the nine suns down the sky
> And rapid as angels before the wings of dragons.
> She began like a thunderbolt, venting its anger,
> And ended like the shining calm of rivers and the sea...[196]

Line 2 of the original is end-stopped, meaning "astonished the whole world";[197] by changing the direct object "四方" to an adverbial adjunct and linking it to the following line, Bynner shows that he has

[195] Hung, 251.
[196] Bynner, 167-68.
[197] Hawkes, 199.

misinterpreted both line 2 and line 3. While "沮喪" refers to a specific and intense state of emotional change, Bynner's "lost in themselves" is general and refers to a vague emotional state which is hard to pin down. "低昂," correctly rendered by Hawkes as "rising and falling," which is vertical, has been mistranslated as "moved back and forth," which is horizontal. In lines 5-8 of the translation, the ferocity of the startling imagery, the grand sweep, and the rise and fall of the rhythm of the original have given place to vague and inaccurate images and a rhythm that sounds more like prose than poetry: "bright," for example, is a much less forceful, much less sharp, and much less startling light image than both Du Fu's "爟" and Hawkes' "flashing"; the word "angels," because of its associations with the lovely or the beneficent, fails to bring out the august and awe-inspiring associations with "群帝"; "驂龍翔," which describes "the lords of the sky driving their dragon teams aloft" (Hawkes' translation), suggesting majesty and grandeur, has been misinterpreted and translated as "before the wings of dragons." Line 7, mistranslating "來" as "began" and converting "收震怒" into its opposite ("venting its anger"), has destroyed the original effect. Similarly, "ended like the shining calm of rivers and the sea," with the catch-all verb "ended," fails to convey the specific and forceful action-verb "凝." With this kind of translation, one cannot, of course, expect it to suggest the cosmic rise and fall described in the original, which Hawkes' translation has succeeded so marvellously in conveying to readers of his version.

Wu, hampered by his deficient command of English and, apparently, by his attempt to rhyme, which he fails to sustain, has produced an even weaker version:

> In former days there was a fair of Gongsun family,
> Her sword dance whene'er played always was a pageantry.
> A mountain of audience was moved, with looks of dismay;
> Even heaven and earth would heave and set their breath all day.
> With flashes like the Archer Yi shot down the nine bright suns,
> And vigour like the Genii drove the dragons on cloud-way,
> She rushed on, and it's the thunders rolling in a fury,
> And when finished, it's the sea calmed down with smooth rays.[198]

In the above lines, meanings are distorted or read into the poem: nowhere in the original does Du Fu say "heaven and earth would [...] set their

---

[198] Wu Juntao 吳鈞陶, trans., *Tu Fu: A New Translation* 《杜甫詩新譯》 (Hong Kong: Commercial Press, 1981), 216.

breath all day"; nor is there "pageantry," much less a "cloud-way"; and "smooth rays" is not "清光." By changing the active voice of line 8 to the passive, the translator has reduced a highly forceful line to something flat. What is even more disappointing is the grammar of lines 5-8, which cannot be disentangled; to make the lines grammatical, one would have to rewrite all of them. The choice of words, too, shows that the translator has difficulty grasping even the most basic denotations of words: it is hard, for example, for the reader to establish any relationship between "Genii" and "群帝"; "calmed down," being in the passive voice, also fails to match the forceful "凝."

In the above discussion, I have examined Hawkes' translations alongside corresponding versions of the same poems by Du Fu, and shown how other versions differ from those by Hawkes, though these other versions may at the same time differ from one another. In the cases studied, Hawkes' versions have proved superior in almost all respects. In the first place, his reading of the original is more meticulous and more accurate; to be sure, his interpretations are not infallible, his errors of interpretation are extremely rare. Second, judging by his translations, he is more sensitive to the poetic qualities of the originals, whether in terms of imagery or in terms of rhythm and the various rhetorical devices used by the poet. Third, his mastery of the target language is unequalled by all the other translators. While many of the other translators appear to be fumbling for the *mot juste*, ending up with the vague, the general, or expressions carrying undesirable connotations or associations, Hawkes is almost always able to employ the right word, the right expression, and the right image, capturing the nuances that prove elusive to less competent or less sensitive translators. Fourth, when he renders Du Fu's imagery, he is equally adept at handling the visual, the auditory, the tactile, the olfactory, the gustatory, the kinaesthetic, and the synaesthetic, often with great felicity. Fifth, with his keen sense of rhythm and his masterly manipulation of syntax, he is able to re-create the syntactic effects of the originals with precision. Finally, he has the widest range of styles, which is beyond the reach of all the other translators.

In the light of these qualities, one feels what he claims in his Introduction to *A Little Primer of Du Fu*, which I have already quoted in footnote 2, is much less than what he has actually achieved:

I have written this book in order to give some idea of what Chinese poetry is really like and how it works to people who either know no Chinese at all or know only a little. To write it I have taken all the poems by Tu Fu contained in a well-known Chinese anthology, *Three Hundred T'ang*

Poems, arranged them chronologically, transliterated them, explained their form and historical background, expounded their meaning, and lastly translated them into English prose. The translations are intended as cribs. They are not meant to be beautiful or pleasing"[199]

From my discussion in this paper, we can see that Hawkes' translations of Du Fu's poems are much more than "cribs"; they are not only "beautiful" and "pleasing," but also unrivalled; for, of all the versions examined in this paper, Hawkes' are the most successful in translating or re-creating the tone, the stylistic features, and the rhetorical devices used by the poet in the source texts. In comparison with Hawkes' versions, many of those in verse and intended to be poetry are nothing more than prose—very often paltry prose—printed in separate lines.

When Hawkes set out to translate Du Fu, the Muses, whether Erato or Clio or Calliope, must have expected him to use verse as his medium, for, in the minds of most translators and readers, verse is the only medium capable of rising to the summit of Mount Parnassus; instead, he used prose—and surprised the Muses.

---

[199] Hawkes, ix.

MIND THE GAP:
THE HAWKES-MINFORD TRANSITION
IN *THE STORY OF THE STONE*

CHLOË STARR
YALE DIVINITY SCHOOL
YALE UNIVERSITY

"At this point," wrote Howard Goldblatt two decades ago, "virtually anything a reviewer could say about the five-volume Hawkes-Minford translation of Cao Xueqin's (and Gao E's) masterly eighteenth century Chinese novel...would be either superfluous or redundant."[1] Goldblatt, like others before and after, argues that the Hawkes-Minford translation is "the one to read."[2] If you had to choose only one of the three good translations, writes Lévy, "il n'y aurait guère d'hésitation."[3] That *The Story of the Stone* has not been superseded since Hawkes published the first volume of the set in 1973 and Minford the last in 1986, indicates something of the "excellence—no, the sheer beauty—of the translation."[4] Is there anything further to say, two score years later, other than to synthesize the adulation?

The existence of this volume suggests an affirmative answer. This paper, rooted in literary rather than translation perspectives, highlights an aspect of confusion in scholarship that gnaws away at the literary/translation interface. The title of the paper is gently misleading: the transition between volumes three and four of *The Story of the Stone*,

---

[1] Howard Goldblatt, Untitled review of *The Story of the Stone* Vol. 5, *The Dreamer Wakes* by Cao Xueqin, *World Literature Today* 63.1 (Winter 1989): 162.

[2] Cf. Andrew Schonebaum and Tina Lu, eds., *Approaches to Teaching the Story of the Stone (Dream of the Red Chamber)*, forthcoming, MLA, 2012. Preface.

[3] André Lévy, Untitled review of *The Story of the Stone* by David Hawkes (translator), *T'oung Pao*, Second Series 70, Livr. 4/5 (1984): 298-302. The other two Lévy compares are those of Gladys Yang and Yang Hsien-yi, and Li Tche-houa and Jaqueline Alézaïs.

[4] Goldblatt, Untitled review, 162.

that is, between David Hawkes' and John Minford's translations (and interpretations) of *Hongloumeng*, is only part of the story. Others have tackled the issue of whether the Hawkes-Minford transition parallels or subverts the Cao-Gao transition, and what the substitution of translator means for the English novel. The widest gap here is not the transition between Hawkes and Minford, although that seam will be unpicked below, but the transition to Hawkes-Minford: to an English language text, and its accompanying critical scholarship.

Scholarship based on the Hawkes-Minford translation has presented a conundrum which those in Chinese literature have yet to face squarely: that much critical literature still confuses the distinction between the translation and the original. The assumption, frequently made, is that in discussing *Stone* we are talking about the Chinese text, a Chinese novel.[5] Students working in an English language medium and writing essays based on *Stone*—even if they cross correlate to *Hongloumeng* pages for purposes of referencing—often write as if they were studying a Chinese novel and rarely acknowledge explicitly that they are working with an English text. This paper draws on the work of textual theorists, and on David Hawkes' own literary critical writings, to explore how the ubiquity of the Hawkes-Minford text among English language readers and students, and particularly its differences from any Chinese *Hongloumeng* edition, means that it should be approached as a separate text, a creative work of fiction, amenable to study in its own right. *Stone* is a work of English-language fiction, an English literary text. Bao-yu is not 寶玉. Or, Bao-yu is not Baoyu, the transliteration of the Chinese character with whom he is often confused.

The paper germinated from the belated realization that to read *The Story of the Stone* in English was an entirely different experience to reading *Hongloumeng* in Chinese, and that to read the two texts in parallel creates a third, different reading experience.[6] With a literary text, the

---

[5] Even where studies acknowledge diverse textual traditions, they may choose to set aside questions of the text(s) and assume one 120-chapter novel for the purpose of analysis. Dore Levy's study, for example, which aims to be a bridge between English language readership and scholarly critical studies, does this, using exclusively Hawkes-Minford, metonymically as that text of *Hongloumeng*. Dore Levy, *Ideal and Actual in* Story of the Stone (New York: Columbia University Press, 1999).

[6] As Venuti notes, translation is a double writing, a "rewriting of the foreign text according to domestic cultural values," that requires a double reading, "as both communication and inscription." The new text holds open the possibility of "exorbitant gain" as well as inevitable reduction in scope from the foreign

versatility and ambiguity of imagery and language means that a translation always brings new possibilities to the imagination of a reader. The principal mode of overcoming the dichotomy between English and Chinese texts has usually been to bring the English language reader to the reading knowledge of a Chinese readership. As Schleiermacher famously noted, there are only two choices in translation: to leave the author in peace, and move the reader towards him, or to leave the reader in peace, and move the author.[7] Critical studies of *The Story of the Stone* have sought to take their readers to Qing China—while working with a text that deliberately domesticates as well as foreignizes. Critical studies by sinologists have perpetuated the notion of an almost transparent English text laid over the Chinese, even as authors are explicitly aware that Hawkes-Minford differs textually from all other editions of *Hongloumeng*.

There are good textual, pedagogical, and translatorly grounds for asserting that we are essentially talking about two separate novels, and reasons for suggesting the Hawkes-Minford translation, *Stone*, is a test case par excellence of the parameters of reading a translated novel. The ramifications are substantial: in terms of curricula, *Hongloumeng* is usually taught in East Asian Studies departments, but the implication here is that an English literature specialist has just as much right or ability to teach *Stone* in English; and that the precious knowledge of Chinese that specialists have vaunted as their raison d'être is at best tangentially useful in teaching the English version, at worst a smoke screen to talk about aspects of Qing life or advocate a New Historicist reading. (I am probably not unique among literature teachers in having taught a work in translation as if I were teaching the original, but merely in a transubstantiated version, and of ignoring the structural and literary impact of the Hawkes-Minford novel qua English novel.) Without a background understanding of the Chinese text, and those cultural references which are not brought out in the English edition, research questions asked of the *Stone* may be quite different, but quite liberating.[8]

---

language novel. See Lawrence Venuti, *The Translator's Invisibility* (London and New York: Routledge, 1995), 312, 18.

[7] Cf. Venuti, *The Translator's Invisibility*, 19.

[8] This works both ways, of course. Hawkes argued as early as 1964 that as world citizens we are all entitled to look to Chinese literature as part of our heritage, and that this new literary world would lead us to ask fundamental questions of our own literature, which might otherwise never be broached. David Hawkes, *Classical, Modern and Humane* (Hong Kong: The Chinese University Press, 1989), 69-72.

[I] Hawkes and Minford: Transition and Translation

But first to the hoary chestnut of the Hawkes-Minford transition. Is there a gap? Does it parallel the Cao-Gao gap, or is it different? Does it matter? The question of whether one mind can inhabit the mind of another teases both characters and author/s throughout the novel. The trope of recognition runs as a leitmotif through *Hongloumeng*: Baoyu recognizes Daiyu on first meeting, and traces of their heavenly pre-encounter echo across the book. The question of authorship parallels this, with its emphasis on one narrating consciousness. The gap in an overtly autobiographical novel is much greater in sequel chapters, and if the elements of regret or shame that critics have imputed to Cao were true, for example, then the shift in psychological motivation might be evident at the join. Should Minford be true to Cao, or to Gao? Or to Hawkes? David Hawkes himself acknowledges a shift in his taskmaster as his translation progressed, and as he realized that creating his own, best-fit eclectic text inevitably left narrative problems and lacunae.[9] There is, it transpires, a whole matrix of Cao-Gao and Hawkes-Minford shifts. One could begin, à la Redological research, by listing the biographical resonances between Hawkes and Minford, as between Cao and Gao, but this plays into notions of a creative author and derivative editor and translator, whereas even Cao Xueqin may have had a source text, and the 120-chapter novel is certainly composite. (For the record, Cao and Gao were both Manchu bannermen, educated in the same classical curriculum, both northerners, and possibly distant kin; Hawkes and Minford were fellow Englishmen, both educated in the Greek and Latin classics, and related by marriage. Both pairs of men are a generation apart. Both switches of writer require a switch of consciousness, of environment, of immediate linguistic heritage.)

Debate since the first 120-chapter editions of *Hongloumeng* appeared has focused on whether Gao E inherited chapter headings and a relatively detailed outline plan from Cao Xueqin, or created the vast majority of the forty sequel chapters himself, with varying degrees of help imputed from Cheng Weiyuan. Scholarly opinion, once divided, has edged towards crediting Gao with an editing role rather than rampant fabrication (the Hu Shi and Yu Pingbo line).[10] This followed debate over whether or not there was a prior text that Cao was drawing on, accounting for many of the

---

[9] Hawkes, *Classical, Modern and Humane,* 159.

[10] Dore Levy notes the divergence between Hawkes and Minford on this question, with Minford – who wrote his doctoral dissertation appraising the last forty chapters of the novel – "more inclined to accept Gao E's role as an editor than as a fabricator," Levy, *Ideal and Actual,* 158 note 2.

timing and spatial non-sequiturs in the manuscript, a theory David Hawkes considers at length in his essay "The Translator, the Mirror and the Dream," but which has lain dormant recently. Those speculating that Gao had a substantial draft to work with for the last forty chapters have been swayed by linguistic analyses (such as that of Bing Chan) which purport to show linguistic homogeneity between the two sections.[11] Chan's statistical tests demonstrate that there is a statistically significant likelihood one hand wrote both parts, showing either that Gao and Cheng's additions to the last forty chapters were not substantial enough to cause differences in vocabulary sampling, or that their editing of the first eighty chapters homogenized the text so as to make their input to the latter parts indistinguishable.[12]

Such data-driven studies have not deterred others who have approached the transition question from different angles. A range of opinions persists over the quality of the later parts, notwithstanding Chan's belief that his data undermined their validity. Haun Saussy, for example, contested in a 1987 article that there is an irremediable structural split between the Cao and Gao portions, between Gao's ending, and vision of the novel's literary structure, and that of Cao Xueqin, predicated on Gao's unwillingness to read Baoyu as Stone, and to render him "man." Gao brings about a happy, Confucian ending, but opts against the radical allegorizing which breaks down the novel's own frame/story construct.[13] In his recent article for the textbook *Approaches to Teaching the Story of the Stone*, edited by Andrew Schonebaum and Tina Lu, Saussy is equally clear, but here appeals to readerly intuition.

> Most readers sense a clear boundary at Chapter Eighty, and feel that the continuation is written in a different authorial voice: one less imaginatively vivid in capturing details of character and action, readier to assimilate story patterns from legends or other vernacular collections, more conformist in morality.[14]

---

[11] Bing C. Chan, *The Authorship of the Dream of the Red Chamber* (Hong Kong: Joint Publishing Co., 1986).

[12] Chan, 20-21. Chan establishes at the outset of his study that Cao had a complete plot worked out at the time of his death, whatever the state of writing, and that, by 1791 there were both 80- and 120-chapter versions extant.

[13] Haun Saussy, "Reading and Folly in *Dream of the Red Chamber*," *Chinese Literature: Essays, Articles, Reviews (CLEAR)* 9, (1987): 23-47.

[14] Haun Saussy, in *Approaches to Teaching the Story of the Stone*, eds. Schonebaum and Lu, forthcoming.

Saussy reminds that the Red Inkstone comments are only present for the first eighty chapters, and that many of the details backed up by Red Inkstone's assertions are incompatible with events in the later chapters. David Hawkes' own position on the question of authorship is broadly in line with the two strand argument, but for different reasons. In a 1963 lecture given in French, he was dismissive of Gao, and proposed studying only the 80-chapter version and ignoring "the forty supplementary chapters added by Gao E a whole generation after Cao had died."[15] Hawkes argued that it was because only two thirds of the chapters received their final form from Cao himself, that very different interpretations of the novel arose. In tracing instances of the various types of pre-figuring that occur by which alert readers are given to see what will happen to characters, and the symbols that forewarn of their eventual destiny, Hawkes suggested that a good deal of the intended outcome of the novel could be conjectured from Cao Xueqin's unfinished version. In a much later essay in 1980, Hawkes had shifted ground somewhat, refuting the notion that narrative problems lay with Gao's editing and the "inauthentic" last forty chapters, since "the incompleteness of *Hongloumeng* goes much deeper."[16] Arguing that the structural problems in the novel persist from the outset, Hawkes draws on Dai Bufan's argument that Cao was utilizing an earlier novel in his rewrites, and suggests that the early chapters reveal the "disiecta membra" of several novels which no amount of editing can reconcile. Hawkes is ambivalent as to whether the earlier text was written by Cao or someone else, but points out that whether or not a prior text is accepted, there is something "gravely wrong" in the sequence of events in early chapters, and that the redaction theory clears up such anomalies as the occasional intrusion of southern vocabulary into an ostensibly northern setting.[17]

If ambiguity persists over where and how in the text(s) Gao takes over from Cao, critics of the Hawkes-Minford linguistic transition have been more unified, with almost all who praised Hawkes seeing Minford's writing in the same vein. Critical acclaim for David Hawkes' translations has from the outset been fulgent. André Lévy acclaims "un tour de force" comparable to Sir Scott Moncrieff's decade long production of volumes of Proust. Hawkes' consummate grasp of grammar meant that he was able to

---

[15] Hawkes, *Classical, Modern and Humane*, 57.

[16] Hawkes, *Classical, Modern and Humane*, 179. Hawkes uses the episodes surrounding the death of You Sanjie (chs 63-69) to show that the chronology of the text is impossible, and argues it is "highly questionable" whether Cao wrote chs 64 and 67.

[17] Hawkes, *Classical, Modern and Humane*, 171 et passim.

manipulate sentences to something approaching Proustian length at times, while retaining the flow of the narrative. Book reviews consistently praise Minford as a worthy continuation of Hawkes, reproducing "not only the tone but the quality of his predecessor's masterful rendering."[18] Goldblatt was right to point to joint honours, noting that the completed five volume set is "virtually assured" classic status. This is not to say, however, that the two translators read as if they are the same hand. Most critical commentators have taken the line that this does not matter, since it parallels the Chinese text where Gao E assumed the task of editing and publishing the last forty chapters.[19]

No-one has yet conducted a statistical semantic study that would "prove" Minford is not Hawkes. I believe it would show a distinct difference in style: in vocabulary, turn of phrase, in the "voice" of characters, from acrolect through to basilect, but the significance of this is not just related to any parallels with the shift between the two Chinese authors. For both David Hawkes and John Minford, there are two types of transposing at work in rendering *Hongloumeng* into *Stone*. The first is textual emendation, a matter which devolved primarily to Hawkes as it required settling at the outset; and the second lies in alterations to the given text and particular vocabulary choices which make cultural aspects of the story familiar to English-language audiences.

If the first act of transposition is textual emendation, it is precisely because Hawkes was eminently qualified by dint of his literary and textual training that the principle of amending the text was accepted by early reviewers. As with any redactor of Cao's novel, editorial choices between multiple circulating MS and printed texts had to be made. Lévy writes of a freedom Hawkes assumed to "transposer, completer, corrigér" which would shock purists, and which would have appeared outrageous in the hands of a lesser connoisseur of the novel.[20] But aside from the decisions about "which text" that have focused critical minds, other aspects of the English text—such as format—affect its reading. The linguistic codes of a novel are far from its entirety. Adopting the format of an English novel in its bibliographic codes, the Hawkes-Minford text excises all commentary,

---

[18] Robert Hegel, Untitled Review of *The Story of the Stone* Vols. 4 and 5, *CLEAR* 8, no. 1/2 (July 1986): 129; Howard Goldblatt, Untitled Review of *The Story of the Stone* Vol. 4. *The Debt of Tears* by Cao Xueqin, *World Literature Today* 57.3 (Summer 1983): 510.

[19] Robert Hegel, for example, takes this position, and in reviewing the Hawkes-Minford line cites Hawkes' own reasoning for passing on the task as the shift in the tone of the last forty chapters to something "more bleak, closer to despair." Ibid.

[20] Lévy, 299.

and prefaces are addended as appendices where they are included, as with Minford's choice in Volume 4. Gone are the illustrations of fine 繡 editions, and eyebrow and interlineal commentary is inserted into text or, more usually, omitted. English-format genealogies have been added, with character lists for ease of reference. It was Hawkes who imposed on Minford the five part division, creating a new reading structure based on the size of an English novel and translation exigencies, one which does not allow for the chapter patterns such as ten chapter highs and lows that have been documented since for earlier Chinese novels such as *Jin Ping Mei*. In return, Minford introduced a significant textual feature when he took over in Volume 4.

Minford's preface to Volume 4 marks a new style, a new era. It is a personal, touristic, tangential discovery of Beijing mansions, a quest for the location of the Cao family home.[21] Whereas Hawkes had given us an introduction to the novel and to Chinese narrative style, Minford strides into the centre of the maelstrom where truth becomes fiction and fiction truth, as he intersects, in person, the reality of contemporary Beijing with the historic setting of the novel. The same process of excavation and of layering takes place as the new translator goes over the first's work. By his venture into old Beijing, Minford establishes communion with Cao Xueqin's world, and asserts symbolically a direct connection to the setting of *Hongloumeng*. There is no need to travel via Hawkes, since through the architecture and atmosphere of the *hutong* and the former mansion we are transported to the source. Penguin proves his accomplice. Penguin, especially in the old format of Penguin Classics gives an instant imprimatur. But Penguin has also chosen to excise any sense of a transition in translation: there is no mention on the jacket that Volume 4 is a continuation of Hawkes' work (neither translator's name appears on the front cover). The elision is near perfect: only an astute reader notices that a significant shift has taken place. It is presumably in the publishing company's interests to downplay the transition.

The second form of transposition, that which critics have emphasized, is the gamut of means, not far from creative imagination, whereby the translator takes the liberty to "moduler, transposer, réduire ou expliciter" the chosen text.[22] Lexicon, syntax, tone, and decisions about closeness or latitude from original are clearly central to a translation's work. Along the two poles of translation style, nearness to target language cedes to nearness to original form and meaning. As Haun Saussy reminds,

---

[21] Robert Hegel makes the point that this is a personal introduction in his review.
[22] Lévy, 300.

paradoxically "The more convincingly the translator observes the protocols of 'nearness,' the more exquisite the readers' sense of strangeness, of distance from the original text."[23] Where the goal is seen as establishing equivalence between two languages, translation has conventionally been esteemed by the ratio of times an author establishes apt and innovative equivalences where none naturally exist. Where a "classic" has been seen as writing which works well in the target language, even at the loss of its original cultural identity, Hawkes-Minford is very deliberately a translation that privileges the richness of the English language, in an attempt to emulate what Cao-Gao do in Chinese. Critics have explicitly called *Stone* a classic—that is, an edition which will endure, a work read for its own sake. Robert Hegel writes that "the universal appeal" of the *Stone* raises it "far above the level of quality in all previous English translations."[24]

Just as *Hongloumeng* required an educated, literate reader, *Stone* requires a reader with a wide humanistic education. Two prominent features of Hawkes' language are lexicon and tone: his vocabulary choice and the voice of characters that emerges. At a distance of thirty plus years, we can see ever more clearly how Hawkes' language represents the genius of a certain era and educational background. Much of the skill turns on a well-honed phrase or particularly resonant image, and often in the very earthly language with which Hawkes renders speech. Hawkes' level of skill and command of English requires something very close to a native speaker to appreciate, much as Cao's Chinese does. This is not to say that his translation is perfect, and errors have been pointed out by native Chinese scholars, but that his grasp of the Chinese is rendered into rich, informed English.[25] In re-creating the text, at times Hawkes simplifies the narrative by reducing levels of meaning, such as by stripping chapter

---

[23] Haun Saussy, "Always Multiple Translation, Or, How the Chinese Language Lost its Grammar," in *Tokens of Exchange*, ed. Lydia Liu, 109. So, for example, Legge makes Mencius speak like Socrates, in Saussy's example, and by doing so, primes us to understand we are reading philosophy.

[24] Robert Hegel, Untitled review of *The Story of the Stone* Vol. 4, Vol. 5 by Cao Xueqin and Gao E, *CLEAR* 8, no. 1/2 (July 1986): 129. This understanding of classic, as working well in the target language, means of course that the canons may not overlap exactly, since Chinese classics in English are thus rated by quality of the English.

[25] The reason, I suspect, why there have been relatively few good translation studies of *Stone* is that a true bilingual scholarly perspective is rare; the alternative would be a native English speaker with a stronger grasp of eighteenth-century Chinese than Hawkes, a degree in linguistics and a poetic turn of phrase, for which there is not a great pool of takers.

headings with recondite allusions of their literary referents, or, throughout the volume, by his decision to translate/interpret the names of minor characters but not the noble born.[26] Elsewhere, Hawkes will amplify a sentence to include an explanation into the translation, as where he inserts an account of the board game "Racing Go" as if a continuation of the voice of the narrator.[27] Lévy argues that Hawkes can be acquitted of superfluous flourishes because "toutes proportions gardées, il recrée le roman en version anglaise." This is the crux: Hawkes' aim is clearly to transpose *Hongloumeng* to an English-speaking, and understanding, readership.

Recent translation theory has imploded the idea of transparency. The effort to find functional equivalence in the target language has been tied to Anglo-American privileging of the author, masking the domestication processes of a foreign text. Fluent translations, writes Venuti, "invisibly inscribe foreign texts with English-language values and provide readers with the narcissistic experience of recognizing their own culture in a cultural other."[28] Venuti calls for a hermeneutic of resistance in the face of this, one which "foreignizes," to allow the foreign to remain different, and/or which highlights the role of the translator in the production of the new text. The question remains: how to produce a readable, enjoyable text which also resists rampant domestication? One could argue that Hawkes is judicious in his balance of domesticizing and foreignizing. Time after time, he attempts to match the polyvalence of *Hongloumeng* and shies away from privileging instant intelligibility, or producing a fluent translation for English reader's ease. That which is culturally other is not always given an English equivalence, and where it cannot be domesticated and replaced with an English object or rendering, may be left in transliteration. Archaisms point to the translatedness of the text. ("after I was cashiered" means little to most contemporary readers, and shows Hawkes' wartime upbringing.)[29] Elsewhere, though, a transposition of setting or character into pre-war England does occur, and is particularly noticeable in school

---

[26] There is no right answer to the dilemma created by allusive names. Hawkes simply acknowledges this by retaining transliterated names for major players, so that their English sobriquets do not detract for their overall characterization, but retaining them for servants and maids, whose names are often chosen for them anyway by their masters and mistresses and therefore relevant to wider characterization, and where, with notable exceptions, their role is not a rounded character but more of a symbolic presence.

[27] Lévy gives this example, from *Stone* Ch. 29.

[28] Venuti, *The Translator's Invisibility*, 15.

[29] Hawkes, *Stone*, I, 80.

boy scenes, such as Chapter Nine. Readers are expected to work hard to read themselves into the world of the text, but once there, to find a credible and consistent universe.

Words for Hawkes are chosen for their precise effect and associations. When Wang Xifeng is described as "distingué," the "sophisticated" French shows off her affect, and this is coupled with a sudden change in her attitude, as she dabs her eyes in an uncharacteristic display of sympathy.[30] Xue Pan shows the callous levity of youth in blurting out in English boarding school-speak. "The old boy obligingly gets himself popped out of the way. Fortune is on my side!" he gloats, delighting in the demise of a relative. Characters are given their flavour by the language used of them: Brother Stone comes across as a curmudgeonly old pedant.[31] Grandmother Jia (the "grannie" of Minford retains the tone of endearment) turns into a buxom Geordie grandma: "My pet. My poor lamb!" in her first words to Daiyu, far from the rather austere figure we encounter in other editions.[32] Occasionally the English reader is left wondering if the tone comes from Cao or Hawkes, when a thirteen year old girl, for example, comments that a poetry club should be formed, as of old, so that "the fleeting inspirations of an idle hour might often be perpetuated in imperishable masterpieces of verse".[33]

Hawkes' tone is frequently jocular, leavened by a humour sometimes sardonic, sometimes colloquial, such as when Yu-cun is "a sheet or so in the wind".[34] Hawkes writes of the monk, in succinct and dismissive humour, that "His toothless replies were all but unintelligible, and in any case bore no relations to the questions".[35] Sometimes the language is too highfalutin, or the transfer to English hits the wrong register or invokes images very different to the Chinese ones, such as the use of "*hetaerae*" for courtesans.[36] The familiarization project for the most part is what makes the English *Stone* so vibrant as a popular, accessible rendition. Latinate names for religious figures work because they give us to expect a spiritual lesson ahead. Occasionally the effect of familiarization does threaten to reconstitute the entire cultural milieu, as where Buddhist prayers are intoned in the language of the Book of Common Prayer (what

---

[30] Hawkes, *Stone*, I, 92.

[31] Hawkes, *Stone*, I, 50.

[32] Hawkes, *Stone*, I, 88-89.

[33] Hawkes, *Stone*, II, 214.

[34] Hawkes, *Stone*, I, 60.

[35] Hawkes, *Stone*, I, 71.

[36] Hawkes, *Stone*, I, 79.

else? The Prayer Book is the language with which Hawkes' generation prayed). In places, no amount of vestment can hide cultural differences, when young girls cast themselves down wells, or nuns reappear garbed in entirely new symbolic systems.

Sometimes Hawkes' choice is strikingly apt, even if not obvious. What Venuti sees as the "violence" of translation, as the text is reconstituted within a new culture, may also be taken as risk. Hawkes' use of the term Imperial "seraglio," for example, offers an Italianate word, but referring to the nearer East, a Turkish sultanate harem.[37] This is the recognisable East for a European readership, China has shifted longtitude just far enough to be both comprehensible and exotic. The effect is heightened by the mixture of distancing and making near, as where untranslatable terms for Shang Dynasty bronzes and Chinese musical instruments are left in transliteration, while terms deemed to have entered the English language (such as kang) are left in roman case. Fusion language presents a European salon with added orientalia, as in the genius phrase "the sedate twang of the *zheng*'s silver strings".[38] This is a mode of lexical accustoming, or cultural rapprochement. Take, for example, the sentences: "On the left-hand one was a small, square, four-legged *ding*, together with a bronze ladle, metal chopsticks, and an incense container. On the right-hand one was a narrow-waisted Ru-ware imitation *gu* with a spray of freshly cut flowers in it".[39] The description tells us nothing, and yet everything we need to know—that there are some Chinese ornamental vessels which are so distinctly Chinese as to have no functional equivalence in English. We are gently informed that our ceramics knowledge is deficient, and that we might need to brush up on Ru-ware. The translation conveys the scene, without translating. The effect, however, exoticizes, and conveys a different feel and literary function than the Chinese list of objects, problematizing Venuti's push for foreignization. Hawkes is frequently unapologetic that Chinese symbols need learning, just as we learn to understand our own.[40] Erudite and arcane language has the effect of distancing the text for a modern English reader, of giving the sense of a past world, whose daily existence and vocabulary are within our grasp, but slightly removed, say just about as far as Qing China from the Republic.

---

[37] Hawkes, *Stone*, I, 118.

[38] Hawkes, *Stone*, I, 139.

[39] Hawkes, *Stone*, I, 96.

[40] Hawkes, *Classical, Modern and Humane*, 93. He writes, for example, "the problem of allusion… is a product less of Chinese obscurantism than of our own cultural alienation" (p. 92).

Minford cannot be Hawkes; he is from a different generation. Minford could not be true to himself as a translator and follow Hawkes exactly; the thirty year difference in their upbringing across the war years furnishes them with a critical difference in experience, world view and vocabulary.[41] Minford could have patterned his language exactly on Hawkes, but only by doubly effacing himself, as translator and as actor. The reams of poetry that Hawkes versified and rhymed in English begin to look strange in a contemporary translation. Hawkes, whose proficiency in Latin, Greek, and English literature shaped the force of his writing, and whose learning has been described as "phenomenal," was likened to Arthur Waley, another "man of letters" with more than a touch of the pre-war gentleman about him. As Pollard points out, "Hawkes took ALL of Chinese literature as his demesne." This is not to question Minford's academic or literary credentials, but to suggest that in as much as some of the more archaic and school-boy language of Hawkes' own childhood has been toned down, there is a shift in tenor. We find fewer such Anglicisms as "ranting and raving like a lunatic" (I. 98) in Minford, or such elaborate, arch, sentences as "Entrusting everything to his clansmen and a few old and trusty retainers, he then proceeded to depart according to schedule, in company with his mother and sister, on the long journey to the capital, accounting the charge of manslaughter a mere bagatelle, which the expenditure of a certain amount of coin could confidently be expected to resolve" (I. 119).

In pulling back from such particularized language, Minford tempers some of the more extreme Englishness of Hawkes' version. The upper class and public school tone of much Jia family life is not entirely lost, however—to do so would have been to create too sharp a disjunction between the volumes. Jia Zheng is still very much the dismissive, and rather ineffectual, paterfamilias, "Speaking of Bao-yu," he said, in a more serious tone, "the boy spends all his time loafing around in the garden – it simply won't do. With one's daughters – well, one has one's disappointments, I realize, but in the long run girls get married and leave the family anyway" (*Stone* IV. 44). The tone is redolent of TV period dramas. Baoyu's education still takes place in an English public school

---

[41] David Pollard notes in his review of Hawkes' collection of essays *Classical, Modern and humane* (co-edited by John Minford and Siu-kit Wong) that "Hawkes was, however, fortunate that his academic career coincided with some of the best years for British universities, when it was still possible to be a scholar and a gentleman, and, especially in Oxford, to set one's own tasks and pursue them with little disturbance." Untitled review of *Classical, Modern and Humane: Essays in Chinese Literature* by David Hawkes (eds. John Minford and Sui-kit Wong), *CLEAR* 13 (Dec 1991): 191-93.

environment, adroitly depicted by transposing classical Chinese to Latin, in language which is rarefied, but credible for a small sector of upper class schoolboys:

> "Bao-yu, step up here. Oral Exposition of this text."
> Bao-yu walked up. On inspection, he found to his relief that it was a rubric he knew. *Analects*, chapter IX, verse XXII: Maxima Debentur Puero Reverentia – RESPECT DUE TO YOUTH. "What a stroke of luck!" he thought to himself. "Thank goodness it's not from the *Mag* or the *Med*!" (*Stone* IV. 55).

The principle of rendering into culturally familiar form is retained throughout, even to the point where this threatens to alter the effect by the associations of the English, as in this exchange:

> Dai-yu: "The first rule of Zen is not to tell lies."
> Bao-yu: "But it's the truth, so help me Buddha, the Dharma and the Holy Brotherhood" (*Stone* IV. 241).

We can be amused by the triune invocation and court house language, without needing to believe it an exact rendition of the original. Hawkes, who believed in the priority of the poet over the philologist in matters of translation, no doubt approved of Minford's ingenuity.[42]

[II] Text and Edition

If we marry together textual, literary and translation study perspectives we begin to create an appropriately complex frame for studying the question of the Hawkes-Minford transition to an English *Stone*. In terms of text, the research of textual and bibliographic scholars in the 1980s and 90s lays the groundwork for an understanding of text and edition which cuts through casual talk about "the novel *Hongloumeng*," back towards a Chinese heritage of multiple, fluid editions. The achievement of the sociologists of the book school—Jerome McGann, D. F. McKenzie, Greetham et al., has been the systematization of the insight that edition

---

[42] Cf. Hawkes, *Classical, Modern and Humane*, 231. "Too often the philologists, who hold the key to the treasure house, betray their trust by turning to the gold into dross." Admittedly Hawkes is discussing poetry translation here, and he balances it with the astute (if not always followed?) observation that translators should be self-effacing people, "more anxious for the faithful interpretation and good reception of the original than for their own creative development or greater glory." (p. 235.)

matters, that every different edition of a text, every alteration of punctuation or of dust jacket, engenders a different reading.

For much of the twentieth century scholars in the West held that a perfect critical edition consisted of the collation of all prior texts, and only in the last decades of the millennium was this ideal discarded. The text came to be regarded by social textual critics as a series of events, each edition important in its unique circumstances of production.[43] As textual criticism outgrew its position as a subset of historical criticism, it impacted wider literary criticism, but the insights have yet to transfer as forcefully to critical studies of Chinese works in English. In this understanding of the text, the work of editors and publishers is central, as the signifying processes of the text become more collaborative and socialized during transmission and circulation.[44] Texts are made and remade as they are distributed.[45] One of the key tenets of the textual critics' work has been that the prime law of the textual condition is the law of change.[46] Any minor change to a text, down to the addition or subtraction of a comma, produces a new work, to take the theory to an extreme. The quest is no longer to determine the textual version closest to the final intention of the author by combining readings of the earliest extant manuscript and print versions, but to account for the existence and reception of the plurality of texts comprising any given novel.[47]

Such insights matter because how we read the notion of text determines how we read the novel as text. David Hawkes understood this, since he was as much a textual scholar and literary critic as a translator. Hawkes was equally aware that rendering Chinese into English threatens to silence associations, and make monovalent a rich text, as he was that

---

[43] Here "text" denotes both the physical book (Barthes' "work") and the conceptual work of art. For a discussion on the terms "text" and "work" see D. C. Greetham, *Theories of the Text* (Oxford, New York: Oxford University Press, 1999), 26-28, 47-48. This section recapitulates an argument made at the outset of a paper on the novel *Huayue hen*, in *Reading China*, ed. Daria Berg (Leiden: Brill, 2005).

[44] Jerome McGann, *The Textual Condition* (New Jersey: Princeton University Press, 1991), 58.

[45] Joseph Grigely, *Textualterity* (Ann Arbor: University of Michigan Press, 1995), 4.

[46] McGann, *Textual Condition*, 9.

[47] On the "Greg-Bowers Theory of Transmission" where the "substantives" of an edition were taken from the latest authorial edited manuscript version and the "accidentals" from the earliest print version see G. Thomas Tanselle, "The Editorial Problem of Final Authorial Intention," *Textual Criticism and Scholarly Editing*, ed. Thomas Tanselle (Charlottesville: University Press of Virginia, 1990), 27.

readers, commentators and editors all had extensive input into Cao's circulating novel. If we take the recent anthology of critical essays on *Hongloumeng* edited by Andrew Schonebaum and Tina Lu as a base, we can test out some of the arguments on text, readership, and the transition to an English novel. The Schonebaum and Lu volume precisely purports to be answering the need of English-language students of the Hawkes-Minford *Stone*, and uses the *Stone* as its base text. As a teaching aid to the novel, the volume is a wonderfully rich historical, literary, legal, anthropological, even medical digest of the novel. The editors have arrayed a huge selection of many of the best, most lucid, thinkers across a range of sinological fields, distilling their expertise for an undergraduate audience.

In the preface to the anthology, Schonebaum sets out explicitly its goals: an attempt to bring the English-language reader to a better (more Chinese?) understanding of the text, noting that the essays in the collection "serve as extended commentary, providing historical background, contextual and literary approaches for those who wish to have a deeper and broader understanding of the novel than is possible without extensive outside reading." Schonebaum acknowledges that there is a valid input to *Hongloumeng* scholarship, albeit a limited one, outside of sinology: "Students of the English version often have strong opinions and can also have fruitful debate on the issues of Stone's authorship and authority," he writes, and, directly of Hawkes-Minford, that "this is a translation that allows its readers to gain some ownership of the text." The qualification is key: English readers may gain *some* ownership of the text. The statement has to refer to the Chinese originary text to make sense—they can, one would hope, gain purchase on Hawkes' English text. Although authors in the volume acknowledge they are using Hawkes-Minford, they are all aware of, and return repeatedly to, the text behind the text, the Chinese novel(s). While reference is rarely made to a specific Chinese text, this is still understood as a possibility, a text for which, with greater skill or luck, we could construct a genealogy of ascent.

There are two premises here which need teasing out, and which can be accepted singly or in tandem. The first is that the translation refers to the original as a shadow to its form: that when we are discussing the English translation of *Stone*, we actually talking about Cao Xueqin's novel. The second is that the academic study of the Hawkes-Minford *Stone* necessarily also shadows critical study of Cao Xueqin's novel, in exactly the same fashion. The two propositions can be decoupled. It can be shown relatively straightforwardly from study of either the linguistic codes (lexicon, semantics, cultural relocation etc.) or its bibliographical codes (paratextual materials: preface in/exclusion, commentary, line drawings) that the Hawkes-Minford *Stone* is a different book, a different novel, to earlier editions, one more folio in the great bookshop of *Hongloumeng* intertext. But even if this is not accepted, it could still be argued that the critical study of an English language novel (especially one towards the inculturated, nativized pole of translation) is amenable to different forms of critical study than a Chinese language novel.

The writers of the Schonebaum/Lu volume make clear why this is a necessary position. Because we cannot hope to attain a knowledge of the meaning of the Chinese verse through English translation, or the symbolic universe of Chinese décor and material patterns, of the implications and traditional uses of medicines and their revelations about characters, we need a compendium to help us approach the Chinese world of Baoyu's day. Schonebaums' premise makes a literary reading an attempt to understand the "encyclopedic inclusiveness" that he commends as Li Wai-yee's description of the novel. A broader and deeper reading of the novel, suggests the anthology, means a greater contextual knowledge of Manchu customs, of materia medica appearing in the text, of textual editions and their compositors. The question: why read a novel? and discussion of whether the question is the same for a translation, is not examined as such.

The "filling in the gaps" mode comprises both extra-textual materials, such as discussions of what ridge tile ornamentation might mean, and the translations themselves. "It might behoove readers of *Stone* to know what some feel is missing from this great translation" writes Schonebaum, opening up a discussion of both Hawkes-Minford and the Yangs' versions. The "missing" makes explicit that the English *Stone* is the shadow text, the ever-deficient. Some of the contributors are more radically attached to the "original" than others. In a discussion on the material culture of the text, Ni Yibin comments on how the translators have tried to substitute Western metaphors or sayings for Chinese ones to avoid footnotes, but argues that "further elaborations and clarifications" of the background to the novel are "imperatively needed" for readers who wish to appreciate the novel "with its full indigenous flavor." Ni creates two classes of reader, "casual" ones who can enjoy the English version with its best-fit renditions, and a second category of those who seek a real knowledge of China. The position assumes that a perfect reader has a taxonomic cultural knowledge, au fait with all facets of Qing history and society. Pictorial designs and their culturally significant messages "will have immediate impact on the knowing reader," notes Ni. This may be true, but it is open to argument whether extensive knowledge of Manchu medicine or embroidery designs necessarily makes someone a more astute reader of the novel—and of whether this is equally true for the English *Stone*.

An underlying assumption that critics are working from a Chinese text leads to various constraints. In Andrew Schonebaum's essay in the textbook volume, he notes that Baoyu's identification and alienation from the mirror image of the real Baoyu "reads like a formative Lacanian experience" but then retreats, "although Baoyu's 'psychology' cannot be Freudian or Lacanian or a representation of any other Western psychological schema, he clearly has a psychology that is imbued with significance and signification." But why cannot Baoyu's psychology be described in Lacanian or Freudian terms? Because he predated Lacan and Freud, or because as a Chinese boy his psychology must be discussed in (Qing Dynasty?) Chinese psychological terms? We may need to appreciate Qing Dynasty beliefs about the mind and the body to grasp why Baoyu is so particularly constituted, but that does not preclude applying other critical methods to the character—just as different questions may be applied to *Stone* as to *Hongloumeng*.

The assumption of a perfectly knowledgable Ur reader is challenged in an essay in the same volume by Charlotte Furth, which emphasises the history of reading experiences. No contemporary Chinese (let alone culturally illiterate foreigners) can regain the reading experience of Cao Xueqin's contemporaries, no matter how much background knowledge is attained, argues Furth, because we have too much accumulated reading history since then. We cannot cut away the debates, assumptions, and the sheer wealth of culturally embedded readings that have taken hold since publication. Furth shows the gains that can come from an English language reading, such as when the "Anglophone student" can experience that which is near impossible for a Chinese reader: the feeling that the poetic riddles in the Land of Illusion are about unknown characters.[48] Chinese readers cannot undo knowledge gained through wider cultural sources, cannot pare back to a mid-eighteenth century knowledge. As Furth makes clear, we can still distinguish between erroneous and unlikely readings, whether in Chinese or English criticism, including those that derive from translated terms.[49]

---

[48] Charlotte Furth, in *Approaches to Teaching the Story of the Stone,* eds. Schonebaum and Lu. One of the main losses that Furth highlights is where the translation has simplified kinship terms because those relationship terms are themselves meaningless to non-Chinese.

[49] In her discussions of Baoyu's clothing, for example, Furth questions whether a long-haired young man in medallions, a coronet and silks comes across as "profoundly female-identified" within Qing regimes of sexuality, or just our own.

Just as there are multiple texts and editions, there are multiple valid readings. The cumulative weight of research essays geared towards studying "what cannot be translated"—those gaps that need bridging between the two sets of cultural understandings that are not evident from an English translation—may need to cede in English language scholarship to an emphasis on "what has been translated," or, what is, for the English reader.

[III] Reading as English Literature:
Creating New Readings

"Gentle Reader," begins Hawkes' translation of *Stone*, immediately conjuring up the ghost of Jane Austen. Still in the first chapter, Greensickness Peak looms into sight – we are now into Tolkien territory, the landscape of Mordor rising up beyond the Hebei hills. As commentators have pointed out, Hawkes has, by a judicious slip of editing, created a perfect parallel for the Chinese term in his rendition of Greensickness Peak.[50] The Incredible Crags of the Great Fable Mountains are a territory we might well recognise, as the avuncular narrator launches into to what sounds very much like a children's fairy story, "Now this block of stone… possessed magic powers." The narrator's tone is able to be so formed in part because of Hawkes' omission of the preface, an "authorial" reflection on the story's oneiric origins, retained in most published *Hongloumeng* texts. Still in the first few pages, Latinate names take us into Bunyan territory, where we await religious lessons in textual symbols, as the Daoist and Buddhist Impervioso and Mysterioso saunter into view. A few chapters later, we join Baoyu in Frances Hodgson Burnett's *Secret Garden*. When a mustachioed signior appears, Don Quixote hovers, fleetingly.

To appreciate the role of the *Stone* in Chinese culture, writes Dore Levy, "we must imagine a work with the cultural cachet of James Joyce's *Ulysses* and the popular appeal of Margaret Mitchell's *Gone with the Wind*." For a native English reader to read the *Stone* in terms of English literature is inevitable in a two-fold manner: because our own frame of critical reference is drawn from that tradition, and secondly, because Hawkes and Minford are so steeped in Greco-Roman and English literature that their translations deliberately and subconsciously allude to Western literary referents. Take the Qin Shi passage, for example, where even the supernatural can be tamed by familiar referents: we understand

---

[50] Dore Levy, 10.

wronged ghosts, bells, cock crows and other worlds, because we know our Hamlet. When a contemporary non-Chinese speaker reads the *Stone,* tales of Imperial largesse, of palanquins and plush interiors conjure up a distant, or displaced, royal England, or the court of Louis XIV, as much as Qing China. The vocabulary of regal trappings, of opulence and excess is not immediately country specific, but relates to a stratified existence: we infer from our own knowledge of courts, and imprint on them images from our own virtual storehouses.

Hawkes was fully aware of the dangers of unintended associations and new readings being driven by a translation. Writing in another context, in an essay comparing the poetic translations of Waley and Pound, he acknowledges the dissonance that can arise between text and translation in the hands of a free-wheeling poet such as Pound, where "It might, after all, turn out that the kinds of things believed to be most typical of Chinese poetry and therefore most likely to have made some sort of impression on English-speaking poets are not really characteristic of Chinese poetry at all, but are simply atmospherics produced by the translator."[51] In a world of multiple editions and multiple significations, this is not necessarily an inherent evil, but needs acknowledging. The vital phrase here is "believed to be:" if a reader reads Hawkes-Minford trusting it to purvey an unalloyed China, then s/he might be drawn to conclude that a clan school followed the Eton curriculum. The danger, as well as delight, of a nativized translation lies with the reader.

Where might adopting English literature approaches take us? If we followed the logic of sinological readings, it would allow full play to the referents behind Hawkes' allusions and puns—some Chinese, some Greek or Latin, some from English literature. The point is not just to apply to the English text the same forms of criticism as to the Chinese. Levy postulates that *Stone* is underread because of "the inevitable cultural loss that must occur when a work of art becomes distant in time and is by nature distant in culture," and argues that "the major challenge for the comparativist is to understand the internalized assumptions of one culture and articulate them in terms of another." [52] But this overarching method, of finding equivalence, articulated in the ever-inventive, categorical quest to bridge that cultural loss, sets itself up for failure. Levy herself acknowledges that for every theme or topos chosen by the critic, an equal number of paths remain untravelled. We still remain perpetual motion towards a Chinese text, its cultural background and its cultural modes of narrative expression,

---

[51] Hawkes, *Classical, Modern and Humane*, 80.
[52] Levy, *Ideal and Actual*, 3.

always accessing the Chinese through the English. This is not a unidirectional flow: no amount of critical bridging is going to enhance enjoyment of *Stone* as a novel unless it addresses the characteristics that may be easily appreciated in Chinese or English, as well as delighting in the peculiarities of the English text.

There are two possible ways forward to allow for distinctive readings from individual texts. The first is textual, the second thematic. Sinologists have long colluded in the narrowing down of study topics on Cao Xueqin's novel. Haun Saussy wrote in 2003 that *Hongloumeng* began its career in print "as an authorless, somewhat mysterious piece of fiction open to multiple lines of interpretation," but that when a definitive author had been ascertained in Cao Xueqin, a new author-function was created, and readings proceeded along new lines.[53] 1922, notes Saussy, marked a turning point in readings of the novel, to Hu Shi's new, "scientific" methods. The appearance of the English language volumes from 1974, one might argue, marks another interpretive turning point. In contrast to the iconoclasm of 1922, however, many scholars are still clinging on to the old. Saussy argued that it is not just a question of determining an author's name, but "whether there was anything like an author, and how many heads that author might have possessed." This polycephalous being to which he refers comprises the "Red Inkstone" set of family friends, assorted scholarly and official friends whose comments graced circulating manuscripts, as well as later editor/authors Gao E and Cheng Weiyuan.

Drawing on David Rolston and Foucault, Saussy traces a history of readings which privilege the text itself, and a reading community of commentators whose reactions to the protagonist (*Stone*, the book itself) guided later readers. Hawkes himself had undertaken a similar study, thirty years earlier, in the heyday of Marxist readings. The "traditional" readings draw on a reader-response hermeneutic where the onus for a moral reading lay with the reader, not the text. Some of the neglected early commentators align with a mode of reading particularly accessible to English language readers, where the text itself is free to speak as it wills, delighting in "the poetics of pure narrative, the joys of rhetoric freed from obedience to representation, and the artifices and powers of text as such." These analyses are to be read for their own sakes, rather than to access the author or the lessons he may be teaching us.[54] Such readings, which contrast markedly with the later roman à clef historical readings and with early

[53] Haun Saussy, "The Age of Attribution: Or, How the *Hongloumeng* Finally Acquired an Author," *CLEAR* 25 (2003): 119-20.
[54] Saussy, "The Age of Attribution," 125.

twentieth century reconstructions based on Cao Xueqin's environs, offer one route forward.

Thematic studies provide a second channel for work from an English text—if that text is acknowledged as the authority for the ideas constructed. There have been numerous studies of memory, for example, in recent Western literature. A study of a topic like memory in Chinese literature offers insights to readers of either Chinese or English texts, and can work between Chinese and other notions of memory and the construct of the self. How memory is constructed and developed in *Hongloumeng/Stone* intersects with major themes of identity, the supernatural and the textual. Memory in *Stone* is linked to an in-between state, a liminal existence that surfaces in traces of remembrance of the past, in objects that play between worlds, in foreboding, and prognostication, in the linguistic ambiguity of poetry and the conscious ambiguity of dream states. Memory holds Baoyu in its thrall, from his early meetings with his cousins through to his decision to evade human society.

A topic like memory could be equally (but differently) developed in either language text. It is clearly linked to premonition and the non-rational world in both Chinese and English editions, and since the novel is framed by the meeting of the protagonists outside of human time and space, snatches of memory relate to this half state. An episode which explores to the full the force of memory traces occurs when Baoyu is in Qinshi's bedchamber. Like some Jean Cocteau scene, objects from the past are imbued with a numinous force, listed as if in a museum catalogue, and a material history of strong regal women is given through the suggestion of individual ornaments. These symbols, the reification of history, stimulate a responsiveness in Baoyu, although the effect on the English reader of a list of Wu Zetian, Zhao Feiyan, Yang Guifei et al. is more muted (even a contemporary Chinese edition gives footnotes to aid the reader). The psychological realism is acute, as memories of an earlier life surface during a sub-conscious state informed by association of the rich women's objects and sensual descriptions. Baoyu's desire to be memorialized eternally in a sea of tears is frequently cited by critics, but his aim for obliteration, for no memory to be held of him, is of equal force in the novel, and readily apparent in the English text. Critics emphasize the first part of his declaration, the feminine sentimentality, but rarely the annihilation, a "glorious death" where he would "gently decompose there until the wind had picked my bones clean, and after that never, never to be reborn again as a human being" (II. 206). The English reader, clean of two centuries of critical sediment, might forge new meanings in the text.

[IV] Conclusions

Textual, literary and translation scholarship conjoin to show why we should study *Stone* as a unique, English volume. Textually, the novel is distinct, both as an edition in terms of the written content, and in terms of its physical format as a text. Recent translation scholarship has shown that translation is a rewriting, a manipulation, producing a creative new text that cannot just be read as a transparent version of the original. Literary criticism shows how facets such as imagery, or characterization in the novel may produce very different readings in the target language.

The pole has swung too far—in literary critical if not in translation studies—towards viewing a translation as a mere vessel, a vehicle. A translation is yet another step in the transformation of a text, a quantitatively larger stride than to another same-language edition. For many who read the Hawkes-Minford text, the pleasure is in part that of a "betwixt" text, the simultaneous appreciation of two texts: the volume in our hands, and the text it points to. When I once told my doctoral supervisor that I was reading *Hongloumeng* and *The Story of the Stone* in parallel he asked—why? Why would I not just read the Chinese? I read the Chinese to read *Hongloumeng*. I read the English for ease, for fun, because it is a well-written, engaging tale of a rather snotty little boy and his flawed, extended kin. Reading in parallel makes abundantly clear that these are not the same novel, that the process is like, but not identical. Allusions are gained and lost. Characters' personalities shift and evanesce. I skip the poetry in English but wade through the original. My thought processes, stimulated by the text in hand, dart off in different directions depending on the language and its associations.

The obsession with the Hawkes-Minford gap speaks to the value placed on the integrity of a translation, including the notion of one authorial consciousness. Since the transition to an English text is inevitably much greater than any difference between Hawkes and John Minford, the attention paid to their division of labour suggests our continuing desire for the illusion of integrity. The attention to the minor gap obscures the much larger breach that this paper has explored. The anxiety about the Hawkes-Minford transition reveals itself as a symptom of the anxieties we feel about being unable to access any original, ever.

The gap between Cao-Gao and Hawkes-Minford may be noticeable—and differently configured in each—but it is infinitely smaller than the transition from *Hongloumeng* to *Stone*. The standard way of closing the gap has been to draw English language readers towards the Chinese text, to alert them to linguistic plays being missed, to fill in for them with encyclopœdic thoroughness an account of every possible aspect of the author and the text's environment, from historical to ethnographic to suppositional. This may be a laudable pedagogical aim, but the conceit lies in allowing readers to continue to believe that they are reading Cao Xueqin. Guides and notes are valuable for the minority of *Stone* readers who are also students of China, and who want to perform a hermeneutical double-reading, but this is not the only valid reading possible. An alternative approach treats *Stone* as a self-contained, complete text. This model does not continually refer back to an original or excavate examples of poor translation or difference. Critics almost all agree that *Stone* is the best English text approximating to the novel *Hongloumeng* that we have, that it supersedes all others to date. So perhaps we should allow English language readers to develop their own responses to the text as it stands, and rejoice in whatever readings emerge. Although he believed in the self-effacing of the translator, Hawkes may well have approved of this freedom to take his paronomasia and equivoke seriously too.

THE TRANSLATOR AS SCHOLAR AND EDITOR: ON PREPARING A NEW CHINESE TEXT FOR THE BILINGUAL *THE STORY OF THE STONE*[1]

FAN SHENGYU
SCHOOL OF CULTURE, HISTORY AND LANGUAGE
COLLEGE OF ASIA AND THE PACIFIC
AUSTRALIAN NATIONAL UNIVERSITY

More than thirty years after the first volume of *The Story of the Stone* (or *Hongloumeng*《紅樓夢》as it is more commonly known in Chinese) was published in London, a bilingual edition of this version of China's most famous novel will be published in Shanghai. Sadly Professor David Hawkes, the brilliant translator of the novel's first eighty chapters, passed away last year.[2] In the last few months of his life, I had the honour of being given the task of editing this bilingual edition, and as a result exchanged a number of emails with him, in which we discussed some of the problems encountered. I am here today to share with you what I have learned in the process.

I would like to begin by quoting David Hawkes' own words. He became well aware, as he worked on the project, that his translation of the

---

[1] I would like to express my heartfelt thanks to Professor John Minford, for his trust and help both in the process of editing the coming bilingual edition, and allowing me access to the precious letters and diaries, as well as helping with reading the sometimes indecipherable notebooks of Professor David Hawkes.

[2] Another outstanding translator of *Hongloumeng*, Yang Xianyi 楊憲益, also passed away a few months later. The year 2009 brought a huge loss for *Hongloumeng* readers, both Chinese and English. The bilingual edition of David Hawkes' translation will be published by Shanghai Foreign Language Education Press, while the translation by Yang Xianyi and Gladys Yang 戴乃迭 has already had a bilingual edition published by Foreign Language Press in Beijing (although in this case the English and Chinese texts do not match each other exactly).

novel was turning out to be totally different from any done previously. It was for the first time, a complete translation;[3] and he set about translating it in a completely new way. The following words of his amount to both a defence and a declaration, and establish the basic rationale for his own work, for my work as editor, and for this brief paper: "Admittedly the decision where to draw the line between what may and what may not be emended is a somewhat arbitrary one, and to a textual critic the subjective arguments and rule-of-thumb methods of the translator-editor may seem arrogant and unscientific. But a translator has divided loyalties. He has a duty to his author, a duty to his reader and a duty to the text. The three are by no means identical and are often hard to reconcile."[4]

No translator of Chinese fiction had ever dared to do anything like this before, to combine the roles of scholar, editor and translator, least of all with *Hongloumeng*, which presents some of the most complicated editorial and textual problems in the whole of Chinese literature. The study of the novel itself has become an academic discipline in its own right. There have been many "Redologists" (*hongxuejia* 紅學家, scholars of *Hongloumeng*) in the past, and many more will undoubtedly continue to appear. It is certainly interesting that David Hawkes never called himself a "*hongxuejia*," even though others were only too proud to claim this title. Madame Jiang Qing called herself "half-a-*hongxuejia*," even though she succeeded in confusing some of the novel's main characters, and could never master the novel's basic plot. As we can see clearly in his 32-page Introduction to Volume One, the rapid development of *Hongxue* 紅學 had already filled Hawkes with apprehension: "It is difficult to give an account of the novel that will not seem dated in a year or two's time."[5] In reality, although that Introduction was written in 1972, it is still hard to find a better general introduction to the novel written in English. It provides the reader with an excellent survey of the history of the author's family, the Bannermen, and the Qing Dynasty background, the questions of authenticity and authorship, and the complex story of the various transcriptions and printed versions. He goes on to discuss some of the novel's complex themes and the author's use of symbolism and rhetoric. Even today, it can still serve as a useful reference.

---

[3] Yang Xianyi and Gladys Yang's first volume was published in 1978 by Foreign Language Press in Beijing.
[4] David Hawkes, Preface to *The Crab-Flower Club*, volume two of *The Story of the Stone* (Harmondsworth: Penguin Books, 1977), 20.
[5] David Hawkes, Introduction to *The Golden Days*, volume one of *The Story of the Stone* (Harmondsworth: Penguin Books, 1973), 17.

[I] The Scholar

Let us first discuss David Hawkes as a scholar. In order to do so, we need to briefly examine the novel's evolution. Before the author Cao Xueqin 曹雪芹 died in 1763, the novel was already circulating among friends and relatives in various transcribed forms, most of them with commentaries by a certain *Zhiyanzhai* 脂硯齋 (Red Inkstone) and other members of the author's inner circle. But none of these transcriptions went beyond chapter 80. They all ended up abruptly just as the plot seemed to be reaching a climax. Subsequently, the Chinese Bannerman Gao E 高鶚, together with his collaborator Cheng Weiyuan 程偉元, edited and published the first 120-chapter version of the novel. He claimed that he and his friend got hold of the legendary lost conclusion, the last forty chapters of Cao Xueqin. They then edited and polished this "ending" and finally published their new edition, in the first days of the year 1792. But to return to the earlier transcriptions, up to the present, at least twelve of these have been discovered and reproduced. In addition, there are several early printed editions, which differ to a greater or lesser extent from each other.[6] Hawkes was surrounded by copies of at least six or seven varying versions of the novel when he began translating in the 1970s. It is important to note that when confronted with this hugely rich but complicated textual corpus, Hawkes chose not to ignore the difficult issues raised, but instead, to master the necessary scholarship.

What kind of scholarship was it that Hawkes aspired to? When asked in 2007 who had influenced him the most in his entire academic life, Hawkes replied that it was the Chinese scholar Wen Yiduo 聞一多.[7] The other scholar who influenced him deeply was Arthur Waley. It is interesting to note that Wen Yiduo himself was not only a highly original scholar of the Chinese classics, but also a passionate poet and an accomplished translator.[8] David Hawkes certainly benefited a lot from

---

[6] Actually one of the 12 manuscript editions was found and then lost. We can in fact never be sure that it actually existed. We only have a certain scholar's copied version of the commentaries in that particular edition. It might be simpler to say that there are only eleven, not twelve. These transcriptions vary in length and importance. The careful study of these variations will be the topic of another article, and I will not elaborate on them here.

[7] This statement was made during a video interview, conducted by Prof. John Minford in Oxford in July 2007.

[8] Wen Yiduo translated, among other things, A. E. Housman's *A Shropshire Lad*. Interestingly enough, Housman himself was a great poet-scholar, and a fastidious editor of the classics.

Wen Yiduo's *Chuci*《楚辭》annotations when he was translating *The Songs of the South*.[9] As a textual scholar, Hawkes had already served a rigorous apprenticeship in the 1950s, tackling the complex problems of authorship of *The Songs of the South* for his Oxford D. Phil. dissertation. When in the early 1970s he turned his attention as a translator to *The Story of the Stone*, he first set about, as we have already mentioned, mastering the intricate details of the many early manuscript transcriptions and printed editions of the novel, including the then newly published and still controversial 120-chapter *Qianlong chaoben*《乾隆鈔本》(Gao E's draft). As he translated, he consulted all of these versions, carefully listing the differences, sometimes even variations in a single word, as I will show you presently. Luckily we still have his notebooks, which provide invaluable evidence of his methods of work.[10] Few translators have ever spent so much time laying such meticulous textual foundations for their work. Indeed, often where translators are also textual scholars, the resulting translation turns out to be unreadable. Here lies one of the essential qualities of Hawkes' scholarship: it always served the broader goal of literature.

The textual problems of *Hongloumeng* are never problems about editions only. They inevitably involve other matters, such as the identity of the author, the nature and authenticity of the Red Inkstone commentaries, the relationships between the novel and the autobiographical reality it reflects, the reliability of Gao E's declarations as editor, etc. Again, let me quote Hawkes himself from an interview conducted in 1998:[11] "But it was really only much later that I started getting really interested and involved in the textual side of things. The reason for that is, when you start working closely with *Hongloumeng*, all the problems, the inconsistencies, the sort of tangles and so on, and the differences, they start mattering and then of course [new]stuff was coming out gradually."

The problems involved in these editions themselves became the topics for repeated debates between renowned scholars such as Hu Shi 胡適, Yu Pingbo 俞平伯, Wu Shichang 吳世昌 and Zhou Ruchang 周汝昌. A strong bias against Gao E soon became one of the key issues in the debates.

---

[9] Preface to 1959 edition of *The Song of the South*, viii.

[10] These were published as *The Story of the Stone: A Translator's Notebooks*《紅樓夢英譯筆記》by the Centre for Literature and Translation of Lingnan University in Hong Kong in 2000.

[11] This is from an audio interview conducted by Connie Chan in Oxford on 7 December 1998. The interview was included as an appendix in her M. Phil. Dissertation at the Hong Kong Polytechnic University, 2000.

There was a distinct demarcation between two major groups of *Hongxuejia*: those who supported Gao E (a tiny minority) and those who accused him of dishonesty and forgery. Gao himself, the poor editor who brought the printed novel into the world, claimed that he did nothing more than edit the last forty chapters. Hawkes, while working on his translation, came to a stonger and stronger vindication of Gao's work as editor.

But to call Hawkes a *Hongloumeng* scholar is an inadequate description of the man. He never seemed to care too much for the values of the academic world around him. He seems to me, though I never met him personally, someone who while himself a master of the relevant scholarship, rose above it to a higher calling. I mean he was a true scholar, one who knew how to use his knowledge and wit but was never encumbered by them. Here again is what Hawkes said about himself and his decision to resign the Oxford professorship: "I don't think it was that I wanted to give all my life to *Hongloumeng*, that it was so important, so I must give everything else up; it wasn't really that. I mean, that would be pretentious, it makes it sound as if I think my translation is so wonderful; it was really more that I felt, when I started translating this, I enjoyed it so much, that I thought well – and I never saw myself as a very good Professor; and I thought, this is really my metier, I really ought to be a translator and not a Professor. So I decided to give the Professorship up."[12] From my own limited encounter with him through emails, and through reading his *Notebooks* and letters,[13] I have found myself agreeing with his friend, Professor Pang Bingjun who in *A Birthday Book for Brother Stone* called Hawkes: "a perfect gentleman-scholar, both in the English and Chinese sense of the word."[14]

[II] The Editor

As David Hawkes was mastering the problems of *Hongloumeng* editions and wrestling with the subtle differences between the Red Inkstone transcriptions and the printed versions, he gradually realized that he was creating a totally new edition of his own, to serve the purpose of his translation. This new edition existed nowhere but in his mind. It was never written down. The most important feature of the new bilingual

---

[12] Connie Chan's interview, Oxford, 1998.

[13] By letters, I am referring to the extended unpublished correspondence between David Hawkes and his collaborator John Minford from 1970 onwards.

[14] Pang Bingjun, "Following the Steps of Karma," in *A Birthday Book for Brother Stone*, eds. Rachel May and John Minford (Hong Kong: The Chinese University Press and The Hong Kong Translation Society, 2003), 64.

edition will be that it traces what he did and why he made those choices and decisions, which are reflected in the English translation but which Hawkes himself never spelled out. As he said, "In translating this novel I have felt unable to stick faithfully to any single text. I have mainly followed Gao E's version of the first chapter as being more consistent, though less interesting, than the other ones; but I have frequently followed a manuscript reading in subsequent chapters, and in a few, rare instances I have made small emendations of my own."[15] In other words, he was following the basic text established by Gao E (specifically, the so-called Cheng-yi text 程乙本, as reproduced by Renmin wenxue Press 人民文學出版社 in 1964), but every now and then, allowing himself to deviate from that basic text for a number of different reasons. So my own job as editor has turned out to be somewhat like that of Sherlock Holmes, collecting evidence of details at the "crime scene," in order to reconstruct what happened forty years ago.

[III] Editorial Procedures for the Bilingual Edition

I have used a number of editorial symbols to mark some of these decisions taken by David Hawkes:

(1) < > Triangular brackets
These will indicate that the translation has followed a text other than the basic Cheng-yi text. We will not specify which text. Since this bilingual edition is not aimed at *Hongxuejia*, such details would simply be too cumbersome.

(a)
Original (Renmin wenxue, 1964, Vol. 1, p. 114):
第九回：秦鐘哭道：「有金榮在這裡，我是要回去的了。」
Hawkes (Penguin, 1973, Vol. 1, p. 214):
"If Jokey Jin stays here," wailed Qin Zhong tearfully, **"I'm not studying in this school any longer."**
第九回：秦鐘哭道：「有金榮在這裡，**<我是不在這裡念書的。>**」

---

[15] Hawkes, Introduction to *The Golden Days*, 45-46.

(b)
Original (Renmin wenxue, 1964, Vol. 1, p. 153):
第十四回：眾人連忙讓坐倒茶，一面命人按數取紙；來旺抱著同
來旺媳婦一路來至儀門，方交與來旺媳婦自己抱進去了。
Hawkes (Penguin, 1973, Vol. 1, p. 270):
The man pressed round her offering her a place to sit and a cup of tea
to drink while **one of them hurried off with the list to fetch the
needed items. Not only that, but, having fetched them, he carried
them for her** all the way to the inner gate of the mansion, only
handing them to her then so that she could take them in to Xi-feng.
第十四回：眾人連忙讓坐倒茶，<**一面命人按數取紙來抱著，**同來
旺媳婦>一路來至儀門，方交與來旺媳婦自己抱進去了。

(2) [ ] Square brackets
These will indicate either deliberate or inadvertent omissions by the
translator.

(a)
Original (Renmin wenxue, 1964, Vol. 2, p. 494):
第四十回：[只聽外面亂嚷嚷的]

(b)
Original (Renmin wenxue, 1964, Vol. 1, p. 61):
第五回：[卻說寶玉聽了此曲，散漫無稽，未見得好處；但其聲韻
淒婉，竟能銷魂醉魄。因此也不問其原委，也不究其來歷，就暫
以此釋悶而已。因又看下面道：]

(3) { } Angle brackets
These will indicate the translator's own editorial emendations or
creative additions, again, for a number of reasons, mostly connected with
the translator's detailed study of the plot.

(a)
Original (Renmin wenxue, 1964, Vol. 1, p. 266):
二十三回：寶釵住了蘅蕪院，黛玉住了瀟湘館，迎春住了綴錦
樓，探春住了秋掩書齋，惜春住了蓼風軒，李紈住了稻香村，寶
玉住了怡紅院。

Hawkes (Penguins, 1973, Vol. 1, p. 459):
It was finally settled that Bao-chai should have All-spice Court, Dai-yu the Naiad's House, Ying-chun the building on **Amaryllis Eyot**, Tan-chun **the Autumn Studio**, Xi-chun **the Lotus Pavilion**, Li Wan Sweet-rice Village, and Bao-yu the House of Green Delights.
二十三回：寶釵住了蘅蕪院，黛玉住了瀟湘館，迎春住了**{紫菱洲}**，探春住了<**秋爽齋**>，惜春住了**{藕香榭}**，李紈住了稻香村，寶玉住了怡紅院。

(b)
Original (Renmin wenxue, 1964, Vol. 1, p. 283):
二十四回：秋紋、碧痕兩個去催水，檀雲又因他母親病了，接出去了，麝月現在家中病著。
Hawkes (Penguin, 1973, Vol. 1, p. 483):
Ripple and Emerald had gone off to see about the water. Of the other senior maids, **Skybright had been fetched home for her cousin's birthday** and Musk was away ill;…
二十四回：秋紋、碧痕兩個去催水，**{晴雯因他表哥生日接了出去}**，麝月現在家中病著。

(c)
Hawkes (Penguin, 1980, Vol. 3, p. 332):
This was because Er-jie, she had discovered, had not long since suffered a second and greater bereavement: old Mrs You, who had never quite recovered from the shock caused by her third daughter's suicide, had, only two or three weeks previous to this date, taken a nap which turned out to be her last.
六十八回：**{原來熙鳳已經得知，二姐尚在孝中，卻是尤老娘因三姐兒自盡，受了驚嚇，半個月前已在睡夢中過世了。}**

[IV] A Second Gao E

As he proceeded with his own process of editing, Hawkes became more and more convinced, as we can read in his *Notebooks*, letters and interviews, that Gao E was not the villain that the mainstream *Hongxuejia* had accused him of being, but rather a conscientious and often skilful editor. As he said in the interview in 1998, "it seems to me ridiculous to try to believe that Gao E sat down and wrote the last 40 chapters. I'm sure that's not true. Because you can see the way Gao E works. Gao E is trying I think just to reconcile – he's not altering, I think he doesn't feel he can alter what's been found. I think he tried to alter things occasionally to square one thing with another. If you're just making something up, forging something, you wouldn't be bothered about trying to reconcile inconsistencies. You'd make jolly well sure that they didn't occur."[16] David Hawkes was basically carrying on in the tradition of Gao E. As a conscientious editor, he was in no way inferior to Gao E.

But Hawkes was going one step further, he was trying to reconcile the inconsistencies and discrepancies between the Red Inkstone transcriptions and Gao E's printed text, as it had become accepted by the general reading public. Hawkes wanted, above all, to come up with a convincing and consistent novel for his English public, a version that would be at once true to the Chinese original and yet accessible to the new readership. He wanted to create a novel that worked in English, and in order to achieve this he found it necessary to create an edition that worked in Chinese! As a foreigner, he was not constrained by the almost religious taboos of Chinese *Hongxue*. This edition of his differed from all previous Chinese editions. But he himself was too modest to make any such claims. Again, in the 1998 interview: "I was simply eclectic. I just went for whatever made a good story, I did that. It's very unscholarly, it's not the sort of thing that a serious scholar would do. Another thing that I must correct. I never did any editing of manuscripts. A lot of work has been done on this by very high-powered scholars. If you attribute that work to me I become ridiculous."[17]

"I didn't do any editing at all. In so far as you can call it editing, it's just choosing this and choosing that from different texts. I think to start with I wasn't thinking about that very much. If you were to do a very careful study – it wouldn't be worth your while – but if you *did* study my translation with the texts all along you'd probably find that it follows one popular edition [Cheng-yi text] much more closely and gets more eclectic as it goes along, as I was learning more about it and becoming more aware of the problems involved."[18] I must dare to contradict Professor Hawkes! He did create a new text, and studying it has been extremely worth my while!

---

[16] Connie Chan's interview, Oxford, 1998.
[17] Connie Chan's interview, Oxford, 1998.
[18] Connie Chan's interview, Oxford, 1998.

[V] The Translator

As we can see clearly from his own remarks, with all of his scholarship and editorial expertise, in the end David Hawkes made his editorial choices ultimately neither as a scholar nor as an editor, but as a literary translator. In other words, all his previous efforts combined together to serve one ultimate goal: the creation of a reader-oriented translation, "a real novel for reading."[19] He wanted more than anything else to convey the greatness of China's finest novel to the English-speaking world. "If I can convey to the reader even a fraction of the pleasure this Chinese novel has given me, I shall not have lived in vain."[20]

Again, Hawkes' own informal explanation given in the 1998 interview is to the point: "I'd thought that what I'd like to do is a translation where I don't have to think about academic considerations. Scholarly considerations. I'll just think about how to present – this is Penguins, after all – how to present this book in such a way that I do the whole of it but at the same time it's enjoyable for the English reader, if possible, and they can get some of the pleasure out of it that I got myself. So it's in a different sort of – the way that I went about that, my attitude to it, was very very different from when I was doing *Chuci*."[21]

My concern in this paper has been to describe the manner in which David Hawkes the translator was also a scholar and an editor. His strategies as a literary translator, which I will be addressing in a separate paper, are reflected in some of the emendations that he made in the process of editing his text. He chose to correct errors and inconsistencies in the original text in order to make a more convincing story, rather than follow the basic text automatically.

In rummaging through David Hawkes' notebooks, diaries, letters and papers, I have never once come across a single fanciful or pretentious remark on the subject of his own translation. His is an outstanding example of the humility illustrated in the Chinese saying: "Peach and plum trees do not speak, but a well-trodden path appears beneath (桃李不言，下自成蹊)."

---

[19] From John Minford's obituary, "David Hawkes: Scholar whose superb translation of the lyrical Chinese novel *The Story of the Stone* is regarded as a masterpiece in its own right," *The Times,* Friday 28 August 2009.

[20] Hawkes, Introduction to *The Golden Days*, 46.

[21] Connie Chan's interview, Oxford, 1998.

Translation as Access
to Unfamiliar Emotions

Mark Elvin

School of Culture, History and Language
College of Asia and The Pacific
Australian National University

Tao Tao Liu asked me some time ago why I spent so much time translating from Chinese. My answer was that I had two main motives. In the first place, as a historian of China, I wanted to make *intellectually* accessible to English-speaking readers samples of the type of documentation on which I was basing my historical arguments. It should be added that that the discipline of always having to relate what I am saying to these materials has on the whole kept me from wandering too far into prejudice and distortion, not that one can ever avoid these entirely.

The second reason was that I wanted to make *emotionally* accessible to English-speaking readers the feelings that inspired actions in a historical past with which they were normally unfamiliar. Conveying such feelings is useful in making actions more intelligible. This presented a literary challenge of a particular kind: I was *not* translating to be psychologically moving, or entertaining, but to be informative. At the same time, though, I had to transfer *some* resonances of these feelings so that they also stirred to life at least a little in my readers.

The first type of translation required as much precision as I was capable of; and it allowed only as much stylistic concession to easy reading as was necessary for the type of audience to which it was addressed. The second type had, in contrast, to be an emotional and conceptual conjuring that would let readers almost instinctively feel what was going on in other minds at other times. These were different goals. Even if sometimes they interacted positively with each other, they also could, and sometimes did, conflict.

Tao Tao then talked me into writing a paper about it. I agreed, but did not realize it would prove so much more difficult than I had imagined. The best I can offer in the space available is a collage of fragments of my own work.[1] Though I hope they are interesting fragments, or at least suggestive. I have used poetry to what seems to me, and will almost certainly seem to you, an extent that is disproportionate. The reason is that it is more compact than prose, so one can, overall, include more examples this way. If you dislike poetry, or have little taste for it, bear with me if you can. It can be revelatory.

In second place, I am only going to discuss the second type of translation here, as its role in conveying the flavour of, and the human reality of, the concepts and attitudes of individuals from one culture to those of another is one of translation's most important, but difficult, functions.

◇ ◇ ◇

A simple example is translating something written by a historical figure who comes from a culture or a time not one's own, in order to help oneself and one's readers to imagine the nature of the feelings that may have been at work behind his or her actions and arguments. It also often happens that these are justified—by the historical figure—in terms that are strange to those of us from outside his or her world; and perhaps also different in reality from what is at first presented to us on the surface. As a modest tribute to Professor Chan Sin-wai, who is an expert on Tan Sitong 譚嗣同, that physically and intellectually impetuous as well as eagerly and deliberately self-sacrificing late-nineteenth century advocate of reform, let me give as my first illustration a translation of one of Tan's poems. At a surface level it is no problem to understand.

Yet it begins to open the door into his mind, even if only a crack. It hints at what touched and inspired him, but even so slight an insight as this can lead us a long way. His deeper poems, with their focus on suffering, death, and the Buddhist themes of reincarnation, and the illusory nature of the so-called world, reveal more violently the disturbing intensity of his character, and its at times abrupt compassion for the sufferings of sentient creatures. In the days when I was working on him, now more than thirty years ago, I was never able to produce a convincing translation of these harder pieces and their tangled references.

---

[1] Why only my own, and not others'? Simply because I am intensely familiar with the original texts and with the various struggles that they provoked inside me.

This poem is called "The Boy who Hauled the Boat."[2] It relates what Tan says was a real event in which a young boat-puller saved his passengers from probable death:

北風蓬蓬。大浪雷吼。
小兒曳纜逆風走。
惶惶船中人。生死在兒手。
纜倒曳兒兒屢仆。持纜愈力纜靡肉。
兒肉附纜去。兒掌惟見骨。
掌見骨。兒莫哭。
兒掌有白骨。江心無白骨。

Wind from the north
Gust after gust,
Mounting swell
Thunder-throated,
A mere boy dragging
The long tow into the wind.

The long tow to the boat of people
where fear shivers,
for living or dying
lie in the boy's hands.

Dragged from his feet
he rises and falls
dragged from his feet
again and again,
but his grip grows tighter
though the cords bite flesh from his palms.

The bones start through
yet he keeps his silence.
Hands that are bones
lest other bones
lie in the river's depths.

---

[2] "Er lan chuan bing xu" 〈兒攬船并敍〉, in *Tan Liuyang quanji* 《譚瀏陽全集》 (*Complete Works of Tan Liuyang* (Sitong)) (Taibei: Wenhai chubanshe, 1962), 161-62. This translation was first published in *Other Poetry* 1, eds. A. Stevenson, G. S. Fraser, J. Campbell-Kease, P. J. Foss, and J. Parini (1978). It also appeared as part of endnote 3 in M. Elvin, *Self-Liberation and Self-Immolation in Modern Chinese Thought*, 39th Morrison Lecture in Ethnology (Australian National University: SocPac Printery, 1978), 22-23.

This heroism seems straightforward enough to a European-American mind, even if humbling; but it was also a metaphor for Tan's vision of his own life as a political activist.

A deeper and quite different gulf separates Western readers from the feelings of faithful widows 節婦 in late-imperial China who committed suicide in order to rejoin their husbands in the other world. Here is a poem written by Zeng Rulan 曾如蘭 who stayed alive after her husband's death, in obedience to a magistrate's order, to care for her parents-in-law.[3] Once they had died, she said goodbye to her sisters-in-law and took her leave of the family's ancestors. Then, sitting flawlessly dressed, she wrote the poem that follows, flung aside her writing-brush, swallowed a little metal ball she had prepared beforehand, and passed away. A couple of words of textual explanation before her farewell poem may be helpful: the phrase "a water-chestnut-flower mirror" was a lady's vanity glass; and the "Western Slopes" were the land where, in the dawn of the Chinese race, the Yellow Emperor married his wife Leizu 嫘祖. Rulan's lines are almost exultant:

鏡裡菱花冷。三年淚未乾。已終姑舅老。復嗟雪霜寒。
我自歸家去。人休作烈看。西陵松柏下。夫婦共盤桓。

Like the water-chestnut's blossom, cold my face in the looking-bronze,[4]
and never, through these last three years, have my tears been dried away.
In the fullness of their old age, my parents-in-law have gone.
Once more I taste the frost and snow, the chill of the widow's estate.

---

[3] Zhang Yingchang 張應昌, ed., 1960 (1869) *Qing shiduo* 《清詩鐸》 (*Warning-Bell of Poesy for the Qing Dynasty*. Originally *Guochao shiduo*《國朝詩鐸》). Hereafter cited as *QSD*. (Beijing: Zhonghua shuju), 726-727. Translation slightly changed from M. Elvin, "Unseen Lives. The Emotions of Everyday Existence Mirrored in Chinese Popular Poetry of the Mid-Seventeenth to the Mid-Nineteenth Century," in *Self As Image in Asian Theory and Practice*, eds. Roger Ames, Thomas Kasulis, and Wimal Dissanayake (Albany: State University of New York Press, 1998), 176. Hereafter cited as "Ames et al. (1998)."

[4] I originally translated *jing* 鏡 as "looking-glass," but this is unlikely to be right at this date. Most mirrors were still made of highly polished metal. As poetry, this first version sounded better; and, regrettably, the smooth vowel-rhyme "departed" in the third line had to be replaced by the more staccato "gone." Historical accuracy came before the word-music.

But now, I myself am returning, to that place for all time my home.
You, whom I leave behind me, don't think I'm heroic. Not so.
Under the faith-keeping pines and cedars that rise on the Western Slopes,
husband and wife, we roam together, where delight has bidden us go.

To turn to another cruel subject but one ungilded by any self-delusion,
what does it feel like to sell one's own children, or, as a child, to be sold?
Something of both are expressed in a poem by Ni Shui 倪蛻, "Tears at the
Sign 'For Sale'."[5] Ni makes the passion of the son all but obliterate his
father's worldlywise reasoning. One also senses, I think, an undercurrent
of helpless hatred of the custom on the writer's part. Note that sticking a
stalk of grass in someone's hair was a way of showing that they were for
sale.

旱潦不常畿輔饑。流民乞食來京師。草標插頭淚滿眼。凍餓迫人行賣
　　兒。
阿兒向父言。
人家生兒望成立。父今棄兒又奚為。
阿父向兒言。
兒年猶小兒不知。凶荒不得保軀命。安能望爾成立時。
貴家大宅有衣食。兒去得飽父有貲。兒住同死去同活。事勢至此將何
　　之。
阿兒乃大哭。委擲草標當路歧。
同活不相見。不如同死還相隨。
草標泣。真可悲。

As droughts alternated with floods, hunger gripped the Capital area.
People came fleeing into the city to beg for some scanty fare,
sticking, as tears welled up in their eyes, telltale straws in their youngsters'
　　hair,
being driven by cold, and lack of food, to put the kids up for sale.

There spoke a lad to his father:
"People give birth to their sons in the hope that they'll grow up.
Why is it, Father, then that now—you're abandoning your son?"

The father said to his son in answer:
"My boy, you are still too young to have a true sense of such things.
It's impossible, when a famine's severe, to preserve one's body's
　　existence.
How then can I ever hope for a day when *you* will become an adult?

---

[5] "Caobiao qi" 〈草標泣〉, *QSD*, 566.

But families of rank and wealth—*they* have victuals and apparel.
If you go *there*, you'll be fed your fill, and your father will get some assets.
If *you* stay here, we will perish together. If you leave, we'll both get
    through.
When circumstances have come to this pass, what else *is* there we can do?"

At this the boy gave a cry of pain,
ripped out and threw down the straw sign "For Sale."
"If we both live on, then—we part forever,
to stay together—in death—is better."

Truly, one can only sigh
at the tears, oh, the tears! of the straw sign.

It was quite widely believed that members of a family who died
together would stay together in the world of spiritual existence. At the end
of his *Ballad of Date-tree Lane* Li Fuqing 李孚青 wrote of parents and
their son who had all committed suicide out of love for each other in a
famine: the mother first, to save food, her husband and son next so as to be
with her:

在天為比翼。在地為連枝。精魄不相失。殊勝生別離。

Like wings that support each other in flight, they soar now in Heaven
    above.
On this Earth beneath they are linked each with each, like intertwining
    branches.
The physical souls of their essences keep—forever—in touch with each
    other,
which far surpasses living on, if they'd had to live apart.[6]

This premodern Chinese emotional and conceptual world is in many ways
strange to the uninitiated modern European mind, but at the same time
partially accessible, partially imaginable, and partially rebarbative, even
abhorrent.

◇ ◇ ◇

So far we have touched mainly on the feelings and experiences of
individuals, and opened the window on relatively simple, if different,

---

[6] "Zaojiang xing" 〈棗巷行〉, *QSD*, 963. The full version originally appeared in
Ames et al. (1998), 172-73.

conceptions of the world. In "The Old Farmer" written by You Tong 尤侗 in the later seventeenth century we meet with a more complex interplay of conflicting emotions that relate both to individual and to collective destinies.[7] This clash of viewpoints, which is also a clash in the author's own mind, takes the form of a dialogue. It further raises the critical question, not infrequently found in poetry in Qing times, but largely neglected by critics, as to whether "Heaven" or "Heaven-Nature" (*Tian* 天) should be considered as just or unjust. Note that the "River of Stars" "雲漢" (Yun Han—the Han River in the Clouds) refers to the Milky Way as the emblem of the Zhou-Dynasty emperor Xuan after he had quelled a rebellion, but social conditions remained painful. The poem begins in a sympathetic but humdrum way; then it changes register in midcourse; and, in one version, ends with a somewhat shocking conclusion. In an alternative version, two additional gentler lines at the end ease the abruptness, suggesting that the writer is not altogether happy with what he has said, even if he feels that he has *had* to say it.

披衣過東郊。倚杖問秋穀。荒草滿溝涂。老農相對哭。

「二月響春雷。三月霖春霂。四月荷鋤來。小雨如珠玉。
五月旱既甚。蘊隆至三伏。萬里曠無雲。赤日燒茅屋。
青苗元以黃。滄海變為陸。我耕數畝田。三年無私蓄。
…… ……
為我與天言。何故欺煢獨。徒空野人家。豈減縣官粟？」

吾謂「若毋聲。何不食糜肉。公卿不撫髀。有司不蒿目？
一夫田幾何？嗷嗷愁容蹙。秦楚多大兵。盜賊空城宿。
白骨半邱墟。何處問穜穋。餓死事極小。苟安心亦足。
誰將雲漢詩。補入流民牘？」〈嘆息歸來臥，青風起疏竹。〉

Mantle over my shoulders, I roamed through the city's outskirts.
Then leaning upon my staff, I asked: "How's the autumn's rice?"
The muddy ditches were choked—full of rank and fruitless herbage—
while before me there stood an agèd man, the tears welling up in his eyes.

---

[7] "Lao nong" 〈老農〉, *QSD*, 156. The discussion of the two endings is based on Xue Ruolin, *You Tong lungao* 《尤侗論稿》 (*Draft Essays on You Tong*) (Beijing: Zhongguo xiju chubanshe, 1989), 128. I am grateful to Dr. Warren Wanguo Sun for drawing this book to my attention. There is clearly more to be clarified about You's motivation in this case and the writing of this alternative version; and, conceivably, about interventions by editors.

"All through the second lunar month, the springtime thunder rattled,
while, in the third, the springtime drizzle—dripped on, and on,
   interminably.
During the fourth, as we trudged along, bearing our hoes on our backs,
fine-textured showers were still at least *falling*, drops precious as jades or
   pearls.

But following that, in the *fifth* moon, we met with a total drought,
oppressive weather that would not lift, and dragged on and into the
   dog-days.
For mile after mile the land lay waste, the sky without a cloud,
and held but a reddened sun that burned—down onto our reed-thatched
   cottages.

The fresh green sprouts, on a sudden—changed in colour to brownish
   yellow.
It seemed as if what was an ocean once—had now turned into dry land.
I've a handful of fields for growing crops, and I cultivate them myself,
but these last three years I've not reaped enough to store in my family's
   granary.
... ...
   Would you be willing, on my behalf, to speak to Heaven-Nature?
To ask why It should play these tricks on the poor and the unsupported?
Inflicting upon us countryfolk our total ruination,
yet hardly cutting—if at all—into official resources?"

I answered him: "Such matters as these—are not *your* business to mention.
Why do you think it is that *you*—don't sup on fine-hashed meat?
Why it is that the high officials—are not sympathetic in temper?
Why the powers-that-be don't notice *you*, their eyes disturbed with grief?

Think! How many acres of farmland does a commonplace person have?
Yet he worries and whimpers about them, his forehead puckered with
   wrinkles,
though Qin in the West and, southwards, Chu, are filled with our massive
   battalions,
and robbers and brigands pitch camp overnight in our no more inhabited cities.

Our townships in hummocked ruins are half-covered with whitening bones,
so *who* is concerned how amply—*your* quick and slow millets are
   growing?
It's a wholly trivial matter if *you* should expire from hunger.
It's enough if, however undeserved, you still enjoy some security."

—How could lines on suppressing rebellion, on that River of Stars above,
Be patched up with such information on the fates of displaced persons?

In the gentler version, the dismissive phrase *gou an* "苟安" (undeserved peace) has been replaced by *an zhai* "安宅" (a peaceful homestead,) and two final lines seemingly added:[8]

> I sighed in my sadness, came home—and laid myself down to sleep,
> as, through the sparsely-set glades of bamboos, stirred breaths of relieving breeze.

The question that tormented people here was whether or not a natural disaster was a morally deserved punishment. The spiritual agency most often questioned was Heaven, but could also be other deities. But what *was* "Heaven?" Not quite "God," not quite "Nature," as we would understand these ideas, and even, since humans of indomitable will could on rare occasions allegedly overcome It, not quite a composite of these two either. It was more elusive than we are inclined to think.

The problem of moral justification, though often raised, was almost never explicitly answered, but scepticism is evident enough. Sometimes, though, they reply could indeed be negative. This can be seen in part of "The Scream of the Sea" by Zhang Yongquan 張永銓 on the storm that smashed through the seawalls south of the mouth of the Yangzi River in 1696, drowning large numbers of the coast's inhabitants:[9]

> ...... 數口同將繩繫身。猶冀相依或相挈。那知同泛竟同沈。
> 或鑽屋頂求身脫。身隨茅屋偕飄泊。或抱棟梁任所之。風來衝激東西撒。
> 或攀樹杪得暫浮。蛇亦怖死緣樹頭。人怕蛇傷手自釋。人蛇俱已赴滄洲。...
> 黎明雨息風不定。未沒人家歡相慶。遙見波中有一沙。千人沙上呼救命。
> 潮來一捲半云亡。再捲沙沈人已竟。...
> 一日二日面目在。浮屍填積如邱山。三日四日皮肉爛。臭聞百里真心酸。...
> 半月海塘人裹足。天昏地黑驚心目。子夜時聞怨鬼號。日中還聽游魂哭。

---

[8] This could then read "It's enough if in your peaceful home you still enjoy security."

[9] "Hai xiao xing" 〈海嘯行〉, *QSD*, 472-73. A translation of the first two-thirds of this poem appears in M. Elvin, *The Retreat of the Elephants: An Environmental History of China.* (New Haven CT and London: Yale University Press, 2004), 172-73. Hereafter *RE*. The translation of the final lines given here is new.

嘗考邑乘紀災祥。嘉隆暨萬海波揚。人畜淹沒稱無數。百年未滿復遭
殃。
嗚呼海民獨何辜？賢愚老幼忽同徂。天吳海若何殘暴？布此虐令傷太
和。⋯⋯⋯⋯
嗟哉閭里遭顛連。越瘠秦視人胡然。自古陰陽憑爕理。漫將劫數諉蒼
天。

⋯⋯

Some of the people used ropes, to tie themselves together,
hoping this way to support each other, or give each other help.
How were *they* to know that, together, they'd be swept away and drowned?
Some of them sought to escape, boring holes in the rooves of their houses,
but their bodies, along with their reed-thatched shacks, were borne off, and
    tossed about.
Some clutched at beams and rafters, and let themselves go where these
    went,
but the wind pounded and battered them, and scattered them east and west.
Some clambered to the tops of trees, where they floated for a time,
but snakes climbed up to the treetops, too,—anguished with fear of dying.
Men's hands, seized with panic the snakes would bite—of themselves
    released their hold.
Men and snakes have gone, together, into the other world....

The downpour ceased at dawn, but the storm did not let up.
Those people who had not been drowned congratulated each other.
Then they saw a sandbank far away, among the rolling waves,
where a thousand others called for help, that their lives, too, be saved.
The tide came in, then, with a swirl, and half of them went down.
With the second swirl the bank submerged, and every one was drowned....

Their faces, a few days later on, were still easy to recognize,
while, like mounds or hillocks, their washed-up corpses had stacked
    themselves in piles.
By the third day, or the fourth, skin and flesh were soggy-rotten.
One could smell the stench some thirty miles. It made one want to
    vomit....

Half a month later, beside the seawall, folk dragged along, barely mobile;
dark was the Heaven, and black the Earth, hearts with apprehension
    hopeless.
At the hour of midnight their ears were filled—with howls from resentful
    ghosts,
and at noontide they still continued to hear—the wails from these
    wandering souls.
Disastrous events, and auspicious omens, in the county records consulted,

showed in *three* reigns under the later Ming—storm surges had risen up,
drowning the livestock, and humans too, in numbers declared past number,
yet before a hundred years have gone, we are once *more* being punished.
Why are *only* those who live by the sea guilty—alas!—of transgressions?
Evil and virtuous, agèd and youthful, met their deaths at once and *together*.
Why would Tianwu and Hairuo, the sea-gods, have acted in fashion so
    venomous,
giving orders so harsh that the *yin-yang* balance—was lethally thereby
    unsettled? ...
The country people have, sadly, now suffered—destruction *so*
    overwhelming
that those far remote, in distant places, gaze at it without comprehending.
As of old, *yin* and *yang* coordinate patterns in the ways that, *to them*, are
    inherent;
catastrophic conjunctions induce folk to blame—in their *folly*—Caerulean
    Heaven.

Zhang's concern in writing of the causes as purely natural in Chinese
metaphysical terms was probably to persuade the local people to give a
decent burial to the remains of those who had died. We may suspect that
he was anxious to combat any tendency to suspect that the victims of the
storm-surge had *deserved* their deaths. Against any belief that it might
have been justified action on the part of the lesser deities, let alone a
morally conscious Heaven, he argued—if I have correctly understood his
final lines—that it was the more or less *mechanical* result of the
interactions of the cycles of situations all but inexorably generated by the
Bright Force and the Dark Force. Was the cosmos then amoral? Or were
these forces, the *yin* and the *yang*, perhaps somehow independent of
Heaven?

The belief that human resolve could sometimes prove stronger than
Heaven-Nature and the spirit world is evident from a number of
Qing-Dynasty poems. Thus Li Zhan 李栴, writing in the mid-nineteenth
century about the clearance by Li Benzhong 李本忠 of rocks that were a
danger for shipping on the upper Yangzi, could declare:[10]

當其熾炭頑石裂。火光下徹馮夷宮。椎聲丁丁徧崖谷。夫役擾擾團沙
    蟲。
夔歸諸險次第盡。人志一定天無功。

---

[10] "Ping xingtan"〈平行灘〉, *QSD*, 13. "Clasts" are fragments of sedimentary rocks
ranging in size from pebbles to boulders. This partial translation also appears in *RE*,
445.

By heating them with fiery coals he split stubborn rocks to clasts,
their flame-lights flashing downwards to the River God's palaces;
as his ringing hammers echoed through the precipice-walled valleys,
grim beasts, rounded up in mud-shoals, fled his work-force in their panic.

He cleared away the hazards on these two routes step by step.
When once the human will is fixed, Heaven-Nature has no effect.

Tian was not always omnipotent. Conveying the Chinese sense of
"Heaven" in a given context is thus a matter of highlighting aspects,
selected as judgement indicates, of a varying composite intuition rather
than giving a precise translation of a precise doctrine.

◇ ◇ ◇

Let us now explore more deeply a theme hinted at in the foregoing.
This is the variety of possible scenarios competing in the late-imperial
Chinese mind to describe what happens to the human soul after death. Or
rather *souls*, since there were always deemed to be at least two per person.
Many of these scenarios, as specialists are aware, seem to be in
contradiction with one another. Rather than trying to disentangle all the
threads interwoven over the millennia, let us look at two further examples.
There are at least three others implied in parts of the other items cited, as
attentive readers will spot for themselves. The first of our two explicit
illustrations is of the view that the dead were living in a shadowy mirror of
the everyday world.

For example, most Chinese of those times thought that a form of
otherworldly "money" could be transmitted to the spirits of the dead for
them to use. This was commonly done by burning special printed paper
representations of copper cash (*zhiqian* 紙錢), to be spent at
"ghost-markets." The practice sometimes provoked sarcastic comments
from sceptical scholar-poets, but it was taken seriously by ordinary people.
Here is the "Song on the Burning of Paper" by Yuan Shouling 袁壽齡.[11]
Note the shift at the end from the descriptive, mildly mocking, mood to a
pious, didactic, tone. He was also clearly aware of, and unhappy about, the
existence of alternative post-mortem scripts:

世間第一可怪事。鬼神亦受飢寒累。年年七月送紙錢。人到重泉猶嗜
　利。
金銀衣裳并宮室。一身所須共一紙。深山窮谷人不到。此中想亦開墟

---

[11] "Shao zhi ge" 〈燒紙歌〉, *QSD*, 894.

市。
鬼神貧富之權操人間。祖宗貧富之境隨孫子。
豪家紛紛信僧道。堆聚如山煙焰起。老年寄庫數百萬。臨終送錢布大
　地。
人世富貴有代謝。冥漠富貴無窮已。古人一事有一義。致死致生非仁
　智。
神明之道惟明器。報本追遠教萬世。今日孝子無忝不匱心。祭葬盡禮
　乃在是。

Among all the phenomena in this world, the foremost cause for our wonder
is that ghosts, too, grow weary, and suffer from cold and hunger.
In the seventh month of each lunar year, they're presented with paper
　money,
for even the dead in the world below—have a taste for money-grubbing.

Dwellings and palaces, gold and silver, as well as splendid raiment
—all that a person could require—are combined *on a sheet of paper.*
In the depths of the hills and the barren valleys, where nobody ever goes,
the people believe that here, as elsewhere, there are market-places open.

Power to make ghosts rich or poor—lies in *living* people's hands.
Ancestors' poverty, or wealth, *follow* that of their sons and grandsons.
Countless numbers of powerful families—trust in Daoists and Buddhist
　monks
from whose offerings, piled as high as hills, the smoke and flames leap up.

The old remit several millions of cash through the *post-mortem treasuries,*
everywhere squandering transferred funds, as they face the approach of
　death.
In the world of the *living*, riches and honours—are always in transition.
In the boundless darkness of the *dead*, they perdure, and never finish.

Each event, for the men of ancient times, had only a single *sense.*
But to cause the deceased to become alive—shows neither wisdom nor
　empathy.
The way of the Spirits Bright prescribes—only burying goods *with the*
　dead,
and, requiting one's forebears by sacrifice, to teach numberless
　descendants.

For a filial son with no cause for shame, and every duty fulfilled,
the rites for interment and sacrifice—for perfection need only this.

The remittances through the post-mortem treasuries (*ji ku* 寄庫) may be
thought of as an analogy to bank transfer: sending spirit money to the

other world to await the arrival of its owner there, in due course, to collect it, and go shopping.

◇   ◇   ◇

Our second example is more complex, and embedded in a longer narrative more complex still: it is part of an extended tableau from the early-nineteenth-century novel *The Destinies of the Flowers in the Mirror,* the *Jinghua yuan*《鏡花緣》by Li Ruzhen 李汝珍.[12] Even the title here presents a problem of translation: *yuan* 緣 signifies an invisible but powerful causal affinity across time and space between two entities, often people or spirits, but also domains of activity or events, linked by shared origins or past history, or some other common character.

We are eavesdropping, in imagination, on the party allegedly held some time during the reign of the Empress Wu Zetian in the later seventh century to celebrate the success of the hundred girls who have taken part in a great—but regrettably fictitious—event, the first imperial Palace examinations ever held for talented women. The successful candidates are all the reincarnated spirits of flowers that a superior but not supreme numinous authority, the Queen Mother of the West, has capriciously commanded for a certain time to walk the earth in human form as a punishment. This section of the book interweaves several themes with which Western readers are rarely comfortable. These include a belief in the unending reincarnation of the dead not only in the form of people but also as animals and even parts of animals; an obsession with the sexual allure of women's feet, and parodies of the Confucian scriptures. Pervading everything is learning mixed with a mischievous sense of humour that is remorselessly scatological and sexual, but delicately expressed by playing scholarly games with words and allusions. In places my rendering is still uncertain: we are close here to the limit of what translation, in general, and the present translator, in particular, can hope to convey, maybe even to comprehend. The personal names in what follows, it should be noted, are all of females.

…只見彩雲同著林婉如、掌浦珠、董青鈿遠遠走來。呂堯蓂道：「四位姐姐却到何處頑去，臉上都是紅紅的？」掌浦珠道：「我們先在海

---

[12] Li Ruzhen 李汝珍, *Jinghua yuan*《鏡花緣》, 1955. Originally perhaps 1828. Modern edition used here (Beijing: Zuojia chubanshe, 1955). The text translated is a composite assembled from chapters (*hui* 回) 80, 81, and 87. There being a number of editions, I have not given specific page-references.

棠社看花，後來四個人就在花下拋毬，所以把臉都使紅了。」彩雲道：
「告訴諸位姐姐：我們不但拋毬，內中還帶著飛個鞋兒頑頑哩。」瓊
芝道：「這是甚麼講究？」彩雲只是笑。婉如指著青鈿道：「你問青
鈿姐姐就知道了。」青鈿滿面緋紅道：「諸位姐姐可莫笑。剛才彩雲
姐姐拋一個『丹鳳朝陽』式子，教妹子去接，偏偏離的遠，穀不著，
一時急了，只得用腳去接，雖然踢起，誰知力太猛了，連毬帶鞋都一
齊飛了。」眾人無不掩口而笑。紫芝道：「這鞋飛在空中，倒可打個
曲牌名。」青鈿道：「好姐姐！親姐姐！你莫罵我，快些告訴我打個
甚麼？」紫芝道：「你猜。」青鈿道：「我猜不著。」紫芝道：「既
猜不著，告訴你罷，這叫做…。」

... Just then Rainbow Cloud came running towards them from a distance,
together with Complaisant, Inlet Pearl, and Blue Brooch.

"Where," demanded Lü Yaoming, "have you four young ladies been
off amusing yourselves so that your faces are flushed?"

"First of all," said Inlet Pearl, "we looked at the blossoms in the
Crab-Flower Club,[13] and then later the four of us played beneath the
blossoms at tossing the ball. That's why we've made our faces go red."

"Let me tell you all," added Rainbow Cloud, "that we didn't *just* play
ball. We had fun as well with flying the shoe."

"What does *that* mean?" asked Precious Mushroom.

Rainbow Cloud merely smiled.

"Ask sister Blue Brooch," said Complaisant, pointing at Blue Brooch.
"Then you'll know!"

Blue Brooch's face went bright scarlet all over.

"Sisters," she said, "you shouldn't be laughing at me. What sister
Rainbow Cloud threw to me just now was a 'phoenix facing the sunlit
slope'-style swinger[14] and, as bad luck would have it, too far away for me

---

[13] *Haitang she* 海棠社. This is one of Li Ruzhen's characteristic time-inversion
jokes. The literary club is a feature of Cao Xueqin 曹雪芹 and Gao E 高鶚's *The
Story of the Stone* 《石頭記》 (*Hongloumeng* 《紅樓夢》 in customary Chinese
usage) written in the eighteenth century (see chapter 37), with a somewhat similar
focus on upper-class young ladies conversing in a magnificent garden. Li was
writing in the early nineteenth century but, *purportedly*, about events in the reign
of the Empress Wu Zetian 武則天 at the end of the seventh, more than a
millennium *earlier*.

[14] *Danfeng chao yang shizi* 丹鳳朝陽式子 ("set form [named for] the
cinnabar-hued phoenix facing the sunlit [morning] slope.") This was a term applied
to a particular type of fixed-pattern body-movements, members of a wider range
practised in the traditional martial arts and related exercises, sometimes intended to
strengthen the physique or improve the health, and having Daoist symbolical and
metaphysical overtones. How far the various types bearing this specific label had

to reach. I wasn't up to catching it; and, in the hurry of the moment, could only use my *foot* to cut it off. I did no more than kick out, but who'd have guessed— I did it so violently that the ball and the shoe both flew off *together*!"

Everyone there covered their mouths and giggled.

"On the other hand," said Purple Mushroom, "this shoe flying through the air would make a clue for the title of a song."

"Good sister," said begged Blue Brooch. "*Dear* sister, don't tease me. Hurry up and tell me what it's the clue for."

"You have a guess," said Purple Mushroom.

"I can't."

"Seeing you can't guess," said Purple Mushroom, "let me tell you: it's called…."

The chapter ends at this point in the conventional tantalizing way, and we have to go on to the next one to learn the answer. This is a pun based on what may have been Li Ruzhen's own reconstruction of the Tang pronunciation of the term for "flying shoe." He was an expert on historical phonetics. We may further guess that this sound, in his view, was roughly

---

distinctive common elements requires further examination, and probably more expertise than I possess. It is also a matter for speculation whether there are overtones of what seems to be the earliest classical source of the two key components, namely the phoenix or phoenixes (*fenghuang* 鳳凰) and facing toward the the sunlit slope (*chao yang* 朝陽). This is ode 252 in Bernhard Karlgren's edition of the *Book of Odes* (Museum of Far Eastern Antiquities: Stockholm, 1950), and commonly referred to under the title "Juan E" 〈卷阿〉 ("The Sinuous Hill-slope.") The opening lines are:

There is a sinuous hill
where a turning wind blows from the south.

The other relevant lines are:

Male and female phoenix sing
from that ridge high above,
a *wutong* tree's grown up there
its face turned toward the dawn.

—Traditionally, a *wutong* (*Firmiana simplex*) was thought to be the only tree on which a phoenix would alight. At all events, the context of the curved hill and the turning wind, and perhaps also the sinuosity of the phoenix as conventionally painted, makes the idea of this being a reference to a swerving throw conceivable, though it in no way proves it. Or the terminology here may be strictly technical, but beyond reach for the moment.

like *fei-xia.[15] To resume:

> 話說青鈿道：「我這『飛鞋』打個甚麼？姐姐告訴我。」紫芝道：「只打四個字。」青鈿道：「那四個字？」紫芝道：「叫做『銀漢浮槎』。」題花笑道：「若這樣說，青鈿妹妹尊足倒是兩位柁工了。」眾人聽著，任不住笑。

As we were just saying, then—
> Blue Brooch asked: "What does my 'flying shoe' [*fei-xia*] give a clue for? Tell me, elder sister."
> "It only indicates four words," Purple Mushroom replied.
> "But which four?"
> "The solution comes out as 'The Floating Raft [likewise *fei-xia*][16] on the Milky Way'."[17]
> "If one follows up on this idea," said Flower-Gazer with a laugh, "younger sister Blue Brooch's honourable feet turn out to be *a couple of steersmen*."
> When everyone heard this they could not stop themselves sniggering.

Let us pause and ask ourselves why these well-bred young ladies reacted in this vulgar way. I can only guess that "steersman" *duo gong* 柁工 = 舵公 was a way of referring to a husband or lover. In Qing times the phrase *wu duo zhi zhou* 無舵之舟 "a boat without a rudder or steering-oar" meant "a widow,"[18] though it has the more general meaning in modern times of simply being "purposelessly adrift." Blue Brooch has just been gratuitously assigned *two* of the gentlemen who do this sort of steering, and not unnaturally she wants her revenge on those playing at impugning her reputation. The tale continues:

> 青鈿呆了一呆，因向眾人道：「妹子說件奇事：一人飲食過於講究，

---

[15] A possible old-style *fanqie* "spelling" being 甫微 + 懸佳, following the *Kangxi Reign-Period Dictionary*《康熙字典》. The asterisk * indicates a reconstructed pronunciation.

[16] A possible *fanqie* spelling being 符非 + 仕下, with the first of these pairs a so-called "forced" reading allowed for the purposes of rhyming.

[17] The Milky Way was thought to join the sea at the point where people living on the nearby coastal islands observed it to seem to reach the horizon. See the *Zhongwen da cidian*《中文大辭典》(*Great Dictionary of the Chinese Written Language*), 8173.

[18] See Herbert Giles, *A Chinese-English Dictionary*, 2nd ed. (Shanghai and London: Kelly and Walsh, 1912), 1406, entry 11,331.

死後冥官罰他去變野狗嘴，教他不能吃好的。這人轉世，在這狗嘴上
真政熬的可憐。諸位姐姐，你想：變了狗嘴，已是難想好東西吃了，
況且又是野狗嘴，每日在那野地吃的東西可想而知。好容易那狗才死
了。這嘴來求冥官：不論罰變甚麼都情願，只求免了狗嘴。冥官道：
『也罷！這世罰你變個猴兒屁股去！』小鬼道：『稟爺爺，但凡變過
狗嘴的再變別的，那臭味最是難改，除非用些仙草搽上方能改哩。』
冥官道：『且變了再講。』不多時，小鬼帶去，果然變了一個白猴屁
股。冥官隨命小鬼覓了一枝靈芝在猴兒屁股上一陣亂揉，霎時就如胭
脂一般。冥官道：『他這屁股是用何物揉的？為何都變紫了？』小鬼
道：『稟爺爺：是用紫芝揉的。』」

紫芝道：「他要搽點青還更好哩。」題花道：「只怕還甜了。」

Blue Brooch was stupefied for a moment. Then she said to the company:

"Let *me* tell *you* a strange story. There was a gourmet once who was
excessively fastidious about what he drank and ate. After he had died, the
authorities in the underworld punished him by sending him back into our
world as the lips of a wild dog, so he could not get a good meal. When this
fellow returned to life he suffered really pitiably in the form of those dog's
lips! Think on it, ladies, when one has changed into the muzzle of an
ordinary dog it is already hard enough to think of good things to eat, but
how much more was this so for a *wild* dog's lips. One has only to imagine
what there is to eat every day in those wastelands! He did *not* have an easy
time of it before he died! He then went to beseech the underworld officials,
saying he was willing to accept *anything* they turned him into as a
punishment, just so long as he was spared being a dog's lips. 'So be it!'
said the authorities. 'We'll punish you for this next life by turning you into
a monkey's buttocks.'

'I beg permission to speak to Your Honour,' said a little demon at this
point, 'but when we merely change the everyday earthly *form* of someone
who has been a dog's muzzle into something else, the stinking *odour*
remains *very* difficult to remove. Only if we rub it with a bit of a herb of
the immortals can we alter it.'

'Once he's been transformed, we'll discuss it again,' said the
underworld official.

Shortly afterwards, the little demon took the man away and actually
changed him into the buttocks of a white ape. The underworld official then
told the little demon that once he'd found a stalk of magic fungus he was to
give the monkey's rump a vigorous pummeling with it; and in next to no
time it looked as if it had make-up on it.

'What *did* you rub on these buttocks,' asked the official, 'and why
have they all changed to a *purple* colour?'

'I beg permission to speak to Your Honour,' said the little demon. 'I
rubbed them with a *purple mushroom.*'"

"It would have been even better if he'd rubbed them with a bit of
blue," said Purple Mushroom.

"In all likelihood," said Flower-Gazer, "that would have made him even nicer."

Blue Brooch tells them all to stop laughing, and then tears Flower-Gazer to shreds with some pleasantries equally nasty, dirty, and ingenious. At the end Purple Twig comments that both jokes were "provoked by the two steersmen on the Raft Floating on the Milky Way."

This is a world that has aspects with which most of us are, to some degree, familiar. Upper-class young women are often catty towards each other, frequently with a dexterous indirectness, while concealing their competitiveness, and feigning a well-brought-up amiability. Li Ruzhen, who must have spent many years observing this sort of behaviour, is clearly rather intrigued by it, for all its lack of human warmth, seeing how long he spends describing it.

The shoe theme is pursued on and off for more than fifty pages more. It culminates with some parodies of the Chinese Scriptures or Classics, and their commentaries. That the young ladies should compete in composing these mocking imitations is proposed by Spring Brightness as a way of "clearly expounding the inner meaning" of these books. The term she uses is *biaobai* 表白, a Buddhist phrase that indicates a clarification of the mysteries of the faith at a popular level.[19] It would, she suggests, provide their gathering with a "refined amusement" (*yaxing* 雅興). They begin with ancient canonical but *not* scriptural books: thus Little Spring mimics the "Responses to the Questions to the King of Chu" 〈對楚王問〉 by the Chu poet Song Yu 宋玉:

「巨屨上擊九千里，絕雲霓，入青霄，飛騰乎杳冥之上；
夫凡庸之屨，豈能與之料天地之高哉！」

"Nine thousand miles upwards strikes the Great Brogue,
clouds cleaving, and rainbows,
entr'ing *blue* empyrean,
soaring on high, above darkness unceasing!
How could a commonplace brogue
delimit, like this, Sky above, Earth below?"

Purple Mushroom says that it is not difficult to trump this for "strength." She then parodies the celebrated opening section of the philosophical masterwork *Zhuangzi* on the giant roc-like bird of legend:

---

[19] Morohashi Tetsuji 諸橋轍次, *Dai Kan-Wa jiten* 《大漢和辭典》(*Great Sino-Japanese Dictionary*), X.10622. i.

「其名為屨，屨之大不之其幾里也。怒而飛，其翼若垂天之雲…」

"'Sandal' is its name. It is I know not how many thousands of miles in size. When with impetuous ardour it takes flight, its wings are like the clouds that hang down in the heavens...."

And so on, rather predictably.

Flower-Gazer then suggests that it would be better to parody some of the Five Classics, the core scriptures. Jade Mushroom tackles *The Book of Changes,* the numerically based divining manual interpreting particular human situations, and foretelling the consequences of particular envisaged actions:

「初九，屨：履之則吉，飛之則否。象曰：履之則吉，行其正也；飛之則否，舉趾高也。」

"Nine at the beginning: shoes. *Walking* in them brings good fortune, but *flying* in them entails *mis*fortune. The image: walking in them brings good fortune, one's conduct is correct; flying in them is *mis*fortune, one is lifting up one's feet and walking pretentiously."

Finally, Purple Mushroom makes fun of the venerable *Book of Odes* and inserts a delicate hint that Blue Brooch's foot has a nasty smell:

「巨屨颺矣。於彼高岡。大足光矣。於彼馨香。」
春輝道：「『馨香』二字是褒中帶貶，反面文章，含蓄無窮，頗有風人之旨。…」

"Tempest-borne the vasty shoe
o'er that high ridge aloft ,
and bared to view the *giant* foot
— *sweet* reek from *so* far off."

"The two words 'sweet reek'," observed Spring Brightness, "are criticism concealed in praise. There are limitless hidden implications in a style that explains by means of contraries. What is said here conveys in good measure the purport the poet intends to express."

The resilient Blue Brooch counter-attacks yet again, raising the stakes:

「你們變著樣兒罵我，只好隨你嚼蛆，但有侮聖言，將來難免都有報應。」眾人道：「有何報應？」青鈿把舌一伸，又把五個手指朝下一彎道：「只怕都要『適蔡』哩。」眾人聽了，一齊發笑。

"When you abuse me in one way and then another, all I can do is follow *your* example and talk nonsense back at *you*, but, when you insult the words of the Sages, then in the future you will, *all of you*, find it difficult to avoid retribution."

"What sort of retribution?" everyone demanded.

Blue Brooch uneasily pushed out her tongue and clenched five fingers in an arc before she said: "Probably—that you will be married to sick husbands for whom you will be obliged to care."[20]

When they heard this, they all of them tittered.

Non-believers find it all but impossible to imagine, let alone feel, the depth of the shock that sacrilege can inflict on those brought up in a tradition of certain beliefs, even if, as here, these believers are sophisticated, having acquired some psychological distance from their original indoctrination. Probably even the best of translations cannot make such impacts *intrinsically* comparable to the original, but a workaday one can at least draw attention to their presence and general nature. And responding to humour, which relies on the *unspoken shared assumptions* of the members of a culture, or subculture, to work its effects—the deliciously instantaneous closure of the circuits between aligned minds, where there is no need for tedious explanation—is the litmus-test of one's intimacy with that culture or subculture. It is, notoriously, the trickiest mood for the translator to convey to the uninitiated.

It is worth adding a final observation that applies both to the translator and readers. The type of translation that I have discussed here can also be of value in gaining insights into more modern history, perceptions hard to access in any other way. An illustration of this can be found in the third chapter of my *Changing Stories in the Chinese World*. I suggested there that there was a "crisis of absurdity" in China in the first third of the twentieth century, when social and psychological realities began to diverge in mind-torturing fashion from deeply rooted cultural expectations, still alive but already discredited. I compared this to the somewhat similar, though not identical, crisis in pre-Hitlerian Germany at about the same time. A common reaction of many people and movements, when a sense of pervasive absurdity seems to have taken hold of their lives and their thinking, is to attack perceived scapegoats with a dogmatic savagery, and to attempt to reshape an unsatisfactory society and ways of thought by

---

[20] See the entry under 蔡人妻 in the *Zhongwen da cidian*《中文大辭典》.

violent political and ideological orthopaedics. If necessary, facts get pushed aside to meet the demands of abstract formulations that seem to restore some degree of conceptual order, and to exorcise absurdity. This process can nonetheless have fearful consequences.

Much of my evidence for this psychological syndrome in educated city-dwellers in the early decades of modern China was drawn from my efforts to translate the Shanghai-flavoured Chinese that expressed the grotesque picture of late 1920s Chinese society summoned into life by the surreal realism of Ping Jinya 平襟亞,[21] both mocking and macabre, rational and mad, in his novel *The Tides in the Human Sea* 《人海潮》[22] probably published in 1927.[23] You can find a few lines of of it in my chapter in Rachel May and John Minford's elegant *Birthday Book for Brother Stone*, the Festschrift for the late Professor David Hawkes to whom our conference is dedicated.[24]

I did not complete this translation because the mixed oddity, vulgarity, preposterous inventiveness, and psychological virtuosity of the text seemed to be too difficult for almost any Western readers to grasp, let alone enjoy, or at least to the inadequate extent that I was capable of conveying it. So I never examined this hypothesis more deeply, and it remains just a hypothesis. I mention it here as an example of the ideas that can emerge through the translator him- or herself being forced to wrestle

---

[21] The real name of Wangchu Sheng 網蛛生 (Master Spider-in-the-Web), his *nom-de-plume*.

[22] Subtitle *Shanghai shehui zhenxiang* 《上海社會真相》(*The True Face of Shanghai Society*). There are five volumes in the 1936 edition that I have used. It was published by the Shanghai zhongyang shudian 上海中央書店.

[23] The first point is the 1935 version commonly available was not the first. It contains the statement "*Reprinted* in the first month of 1935" 民國二十四年一月重版 at the back of the fifth volume. The identification of the actual date of the first edition rests mainly on the dates in the prefaces by various friends of the author in the first volume (*xuwen* 序文) pages 1-4, which range from 1926 through 1927, and the author's own "Repetitious Words" (*zhuiyan* 贅言) just before the table of contents, but also on tracing a reference in online booksellers' catalogue to one volume of a 1927 edition. I would like to express my thanks to Professor Rudolph Wagner who urged a re-examination of the date of publication, and supplied the reference to the catalogue just mentioned: 网罗天下图书 传承中华文明 (網羅天下圖書 傳承中華文明), accessed on or just before 18 June 2011.

[24] Rachel May and John Minford, eds., *A Birthday Book for Brother Stone—for David Hawkes at Eighty* (Hong Kong: The Chinese University Press, and the Hong Kong Translation Society, 2003), 263-81.

with the problems of translating, and hence interpreting, intriguing but often baffling material. In this case, the history of the emotions as they affected the psychological foundations of politics. And sometimes, just sometimes, I wonder if it could be, that, as the traditional proverb has it, it is the *outsider* 旁觀的 who sees some things most clearly, or, at least, with a vision that is provocatively, but usefully, different.

Note on the main source of the poems, and the style of translation
The principal source of the poems used here is anthology *Qing shiduo* 《清詩鐸》 or *Warning-Bell of Poesy for the Qing Dynasty* which was compiled by Zhang Yingchang 張應昌 and first published in 1869 under the title The *Warning-Bell of Poesy for the Present Dynasty*《國朝詩鐸》. It was reprinted under the present title, with a few ideologically motivated excisions, by the Xinhua shudian in Beijing in 1960. It contains over 2,000 poems by 911 authors who lived in, or at least on into, the Manchu-Qing Dynasty. The contents were chosen mainly but not exclusively to reflect the severity of the impending crisis emerging from the worsening social, economic, environmental and political circumstances of these times. The poets were mostly of gentry and official status, though some came, in their own terms, from fairly impoverished backgrounds, and the language used is basically literary. It is not, strictly speaking, popular verse.

With one exception, the poem by Tan Sitong, which is taken from his collected works, the translations attempt to reflect something of the basic prosodic and metrical structure of the originals. They use English *vowel-rhymes* between the last *stressed* syllables in lines to suggest the Chinese full rhymes, though often with some liberties as regards the pattern. They use the English *stressed* syllable as a rough metric equivalent of the Chinese syllable; this enables an approximation of the effect of the mid-line *caesura* or fleeting pause, which usually occurs after the fourth syllable in a seven-syllable Chinese line, and after the third in a five-syllable line. If not obvious, this may be marked with an em-dash "—." The object is to create an echo of the almost crystalline *structural regularity* that is a distinctive characteristic of the great majority the Chinese verses and verse-styles. This feature is generally lost in the "sprung rhythm" employed in most English translations. —At its rare best this can of course have its own power and charm. In general, the Chinese originals drawn on here are not literary masterpieces. Something has undoubtedly been lost in translation, but perhaps somewhat less than where works of genius are concerned.

ENGLISH TRANSLATIONS OF THE *SHIJI*: A PRELIMINARY STUDY

JOHN C. Y. WANG

DEPARTMENT OF EAST ASIAN LANGUAGES AND CULTURES
STANFORD UNIVERSITY

The *Shiji* in one hundred and thirty chapters is of course one of the most important texts in the entire Chinese tradition. Written by Sima Qian (145-c. 86 B.C.) of the Han Dynasty, it is not only the first comprehensive history of China (and some of its neighboring peoples) from the legendary past to the author's own time, it has also been admired as a literary masterpiece. As such, it has exerted immense influence on later historians and literary scholars alike not only in China, but also in countries within the Chinese cultural sphere, such as Korea and Japan. English translations from the work go back to the nineteenth century. But as can be seen in the partial translation of the "Biography of Laozi" (first part of Chapter 63) by James Legge in his *The Texts of Taoism* in *The Sacred Books of the East* 39 edited by F. Max Muller[1] and the translation of the "Basic Annals of the Five Emperors" (Chapter 1) by Herbert J. Allen and Leon Rosny under the title "*Historical Records*, Chapter 1—Original Record of the Five Gods" in the *Journal of Royal Asiatic Studies*,[2] these early pioneering efforts are haphazard and piecemeal at best. Most of the translations of specific individual chapters from the *Shiji*, including those by some later scholars, could be characterized this way.

It was not until the 1930s and 1940s that we began to see more serious and earnest attempts to translate from the *Shiji*. Still, these early efforts, such as Derk Bodde's *China's First Unifier, A Study of the Ch'in Dynasty as Seen in the Life of Li Ssu*[3] with a full, annotated translation of Chapter 87 and *Statesman, Patriot, and General in Ancient China*,[4] which contains

---

[1] Oxford: At the Clarendon Press, 1891, 34-36.
[2] 1894, 278-95.
[3] Leiden: E. J. Brill, 1938.
[4] New Haven: American Oriental Society, 1940.

annotated translations of Chapters 85, 86 (the part on Jing Ke), and 88, should perhaps not be regarded as translations per se since they were done as part of studies on topics that go beyond just the translations themselves. Frank Kierman Jr.'s *Ssu-ma Ch'ien's Historiographical Attitude as Reflected in Four Late Warring States Biographies* [5] with annotated translations of Chapters 80, 81, 82, and first half of Chapter 83, which began in 1949 but was not finished and published until 1962, may be said to belong to the same category.

The situation changed dramatically in 1961, when Burton Watson's monumental 2-volume translation known as *Records of the Grand Historian of China* was published by Columbia University Press with fifty-six fully translated and nine partly translated chapters from the *Shiji*. Most of the chapters deal with the Han Dynasty. In 1969, Columbia University Press issued a paperback edition, entitled *Records of the Historian, Chapters from the* Shi chi *of Ssu-ma Ch'ien*, with fourteen chapters from the original 2-volume work plus five newly translated ones dealing with the pre-Han period. Finally, in 1993 The Research Centre for Translation of The Chinese University of Hong Kong and Columbia University Press jointly published Watson's third volume of translations from the *Shiji* with ten full and three partial chapters all dealing with the Qin Dynasty under the title, *Records of the Grand Historian: Qin Dynasty*. At the same time, a revised version of the original 2-volume translation using the new romanization system of *pinyin* was also published by the two organizations. Thus altogether now Watson has translated seventy-one chapters in full and twelve chapters in part of the one hundred and thirty chapters into English—a truly remarkable feat for a single translator. What is even more remarkable is that the first two volumes were done in just a little over three years as he tells us in his essay "The *Shi Chi* and I" [6]— much less than the thirty years Professor Francis Cleaves of Harvard envisioned for him.

Watson's interest in the *Shiji* has been deep and enduring. His first serious encounter with the *Shiji*, he tells us in the aforementioned *CLEAR* essay, came in the fall of 1950, "when I was working toward an MA degree in Chinese studies at Columbia University and casting around for a topic for my MA essay." [7] He finally settled on the two respective chapters on the *yu-hsia* or "wandering knights" in the *Shih Chi* (*Shiji*) and *Han Shu* and did a translation and study of both in 1951—well over forty years

---

[5] Wiesbaden: Otto Harrassowitz, 1962.
[6] Watson, *Chinese Literature: Essays, Articles, Reviews* 17, (1995): 199-206. Hereafter referred to as *CLEAR* essay.
[7] Watson, *CLEAR*, 199.

before the appearance of the third volume of his *Records of the Grand Historian* in 1993. Five years later, in 1956, he finished writing a Ph.D. dissertation on Sima Qian, the historian himself, which was subsequently published by Columbia University Press under the title *Ssu-ma Ch'ien: Grand Historian of China* in 1958. Given his long-term relationship with the *Shiji* and his solid grounding in its scholarship, had Watson chosen to do so, he would have been able to produce a fully annotated translation of the work—the kind the sinological field is more accustomed to. But as Professor Wm. Theodore de Bary points out in his Foreword to Watson's 1961 translation, it is meant primarily for the general reader rather than other specialists: "This translation has been undertaken for the Columbia College Program of Translations from the Oriental Classics in the belief that Ssu-ma Ch'ien's monumental *Shih chi*... can be read not only as history but as literature, and not by the China specialist alone but by the educated reader in general."[8] Accordingly, Watson's main concern in his translation is readability and literary effect as he writes in his Introduction to his original 2-volume work:

> "In the two thousand years since its appearance, the *Shih chi* has been widely and affectionately read not only by educated Chinese but by men of learning in Korea and Japan, as well. The reason for its continued popularity and incalculable influence it has had upon the literatures of these countries lies undoubtedly in its moving portraits of the great men of the past, its dramatic episodes and deft anecdotes. Accordingly, it is these aspects of the *Shih chi*—giving it interest as a collection of good stories—which I have been most concerned to reproduce in the translation."[9]

Notes and annotation are thus kept to a minimum.

To do a translation of a classical text like the *Shiji* for a general reading public, however, is easier said than done. First of all, as Watson points out in the same Introduction, "Classical Chinese... is capable of a breathtaking economy and vigor of expression. Chinese historians in particular prize terseness above almost any other quality of style, and though the *Shih chi* is relatively verbose compared to other early historical works, its narrative still maintains a swiftness and leanness that can seldom be produced in another language."[10] Then there are the plethora of names and titles by which the main figures are referred to at various times and the elaborate set of pronouns and polite terms of address found in direct discourse. In

---

[8] Burton Watson, *Records of the Grand Historian of China* (New York: Columbia University Press, 1961), vii.
[9] Watson, *Records of the Grand Historian of China*, 6.
[10] Watson, *Records of the Grand Historian of China*, 6.

addition, there are set formulas in the original, "such as the ubiquitous 'he said' or 'he asked saying'." To overcome these obstacles, Watson decided to sacrifice "strict fidelity to readability."[11] In the case of formulaic expressions, for example, he has attempted to vary in his renderings because while good Chinese permits such formulas, good English demands variety, "and it seems pointless, merely for the sake of literalness, to make Ssu-ma Ch'ien sound like a clumsy schoolboy."[12] And in the case of allusions with hidden meanings (or perhaps, we should add, elliptical sentences as well), "I have, as Robert Graves would say, 'brought up' into the translation whatever information is necessary to make their meaning comprehensible."[13]

However, according to Watson, most reviewers seem to have failed to see what he was trying to do and had thus taken him to task for his "unscholarly approach to the text" and particularly for "the paucity of annotation."[14] Watson seems to have anticipated such criticisms as he says almost in self-defense in the same Introduction mentioned above, "… any attempt to please all readers, specialists and non-specialists alike, would almost certainly end by pleasing none. Michael Grant, in the introduction to his translation of Tacitus' *Annals*, states his opinion that 'except as a mere crib, an unreadable translation is useless.' Though the wording is perhaps a bit drastic, I fully agree with this dictum in principle, and ask the reader to keep it in mind in judging what follows."[15]

For an author, perhaps nothing is more frustrating than to have one's objective in writing misunderstood or simply ignored. Writing thirty some years later in the *CLEAR* essay, "The *Shih Chi* and I," already referred to above, Watson still feels the urge to devote considerable space in explaining his purpose in translation. He tells us how he struggled with both the Chinese and the English when he was translating the chapters on the *yuxia* from the *Shiji* and *Hanshu*, respectively, under the stern guidance of Professor Chi-chen Wang who, as an acclaimed translator of traditional and modern Chinese literature himself, not only found fault with his understanding of Classical Chinese, but also "had little patience with my often painfully literal renderings of the *Shih Chi* and *Han Shu* texts."[16] He goes on:

---

[11] Watson, *Records of the Grand Historian of China*, 6.
[12] Watson, *Records of the Grand Historian of China*, 7.
[13] Watson, *Records of the Grand Historian of China*, 7.
[14] Watson, *CLEAR*, 203.
[15] Watson, *Records of the Grand Historian of China*, 8.
[16] Watson, *CLEAR*, 199.

"The hours spent with him that year left me with the conviction that in translating such texts, it is not enough merely to bring across the meaning of the Chinese; one must do so in a manner that reads like natural, idiomatic English. This conviction has remained with me through the years and informed all my work as a translator of Chinese and Japanese. I am of course aware that there are other approaches to the task of translation, doubtless valid in their own way. But I have never wavered in my dedication to this one."[17]

He also tells us in the essay how Homer H. Dubs' "lumbering and bracket-ridden" [18] translation of the *Hanshu* served as a negative example for him:

"My approach to *Shih Chi* translation was very much influenced, mostly in a negative way, by Professor Homer H. Dubs' three volumes of translation from the *Han Shu*. In my youthful intolerance, I was outraged by what struck me as the extremely stiff and awkward tone of the translation, which seemed to constitute an affront both to the nobility of Pan Ku's original and to the spirit of the English language. I was determined that, if I could not make Ssu-ma Ch'ien sound like a Gibbon or a Macaulay, I would at least do my best to render him in language that suggested the work of a major stylist."[19]

He is aware of the importance of a more scholarly translation of the *Shiji*, he says, but to him style remains paramount:

"I think, particularly now that I am a good deal older, that I can appreciate the importance and excellence of Dubs' work; and, as I have indicated elsewhere, I am fully aware of the need for a scholarly and copiously annotated translation of the *Shih Chi* such as Dubs produced for the *Han Shu* chapters, and that Professor Nienhauser and his colleagues are now in the process of producing. Despite the undeniable usefulness of Dubs' translation, however, I have never quite been able to overcome my initial antipathy to the woodenness of his language."[20]

The aspects of *Shiji*'s style that Watson is most interested in capturing in his translation are what he calls the "epic or operatic quality in the dramatic sweep" of its narratives, "the rhythm of their reiterated cycles of

---

[17] Watson, *CLEAR*, 199.
[18] Burton Watson, "Some Remarks on Early Chinese Historical Works," in *The Translation of Things Past: Chinese History and Historiography*, ed. George Kao (Hong Kong: The Chinese University Press, 1982), 36.
[19] Watson, *CLEAR*, 202.
[20] Watson, *CLEAR*, 202.

florescence and decay, and the sonority of their language." The end result may be just a "pale reflection" of the beauty and power in the original, as Watson acknowledges a point made by one of his reviewers. Still, he hopes that other readers of his translation "have not only been able to appreciate the factual flow of the narratives, but have also caught some of the music that I was endeavoring to convey."[21]

For all his emphasis on style and literary effect, Watson does not neglect the importance of a good grasp of the meaning of the original based on sound textual scholarship. For this, he has the solid scholarship of the many China scholars in Japan to thank. As he states in the Translator's Note on the Text that precedes the various editions of his translation, he followed mainly the text of the *Shiji* as it appears in the edition entitled *Shiki kaichu kosho* (1934), edited and with a commentary in Chinese by Takikawa Kametaro, while consulting the various new modern-language Japanese translations. Anyone who has made an effort to check Watson's translations against the original would be impressed by his overall accuracy. In fact, as he says in the *CLEAR* essay, he actually had more trouble with his English than the Chinese of the original: "My real problems in translation... were not so much with the Chinese of the original—I was not interested in putting forth any innovative interpretations, but simply in rendering the text as it had traditionally been understood in China and the countries in the Chinese cultural sphere—as with the appropriate type of English to be employed."[22] Maybe this is why, as we have seen above, the reviewers can criticize him for his "unscholarly approach," but cannot really attack him for his command of the original language. Both his *Records of the Grand Historian of China* in two volumes and his *Records of the Historian, Chapters from the* Shih chi *of Ssu-ma Ch'ien* are included in the Columbia College Program of Translations from the Oriental Classics series. According to the Foreword to the latter title, the purpose of the series "is to provide translations based on scholarly study but written for the general reader rather than primarily for other specialists." It would be difficult to find a more apt characterization of Watson's two translations.

Not long after the appearance of Watson's one volume paperback edition of *Records of the Historian* in 1969, two collections of translations from the *Shiji* appeared in 1974: Yang Hsien-yi and Gladys Yang's translation also known as *Records of the Historian* [23] and William Dolby

[21] Watson, *CLEAR*, 205-206.
[22] Watson, *CLEAR*, 203.
[23] Hong Kong: Commercial Press.

and John Scott's *War-Lords*.[24] Based on Wang Boxiang's 王伯祥 *Shiji xuan* 《史記選》 (1957), the Yangs' work contains altogether thirty-one chapters from the original—"two of the Basic Annals, five of the Hereditary Houses, and Twenty-four Lives."[25] Dolby and Scott's work, on the other hand, contains only seven chapters (Chapters 65, 75, 76, 77, 78, 86, 126) from the original. Like Watson's, both titles are meant for the general reading public with minimal annotation.

Writing in 1962 in an article entitled "The Present State of the Translations from the Shih chi," Timoteus Pokora expresses the hope that someday a scholarly full translation of the *Shiji* would be undertaken. "But what is most needed," he remarks, "is a new full translation of the *Shih chi* which should be executed preferably under the auspices of some learned body according to the high standards reached by the best translators."[26] Almost as though in response to this call for action, William H. Nienhauser, Jr. and his collaborators started publishing in 1994 their gigantic project of a fully annotated translation of the entire *Shiji* under the title *The Grand Scribe's Records*. So far five of the projected nine volumes have been published by Indiana University Press in the following sequence:

Volume I	The Basic Annals of Pre-Han China (1994)
Volume VII	The Memoirs of Pre-Han China (1994)
Volume II	The Basic Annals of Han China (2002)
Volume VI	The Hereditary Houses of Pre-Han China, Part 1 (2006)
Volume VIII	The Memoirs of Han China (2008).

In addition to footnotes which sometimes can take up more space than the individual texts themselves, the translation is laden with an elaborate scholarly apparatus. In Volume I, for example, we have an Introduction that consists in six parts: Prolegomena, The Authors of the *Shih chi*, Reception of the *Shih chi* (A. History of the Text; B. Modern Translations of the Text), History and Description of Our Project, A Brief Comment on Ssu-ma Ch'ien's Historiography, and The *Pen-chi* as a Genre. This is followed by four sections entitled On Using This Book, A Note on Chronology, Weights and Measures, and List of Abbreviations. In the main text, each translation is followed by a Translator's Note and a short

---

[24] Edinburgh: Southside.
[25] Yang Hsien-yi and Gladys Yang, *Records of the Historian* (Hong Kong: Commercial Press, 1974), vi.
[26] *Oriens Extremes* 9, 157.

Bibliography. "The former may provide a summary of analyses from traditional commentators, point out problems in the text, or discuss its relations to other chapters. The latter includes the major studies and translations."[27] The volume ends with a general bibliography, an index, and maps. The general bibliography is further divided into eight parts: Texts of *Shih chi*, Reference Works on *Shih chi*, Translations of *Shih chi*, Commentaries on *Shih chi*, Studies of *Shih chi* and Ssu-ma Ch'ien, Comparisons of *Shih chi* and *Han shu*, Other Chinese and Japanese Works, and Other Western Language Works. The other volumes follow more or less the same format.

The first two volumes (I and VII) were the results of truly collaborative work as we are told in the Introduction to Volume I, "Our normal procedure is for each of the translators to prepare several drafts during the academic year. These translations are distributed to the other participants and, after we have all had a chance to study the texts and offer written comments on each other's work, we meet to discuss problems and to revise the translation."[28] Sometimes, as we learn in the Introduction to Volume VII, drafts of a number of chapters were also sent to various colleagues elsewhere with expertise in the *Shih chi* for comments and suggestions.[29] This procedure seems to have undergone some change in subsequent volumes. In Volume II, for example, names of authors for all the translations as well as the Introduction and other paraphernalia are specified. A highly useful selection of a still expanding Glossary of the most often used and/or troublesome terms is also added.

From what we have seen above, the two respective translations of the *Shiji* by Watson and Nienhauser et al. could not be more different in approach and style. To make this more apparent, let us cite for illustration one passage from Chapter 61 ("The Biography of Bo Yi") in the original accompanied by the two translations (with Nienhauser's first):

---

[27] William Nienhauser, Jr., *The Grand Scribe's Records*, Vol. I (Bloomington: Indiana University Press, 1994), xxv.
[28] Nienhauser, *The Grand Scribe's Records*, Vol. I, vxii.
[29] William Nienhauser, Jr., *The Grand Scribe's Records*, Vol. VII (Bloomington: Indiana University Press, 1994), ix.

或曰：「天道無親，常與善人。」若伯夷、叔齊，可謂善人者非邪？
積仁絜行如此而餓死！且七十子之徒，仲尼獨薦顏淵為好學。然回也
屢空，糟糠不厭，而卒蚤夭。天之報施善人，其何如哉？盜蹠日殺不
辜，肝人之肉，暴戾恣睢，聚黨數千人橫行天下，竟以壽終。是遵何
德哉？此其尤大彰明較著者也。若至近世，操行不軌，專犯忌諱，而
終身逸樂，富厚累世不絕。或擇地而蹈之，時然後出言，行不由徑，
非公正不發憤，而遇禍災者，不可勝數也。余甚惑焉，儻所謂天道，
是邪非邪？（《史記・伯夷列傳第一》）

    "Some say, 'Heaven's way favors none, but always sides with good men.'[29] Can men such as Po Yi and Shu Ch'i be called good then, or bad? They accumulated such virtue, kept their actions this pure, and died of starvation."

    "Of his seventy disciples, Confucius recommended only Yen Yuan 顏 淵 as 'fond of learning.'[30] But 'Hui 回 [Yen Yuan] was often poor,' and did not get his fill of even rice dregs and husks, finally dying young.[31] How then does Heaven repay good men?"

    "The Bandit Chih 盜跖 killed innocent men daily, made delicacies from men's flesh,[32] was cruel and ruthless, willful and arrogant, gathered a band of thousands of men and wreaked havoc across the world, yet finally died of old age.[33] From what virtue did this follow?"

    "These are just the most notorious and best known examples. As for more recent times, men who do not follow what is proper in their actions, and do nothing but violate taboos are still carefree and happy for all their lives and wealthy for generations without end; men who choose carefully how they tread, wait for the right time to offer their words,[34] in walking do not take shortcuts,[35] and except for what is right and fair do not vent pent-up emotions, still encounter disaster and catastrophe in numbers beyond counting. I am deeply perplexed by all this. Perhaps this is what is meant by 'the Way of Heaven.' Is it? Or isn't it?"[36]

---

[29] *Lao Tzu*, section 79. Wang Shu-min (61: 2000) cites several other pre-Ch'in and early Han works which express similar sentiments.

[30] In *Lun yü*, 6/3 and 11/7.

[31] See *Lun yü*, 11/7 and 11/18; on Yen Yüan see also *Shih chi* Chapter 67.

[32] The phrase *kan jen chih jou* 肝人之肉 is difficult to interpret. The "Tao-chih" 盜跖 chapter of *Chuang Tzu* (9:18a, *SPPY*) says "[he] minced men's livers and ate them." 膾人肝而餔之. Takigawa (61:12) would thus read *kan* 肝 in the *Shih chi* as an error for *kuai* 膾. Our translation is an attempt to take *kan* in a putative sense: "he treated men's flesh as [a delicacy or snack similar to] liver."

[33] The Bandit Chih is a stock figure in philosophical literature of the Warring States period. The longest essay on him is found in chapter 29 of the *Chuang Tzu* (9:17b-25a, *SPPY*). We have found no other reference to

the Bandit Chih dying of old age. The "P'ien-mu" 駢拇 chapter of *Chuang Tzu* (4:4b, *SPPY*) says that "the Bandit Chih died for the sake of profit on the Eastern Hill," contradicting Ssu-ma Ch'ien's claim.
[34] Perhaps derived from *Lun yü*, 14/13: "The master waited for the right time and only then spoke."
[35] *Lun yü*, 6/14.
[36] The interpretation of the word *tang* 儻 is problematic. One common meaning of *tang* is "if." This would require us to read *so-wei t'ien Tao* 所謂天道 as one clause, and *shih yeh fei yeh* 是邪非邪 as a second clause: "If this is the so-called Way of Heaven, is it right, or wrong?" This is the most common interpretation. Another meaning for *tang*, however, is "perhaps." Thus "Cheng-yi" says "*tang* is a particle indicating uncertainty." 儻，未定之詞。Such a usage is also found in *Shih chi*, 47:1914: "Although Pi is small, perhaps it is close enough!" 今費雖小，儻庶幾乎 (see also Wang Yin-chih 王引之 *Ching-chuan shih-tz'u* 經傳釋詞 [Peking, Chuang-hua shu-chü, 1956], p. 138). Our translation follows this interpretation. Wang Shu-min (61:2006) notes that a T'ang mss. of this chapter reads 儻所謂天道邪，非是邪, but regards this as an error for 儻所謂天道，是邪，非邪。

[30]

Some people say, "It is Heaven's way to have no favorites but always to be on the side of the good man."[6] Can we say then that Po Yi and Shu Ch'i were good men or not? They piled up a record for goodness and were pure in deed, as we have seen, and yet they starved to death.

Of his seventy disciples, Confucius singled out Yen Hui for praise because of his diligence in learning, yet Yen Hui was often in want, never getting his fill of even the poorest food, and in the end he suffered an untimely death. Is this the way Heaven rewards the good man?

Robber Chih day after day killed innocent men, making mincemeat of their flesh. Cruel and willful, he gathered a band of several thousand followers who went about terrorizing the world, but in the end he lived to a ripe old age. For what virtue did he deserve this?

These are only the most obvious and striking examples. Even in more recent times we see that men whose conduct departs from what is prescribed and who do nothing but violate the taboos and prohibitions enjoy luxury and wealth to the end of their lives, and hand them on to their heirs for generations without end. And there are others who carefully choose the spot where they will place each footstep, who "speak out only when it is time to speak," who "walk no bypaths"[7] and expend no anger on what is not upright and just, and yet, in numbers too great to be reckoned,

---

[30] Nienhauser, *The Grand Scribe's Records,* Vol. VII, 4.

they meet with misfortune and disaster. I find myself in much perplexity. Is this so-called Way of Heaven right or wrong?

6 *Tao-te-ching* 79.
7 *Analects* XIV, I4; VI, I2

31

"The Biography of Bo Yi" is the first in the biography or memoir section. After providing the little information that was known of the high-principled Bo Yi and his brother Shu Qi, who chose to starve themselves to death rather than serve under the new and what they considered violent dynasty of Zhou, Sima Qian took the opportunity to raise a tough and unsettling question about justice in life. Given the terribly unfair punishment that befell Sima Qian himself, it is highly significant to see him raise such a provocative question at the very beginning of the biography section. For our immediate purpose here, however, let us just do a quick comparison between the two translations in terms of approach and style.

Niehhauser and his colleagues' translation demonstrates clearly a more scholarly approach. There are eight notes to their translation, including 3 long ones (notes 32, 33, and 36), compared to only two short ones to Watson's. Typical of a scholarly translation, Nienhauser's tends to be more literal overall. For example, Confucius' favorite disciple is referred to in paragraph 2 first as Yen Yuan and then as Hui. Nienhauser follows the original faithfully but adds the name Yen Yuan in brackets after Hui to indicate that it is the same person, whereas Watson simply uses the name Yen Hui in both places. Similarly, following the word order of the original, Nienhauser puts the phrase "in numbers beyond counting" at the end of a long sentence toward the end of the final paragraph, whereas Watson breaks up the sentence into two and places his rendering of the phrase—"in numbers too great to be reckoned"—before the second sentence. "From what virtue did this follow?" at the end of paragraph 3 in Nienhauser, to give another example, is a more exact translation than Watson's freer but clearer and more readable "For what virtue did he deserve this?" In places where different interpretations of individual words exist, such as the meaning of *gan* "肝" in the third paragraph and that of *tang* "儻" at the end of the final paragraph, notes are provided by Nienhauser to explain why a particular reading is adopted in their translation. By contrast, with problematic words such as *gan* and *tang*

---

[31] Burton Watson, *Records of the Historian* (New York: Columbia University Press, 1969), 13-14.

Watson would simply choose a reading suitable to his purpose without any explanation. Sometimes, to avoid awkwardness and ensure the natural flow of his narrative, he would give a looser rendering instead. Thus for Nienhauser's "rice dregs and husks" in paragraph 2, which is a literal rendering of *zaokang* "糟糠" in the original, he just has "the poorest food." In fact, sometimes, in order to accomplish his purpose, he would even add things not found in the original, such as the phrase "as we have seen" toward the end of the first paragraph. As a result, Watson's language sounds more idiomatic and fluent, and gives a good approximation of Sima Qian's eloquent and emotion-laden questioning in the original. Overall, there is a natural, smooth, and melodious quality to Watson's translation that is missing in Nienhauser's more literal rendering.

Be this as it may, we have to conclude that both translations are well-done in accomplishing what hey have set out to do. Any evaluative comparison of the two would be quite pointless. Just as Watson has observed in a comment quoted above, there are different approaches to the task of translation, and they are "doubtless valid in their own way."[32] Moreover, Watson and Nienhauser themselves seem to have undertaken their respective translation task well aware of the limitations imposed by the approach they have each adopted. Watson, for example, writes not without some chagrin in "Some Remarks on the Early Chinese Historical Works" cited above:

> "In my translations from the *Shih chi* and *Han shu* I attempted to concentrate on the literary appeal of the works, keeping annotation to a minimum… Since the famous Greek and Roman historians are available to the general English reader in such translations, it seemed reasonable to me to present Ssu-ma Ch'ien and Pan Ku in the same fashion. What I failed to consider was that 'popular' translations of Greek and Roman historians are acceptable in English because scholarly and heavily annotated translations of such works already exist and can be consulted by those in search of more detailed information, whereas that of course is not the case with most Chinese historical works."[33]

This sentiment is repeated later in the *CLEAR* essay already cited several times above. When he was working on his translation in Kyoto, he informs us, several new modern language Japanese translations of the *Shiji* appeared:

---

[32] Watson, *CLEAR*, 199.
[33] Watson, "Some Remarks," 36.

"These translations, like the one I was preparing, had relatively little annotation and were designed for general readers, and they encouraged me to think that, if there was much demand for a modern language translation of the *Shih Chi* in Japan, there would surely be some sort of comparable demand for my translation in America. What I failed to consider, of course, was the fact that most educated Japanese have at least heard of the *Shih Chi* and have some idea of its importance, while this was not true of most readers of English in the 50s and 60s, if indeed it is now."[34]

Nienhauser, on his part, readily admits the sometimes awkward literalness in his translation in a short prefatory note to the Glossary in Volume II of his translation. He says: "This list is not intended to be complete, but rather a sampling of some of the most often and/or troublesome terms and phrases which should give the reader an idea of the sources of our admittedly sometimes awkward, but literal translations."[35]

At the same time, Nienhauser fully recognizes the value of Watson's translation. After citing the passage quoted earlier, in which Watson acknowledges the need of "a scholarly and heavily annotated" translation of the *Shiji*, he says: "Watson is too hard on himself. His translations of the *Shih chi*—as most of his work on early Chinese texts—have been vital in introducing this literature to the general English public while also serving scholars well. As Watson implies, however, 'scholarly and heavily annotated translations' would complement, not in any way replace, his own efforts."[36] In fact, Nienhauser has such high regard for Watson's achievement in the translation of the *Shiji* that he has dedicated Volume II of his own translation to him. In the Acknowledgements he writes:

"Finally, our debt of gratitude to Burton Watson has been clear from the first months we worked on this text nearly thirteen years ago. What is amazing about Burton Watson's translation work with the *Shih chi* is not that he did so much, but that he did so much so quickly. Like Chavannes, Watson's *Shih chi* work was his first major sinological project; yet within a little over three years (a period not unlike that which Chavannes devoted to the text) he had produced a masterpiece not only for Sinology, but for those general readers interested in China's most important history. This volume is dedicated to Professor Watson and his accomplishments in making the *Shih chi*... a part of world history."[37]

---

[34] Watson, *CLEAR*, 202-203.
[35] William Nienhauser, Jr., *The Grand Scribe's Records,* Vol. II (Bloomington: Indiana University Press, 2002), 269.
[36] Nienhauser, *The Grand Scribe's Records,* Vol. I, xviii-xix.
[37] Nienhauser, *The Grand Scribe's Records,* Vol. II, xi.

Nienhauser has said it well. In the final analysis, in terms of cultural interactions, which is the main theme of this conference, Professor Watson's translation, by its very nature, would most likely work better—especially if public interest in China's past ever catches on in the West. Still, we should be grateful for the more scholarly translation by Nienhauser himself and his collaborators: readers whose interest in the *Shiji* is aroused from reading Watson now finally may have a place to go to for more detailed information. We are indeed fortunate to have two translations of China's "most important history" complementing each other so nicely. We can only wish Professor Nienhauser and his colleagues Godspeed in completing their monumental undertaking.

SEARCH AND RE-SEARCH:
TRANSLATING *FAMOUS CHINESE SAYINGS QUOTED BY WEN JIABAO* INTO ENGLISH

CHAN SIN-WAI
DEPARTMENT OF TRANSLATION
THE CHINESE UNIVERSITY OF HONG KONG

我仰望星空，
它是那樣寥廓而深邃；
那無窮的真理，
讓我苦苦地求索、追隨。
我仰望星空，
它是那樣莊嚴而聖潔；
那凜然的正義，
讓我充滿熱愛、感到敬畏。
—溫家寶：〈仰望星空〉

I look up at the starry sky,
which is so vast and profound;
The infinite truth
attracts my persistent search and pursuit;
I look up at the starry sky,
which is so pure and dignified;
The awe-inspiring justice
commands my devotion and reverence.
— Wen Jiabao: "Looking up at the Starry Sky"

[I] Introduction

The idea of translating《溫家寶總理經典引句解說》(*An Explanation of the Classical Quotations Cited by Premier Wen Jiabao*) by Wang Chunyong 王春永 into English was initiated by Mr Zhai Defeng, Managing Director and Chief Editor of Chung Hwa Book Co. (H.K.) Ltd. in December 2008. I was given five months to translate the entire book, single-handedly or with the help of colleagues, so that it could feature on the China Exhibition Stand at the Frankfurt Book Fair, which had China as the Guest of Honour for the first time.

As the annual book fair was to be held from 14 to 18 October 2009, the actual translating of the book began in April, the plan being to complete the translation in mid-June to allow time for the printing and production of the book. In the process of translating the book, the methods of search and re-search, mostly in the computational sense, have clearly been used to help complete the translation work. This paper, therefore, examines the role of technology in translating a book on a prominent Chinese leader. Before sharing my experience in translating Wen Jiabao, perhaps it would be useful to examine the reasons for translating quotations cited by the Chinese Premier, and how these quotations have been treated in the book.

[II] Reasons for Translating Quotations Cited by Wen Jiabao

There are at least two reasons for translating the quotations cited by Wen Jiabao into English. Firstly, Wen is a man of integrity and noble character and his quotations reflect his great love for China and his fellow compatriots. As stated by Zhai Defang in his preface:

> Premier Wen is a man of noble character and integrity. He always acts for the benefit of the country and the people regardless of the personal cost. He is able to freely express his views on various occasions by an appropriate reference to the classics in a manner befitting the premier of a large country. It is this latter point that has become the feature of Premier Wen's public speeches and the focus of attention of local and foreign reporters.[1]

Secondly, Wen Jiabao is a learned person who is capable of transmitting Chinese culture to the world through his quotations. It was mentioned in the book that a student of Renmin University said to Wen Jiabao when he visited the University: "In your speeches, you often cite poems and prose, and you have great literary attainments."[2] It has often been pointed out that the scholarly premier usually prefers to use poems to express his feelings. No wonder the *Times* stated that "Wen Jiabao is the only leader in China who can, after Mao Zedong, show his profound knowledge of classical Chinese literature in public." In his Preface, Zhai

---

[1] Chan Sin-wai, trans., *Famous Chinese Sayings Quoted by Wen Jiabao* (Hong Kong: Chung Hwa Book Co. (H.K.) Ltd., 2009), 3.
[2] Chan, *Famous Chinese Sayings*, 43.

also points out that:

> He is able to freely express his views on various occasions by an appropriate reference to the classics in a manner befitting the premier of a large country. It is this latter point that has become the feature of Premier Wen's public speeches and the focus of attention of local and foreign reporters.
>
> Whether on the ever-changing world stage or at press conferences in China's Great Hall of the People, Premier Wen naturally and effortlessly quotes famous poems and lines of the ancient sages of China and other countries. With a mild manner, this leader of China, by speaking freely and elegantly to the world, reveals the longstanding culture and tradition of the Chinese people.[3]

This is also evident in the remarks made by Wang Chunyong:

> As a statesman, Wen Jiabao fully understands the idea of literature being a vehicle of the Way. As the premier of a large country, he is immersed in a myriad of state affairs every day. But he never forgets to re-read the classics, and frequently quotes famous poems to explain his ideas. This is far more effective than lecturing with a stern face.[4]

His knowledge of classical Chinese might have a lot to do with his family education. The grandfather, father and mother of Wen Jiabao were teachers. His grandfather Wen Yingshi 溫瀛士, who founded the Puyu Private Primary School for Girls, was engaged in education all his life. He fostered a team of primary teachers loyal to education, including his eldest son Wen Gang 溫剛 and his wife Yang Xiuan 楊秀安 (parents of Wen Jiabao), his second eldest son Wen Qiang 溫強, and his five daughters, including Wen Keqin 溫克勤, Wen Keqian 溫克儉, Wen Keran 溫克讓, Wen Keliang 溫克良, and Wen Kezhuang 溫克莊. Brought up in a family of teachers, Wen Jiabao is well versed in Chinese classics and has great expectations of teachers, as shown by his speech on the Teachers' Day on 9 September 2008:

> I would like to take this opportunity to express my hopes to teachers. First, they must have high aspirations, love their country and respect their profession. Second, to be a teacher, to teach and educate people, they must make efforts to learn so as to teach others, and act so as to serve as an example to all. Teachers should conscientiously enhance their moral

---

3 Chan, *Famous Chinese Sayings*, iii-iv.
4 Chan, *Famous Chinese Sayings*, 185.

cultivation to set a model, educate and influence students with their noble character, make efforts to be good teachers and friends to their teenage students, and be respected by the entire society. Third, be inspective in learning and advance with the times. Teachers are important transmitters and creators of knowledge, and linked to the past, present, and future of the progress of civilization. They should keep pace with the times, continue to enrich themselves with new knowledge, and become models for those who love to learn.[5]

[III] A Textual Analysis of the Chinese and English Versions of the Book

As the English version of the Chinese original text has undergone considerable changes, it is necessary to make an analysis of the textual differences before translating. We will look at the structure of the book, the changes made, the popularity of the quotations, the modifications of the quotations, and the authors and works quoted in the book.

(1) Structure of the Book

The book 《溫家寶總理經典引句解說》 (*An Explanation of the Classical Quotations Cited by Premier Wen Jiabao*) by Wang Chunyong 王春永 has 120 articles in seven parts. The seven parts, which are given below, remain the same for both the Chinese original and its English translation.

Part 1: Feelings and Aspirations 情懷・抱負
Part 2: Responsibilities and Hardships 責任・憂患
Part 3: Economy and Livelihood 經濟・民生
Part 4: Education and Culture 教育・文化
Part 5: Democracy and Listening to the People 民主・納言
Part 6: Across the Taiwan Straits, Hong Kong and Macao 兩岸・港澳
Part 7: The International Situation and Diplomatic Relations 國際・邦交

The structure of each article is also the same. Each article begins with a numeral. This is followed by a quotation. Then the article has four sections. Section One is "Source and Explanation" (*chu chu ji shi yi* 出處及釋義),

---

[5] Chan, *Famous Chinese Sayings*, 187-88.

citing the original source of the quotation, author of the source, and title of the source, with a modern Chinese translation of the cited classical source. Section Two is "About the Author" (*zuo zhe jian jie* 作者簡介), introducing the author of the quotation. Section Three is "Background to the Quotation" (*yin ju bei jing* 引句背景), describing the specific context in which Wen Jiabao cited the quotation. The last section, Section Four, is "Remarks" (*yi jing dian ping* 意境點評) in which the vision and conception of Premier Wen are explained by the author.

It occurred to the translator that it was not necessary to translate the *shi yi* 釋義 (Explanation) into English. As the target readers are no longer the Chinese-reading but the English-reading public, there is no need to translate the modern Chinese version of the classical source. The quotation of Article 8 is given as an example:

(8) 先天下之憂而憂，後天下之樂而樂。

[出處及釋義]
嗟夫！予嘗求古仁人之心，或異二者之為，何哉？不以物喜，不以己悲；居廟堂之高則憂其民；處江湖之遠則憂其君。是進亦憂，退亦憂。然則何時而樂耶？其必曰「先天下之憂而憂，後天下之樂而樂」乎。噫！微斯人，吾誰與歸？

              — 范仲淹〈岳陽樓記〉

我曾經探求古代品德高尚的人的思想感情，或許跟上面說的兩種思想感情的表現不同，為什麼呢？他們不因為環境好而高興，也不因為自己遭遇而悲傷；在朝廷裏做高官就擔憂他的百姓；處在僻遠的江湖間就擔憂他的君王。這就是進入朝廷做官也擔憂。那麼什麼時候才快樂呢？他們大概一定會說：「在天下人憂愁之先就憂愁，在天下人快樂之後才快樂」吧？唉！如果沒有這種人，我同誰一道呢？[6]

Despite the fact that the quality of this piece of intralingual translation may not be totally acceptable, it is by and large comprehensible. There is no need to translate both the Chinese source and its modern version. The English version is as follows:

---

[6] Wang Chunyong 王春永，《溫家寶總理經典引句解說》(*An Explanation of the Classical Quotations Cited by Premier Wen Jiabao*) (Hong Kong: Chung Hwa Book Co. (H.K.) Ltd. 中華書局（香港）有限公司, 2008), 18-19.

(8) To worry before the whole world worries, and to rejoice after the whole world rejoices

[Source]
But again when I consider the old men who possessed true humanity, they seem to have responded quite differently. The reason may be this: natural beauty was not enough to make them happy, nor their own situation enough to make them sad. When such men are high in the government or at court, their first concern is for their sovereign. Thus they worry both when in office and when in retirement. When, then, can they enjoy themselves in life? No doubt they are worried before the whole world worries and they rejoice after the whole world rejoices. Surely these are the men whose footsteps I should follow.
—Fan Zhongyan, "On Yueyang Tower"

(2) Changes Made to the Contents of the English Version

Before the work of translation began in March, it was decided by the editor of Chung Hwa Book Company that it was necessary to make several changes to the book's contents. The articles to be removed, replaced or amended include the following:

(18) We should never shy away from difficult decisions 事不避難；
(28) We need to be cautious and prudent 尤須兢慎；
(30) The causes of concern 憂患與故；
(31) When you know it is difficult, it may be less difficult 知難不難；
(34) Concern about adversity will lead to a solution 患生治；
(40) People are the basis of a nation 民為邦本；
(44) If we knew the economics of being poor 如果你懂得了窮人的經濟學；
(49) View the light of the country 觀國之光；
(63) The mystic chords of memory 記憶的神秘琴弦；
(75) All men are created equal 人生而平等；
(76) The free development of everyone 每個人的自由發展；
(91) A house divided against itself will not stand 自相分裂的家庭是站立不住的；
(92) The narrow Taiwan Strait is the deepest sadness for our nation 淺淺的海峽，是最大的國殤;
(93) Only when the blood of the native son flows back to his native place will it stop boiling 原鄉人的血，必須流返原鄉，才會停止沸騰;
(98) A distant relative is not as good as a near neighbour 遠親不如近鄰；
(117) No matter how far you go, your heart is always linked with your

homeland 無論你走得多麼遠，你的心總和我連在一起；

(118) Leaves must be green in Spring 樹木逢春便會綠葉招展；

(119) To build a bridge for knowledge and skills interflow for peoples in distant places 在距離遙遠的民族間建設一座相互交流的知識與技能的橋樑；

(120) This chance exists only instantly 這個機會只存在瞬間。

These editorial changes are understandable as the editors believed that the English version should include only quotations by Chinese authors. In other words, the original Chinese title of this book,《溫家寶總理經典引句解說》(*An Explanation of the Classical Quotations Cited by Premier Wen Jiabao*), has now been changed to《溫家寶所引用的中國經典名句》(*Famous Chinese Sayings Quoted by Wen Jiabao*). It was on this rationale that quotations from foreign sources were removed:

(44) "If we knew the economics of being poor" by Theodore W. Schultz (German);

(63) "The mystic chords of memory" by Abraham Lincoln (American);

(75) "All men are created equal" by Thomas Jefferson (American);

(76) "The free development of everyone" by Karl Marx (German);

(91) "A house divided against itself will not stand" by Abraham Lincoln (American);

(117) "No matter how far you go, your heart is always linked with your homeland" by Kalidasa (Indian);

(118) "Leaves must be green in Spring" by Herman Melville (American);

(119) "To build a bridge for knowledge and skills interflow for peoples in distant places" by Gottfried Wilhelm Leibniz (German);

(120) "This chance exists only instantly" by Johann Wolfgang von Goethe (German).

A total of nine quotations by three Americans, four Germans, and one Indian, had been deleted from the book. One possible explanation of the removal of six quotations from Chinese classical works, i.e., (18) We should never shy away from difficult decisions 事不避難；(28) We need to be cautious and prudent 尤須兢慎；(30) The causes of concern 憂患與故；(31) When you know it is difficult, it may be less difficult 知難不難；(34) Concern about adversity will lead to a solution 患生治, is that some of the ideas expressed in these quotations have been covered by other similar expressions. The only quotation that was kept is (40) People are the basis of a nation 民為邦本. But it was changed to read (39) People are the basis of a nation, and only when this basis is stable can the nation enjoy peace 民為邦本，本固邦寧。

In mid-May, some additional quotations were sent for translation. These quotations included:

(1) I have devoted my life to serving the people and will always do my best in the service 鞠躬盡瘁，死而後已;

(2) A spring silkworm keeps producing silk until it dies; a candle keeps giving light until it burns into ashes 春蠶到死絲方盡，蠟炬成灰淚始乾;

(3) A fire on the city gate brings disaster to the fish in the moat 城門失火，殃及池魚;

(4) Its rise is quick; its fall is sudden 其興也勃，其亡也忽;

(5) Don't say that this year's spring is about to end, as the scenery of spring will be twice as enchanting next year 莫道今年春將盡，明年春色倍還人;

(6) It would be better to obtain a fire-maker than beg for fire, better to dig a well ourselves than beg for water from others 乞火不若取燧，寄汲不若鑿井;

(7)Where the hills and streams end and there seems no road beyond, amidst shading willows and blooming flowers there is another village 山重水複疑無路，柳暗花明又一村;

(8) Long-lasting is the spacious heaven, deep are my home feelings 悠悠天宇曠，切切故鄉情;

(9) All people are my brothers and sisters, and all things are my companions 民胞物與;

(10) The side that has superiors and subordinates united in heart will take the victory 上下同心者勝;

(11) Safety or danger does not alter one's will; difficulty or ease does not change one's mind 安危不貳其志，險易不革其心;

(12) From shore to shore it is wide and surgeless, and under a fair wind a sail is lifting 潮平兩岸闊，風正一帆懸;

(13) We should have amity among people and friendly exchanges among nations 百姓昭明，協和萬邦;

(14) Those who are in official positions should be courageous to shoulder responsibilities and should not avoid difficulties 居官者當事不避難;

(15) Crossing the river in the same boat in the gale, one would go to each other's aid like the right hand helping the left 當其同舟而濟，遇風，其相救也如左右手;

(16) People are the basis of a nation, and only when this basis is stable can the nation enjoy peace 民惟邦本，本固邦寧;

(17) Literature is a vehicle of the Way 文所以載道也;

(18) It is not too late to mend the fold even after some of the sheep have been lost 亡羊補牢，猶未為晚;

(19) I will not seek personal gains. But if the gains benefit the world, I will certainly seek them 利在一身勿謀也，利在天下必謀之;

(20) When the Great Way prevails, the world is for the public 大道之行
也，天下為公；

(21) All living creatures grow together without harming one another; ways
run parallel without interfering with one another 萬物並育而不相害，道並
行而不相悖；

(22) Learn, so as to teach others; act, so as to serve as an example to all 學
為人師，行為世範；

(23) If you don't move forward, you will fall behind 不進則退；

(24) A fall in the pit is a gain in your wit 吃一塹，長一智.

Several observations on these new additions of articles can be made.
Firstly, of the 24 additions, only Article 21 (re-numbered 122: All living
creatures grow together without harming one another; ways run parallel
without interfering with one another) was a quotation made in 2004. It was
added to highlight the importance of peaceful coexistence which is
China's basic norm governing state-to-state relations. Secondly, it should
be noted that the Chinese book was published in July 2008. Apart from
Article 20 (renumbered as Article 95: When the Great Way prevails, the
world is for the public), cited in mid-April 2008, Article 22 (renumbered
as Article 68: Learn, so as to teach others; act, so as to serve as an example
to all), published on 9 September 2008, Article 14 (renumbered as Article
34: Those who are in official positions should be courageous to shoulder
responsibilities and should not avoid difficulties), cited on 23 September,
and Article 18 (renumbered as Article 121: It is not too late to mend the
fold even after some of the sheep have been lost), cited on 28 October
2008, were additions for 2008 after the Chinese book was published.
Thirdly, 79.16 percent of the new additions, or 19 articles out of 24, were
quotations cited in 2009 so as to update the English version. These
quotations include Article 17 (renumbered as Article 67, cited on 16
January), Article 16 (renumbered Article 39, cited on 24 January), Article
24 (renumbered as Article 123, cited on 28 January), Article 8
(renumbered as Article 50, cited on 31 January), Article 9 (renumbered as
Article 64, cited on 31 January), Article 10 (renumbered as Article 48,
cited on 1 February), Article 11 (renumbered as Article 78, cited on 1
February), Article 12 (renumbered as Article 124, cited on 2 February),
Article 13 (renumbered as Article 101, cited on 2 February), Article 15
(renumbered as Article 120, cited on 21 February), Article 1 (renumbered
as Article 18, cited on 28 February), Article 2 (renumbered as Article 19,
cited on 28 February), Article 3 (renumbered as Article 46, cited on 28
February), Article 4 (renumbered as Article 30, cited on 28 February),
Article 5 (renumbered as Article 47, cited on 13 March), Article 6

(renumbered as Article 49, cited on 13 March), Article 7 (renumbered as Article 42, cited on 13 March), Article 23 (renumbered as Article 96, cited on 10 April), and Article 19 (renumbered as Article 94, cited on 18 April).

The above shows that a number of changes have been made in each part of the revised and enlarged version of the book as a result of the deletion and addition of articles.

For Part 1: "Feelings and Aspirations," all the articles in the original Chinese version were there, with the exception of Article 18: "事不避難 (We should never shy away from difficult decisions)." Two new articles were added. These included Article 18: "鞠躬盡瘁，死而後已 (I have devoted my life to serving the people and will always do my best in the service)." and Article 19: "春蠶到死絲方盡，蠟炬成灰淚始乾 (A spring silkworm keeps producing silk until it dies; a candle keeps giving light until it burns into ashes)."

For Part 2: "Responsibilities and Hardships," a number of changes were made. Article 28 (*orig*): "尤須兢慎 (We need to be cautious and prudent)," Article 30 (*orig*): "憂患與故 (The causes of concern)," Article 31(*orig*): "知難不難 (When you know it is difficult, it may be less difficult)," and Article 34 (*orig*): "患生治 (Concern about adversity will lead to solution)" were replaced by two new quotations in Article 29: "其興也勃，其亡也忽 (Its rise is quick; its fall is sudden)," and Article 34: "居官者當事不避難 (Those who are in official positions should be courageous to shoulder responsibilities and should not avoid difficulties)."

For Part 3: "Economy and Livelihood," more changes were made. Firstly, Article 40: "民為邦本 (People are the basis of a nation)" (*orig*) has been slightly revised to Article 39: "民為邦本，本固邦寧 (People are the basis of a nation, and only when this basis is stable can the nation enjoy peace)." Secondly, Article 44 (*orig*): "如果你懂得了窮人的經濟學 (If we knew the economics of being poor)," a quotation of Western source, has been removed. So was Article 45 (*orig*): "Go and ask the thawing land; Go and ask the thawing river." Thirdly, five new articles were added, which included Article 42: "山重水複疑無路，柳暗花明又一村 (Where the hills and streams end and there seems no road beyond, amidst shading willows and blooming flowers there is another village)," Article 46: "城門失火，殃及池魚 (A fire on the city gate brings disaster to the fish in the moat)," Article 47: "莫道今年春將盡，明年春色倍還人 (Don't say that this year's spring is about to end, as the scenery of spring will be twice as enchanting next year)," Article 48: "上下同心者勝 (The side that has superiors and subordinates united in heart will take the victory)," and Article 49: "乞火不若取燧，寄汲不若鑿井 (It would be better to obtain a fire-maker than beg for fire, better to dig a well ourselves than beg for water from others)."

For Part 4: "Education and Culture," the changes made were relatively few. Article 49 (*orig*): "觀國之光 (View the light of the country)" was removed as what is said in this article has been adequately covered by the following article (Article 50), the quotation of which is "讀萬卷書，行萬里路 (Read thousands of books and travel thousands of miles)." Article 45 (*orig*): "記憶的神秘琴弦 (The mystic chords of memory)," [7] as it came from the "First Inaugural Address" by American President Abraham Lincoln on 4 March 1861, was also removed.

Four new articles were added to this Part. These included Article 50: "悠悠天宇曠，切切故鄉情 (Long-lasting is the spacious heaven, deep are my home feelings)," Article 64: "民胞物與 (All people are my brothers and sisters, and all things are my companions)," Article 67: "文所以載道也 (Literature is a vehicle of the Way)," and Article 68: "學為人師，行為世範 (Learn, so as to teach others; act, so as to serve as an example to all)."

For Part 5: "Democracy and Listening to the People," four changes were made. Article 75: "人生而平等 (All men are created equal)," a quotation by Thomas Jefferson of the United States and Article 76: "每個人的自由發展 (The free development of everyone)" by Karl Marx of Germany, were removed because these were not Chinese sayings. Article 78: "安危不貳其志，險易不革其心 (Safety or danger does not alter one's will; difficulty or ease does not change one's mind)" was added. Article 81: "如將不盡，與古為新 (Only innovation can sustain the growth and vitality of a nation)," originally Article 42 in the Chinese text, was moved to this Part to be its last article.

For Part 6: "Across the Taiwan Straits, Hong Kong and Macao," three articles were removed, while three articles were added. Article 91 (*orig*): "自相分裂的家庭是站立不住的 (A house divided against itself will not stand)," as it was a saying by the American president Abraham Lincoln, was removed. Article 92: "淺淺的海峽，是最大的國殤 (The narrow Taiwan Strait is the deepest sadness for our nation)" and Article 93: "原鄉人的血，必須流返原鄉，才會停止沸騰 (Only when the blood of the native son flows back to his native place will it stop boiling)" were also removed as the cross-Straits relationship became warmer and exchanges and communications between mainland China and Taiwan became

---

[7] Wang, *An Explanation*, 138-40.

frequent and steady.

The three articles were added for different purposes. Article 95: "大道之行也，天下為公 (When the Great Way prevails, the world is for the public)" was added because *tian xia wei gong* 天下為公 has been a very popular expression in Taiwan due to the fact it was cited by Sun Yat-sen, father of Republican China who is widely respected in Taiwan. Article 94: "利在一身勿謀也，利在天下必謀之 (I will not seek personal gains. But if the gains benefit the world, I will certainly seek them)" and Article 96: "不進則退 (If you don't move forward, you will fall behind)" were added because the publisher wanted to update the book with quotations cited by Wen Jiabao in 2009.

For Part 7: "The International Situation and Diplomatic Relations," which has 28 articles, most of the changes were made in the last section, with the exception of Article 98: "遠親不如近鄰 (A distant relative is not as good as a near neighbour)," which was removed. Also removed were four quotations by foreigners, including Article 117 (*orig*): "無論你走得多麼遠，你的心總和我連在一起 (No matter how far you go, your heart is always linked with your homeland)," Article 118 (*orig*): "樹木逢春便會綠葉招展 (Leaves must be green in Spring)," Article 119 (*orig*): "在距離遙遠的民族間建設一座相互交流的知識與技能的橋樑 (To build a bridge for knowledge and skills interflow for peoples in distant places)," and Article 120 (*orig*): "這個機會只存在瞬間 (This chance exists only instantly)."

The five additions were closely related to the international situation and diplomatic relations, including Article 120: "當其同舟而濟，遇風，其相救也如左右手 (Crossing the river in the same boat in the gale, one would go to each other's aid like the right hand helping the left)," Article 121: "亡羊補牢，猶未為晚 (It is not too late to mend the fold even after some of the sheep have been lost)," Article 122: "萬物並育而不相害，道並行而不相悖 (All living creatures grow together without harming one another; ways run parallel without interfering with one another)," Article 123: "吃一塹，長一智 (A fall in the pit is a gain in your wit)," and Article 124: "潮平兩岸闊，風正一帆懸 (From shore to shore it is wide and surgeless, and under a fair wind a sail is lifting)."

The Popularity of the Quotations

It has been observed that some of the sayings quoted by Wen Jiabao are not well known to the Chinese people at large. According to a study made by a professor in literature at Shenyang Normal University, "95% of

the poems and prose quoted by the premier are not in the textbooks."[8]
Wen Jiabao agreed with this view. He said, "Indeed, the poems and prose
that I quoted are all self-taught, and they are used in the contexts of thing
and time."

Some quotations cited by Wen Jiabao are popular sayings:

(4) 為天地立心，為生民立命，為往聖繼絕學，為萬世開太平
To ordain conscience for Heaven and Earth, to secure life and fortune for
the people, to continue the lost teachings of past sages, and to establish
peace for all future generations;

(6) 路漫漫其修遠兮，吾將上下而求索
The way ahead is long, and I do not see any ending, yet high and low I'll
search with determination;

(7) 誰言寸草心，報得三春暉
Who can say that the heart of inch-long grass will repay the sunshine of
spring;

(8) 先天下之憂而憂，後天下之樂而樂
To worry before the whole world worries, and to rejoice after the whole
world rejoices;

(10) 天行健，君子以自強不息
As Heaven's movement is ever vigorous, a gentleman must ceaselessly
strive along;

(11) 窮則變，變則通，通則久
Coming to a deadlock leads to changes; changes lead to solutions;
solutions lead to sustainability;

(18) 鞠躬盡瘁，死而後已
I have devoted my life to serving the people and will always do my best in
the service;

(19) 春蠶到死絲方盡，蠟炬成灰淚始乾
A spring silkworm keeps producing silk until it dies; a candle keeps giving
light until it burns into ashes;

(20) 生於憂患，死於安樂
We survive in adversity and perish in ease and comfort;

(22) 天下興亡，匹夫有責
Everybody is responsible for the rise or fall of the country;

(24) 居安思危，思則有備，有備無患
When living in peace, we have to think of danger. If we think, then we will
be prepared. If we are prepared, then we will have no worries;

(25) 安危相易，禍福相倚
Safety and danger alternate; misfortune and fortune are mutually
dependent;

---

8 Wang, *An Explanation*, 43.

(26) 逆水行舟，不進則退

A boat sailing against the stream must forge ahead or it will be driven back;

(33) 多難興邦

Difficulties rejuvenate a nation;

(41) 天變不足畏，祖宗不足法，人言不足恤

There is no need to fear changes of the sky, no need to emulate the way of the ancestors, and no need to seek the approval of others;

(42) 山重水複疑無路，柳暗花明又一村

When the hills and streams end and there seems no road beyond, amidst shading willows and blooming flowers there is another village;

(43) 察其言，觀其行

Hear what they say and then watch what they do;

(44) 每逢佳節倍思親

Each time a fete day comes, I yearn doubly for my family;

(46) 城門失火，殃及池魚

A fire on the city gate brings disaster to the fish in the moat;

(51) 讀萬卷書，行萬里路

Read thousands of books and travel thousands of miles;

(54) 師者，傳道授業解惑也

A teacher is one who passes on the truth, imparts knowledge and dispels doubts;

(59) 今人乍見孺子將入於井

If a man were, all of a sudden, to see a young child on the verge of falling into a well;

(67) 文所以載道也

Literature is a vehicle of the Way;

(70) 己所不欲，勿施於人

Do not impose on others what you yourself do not desire;

(77) 水能載舟，亦能覆舟

While water can carry a boat, it can also overturn it;

(83) 上不怨天，下不尤人

One does not complain against heaven, nor does one blame the people;

(84) 疾風知勁草

Strong winds test the strength of the grass;

(87) 士不可以不弘毅

A gentleman must be strong and resolute;

(95) 大道之行也，天下為公

When the Great Way prevails, the world is for the public;

(96) 不進則退

If you don't move forward, you will fall behind;

(98) 時移世易，變法宜矣

As generations change and the seasons replace one another, it was time to reform the laws;

(107) 天時不如地利，地利不如人和
Favourable weather is less important than advantageous terrain, and advantageous terrain is less important than human unity;
(110) 花徑不曾緣客掃，篷門今始為君開
I have not swept the path of fallen petals until today, and I have opened my thatched door just for you;
(113) 路遙知馬力，日久見人心
Distance tests a horse's strength, and time reveals a person's real character;
(116) 與朋友交，言而有信
One should honour commitments made to friends;
(121) 亡羊補牢，猶未晚也
It is not too late to mend the fold even after some of the sheep have been lost;
(123) 吃一塹，長一智
A fall in the pit is a gain in your wit.

Of 124 sayings, 37 are relatively popular, amounting to 29.83 percent. In other words, as far as the Chinese sayings are concerned, slightly less than a third are popular.

Modifications of Quotations

On a few occasions, the quotations cited by Wen Jiabao may not correspond to the original source exactly. Take Article 90 as an example. The quotation cited is: "今年花兒紅了，明年花更好 (The red bauhinia is beautiful this year, and it will be even more beautiful next year)." As explained by the author Wang Chunyong, it was cited from "浪淘沙 (To the Tune of Ripples Sifting Sand)" by Ouyang Xiu 歐陽修:

聚散苦匆匆，
此恨無窮，
今年花勝去年紅。
可惜明年花更好，知與誰同？

Our meeting and our parting are too soon.
My sadness will never go.
Flowers are beautiful this year,
And they will be even more beautiful next year,
I don't know who will be there to share the beautiful scene with me.

Firstly, "今年花兒紅了" is not the same as "今年花勝去年紅," and "明年花更好" is different from "可惜明年花更好." Wen Jiabao has skillfully put together these two sentences as "今年花兒紅，明年花更好." To achieve a close resemblance effect, the translations of these two versions are basically similar.

The modification and translation of this quotation are closely related to the context in which this line was cited. This has to do with the situation of Hong Kong in 2007. On the morning of 16 March 2007, at the conclusion of the Fifth Session of the Tenth National People's Congress, Wen Jiabao held a press conference at the Great Hall of the People to answer questions from the Chinese and foreign journalists.

A reporter of the *Hong Kong Economic Times* asked: "This year marks the Tenth anniversary of Hong Kong's return. What is your assessment of Hong Kong's performance in the past ten years since its return? We know that you care a lot about Hong Kong. What are your expectations of Hong Kong's future growth?"

Wen Jiabao first affirmed the achievements of Hong Kong in the last years, and was confident that the position of Hong Kong is irreplaceable. He then conveyed through the media his greetings to the people of Hong Kong: "On the occasion of the 10th anniversary of Hong Kong's return, I would like to ask you to convey my warm greetings to our Hong Kong compatriots. I sincerely hope that Hong Kong will become more prosperous, open, inclusive and harmonious. The bauhinia flower is in full bloom. The red bauhinia is beautiful this year, and it will be even more beautiful next year."

"Flowers will be even more beautiful next year" is a line in the prose-poem of Ouyang Xiu to express the sorrow of parting between friends. But Premier Wen changed this line slightly in his own way and used the red bauhinia to symbolize Hong Kong, and he wished, on the occasion of the tenth anniversary, Hong Kong will have a better future. And that accounts for the translation of *hua* as "red bauhinia" and not as "flowers."

Another example is Article 47: "莫道今年春將盡，明年春色倍還人 (Don't say that this year's spring is about to end, as the scenery of spring will be twice as enchanting next year)." This quotation was related to Du Shenyan's 杜審言 poem entitled "My Feelings on a Spring Day in the Capital 〈春日京中有懷〉," the source text and translation of which are given below:

杜審言：〈春日京中有懷〉
今年游寓獨游秦，愁思看春不當春。
上林苑裏花徒發，細柳營前葉漫新。
公子南橋應盡興，將軍西第幾留賓。

寄語各城風日道，明年春色倍還人。

This year in my travel I travel alone in Qin
Viewing the spring with sad thoughts, I cannot face this spring.
In the emperor's Shanglin Park flowers blossom in vain,
In front of Thin Willow Camp leaves pointlessly renew.
By the young nobles' south bridge, I'm sure their pleasure is fulfilled.
And in the generals' western mansions, how many guests are detained?
I send word to Luoyang, to roads of fine scenery –
Next year spring's beauty will doubly bring the man home.
—Du Shenyang: "My Feelings on a Spring Day in the Capital"

"I send words to Luoyang, to roads of fine scenery – Next year spring's beauty will doubly bring the man home" is a line of poetry written in a lucid and clear style. When Premier Wen quoted this line, however, he removed "I send words to Luoyang, to roads of fine scenery," which was used by the original author to describe the concrete feelings of Luoyang. He changed it to "don't say that this year spring is about to end" to match the background of the financial tsunami. This, together with the second half of the line "the scenery of spring will be twice as enchanting next year" intends to express something to look forward to, and the confidence of the bright spring next year when all things recuperate. If we say that the key word in the original poem was "thoughts of missing," then the intention of Premier Wen to quote this line of poem was to emphasize confidence. As Premier Wen said in the press conference after the conclusion of the Second Session of the Eleventh National People's Congress on 13 March 2009: "To realize this plan, I still believe, first and foremost, we need very strong confidence. Only when we have confidence can we have courage and strength, and only when we have courage and strength can we overcome difficulties. I hope that this press conference can become a meeting to promote confidence and spread confidence. I believe this should be the conscience and responsibility of each journalist, and this is the aspiration of the people. 'Don't say that this year spring is about to end, as the scenery of spring will be twice as enchanting next year.' I expect that next year both China and the world will be better off."

(3) Authors and Works Quoted in the Book

With the finalization of the table of contents, it is possible to make a statistical analysis of the authors and works.

It can be seen from the above that a total of 79 authors or works of unknown authorship have been quoted, spanning from 1134 B.C. to 1996, a period of 3,130 years. This is a strong indication of the breadth of knowledge of Wen Jiabao. Most of the authors were quoted once, but more popular authors or works have been quoted two times or more.

Works with nine quotations:
  (1) Confucius 孔子(*The Analects of Confucius*《論語》)

Works with five quotations:
  (1) *The Book of Poetry*《詩經》
  (2) Mencius 孟子 (*Mencius*《孟子》)
  (3) Zuo Qiuming 左丘明 (*Zuo's Commentary on the Spring and Autumn Annals* 《左傳》and *Discourses of the States* 《國語》)

Works with four quotations:
  (1) Guan Zhong 管仲 (*Guanzi*《管子》)
  (2) Sima Qian 司馬遷 (*Records of the Grand Historian* 《史記》and "A Letter in Reply to Ren'an"〈報任安書〉)

Works with three quotations:
  (1) Zisi 子思 (*Doctrine of the Mean*《中庸》)
  (2) *The Book of History*《尚書》
  (3) *The Book of Changes*《周易》
  (4) *The Book of Rites*《禮記》
  (5) Liu Xiang 劉向 (*Strategies of the Warring States* 《戰國策》)

Works with two quotations:
  (1) Li Er 李耳 (*Daodejing*《道德經》)
  (2) Sun Wu 孫武 (*The Art of War*《孫子兵法》)
  (3) Zhuangzi 莊子 (*Zhuangzi*《莊子》)
  (4) Qu Yuan 屈原 (*Li Sao*《離騷》)
  (5) Zhang Jiuling 張九齡 ("Strolling at Night in Xijiang 〈西江夜行〉and "Seeing off Mr Li〈送韋城李少府〉)
  (6) Du Fu 杜甫 ("Looking at the Mountain"〈望嶽〉and "Receiving a Guest"〈客至〉)
  (7) Liu Yuxi 劉禹錫 ("A Poem on Meeting Bai Juyi at Yangzhou"〈酬樂天揚州初逢席上見贈〉and "Playing with

the Moonlight in Mid-August"〈八月十五日夜玩月〉)
(8) Zhang Zai 張載 (*Complete Works of Master Zhang*《張子全集》)
(9) Mao Zedong 毛澤東 ("Loushan Pass"〈婁山關〉and "Climbing up Mount Jinggang Again"〈重上井岡山〉)

It can be observed that apart from Mao Zedong, the most quoted works are traditional Chinese classics, such as *The Analects of Confucius*, *Book of Poetry*, *Mencius*, and *Records of the Grand Historian*.

Another observation that can be drawn from the above is Wen's meticulous choice of authors based on political correctness and appropriateness. Authors have been most carefully and properly selected to ensure that their quotations would be acceptable to the recipients. The following is an analysis of all the 79 authors in chronological order.

(1) 《詩經》(*Book of Poetry*) (1134 B.C. – 515 B.C.)
The Book of Poetry is the first anthology of Chinese poems. It contains 305 poems collected for around 500 years from the early years of the Western Zhou Dynasty to the middle of the Spring and Autumn period.
(40) 周雖舊邦，其命維新。
Although Zhou was an ancient state, it had a reform mission.
(57) 言之不足，故嗟歎之。
If words are not sufficient, sighing can be better.
(63) 伐柯伐柯，其則不遠。
In cutting an axe handle, the norm is not far off
(79) 言者無罪，聞者足戒。
The speakers are not to be blamed, while the listeners can introspect.
(80) 嚶其鳴矣，求其友聲。
Long, long, the bird will sing, expecting its mates to echo.

(2) Guan Zhong 管仲 (cir 725 B.C. – 645 B.C.)
He served as Prime Minister of Qi for forty years during which he carried out reforms in various areas, such as politics, economy, and military affairs. His achievements were highly praised by posterity.
(28) 事者，生於慮，成於務，失於傲。
Things are born out of planning, completed in practice, but lost in arrogance.
(62) 和合故能諧。
If there is concord and unity, there is harmony.
(69) 海不辭水，故能成其大；山不辭土石，故能成其高。

The sea does not reject water, so it is able to become great; the mountain does not reject stones, so it is able to become tall.

(119) 召遠在修近，閉禍在除怨。

To win distant friends, one needs, first of all, to have good relations with his neighbours. To avoid adversity, one needs to ease animosity.

(3) Li Er 李耳 (of the Spring and Autumn Period)

Author of *Daodejing*, he was also the forefather of Daoism.

(117) 上德不德。

A person with high virtue does not show off virtue.

(118) 利而不害，為而不爭。

Facilitate and not harm; provide and not compete.

(4) Confucius 孔子 (551 B.C. – 479 B.C.)

Founder of Confucianism, best known for *The Analects of Confucius*.

(43) 察其言，觀其行。

Hear what they say and then watch what they do.

(52) 不憤不啟，不悱不發。

I do not open up the truth to one who is not eager to get knowledge, nor help out anyone who is not anxious to explain himself.

(70) 己所不欲，勿施於人。

Do not impose on others what you yourself do not desire.

(87) 士不可以不弘毅。

A gentleman must be strong and resolute.

(88) 死而後已，不亦遠乎。

Only with death does the road come to an end. Is that not long?

(100) 以和為貴，和而不同。

Harmony is most valuable, but it allows diversity.

(108) 德不孤，必有鄰。

Virtue never stands alone. It is bound to have neighbours.

(114) 言必信，行必果。

Promises must be kept and action must be resolute.

(116) 與朋友交，言而有信。

One should honour commitments made to friends.

(5) Deng Xizi 鄧析子 (545 B.C. – 501 B.C.)

Founder of the "Logician School."

(96) 不進則退。

If you don't move forward, you will fall behind.

(6) Sun Wu 孫武 (?535 B.C. - ?)

He was known for his work *The Art of War*, which has been hailed as the best work of its kind in the world, a bible of military science, the ultimate classic of its genre, and the definitive mode for military training.

(48) 上下同心者勝。

The side that has superiors and subordinates united in heart will take the victory.

(120) 當其同舟而濟，遇風，其救也如左右手。

Crossing the river in the same boat in the gale, one would go to each other's aid like the right hand helping the left.

(7) Zuo Qiuming 左丘明 (502 B.C. – 422 B.C.)

A blind-monk historian of the Spring and Autumn period. He wrote *Zuo's Commentary on the Spring and Autumn Annals*, which is the first annalistic history with a detailed narration and a complete structure.

(24) 居安思危，思則有備，有備無患。

When living in peace, we have to think of danger. If we think, then we will be prepared. If we are prepared, then we will have no worries.

(30) 其興也勃，其亡也忽。

Its rise is quick; its fall is sudden.

(33) 多難興邦。

Difficulties rejuvenate a nation.

(34) 居官者當事不避難。

Those who are in official positions should be courageous to shoulder responsibilities and should not avoid difficulties.

(105) 親仁善鄰，國之寶也。

It is most important to have close and honorable relations with one's neighbours.

(8) Zengzi 曾子 (505 B.C. – 432 B.C.)

He actively promoted Confucianism and spread Confucian. He is known as one of the "Five Great Sages" and is respectfully addressed by Confucianists in later ages as "Master Sage."

(21) 生之者眾，食之者寡，為之者疾，用之者舒。

The way to accumulate wealth is to have many producers but few consumers, and to have activity in the production and economy in the expenditure.

(9) Zisi 子思 (483 B.C. – 402 B.C.)

He was a grandson of Confucius who wrote the *Doctrine of the Mean*. Zisi's idea of *mean* has become the most important method of cultivating the mind in the Confucian School and he was respectfully known as the "Sage of Elaboration 述聖."

(45) 人一之，我十之，人十之，我百之。

If another person succeeds by one effort, I will make ten efforts. If another man succeeds by ten efforts, I will make a hundred.

(83) 上不怨天，下不尤人。

One does not complain against heaven, nor does one blame the people.

(122) 萬物並育而不相害，道並行而不相悖。

All living creatures grow together without harming one another; ways run parallel without interfering with one another.

(10) *The Book of History* 《尚書》(476 B.C. – 221 B.C.)

This is the earliest compilation of historical literature in ancient China. It begins with the legendary times of Yao, Shun and Yu, and ends at the Eastern Zhou Dynasty, covering more than 1,500 years. It became one of the important classics of Confucianism since the Han Dynasty.

(38) 德惟善政，政在養民。

The virtue of the ruler is seen in his good government, which is in the nourishing of the people.

(39) 民為邦本，本固邦寧。

People are the basis of a nation, an only when this basis is stable can the nation enjoy peace.

(101) 百姓昭明，協和萬邦。

We should have amity among people and friendly exchanges among nations.

(11) Mencius 孟子 (372 B.C. – 289 B.C.)

Mencius was a great thinker and educator of the Warring States period. In 1330, he was given the title of "The Second Sage after Confucius," and he was later known as "The Second Sage."

(20) 生於憂患，死於安樂。

We survive in adversity and perish in ease and comfort.

(36) 憂民之憂者，民亦憂其憂。

When a ruler rejoices in the joy of his people, they also rejoice in his joy; when he grieves at the sorrow of his people, they also grieve at his sorrow.

(59) 今人乍見孺子將入於井。

If a man were, all of a sudden, to see a young child on the verge of falling into a well.

(89) 得道者多助，失道者寡助。

One who has the Way will have many to support hi, while one who does not will have few to support him.

(107) 天時不如地利，地利不如人和。

Favourable weather is less important than advantageous terrain, and advantageous terrain is less important than human unity.

(12) Zhuangzi 莊子 (369 B.C. -286 B.C.)

He inherited and elaborated the thought of Li Er or Laozi and wrote his book *Zhuangzi*, an important work in Daoism.

(25) 安危相易，禍福相倚。

Safety and danger alternate; misfortune and fortune are mutually dependent.

(109) 凡交，近則必相靡以信，遠則必忠之以言。

In all intercourse between states, if they are near to each other, there should be mutual friendliness, verified by deeds; if they are far apart, there must be sincere adherence to truth in their messages.

(13) Qu Yuan 屈原 (340 B.C. – 286 B.C.)

A famous patriot and statesman of the State of Chu during the Warring States period. *Li Sao* is one of his representative works.

(6) 路漫漫其修遠兮，吾將上下而求索。

The way ahead is long, and I do not see any ending, yet high and low I'll search with determination.

(13) 長太息以掩涕兮，哀民生之多艱。

Long did I sigh to hold back tears; saddened I am by the grief of my people.

(14) Xun Kuang 荀況 (313 B.C. – 238 B.C.)

He was a great master of the Confucian School in the last phase of the Warring States period, and an outstanding thinker and educator. His book *Xunzi*, in thirty-two chapters, covers the various aspects of philosophy, logic, politics and morality.

(77) 水能載舟，亦能覆舟。

While water can carry a boat, it can also overturn it.

(15) Lü Buwei 呂不韋 (292 B.C. – 238 B.C.)

He was known for keeping three thousand retainers to write *The Annals of Lü Buwei*, a foundation for the "Mixed School."

(98) 時移世易，變法宜矣。

As generations change and the seasons replace one another, it was time to reform the laws.

(16) *The Book of Changes* 《周易》 (223 B.C.)

This is an ancient Chinese book of divination and an important Confucian classic.

(10) 天行健，君子以自強不息。

As Heaven's movement is ever vigorous, a gentleman must ceaselessly strive along.

(11) 窮則變，變則通，通則久。

Coming to a deadlock leads to changes; changes lead to solutions; solutions lead to sustainability.

(32) 夕惕若厲。

In the evening, we are still careful and apprehensive.

(17) *The Book of Rites* 《禮記》 (202 B.C. -220)

This book is about the interpretation of the classic *Etiquette and Ceremonies*. Later, it became so popular that it gained the status of a classic. It is listed as one of the "Nine Classics" by the Tang Dynasty, and one of the "Thirteen Classics" by the Song Dynasty.

(56) 詩言志，歌詠聲，舞動容。

Poetry expresses one's thoughts, singing speaks one's voice, and dancing shows one's colour.

(60) 言有物，行有格。

Speak with substance and act by rules.

(95) 大道之行也，天下為公。

When the Great Way prevails, the world is for the public.

(18) Liu An 劉安 (179 B.C. – 122 B.C.)

A grandson of Liu Bang, the founding emperor of the Han Dynasty, was chiefly responsible for the editing of *Huainanzi* 淮南子 (*The Masters of Huainan*).

(49) 乞火不若取燧，寄汲不若鑿井。

It would be better to obtain a fire-maker than beg for fire, better to dig a well ourselves than beg for water from others.

(19) Sima Qian 司馬遷 (145 B.C. – 89 B.C.)

A historian and essayist of the Western Han Dynasty. His most important work was the *Records of the Grand Historian*.

(58) 詩三百篇，大抵聖賢發憤之所為作也。

The three hundred poems in the *Book of Poetry* were for the most part written out of indignation of the sages.

(73) 言能聽，道乃進。

When words can be heard, the Way will move forward.

(86) 一尺布，尚可縫；一斗粟，尚可舂。同胞兄弟何不容。

When even a foot of cloth can be stitched up, even a kilo of millet can be ground, how can two blood brothers not make up.

(97) 桃李不言，下自成蹊。

Peaches and plums do not speak, yet a path is trampled out beneath them.

(20) Liu Xiang 劉向 (77 B.C. – 6 B.C.)

Liu Xiang was a Confucian scholar, bibliographer, and man of letters. He wrote *Strategies of the Warring States*, which mainly recounts the political ideas and strategies of the School of Negotiation in the Warring States period.

(27) 行百里者半九十。

If a journey is one hundred miles long, travelling ninety is half of it.

(112) 吾有德於人也，不可不忘也。

Do not forget the good given by others and do forget the good given to others.

(121) 亡羊補牢，猶未晚也。

It is not too late to mend the fold even after some of the sheep have been lost.

(21) Liu Xiu 劉秀 (6 B.C. - 57)

The first emperor of the Eastern Han Dynasty.

(84) 疾風知勁草。

Strong winds test the strength of the grass.

(22) Wang Chong 王充 (27-97)

A famous thinker and literary theorist of the Eastern Han Dynasty. His only extant work is the book *Critical Essays*《論衡》, which propounded his views on nature, history, and knowledge.

(75) 知屋漏者在宇下，知政失者在草野。

He who knows the leakage of a house lives under its roof, and he who knows the mismanagement of a state stays on its land.

(23) Cao Cao 曹操 (155-220)

A political leader, military strategist, and poet of the Three Kingdoms period.

(74) 烈士暮年，壯心不已。

A man of heroic spirit, though advanced in years, never abandons his proud aspirations.

(24) Zhongchang Tong 仲長統 (180-220)

A political commentator in the Eastern Han Dynasty.

(78) 安危不貳其志，險易不革其心。

Safety or danger does not alter one's will; difficulty or ease does not change one's mind.

(25) Zhuge Liang 諸葛亮 (181-234)

Well-known statesman, military strategist, and essayist, and also the embodiment of the wise man and loyal minister.

(18) 鞠躬盡瘁，死而後已。

I have devoted my life to serving the people and will always do my best in the service.

(26) Du Bi 杜弼 (?490-559)

An honest and benevolent official of the Eastern Wei Dynasty. He was also a straight-tongued counselor. What he hated most were corrupt officials.

(46) 城門失火，殃及池魚。

A fire on the city gate brings disaster to the fish in the moat.

(27) Yu Shinan 虞世南 (558-638)

Yu was a calligrapher, poet, and one of the twenty-four meritorious officials of the Lingyan Pavilion of the Tang Dynasty.

(99) 結交一言重，相期千里至。

Good friends highly value their words. They travel a thousand miles to keep their promise for a gathering.

(28) Du Shenyan 杜審言 (646-708)

A poet of the early Tang Dynasty and the grandfather of Du Fu. His poetry was known for its simplicity and vigour.

(47) 莫道今年春將盡，明年春色倍還人。

Don't say that this year's spring is about to end, as the scenery of spring will be twice as enchanting next year.

(29) Wu Ke 吳兢 (669-749)

A historian of the Tang Dynasty. He wrote *The Book of Tang* and *The Political Programme in Zhenguan Times*.

(16) 非知之難，行之惟難；非行之難，終之斯難。

The difficult thing is not just to know something, but to do something, the difficult thing is not even to do something, but to be persistent in doing something.

(30) Zhang Jiuling 張九齡 (678-740)

Zhang was known as a "sage chancellor of the Kaiyuan period" of the Tang Dynasty. His poetry was profound in sentiment and longlasting, and played an important role in reversing the embellished but empty style of palace poems.

(50) 悠悠天宇曠，切切故鄉情。

Longlasting is the spacious heaven, deep are my home feelings.

(106) 相知無遠近，萬里尚為鄰。

Distance cannot separate true friends who feel so close even when they are thousands of miles apart.

(31) Wang Wan 王灣 (693-751)

A Tang poet known particularly for his poem "Mooring under the North Fort Hill."

(124) 潮平兩岸闊，風正一帆懸。

From shore to shore it is wide and surgeless, and under a fair wind a sail is lifting.

(32) Wang Wei 王維 (701-761)

A famous poet and painter of the high Tang period. He was best known for his epoch-making landscape quatrains.

(44) 每逢佳節倍思親。

Each time a fete day comes, I yearn doubly for my family.

(33) Du Fu 杜甫 (712-770)

A famous Tang poet. He composed more than 1,500 poems. He was called a "poet-historian" and generally regarded as a "poet-sage."

(3) 會當凌絕頂，一覽眾山小。

When I reach the peak of Mount Tai, all other mountains look so small.

(110) 花徑不曾緣客掃，蓬門今始為君開。

I have not swept the path of fallen petals until today, and I have opened my thatched door just for you.

(34) Sikong Shu 司空曙 (720-790)

Regarded as one of the "Ten Talents of the Dali Years" of the Tang Dynasty.

(102) 故人江海別，幾度隔山川。

After parting in the sea, we two have long been divided by mountains and rivers.

(35) Meng Jiao 孟郊 (751-814)

A poet of the Tang Dynasty, known for "bitter poetry."

(7) 誰言寸草心，報得三春暉。

Who can say that the heart of inch-long grass will repay the sunshine of spring.

(36) Han Yu 韓愈 (768-824)

An essayist and philosopher in the Tang Dynasty and a strong propagator of the Ancient Style Prose Movement.

(54) 師者，傳道授業解惑也。

A teacher is one who passes on the truth, imparts knowledge and dispels doubts.

(37) Bai Juyi 白居易 (772-846)

An outstanding realist poet of the Tang Dynasty and an active promoter of the New Ballad Movement.

(35) 心中為念農桑苦，耳裏如聞飢凍聲。

My mind is on the hardship and suffering of the people, and my ears seem to hear the sighs of the people in hunger and cold.

(38) Liu Yuxi 劉禹錫 (772-842)

A poet and philosopher of the middle and late Tang Dynasty.

(91) 沉舟側畔千帆過，病樹前頭萬木春。

A thousand sails pass by the wrecked ship; ten thousand saplings shoot up beyond the withered tree.

(104) 暑退九霄淨，秋澄萬景清。

The retreat of summer makes the sky clean, and the shiny autumn moon makes everything clear.

(39) Liu Zongyuan 柳宗元 (773-819)

One of the "Eight Great Literary Masters" of the Tang and Song Dynasties.

(72) 啟進善之門。

Open the door for the fine words.

(40) Jia Dao 賈島 (779-843)

A poet of the Tang Dynasty. His poetry is known for its elegance and uniqueness, its sadness and misery.

(55) 十年磨一劍。

It takes ten years to make a sword.

(41) Li Shangyin 李商隱 (812-858)

A famous late Tang poet.

(19) 春蠶到死絲方盡，蠟炬成灰淚始乾。

A spring silkworm keeps producing silk until it dies; a candle keeps giving light until it burns into ashes.

(42) Sikong Tu 司空圖 (837-908)

A Tang intellectual known for his work *The Twenty-four Orders of Poetry*.

(81) 如將不盡，與古為新。

Only innovation can sustain the growth and vitality of a nation.

(43) Liu Xu 劉昫 (887-946)

He was involved in the editing of *The Old History of the Tang Dynasty*.

(68) 學為人師，行為世範。

Learn, so as to teach others; act, so as to serve as an example to all.

(44) Fan Zhongyan 范仲淹 (989-1052)

A prominent politician, strategist, and literary figure of the Northern Song Dynasty.

(8) 先天下之憂而憂，後天下之樂而樂。

To worry before the whole world worries, and to rejoice after the whole world rejoices.

(45) Song Qi 宋祁 (998-1062)

A historian and man of letters in the Song Dynasty. He co-compiled *A New History of the Tang Dynasty* with Ouyang Xiu.

(29) 思所以危則安，思所以亂則治，思所以亡則存。

Only when we think about where danger looms can we ensure our security. Only when we think about why chaos occurs can we ensure our peace. And only when we think about why a country falls can we ensure our survival.

(46) Ouyang Xiu 歐陽修 (1007-1072)

A statesman, man of letters, historian, and poet of the Northern Song period and a leader of the reform movement in poetry and literature. He wrote *A New History of the Five Dynasties*.

(90) 今年花兒紅了，明年花更好。

The red bauhinia is beautiful this year, and it will be even more beautiful next year.

(47) Zhou Dunyi 周敦頤 (1017-1073)

A metaphysicist and the founder of Song-Ming Neo-Confucianism.

(67) 文所以載道也。

Literature is a vehicle of the Way.

(48) Zhang Zai 張載 (1020-1077)

He has an important position in the development of Chinese thought and culture and exerted a great impact on the development of ideology in later ages.

(4) 為天地立心，為生民立命，為往聖繼絕學，為萬世開太平。

To ordain conscience for Heaven and Earth, to secure life and fortune for the people, to continue the lost teachings of past sages, and to establish peace for all future generations.

(64) 民胞物與。

All people are my brothers and sisters, and all things are my companions.

(49) Wang Anshi 王安石 (1021-1086)

A prominent statesman, thinker, writer, reformer, and one of the "Eight Great Literary Masters of the Tang and Song Dynasties."

(103) 不畏浮雲遮望眼，只緣身在最高層。

We have no fear of the clouds that may block our view, as we are already on the summit.

(50) Su Shi 蘇軾 (1037-1101)

Su Shi was renowned for his prose, poetry and prose-poetry and was one of the "Eight Great Literary Masters of the Tang and Song Dynasties."

(31) 名為治平無事，而其實有不測之憂。

A country that appears peaceful and stable may encounter unexpected crises.

(51) Su Zhe 蘇轍 (1039-1112)

An essayist of the northern Song Dynasty and one of the "Eight Great Literary Masters of the Tang and Song Dynasties."

(37) 去民之患，如除腹心之疾。

To remove the calamities of the people is like taking away an illness of the heart.

(52) Hu Hong 胡宏 (1105-1161)

A Neo-Confucianist and famous classicist.
(94) 利在一身勿謀也，利在天下必謀之。
I will not seek personal gains. But if the gains benefit the world, I will certainly seek them.

(53) Lu You 陸游 (1125-1210)

Generally recognized as the best poet of the Southern Song Dynasty. His poems are full of patriotism. His carefree and liberal style of poetry makes him become known as the "Little Li Bai."
(42) 山重水複疑無路，柳暗花明又一村。
Where the hills and streams end and there seems no road beyond, amidst shading willows and blooming flowers there is another village.

(54) Xin Qiji 辛棄疾 (1140-1207)

A famous poet of the Southern Song Dynasty. His poems were mainly about resisting the Jurchens and restoring the country.
(115) 青山遮不住，畢竟東流去。
The green mountain can't stop water from flowing, and the river keeps flowing eastward.

(55) Qiao Xingjian 喬行簡 (1156-1241)

A profound scholar with a broad mind who excelled in selecting men of talents.
(76) 賢路當廣而不當狹，言路當開而不當塞。
The chances for worthy people to advance should be wide but not narrow; the channel of communication with leaders should be open but not blocked.

(56) Chen Yuanjing 陳元靚 (1200-1266)

Author of the very popular book *A Comprehensive Record of Affairs* 《事林廣記》.
(113) 路遙知馬力，日久見人心。
Distance tests a horse's strength, and time reveals a person's real character.

(57) Zheng Sixiao 鄭思肖 (1241-1318)

A painter of the late Song and early Ming period. He also excelled in poetry and essays.
(93) 一心中國夢，萬古下泉詩。
I have always longed to see a reunified China, an aspiration shared by all our people.

(58) Liu Ji 劉基 (1311-1375)

A literary figure and statesman of the late Yuan and early Ming periods.

(23) 安不忘危，治不忘亂。

When safe, don't forget danger; when in peace, don't forget chaos.

(59) Tuo Tuo 脫脫 (1314-1355)

A minister in the late years of the Yuan Dynasty.

(41) 天變不足畏，祖宗不足法，人言不足恤。

There is no need to fear changes of the sky, no need to emulate the way of the ancestors, and no need to seek the approval of others.

(60) Zhu Yuanzhang 朱元璋 (1328-1398)

The founder and first emperor of the Ming Dynasty of China.

(17) 行事見於當時，是非公於後世。

What one did at the time will be judged by history. History is created and written by the people.

(61) Wang Yangming 王陽明 (1472-1529)

The best-known philosopher, thinker, politician, and militarist of the Ming Dynasty. He was a great master of Confucianism after Zu Xi, and was one of the most important founders of the Neo-Confucian School of the Mind.

(123) 吃一塹，長一智。

A fall in the pit is a gain in your wit.

(62) Dong Qichang 董其昌 (1555-1636)

The most important calligrapher and painter in the late Ming.

(51) 讀萬卷書，行萬里路。

Read thousands of books and travel thousands of miles.

(63) *Ancient Chinese Proverbs*《增廣賢文》(1573-1619)

This is an ancient Chinese primer for children.

(26) 逆水行舟，不進則退。

A boat sailing against the stream must forge ahead or it will be driven back.

(64) Huang Zongxi 黃宗羲 (1610-1695)

A prominent thinker, philosopher, historian of the late Ming and early Qing Dynasties.

(9) 萬民之憂樂。

The worries and joys of all the people.

(65) Gu Yanwu 顧炎武 (1613-1682)

A thinker of the late Ming and early Qing period. His best known work is *Notes on the Daily Accumulation of Knowledge*《日知錄》.

(22) 天下興亡，匹夫有責。

Everybody is responsible for the rise or fall of the country.

(66) Zheng Xie 鄭燮 (1693-1765)

A late Qing calligrapher, painter, and essayist known for his unique style in poetry, calligraphy, and painting. He was also an outstanding painter of the Yangzhou School of Painting.

(15) 衙齋臥聽蕭蕭竹，疑是民間疾苦聲。

Lying in bed in my den, I heard the rustling of bamboos outside, and it just sounded like the moaning of the needy.

(67) Lin Zexu 林則徐 (1785-1850)

A patriotic politician, thinker and poet of the Qing Dynasty.

(1) 苟利國家生死以，豈因禍福避趨之。

I'll do whatever is in the interests of my country even at the cost of my own life; I would never shrink back because of personal weal and woe.

(68) Zuo Zongtang 左宗棠 (1812-1885)

A high official in military affairs, a general of the Hunan Army, and an important leader in the Westernization School.

(12)身無半畝，心憂天下；讀破萬卷，神交古人。

I don't have half an acre of land to myself, but I care about my people across the land. I read over ten thousand books and am spiritually attracted to the ancient people.

(69) Huang Zunxian 黃遵憲 (1848-1905)

A patriotic late Qing poet, the first envoy to Japan, and hailed as "a giant of the poetic revolution."

(2) 杜鵑再拜憂天淚，精衛無窮填海心。

The fabled cuckoo weeping blood at China's woe, and the Jingwei bird filling the sea with pebbles untold.

(70) Yan Fu 嚴復 (1853-1921)

A highly influential thinker, translator and educator of the late Qing Dynasty, he was also one of the pioneers in modern Chinese history of the movement to learn from the West.

(71) 身貴自由，國貴自主。

The individual values freedom and the state values autonomy.

(71) Qiu Fengjia 丘逢甲 (1864-1912)

Served as Minister of Education of the Military Government of Guangdong Province of the Republic of China.

(85) 四百萬人同一哭，去年今日割台灣。

Four million people cried the same tears of sorrow as Taiwan was ceded.

(72) Liang Qichao 梁啟超 (1873-1929)

A famous thinker, writer, and scholar in modern China.

(61) 明於識，練於事，忠於國。

Clairty of knowledge, proficiency in affairs, and loyalty to the nation.

(73) Yu Youren 于右任 (1879-1964)

A founding figure of the Revolution of 1911, master calligrapher and celebrated poet.

(82) 葬我於高山之上兮，望我大陸。

Bury me on the highest mountaintop so that I can get a sight of the Mainland.

(74) Lu Xun 魯迅 (1881-1936)

A contemporary writer and translator.

(92) 度盡劫波兄弟在，相逢一笑泯恩仇。

We remain brothers after all the calamities, let's forgo our old grudges with a smile and meet again.

(75) Mei Yiqi 梅貽琦 (1889-1962)

From 1931 to 1948, he was the president of Tsinghua University.

(65) 大學不在於有大樓。

It is not buildings that make a university.

(76) Tao Xingzhi 陶行知 (1891-1946)

A prominent democratic revolutionist, educationist, and one of the leading figures in the China Alliance in modern China.

(53) 千教萬教，教人求真。

Whatever we teach is all about the pursuit of truths.

(77) Mao Zedong 毛澤東 (1893-1976)

One of the founders of Chinese Communism, Chairman of the Central Committee of the Communist Party of China, Chairman of the Central People's Government of the People's Republic of China (1949-1954), and Chairman of the People's Republic of China (1954-1959).

(5) 雄關漫道真如鐵，而今邁步從頭越。

Don't say that this fortified pass is as hard as iron, as we can now cross its summit in one step.

(111) 世上無難事，只要肯登攀。

Nothing is hard under the sky, if we dare to climb up high.

(78) Ye Shengtao 葉聖陶 (1894-1988)

A contemporary author and educator. He served as Vice-minister of the Ministry of Education.

(66) 教是為了不教。

Teaching is in order not to teach.

(79) Ai Qing 艾青 (1910-1996)

Acclaimed as a "lord" and "prince" in the world of Chinese poetry, he was named one of the world's greatest contemporary poets.

(14) 為什麼我的眼裏常含着淚水？

Why are my eyes always filled with tears?

[IV] Translations of Quotations

It can be understood from the above that the contexts in which Wen quotes sayings from Chinese authors are varied. Physically, it depends on whether Wen is in China or abroad. As far as the target audience is concerned, there is a difference between Chinese people in China or abroad and foreigners in China or in other countries. As Wen Jiabao is a very important political figure, virtually all his speeches in Chinese which are targeted at foreign readers are officially translated by official organizations such as the Foreign Office of China for global consumption. On the other hand, all his speeches in Chinese are not translated as these are for the Chinese-speaking audience. As far as translations of quotations is concerned, they basically involve occasions where official translations are provided and occasions in which official translations are not provided.

[a] Occasions with Official Translations

Many official translations are readily available on the Internet. These situations or occasions will be explained in detail. Official translations are on the websites run by official agencies, such as the Foreign Ministry of China and Chinese Embassies in different countries. The Department of Translation and Interpretation of the Ministry of Foreign Affairs has been chiefly responsible for translating and interpreting the speeches and press conferences of Wen Jiabao. According to the Ministry of Foreign Affairs, the Department is responsible for providing English and French translation of important state diplomatic documents and instruments and English and French interpretation service at important diplomatic functions. It offers professional training to high-level English and French translators and interpreters of the Ministry." [http://www.fmprc.gov.cn/eng/wjb/zzjg/fys]

In translating the quotations cited by Wen Jiabao, official translations would be used for this book wherever possible. Changes were made when a better translation could be found or when a new translation suited the context better.

(1) Press Conferences at National People's Congresses

Wen Jiabao was elected Premier of the State Council on 16 March 2003 at the Sixth Plenary Meeting of the First Session of the Tenth National People's Congress. Since then he has continuously held press conferences at the conclusion of the National People's Congresses for six years from 2003 to 2009.

(a) *18 March 2003*: Press Conference after the First Session of the Tenth National People's Congress

During the press conference, three quotations were made. To search for the translations of these quotations, the query "Wen Jiabao 18 March 2003" was keyed into the "Google" search engine.

It can be seen from the above that the official website of the Embassy of the People's Republic of China in China [http://www.chinaembassy canada.org/eng/xw/xwgb/t38896.htm] provided a full English version of the press conference held on 18 March 2003. Three classical quotations

were made by Wen Jiabao at this press conference. The following are the contexts in which these quotations were cited.

(1) 苟利國家生死以，豈因禍福避趨之

I'll do whatever is in the interests of my country even at the cost of my own life; I would never shrink back because of personal weal and woe.

[Context and Official Translation]

DPA (Deutsche Presse-Agentur): When Premier Zhu Rongji just became premier, he said that whatever lies ahead, be it a field of landmines or an unfathomable abyss, he will exert all his efforts and contribute all his best to the country till the last minute of his life. Compared to his working style, what are the features of your working style?

A: I have a lot of respect for Premier Zhu. He has many strong points that I need to learn from him. As for myself, it is generally believed that I am quite mild-tempered. But at the same time, I am someone who deeply believes in his conviction, who holds his ground if it is consistent with principle and who is confident and courageous enough to take up his responsibility. Since I became premier, I've been whispering two lines written by Lin Zexu to myself and they are: *I would do whatever it takes to serve my country, even at the cost of my own life and regardless of fortune of misfortune to myself.* So this will be the attitude in which I will start my work.

It can be seen that my translation did not follow the one provided by the official website.

(21) 生之者眾，食之者寡，為之者疾，用之者舒。

The way to accumulate wealth is to have many producers but few consumers, and to have activity in the production and economy in the expenditure.

[Context and Official Translation]

China National Radio: The rural tax-for-fee reform will be extended across the country this year. You once said that China would definitely be able to break the vicious cycle of the Law of Huang Zongxi. So my question is how can the current tax-for-fee reform break such a vicious cycle?

A: I already talked a lot about this subject, so here I only want to make two points. First, the essence of this reform is to reform the certain links in the rural superstructure that do not serve the development of productive forces. The most important work is to downsize the institutions. In the Book of Learning in China, it talks about the way to accumulate wealth. *There are many people who produce, there are very few people who consume, and people work very hard to produce more financial wealth and people practice economy when they spend.* In this way, wealth is accumulated. However, the situation today in the countryside is just the opposite. There are very few who produce whereas there are a lot who consume. For instance, in a county with a population of only 120, 000 to 130, 000 people, 5,700 people live on taxpayers' money by being on the government's payroll. So I think to find a fundamental way to reduce the burden of farmers, we need to cut down the size of institutional functionaries and to shed the people who are not necessary. At the same time, we must increase financial support to the countryside. Our objective is that we want to ensure that the farmers are not asked to pay taxes that they are not entitled to pay. I know this might take some time. This year, we have adopted a new policy. The additional financial resources earmarked for the undertakings in the fields of science, technology, education, culture, and health care will mainly find their way to the countryside.

(82) 葬我於高山之上兮，望我大陸。

Bury me on the highest mountaintop so that I can get a sight of the Mainland

[Context and Official Translation]

Taiwan: Since the beginning of this year, the Taiwan side has come up with new suggestions and measures to improve the relations across the Taiwan straits. For instance, they have put forward the idea of setting up a mechanism to ensure peace and stability in the cross-strait relationship. They have also done something positive towards the three direct links including the direct shipping and air services. We hope to bring about sound interaction between the two sides of the Taiwan straits. In the past, we have not heard much directly from you on your perspective on the question of Taiwan. We would like to know what is your perspective and what is your knowledge about Taiwan? What will be the major items on the agenda of the new government concerning the work of Taiwan affairs? What expectations do you have on the question of Taiwan?

A: Through you, I would like to extend my best regards to our Taiwan compatriots. The achievement of complete reunification is the common aspiration of all Chinese people, including our Taiwan compatriots. When Taiwan is mentioned, lots of feelings well up. I cannot help thinking of the late Mr. Yu Youren, a founding member of Kuomintang and participant in the Revolution of 1911. He wrote a poem to express his grief over national division. He wrote such a poem: *Burying me on the highest mountaintop so that I can get a sight of my mainland. Mainland I see none, tears of sorrow cascade. Burying me on the highest mountaintop so that I can get a glimpse of my hometown. Hometown I see none, but [it] lives forever in my mind. The lofty sky is deeply blue, the vast wildness not seen through. Oh, boundless universe, would you hear me and this elegy of the nation.* What a touching poem he has written, which strikes a cord on the sentiment of all the Chinese people. The Chinese government will continue to unswervingly pursue the policy of peaceful reunification on the basis of "One Country, Two Systems". We will seek an early resumption of dialogue and negotiation between the two sides on the basis of the "One China" principle. We are against "Taiwan independence." We will continue to support more economic and cultural exchanges between the two sides. We want to bring about the early achievement of three direct links. We hope to make bigger progress in the process towards peaceful reunification.

(20) 生於憂患，死於安樂。

We survive in adversity and perish in ease and comfort

[Context and Official Translation]

CCTV: First of all, many congratulations to you, Premier Wen, on your election as premier. Our warm congratulations also go to the vice premiers. We know you were one of the leading officials of the previous government. Over the past five years, China has accomplished remarkable achievements. We would like to have your comment on the work of the previous government and Premier Zhu Rongji himself. And with the achievements in the past five years, you now face a more demanding job in developing the economy even further. What do you think are the major difficulties and challenges for the new government?

A: The third generation of Chinese leadership with Comrade Jiang Zemin at its core have made enormous and universally recognized contribution to China's reform, development and stability and have, through practice, formed the important thought of "three represents", which is a valuable spiritual asset. The previous government under the leadership of Premier Zhu faithfully performed their duties and did a huge amount of remarkable work. The public are satisfied with what they have done. All of our work will have to be built on what our predecessors have achieved. Our predecessors have already laid a very good foundation for us. Yet we are still faced with numerous difficulties and problems ahead, which requires innovation and creativity as we press ahead. I always pay a lot of attention to the ancient motto, that is, *one prospers in worries and hardships and perishes in ease and comfort.*

(b) *14 March 2004*: Press conference after the Second Session of the Tenth National People's Congress.

When "Wen Jiabao 2004 NPC Press Conference" was searched from Google, what we got was as follows.

提示：如只要搜尋中文（繁體）的結果，可使用使用偏好指定搜尋語言。

NPC & CPPCC Sessions 2004 - [翻譯此頁]
Premier Wen Jiabao answers questions at the press conference after the second ... (NPC) closed at the Great Hall of the People in Beijing, March 14, 2004. ...
english.people.com.cn/zhuanti/Zhuanti_384.html

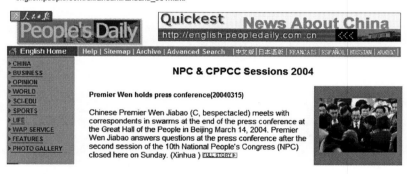

Home>>China

Last updated at: (Beijing Time) Wednesday, March 24, 2004

Full text of Chinese premier's press conference

Premier Wen Jiabao's Press Conference at the Conclusion of the Second Session of the 10th National People's Congress (NPC) on March 14.

This webpage was useful for the translation of four quotations. To save space, only the limited context in which the quotation was made will be displayed.

(69) 海不辭水，故能成其大；山不辭土石，故能成其高。

The sea does not reject water, so it is able to become great; the mountain does not reject stones, so it is able to become tall.

[Official Translation]
A: I think it was in this room last year that I compared socialism to a big ocean. *The ocean never turns away streams, so it becomes wide and deep.* That means socialism can only develop itself by drawing upon all the fine fruits of advanced human civilization. Today I would like to make a further comparison of socialism to a high mountain. *The mountain never turns away stones, so it becomes towering and strong.*

(6) 路漫漫其修遠兮，吾將上下而求索。

The way ahead is long, and I do not see any ending, yet high and low I'll search with determination.

[Official Translation]
And the other is from the ancient poet Qu Yuan: "My way ahead is long; I see no ending; yet high and low I'll search with my will unbending."

(23) 安不思危，治不忘亂。

When safe, don't forget danger; when in peace, don't forget chaos.

[Official Translation]
In terms of the work of the government for this year, we must have a somber mind. *In security, we should never forget the dangers and in times of peace, we should always beware of the potential for chaos.*

(85) 四百萬人同一哭，去年今日割台灣。

Four million people cried the same tears of sorrow as Taiwan was ceded.

[Official Translation]
So I went out sightseeing in the mountain, however, my mind always went back to this day last year when *4 million people on Taiwan cried the same tears of sorrow as Taiwan was ceded.*

(5) 雄關漫道真如鐵，而今邁步從頭越。

Don't say that this fortified pass is as hard as iron, as we can now cross its summit in one step.

[Official Translation]
The first quotation is from Chairman Mao. He wrote in a poem: "*The strong pass of the enemy is like a wall of iron, yet with firm strides, we are conquering its summit.*"

(c) *14 March 2005*: Press Conference after the Third Session of the Tenth People's National Congress;

When the link was clicked, an official website carrying a full English translation of the press conference on 14 March 2005 appeared, a part of which was shown below. [http://www.gov.cn/english/official/2005-07/26/content_17188.htm]

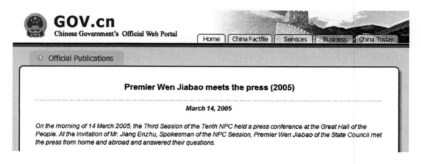

(86) 一尺布，尚可縫；一斗粟，尚可舂。同胞兄弟何不容。
When even a foot of cloth can be stitched up, even a kilo of millet can be ground, how can two blood brothers not make up.

[Official Translation]
A Chinese saying goes "*Even a foot of cloth can be stitched up. Even a kilo of millet can be ground. How come two blood brothers cannot make up?*" The Taiwan compatriots are our own brothers.

(27) 行百里者半九十。
If a journey is one hundred miles long, travelling ninety is half of it.

[Official Translation]
"If the journey is 100 miles, traveling 90 is only half of it" says a Chinese proverb.

(29) 思所以危則安，思所以亂則治，思所以亡則存。
Only when we think about where danger looms can we ensure our security. Only when we think about why chaos occurs can we ensure our peace. And only when we think about why a country falls can we ensure our survival. An official translation of the above quotation could not be found.

(d) *14 March 2006*: Press Conference after the Fourth Session of the Tenth National People's Congress

An official translation of one of the quotations cited in Wang's book, (89) "得道者多助，失道者寡助 (One who has the Way will have many to support him, while one who does not will have few to support him)" could not be found in the "gov.cn" official website. Its translation had to be taken from D.C. Lau's translation.[9]

(e) *16 March 2007*: Press Conference at the Great Hall of the People;
For this particular press conference, by searching with "Wen Jiabao 2007 NPC Press Conference," we found its full translation provided by the Ministry of Foreign Affairs of the People's Republic of China. In this press conference, Premier Wen quoted 4 Chinese sayings from various sources.

---

[9] D.C. Lau, trans., *Mencius* (Hong Kong: The Chinese University Press, 2003), 79.

简体中文 繁体中文 Français РУССКИЙ Español

中华人民共和国外交部
Ministry of Foreign Affairs of the People's Republic of China

Peace

| HOME | The Ministry | Policies and Activities | Press and Media Service | Countries and Regions | International Issues | About China | Resources |

search

Contact Us
Subscribe
Print
Suggest To A Friend

HOME > Latest News

Premier Wen Jiabao's Press Conference

2007/03/17

Wen Jiabao, Premier of the State Council, met the Chinese and foreign press and answered their questions at a press conference of the Fifth Session of the Tenth National People's Congress (NPC) held at the Great Hall of the People on the morning of 16 March at the invitation of NPC Spokesman Jiang Enzhu.

(119) 召遠在修近，閉禍在除怨。
To win distant friends, one needs, first of all, to have good relations with his neighbours. To avoid adversity, one needs to ease animosity.

[Official Translation]
As the ancient Chinese philosopher Kuan-tzu observed: "To win distant friends, one needs, first of all, to have good relations with his neighbors. To avoid adversity, one needs to ease animosity."

(77) 水能載舟，亦能覆舟。
While water can carry a boat, it can also overturn it.

[Official Translation]
Every cadre and leading official should know that "while water can carry a boat, it can also overturn it."

(91) 沉舟側畔千帆過，病樹前頭萬木春。
A thousand sails pass by the wrecked ship; ten thousand saplings shoot up beyond the withered tree.

[Official Translation]
This is a trend no one can reverse, as described in a classical Chinese poem: *A thousand sails pass by the wrecked ship; ten thousand saplings shoot up beyond the withered tree.*

(90) 今年花兒紅了，明年花更好。
The red bauhinia is beautiful this year, and it will be even more beautiful next year.

[Official Translation]
The bauhinia flower is in full bloom. *The red bauhinia is beautiful this year, and it will be even more beautiful next year.*

(f) *18 March 2008*: Press Conference after the First Session of the Eleventh National People's Congress.

Premier Wen Jiabao Answered Questions at Press Conference

2008-03-18

One of the websites that provided a full translation of the questions and answers in Premier Wen's press conference on 18 March 2008 is "The Commissioner's Office of China's Foreign Ministry in the Hong Kong SAR," an official web portal. For this particular press conference, six quotations were mentioned.

(100) 以和為貴，和而不同。
Harmony is most valuable, but it allows diversity.

(81) 如將不盡，與古為新。
Only innovation can sustain the growth and vitality of a nation.

[Official Translation]
The other is that *only innovation could sustain the growth and vitality of a nation.*

(93) 一心中國夢，萬古下泉詩。
I have always longed to see a reunified China, an aspiration shared by all our people.

[Official Translation]
I always think of lines such as *"I have always longed to see a reunified China, an aspiration shared by all our people."*

(41) 天變不足畏，祖宗不足法，人言不足恤。
There is no need to fear changes of the sky, no need to emulate the way of the ancestors, and no need to seek the approval of others.

[Official Translation]
One should not fear the changes under the heaven. One should not blindly follow past conventions. And one should not be deterred by complaints of others.

(17) 行事見於當時，是非公於後世。
What one did at the time will be judged by history. History is created and written by the people.

[Official Translation]
What one did at the time will be judged by history. History is created and written by the people.

(92) 度盡劫波兄弟在，相逢一笑泯恩仇。
We remain brothers after all the calamities, let's forgo our old grudges with a smile and meet again.

[Official Translation]
"we remain brothers despite all the vicissitudes and let's forgo our grudges when smiling we meet again."

(g) *13 March 2009*: Press Conference after the Second Session of the Eleventh National People's Congress

For this particular press conference, most of the websites that were searched only provided highlights of Wen's remarks at the press conference, as shown in the website of the NPC and CPPCC Annual Sessions 2009.

Highlights of Premier Wen's remarks at March 13 press conference

BEIJING, March 13 (Xinhua) -- Chinese Premier Wen Jiabao met the press Friday after the annual session of the National People's Congress concluded. Following are highlights of Wen's remarks: >>>

A detailed Chinese version was available from the official website: [http://www.npc.gov.cn/pc/11_2/2009-03/14/content_1493227.htm], as shown below.

在十一届全国人大二次会议记者会上
温家宝总理答中外记者问

(49) 乞火不若取燧，寄汲不若鑿井
It would be better to obtain a fire-maker than beg for fire, better to dig a well ourselves than beg for water from others.

(47) 莫道今年春將盡，明年春色倍還人。
Don't say that this year's spring is about to end, as the scenery of spring will be twice as enchanting next year.

(42) 山重水複疑無路，柳暗花明又一村。
Where the hills and streams end and there seems no road beyond, amidst shading willows and blooming flowers there is another village.

Besides official websites, there are websites in which bilingual versions of Wen's quotations are available, mostly as model translations to be learned. The following are some examples.

(1) 盤點歷年溫總理兩會答記者問經典語錄(雙語)
    (http://www.youth.cn 中國青年網 English Corner 英語角)
(2) 溫總理答記者問引用詩句及翻譯
    (http://hefei.neworiental.org/publish/portal63/tab4014/info326458.ht
    m 新東方)
(3) 溫總理歷屆兩會答記者問引用詩文及英譯 (HJEnglish.com 滬江
    英語)
    (Translation provided by the Administration Bureau of Foreign Expert
    Affairs of Jinan City 濟南市外國專家局
    http://jinan.caiep.org/forum/content.php?id=41692)

(2) Press Conferences in Foreign Countries

A typical example of Wen's press conference in a foreign country is the one he gave in Cairo on 18 June 2006. When "Wen Jiabao 18 June 2006" was searched, a full translation of the press conference on that date was given by the Embassy of the people's Republic of China in the Arab Republic of Egypt.

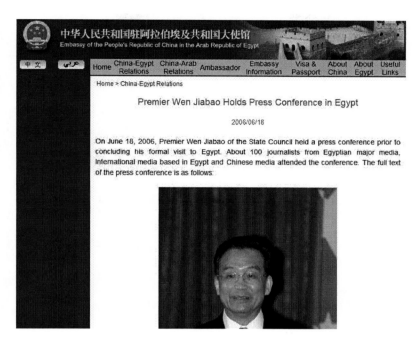

(112) 吾有德於人也，不可不忘也。
Do not forget the good given by others and do forget the good given to others.

[Official Translation]
Here, I wish to stress that the African people also provided China with valuable support over the past years. In Chinese, we say the African people do "Good" to China. An ancient Chinese thinker once said, *"Do not forget the Good given by others and do forget the Good given to others."*

(3) Interviews by News Organizations

Premier Wen often has interviews with different news organizations, including newspapers and television stations both in China and overseas. In the Chinese book, two interviews in China are mentioned. The first one was an interview by the *Washington Post* on 21 November 2003, in which two quotations were cited.
[http://big5.fmprc.gov.cn/gate/big5/no.china-embassy.org/eng/dtxw/t11055 7.htm]

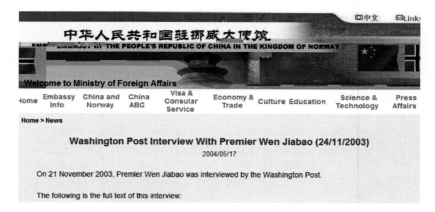

(43) 察其言，觀其行。
Hear what they say and then watch what they do.

[Official Translation]
We have *taken note of the recent remarks* by the Dalai Lama but we still
need to *watch very carefully what he really does.*

(99) 結交一言重，相期千里至。
Good friends highly value their words. They travel a thousand miles to
keep their promise for a gathering.

[Official Translation]
I can quote one fitting ancient Chinese poem to describe our meeting:
"*Good friends highly value their words. They travel a thousand li to keep
their promise for a gathering.*"

Another interview that was conducted in China was made on 5
September 2006 when Wen Jiabao was interviewed by five European news
organizations, including *Helsingin Sanomat* in Finland, *Reuters* and the
Times of London, *Deutsche Presse-Agentur* and *Frankfurter Allgemeine
Zeitung* in Germany. By searching with the query "Wen Jiabao 5
September 2006 European media interview," the following webpage
(gov.cn) was displayed on the screen:

(13) 長太息以掩涕兮，哀民生之多艱。
Long did I sigh to hold back tears; saddened I am by the grief of my people.

[Official Translation]
"Long did I sigh to hold back tears; saddened I am by the grief of my people."

(110) 花徑不曾緣客掃，篷門今始為君開。
I have not swept the path of fallen petals until today, and I have opened my thatched door just for you.

[Official Translation]
"*The path of fallen petals I have not swept until today, when I open my thatched door, just for you.*" I have quoted these lines from a Chinese poem by way of welcome, and I am pleased to give you this interview.

(12) 身無半畝，心憂天下；讀破萬卷，神交古人。

I don't have half an acre of land to myself, but I care about my people across the land. I read over ten thousand books and am spiritually attracted to the ancient people.

[Official Translation]
"While I have little possession at hand, I care deeply about my people across the land. Having devoured ten thousand books and drawing inspiration from ancient thinkers, I have the whole world in my mind."

(14) 為什麼我的眼裏常含着淚水？

Why are my eyes always filled with tears?

[Official Translation]
"You ask why my eyes are always filled with tears. It is because I love my land dearly."

Yet another interview that was conducted in China was an interview with Wen Jiabao by the Deputy Editor-in-chief Pierre Rousselin and Head of the Beijing Office Jean-Jacques Mevel of the French newspaper *Le Figaro*.

Premier Wen Jiabao Accepts the Interview of Deputy Editor-in-Chief Pierre Rousselin and Head of the Beijing Office Jean-Jacques Mével of Le Figaro

2005/12/03

(71) 身貴自由，國貴自主。

The individual values freedom and the state values autonomy.

[Official Translation]
Yan Fu, the great thinker of China at that time raised the idea that *the most important thing for a country is independence and the most important thing for a person is freedom.*

Included in the book is an interview that was conducted in a Thailand hotel on 10 April 2009.

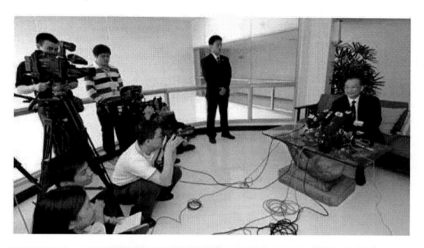

China View

Publicize Chin
Report the

Home | China | World | Business | Culture & Edu | Sports | Entertainment | Sci & Tech | Heal

WINDOW OF CHINA

Premier: Chinese economy shows signs of positive changes

www.chinaview.cn   2009-04-12 01:17:19   Print

Special Report: Global Financial Crisis

┌─ **STORY HIGHLIGHTS** ──────────────────────────────────
· Chinese economy showed signs of better than expected positive changes in first quarter.
· Chinese Premier Wen Jiabao listed four positive performances in economic fields.
· Wen said these performances suggest policies have led to successes.
└──

PATTAYA, Thailand, April 11 (Xinhua) -- Chinese Premier Wen Jiabao, in an interview with Hong Kong and Macao reporters here Saturday, said that the Chinese economy showed signs of better than expected positive changes in the first quarter as a result of the economic stimulus package adopted by China.

It is obvious that an English version of the interview was provided by Xinhua.net.   [http://news.xinhuanet.com/english/2009-04/12/content_111 70833.htm], but only in a paraphrased way. There was only a quotation cited, which is as follows:

(96) 不進則退。
If you don't move forward, you will fall behind.

(4) Meetings with Leaders of Foreign Countries or International Organizations

Quotations that were cited during Wen's meetings with leaders of foreign countries or international organizations were also translated by official agencies. Three examples can be cited. The first is Wen's meeting with Kofi Annan, then Secretary-General of the United Nations (UN), at UN headquarters in New York. When we searched by "Wen Jiabao 7 December 2003 Annan," the following website was found, as shown below.

(98) 時移世易，變法宜矣。
As generations change and the seasons replace one another, it was time to reform the laws.

Another example is the meeting with the new Japanese Prime Minister Shinzo Abe in Beijing on 8 October 2006. When searched with "Wen Jiabao 8 October 2006 Shinzo Abe," the following website provided by the Embassy of the People's Republic of China in Jamaica and the Permanent Mission of the People's Republic of China to the International Seabed Authority" appeared on screen.
[http://jm.chineseembassy.org/eng/xw/t277484.htm]

Home > News

Premier Wen Jiabao Holds Talks with Japanese Prime Minister Shinzo Abe
2006-10-08

On October 8, 2006, Chinese Premier Wen Jiabao held talks with Japanese Prime Minister Shinzo Abe at the Great Hall of the People.

(114) 言必信，行必果。
Promises must be kept and action must be resolute.

[Official Translation]
"*Promises must be kept and action must be resolute*," Wen said, noting that that is an important guarantee for pushing forward China-Japan relations.

(115) 青山遮不住，畢竟東流去。
The green mountain can't stop water from flowing, and the river keeps flowing eastward.

The third example is Wen's meeting with Hillary Clinton, the United States Secretary of State, in China. The citation of a saying from *The Art of War* is contextual. On 15 February 2009, the United States Secretary State Hillary Clinton began her visit to Japan, Indonesia, Korea and China. This was her first foreign trip since she assumed the post of secretary of state of the Obama government.

On 13 February, on the eve of her trip, Hillary Clinton went to the Asia Society in New York and gave a speech. In the speech, she cited a Chinese idiom "as we are in the same boat we have to help each other" to set the tone for Sino-American relationship: "'When you are in a common boat, you need to cross the river peacefully together.' The wisdom of that aphorism must continue to guide us today."

On the afternoon of 21 February, Premier Wen Jiabao met with Hillary Clinton at the Purple Light Hall of Zhongnanhai. Wen Jiabao firstly extended his congratulations to Hillary Clinton for attaining such an important post, and also extended his warmest welcome to her on her visit to China. Wen Jiabao said, "As the world is faced with the grim impact of the financial crisis, I very much appreciate a Chinese proverb you quoted that 'all countries should cross the river peacefully as they are in a common boat.' The proverb is from *The Art of War* by Sunzi, an ancient Chinese military strategist. Another saying in the book goes as 'progress together hand in hand.'" [http://news.xinhuanet.com/english.htm]

It was, however, in another website that the proverb Wen cited was found, as shown below.

[http://news.xinhuanet.com/english/2009-02/21/content_10863097.htm]

WINDOW OF CHINA

Wen, Clinton underline bilateral relations by citing Chinese proverbs▣

www.chinaview.cn   **2009-02-21 16:42:05**   ▭ ✚ Print

(120) 當其同舟而濟，遇風，其救也如左右手。
Crossing the river in the same boat in the gale, one would go to each other's aid like the right hand helping the left.

[Official Translation]
"As the world is faced with the grim impact of the financial crisis, I very much appreciate a (Chinese) proverb you quoted that *all countries should cross the river peacefully as they are in a common boat*," Wen said. The proverb is from *The Art of War* by Sunzi, an ancient Chinese military strategist.

(5) Speeches at International Meetings Held in China

As the Premier of the State Council, Wen has to make a number of speeches in China that are targeted at an international audience. His speeches are usually translated by official agencies.

The first speech is the one he delivered at the World Tourism Organization held on 19 October 2003 in China. A full translation of Wen's speech was provided by the Ministry of Foreign Affairs of the People's Republic of China.
[http://www.mfa.gov.cn/eng/xwfw/zyjh/t40147.htm]

(51) 讀萬卷書，行萬里路。
Read thousands of books and travel thousands of miles.

[Official Translation]
Ancient People also proposed to "*travel ten thousand* li *and read ten thousand books*," which shows they found pleasure in enriching themselves mentally and physically through traveling over famous mountains and rivers.

The second speech is Wen's keynote speech delivered at Boao Forum on 2 November 2003.

Home>>Business

Last updated at: (Beijing Time) Monday, November 03, 2003

Premier Wen calls for win-win development path for Asia

Chinese Premier Wen Jiabao said Sunday that to create a win-win situation through closer cooperation and stronger efforts for development is the only way to make Asia's renewal possible. He also outlined China's policy to promote cooperation, development and a win-win situation in Asia.

Carrying Forward the Five Principles of Peaceful Coexistence in the Promotion of Peace and Development*

WEN Jiabao**

Distinguished Diplomatic Envoys,
Friends and Comrades,

Fifty years ago, the late Premier Zhou Enlai paid separate visits to India and Myanmar, during which joint government statements were issued to define and

(97) 桃李不言，下自成蹊。
Peaches and plums do not speak, yet a path is trampled out beneath them.
[No official translation found]

The third example is a speech Wen delivered at the Great Hall of the People in Beijing on 28 June 2004 to commemorate the fiftieth anniversary of "the Five Principles of Peaceful Coexistence." A full translation of Wen's speech was found, after searching and researching, at the following website:
[http://chinesejil.oxfordjournals.org/cgi/reprint/3/2/363.pdf]

(122) 萬物並育而不相害，道並行而不相悖。
All living creatures grow together without harming one another; ways run parallel without interfering with one another.

[Official Translation]
The ancient Chinese thinker Confucius once said, "*All living creatures grow together without harming one another; ways run parallel without interfering with one another.*"

The fourth example is Wen's speech at the Finance Ministers' Meeting of the Sixth Asia-Europe Meeting held on 26 June 2005 in Tianjin, China. In the website of the "Economic and Commercial Section, Consulate General of the P.R. China in Gothenburg" is a full translation of his speech.
[http://gothenburg2.mofcom.gov.cn/article/chinanews/200506/20050600135332.html]

Economic and Commercial Section, Consulate General of the P.R.China in Gothenburg
中华人民共和国驻哥德堡总领馆经济商务室

Commercial News : Bilateral Visits : Supply & Demand : Exhibition Info : About Us : Bilateral Cooperation : About China
China Law : Host Country : Laws of Host Country : Enquiry Online

Current Location: Homepage > Commercial News > Text

Premier Wen Jiabao Strengthened the Asia-Europe Meeting economic co-operation
Monday,June 27,2005 Posted: 16:41 BJT(0841 GMT) China Daily

Chinese Premier Wen Jiabao delivered a speech yesterday at the opening ceremony of the Sixth ASEM Finance Ministers' Meeting (FMM) of the Asia-Europe Meeting (ASEM) in the northern Chinese port city of Tianjin. The following is the full text of the speech:
Distinguished guests, ladies and gentlemen,
I would like to begin by expressing, on behalf of the Chinese Government, our warm congratulations on the opening of the Sixth ASEM Finance Ministers' Meeting (FMM) in

(106) 相知無遠近，萬里尚為鄰。

Distance cannot separate true friends who feel so close even when they are thousands of miles apart.

[Official Translation]
There is an old saying in China: *"Distance cannot separate true friends who feel close even when they are thousands of miles apart."*

The last example is Wen's speech at the Twenty-first Century Forum in China on 5 September 2005. The following is the quotation cited.

(104) 暑退九霄淨，秋澄萬景清。

The retreat of summer makes the sky clean, and the shiny autumn moon makes everything clear.

(6) Speeches at Meetings Held in Foreign Countries

In the following, there are six speeches by Wen Jiabao which were delivered in Thailand, United States, Malaysia, Fiji, South Africa, and Russia respectively. The first speech was made at the meeting of ASEAN countries in Thailand on SARS on 29 April 2003. It was available from the website of "the Consulate General of the People's Republic of China in Los Angeles."
[http://losangeles.china-consulate.org/eng/news/topnews/t27622.htm]

(a) *29 April 2003*: Speech at the meeting of ASEAN countries in Thailand on SARS;

(25) 安危相易，禍福相倚。

Safety and danger alternate; misfortune and fortune are mutually dependent.

[Official Translation]
As an old Chinese saying goes, *"Danger and safety are often interchangeable, as it is with disaster and happiness."*

The second such speech was delivered by Wen Jiabao at the American Banks Association in New York on 8 December 2003. A full translation of his speech was provided in the website of "The Consulate General of The People's Republic of China in Los Angeles. [http://losangeles.china-consulate.org/eng/news/topnews/t56330.htm] This is the first "search."

Then came the next "search," or "re-search," using the keyword "mountain."

Then the translation of the quotation 會當凌絕頂，一覽眾山小 was found.

(3) 會當凌絕頂，一覽眾山小。
When I reach the peak of Mount Tai, all other mountains look so small.

[Official Translation]
Depicting how climbers of the towering Mount Tai feel, an ancient Chinese poem goes, *"I must ascend the mountain's crest; it dwarfs all peaks under my feet."*

The third speech was given on 14 December 2005 in Kuala Lumpur, Malaysia. A summary of his speech was given on the website of the "Ministry of Foreign Affairs of the People's Republic of China," as shown below.

But this would not help as far as the translation of the quotation is concerned.

(103) 不畏浮雲遮望眼，只綠身在最高層。
We have no fear of the clouds that may block our view, as we are already on the summit.

The fourth speech was delivered by Wen Jiabao at the China-Pacific Island Countries Economic Development and Cooperation Forum held in Fiji on 5 April 2006. A full translation of Wen's speech was given in the website "Gov.cn." [http://www.gov.cn/english/2006-04/05/content_245 681.htm]

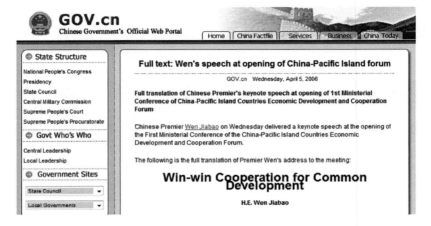

(113) 路遙知馬力，日久見人心。
Distance tests a horse's strength, and time reveals a person's real character.

[Official Translation]
As a Chinese saying puts it, *"Just as distance tests a horse's strength, time will show a person's sincerity."*

The fifth speech was given by Wen Jiabao at the First China-South Africa Business Cooperation Forum in Cape Town, South Africa on 22 June 2006.

A summary of Wen's ideas in the speech was provided by the website of the "Ministry of Foreign Affairs of the People's Republic of China." A full translation of his speech was given at
http://capetown.china-consulate.org/eng.htm.

(111) 世上無難事，只要肯登攀。
Nothing is hard under the sky, if we dare to climb up high.

[Official Translation]
"*Nothing is difficult to the man who will try*. To strengthen China-South Africa and China-Africa cooperation *is like climbing a mountain*. I hope you will race against time and forge valiantly ahead.""

The last speech was delivered by Wen at the Third China-Russia Economic and Trade Summit Forum on 28 October 2008.

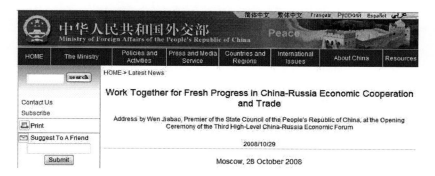

(121) 亡羊補牢，猶未晚也。
It is not too late to mend the fold even after some of the sheep have been lost.

[Official Translation]
As the Chinese saying goes, "it is not too late to mend the fold even after some of the sheep have been lost."

(7) Speeches at Institutions in Foreign Countries

Most of the speeches in this category are those given at educational institutions, such as Harvard and Cambridge, and there was a speech given at the Japanese Diet. As far as educational institutions are concerned, Wen has given speeches at Harvard University in the United States, Ecole Polytechnique in France, Instituto Cervantes in Spain, and Cambridge University in the United Kingdom.

The quotations that Wen cited at Harvard were fully translated by the official agency.

Last updated at: (Beijing Time) Friday, December 12, 2003

Full text of Premier Wen's speech at Harvard

The following is the full text of Chinese Premier Wen Jiabao's speech delivered at Harvard University, December 10, entitled "Turning Your Eyes to China".

(4) 為天地立心，為生民立命，為往聖繼絕學，為萬世開太平。
To ordain conscience for Heaven and Earth, to secure life and fortune for the people, to continue the lost teachings of past sages, and to establish peace for all future generations.

[Official Translation]
Chinese forefathers formulated their goals as follows:
To ordain conscience for Heaven and Earth,
To secure life and fortune for the people,
To continue lost teachings for past sages,
To establish peace for all future generations.

(22) 天下興亡，匹夫有責。
Everybody is responsible for the rise or fall of the country.

[Official Translation]
Especially, patriotism as embodied in the saying *"Everybody is responsible for the rise or fall of the country;"*

(15) 衙齋臥聽蕭蕭竹，疑是民間疾苦聲。
Lying in bed in my den, I heard the rustling of bamboos outside, and it just sounded like the moaning of the needy.

[Official Translation]
A Chinese poet-magistrate of the 18th century wrote:
The rustling of bamboo outside my door,
Sounds like the moaning of the needy poor.

Chronologically, the second speech Wen gave at an educational institution was at the Ecole Polytechnique in Saclay, France on 6 December 2005. There was a summary of Wen's speech at "people.com.cn."

English home   Forum   Photo Gallery   Features   Newsletter   Archive

▶ China
▶ World
▶ Opinion
▶ Business
▶ Sci-Edu
▶ Culture/Life
▶ Sports
▶ Photos

Services

- Newsletter
- Online Community
- China Biz Info

Home >> China   UPDATED: 09:30, December 07, 2005

Chinese premier calls for respect of civilizations, vows to stick to reform, opening up

Visiting Chinese Premier Wen Jiabao on Tuesday called for respect for different civilizations in efforts to build a harmonious world, and vowed that the policy of reform and opening up will continue in his country's modernization drive.

In a speech delivered at Ecole Polytechnique, a leading university in France, Wen said harmony is the ultimate source of coexistence and development of the world's civilizations.

(107) 天時不如地利，地利不如人和。

Favourable weather is less important than advantageous terrain, and advantageous terrain is less important than human unity.

(11) 窮則變，變則通，通則久。

Coming to a deadlock leads to changes; changes lead to solutions; solutions lead to sustainability.

On 31 January 2009, Wen also talked with students of Instituto Cervantes in Madrid in Spain.

中华人民共和国驻爱尔兰共和国大使馆
EMBASSY OF THE PEOPLE'S REPUBLIC OF CHINA IN IRELAND   中文

Home Embassy Info News Spokesperson's Remarks Sino-Irish Relations Visa&Consular Economy&Trade Education Science&Tech About China

Home > News

Remarks by Premier Wen Jiabao During Discussion with Representatives Of the Cultural Community and Young Students of Spain

2009-01-31

31 January 2009

Madame Director,
Dear Students and Faculty Members,
Ladies and Gentlemen,
Friends,

It gives me great pleasure to meet with you at the renowned Instituto Cervantes. Both China and Spain are major

(64) 民胞物與。

All people are my brothers and sisters, and all things are my companions.

[Official Translation]
The belief is that nature has created and nurtured all men and all things on earth, and that *every man is my brother and every object is my friend.*

What is of particular interest, due partly to the shoe-throwing incident, is Wen's Rede Lecture at the University of Cambridge entitled "See China in the Light of Her Development," a full translation of which was provided by the "Ministry of Foreign Affairs of the People's Republic of China" in its official website:
[http://www.fmprc.gov.cn/eng/zxxx/t535283.htm]

(101) 百姓昭明，協和萬邦。
We should have amity among people and friendly exchanges among nations.

[Official Translation]
The Book of History, an ancient classic in China for example, advocates *amity among people and friendly exchanges among nations.*

(124) 潮平兩岸闊，風正一帆懸。
From shore to shore it is wide and surgeless, and under a fair wind a sail is lifting.

[Official Translation]
I want to quote from a Tang Dynasty poem to describe what is happening in China, "*From shore to shore it is wide at high tide, and before fair wind a sail is lifting.*"

Wen Jiabao also gives speeches at political institutions, such as his speech at the Japanese Diet in Japan on 12 April 2007.
[http://www.fmcoprc.gov.hk/eng/zgwjsw/t311107.htm]

The Commissioner's Office
of China's Foreign Ministry in the Hong Kong SAR

About Us | Consular Services | Visa to China | Media Services | Policies | Resourses | 简体中文 | 繁體中文

Home > China's Foreign Affairs

Speech by Premier Wen Jiabao of the State Council of The People's Republic of China at the Japanese Diet
2007-04-12
Tokyo, Japan, 12 April 2007

(116) 與朋友交，言而有信。
One should honour commitments made to friends.

[Official Translation]
An ancient Chinese sage said that "one should value credibility in relations with others" and that "*one should honour commitment made to friends.*"

(8) Speeches at International Meetings in Foreign Countries

A speech that falls into this category is Wen's keynote speech at the World Economic Forum on 28 January 2009 at Davos in Switzerland. The title of his speech was: "Strengthen Confidence and Work Together for A New Round of World Economic Growth."

Home | China | World | Business | Culture & Edu | Sports | Entertainment | Sci & Tech | Health

WINDOW OF CHINA

Full text of Chinese premier's speech at World Economic Forum Annual Meeting 2009

(123) 吃一塹，長一智
A fall in the pit is a gain in your wit.

[Official Translation]
As the saying goes, "A fall in the pit, a gain in your wit," we must draw lessons from this crisis and address its root causes.

(9) Meeting Incoming Ambassadors from Foreign Countries

When Wen Jiabao welcomed incoming ambassadors, he occasionally quoted Chinese sayings to put forth his ideas. This is very much in evidence when he welcomed the incoming ambassadors from thirty-three countries on 28 January 2005.

(105) 親仁善鄰，國之寶也。
It is most important to have close and honorable relations with one's neighbours.

The above shows that when Wen Jiabao quoted Chinese sayings to convey his points in speeches and talked that were targeted at foreigners or international audience in general, the official websites, such as "gov.cn." and "xinhua.net," always provide official translations of the Chinese texts that Wen used at these occasions. It is always advisable to use them as far as possible, but when they may not suit the contexts, they have to be modified slightly.

[b] Occasions without Official Translations

Wen Jiabao is the Premier of the State of the People's Republic of China. He attends many functions attended mainly by Chinese people. The necessity of translating officially his speeches is extremely low. The event may be reported in the media, but the texts of his speeches or talks are not translated. In this book *Famous Chinese Sayings*, there are 16 situations in which translations of the Chinese sources are not provided. Research on the existing translations of the original works and skills of translating quotations properly to suit the contexts is essential.

(1) Speeches to Chinese Audience at Major Festivals

One of the major festivals is the Spring Festival. Every year, leaders of the Chinese Communist Party go the Great Hall of the People to meet with more than 4,000 people from different sectors of the society to celebrate the lunar New Year. These activities are normally reported in the media in English, but they seldom include translations of quotations cited by leaders, such as Wen Jiabao. In this and the following sections, translations by other hands, whose names are put in brackets, will be included.

Three of the speeches made at these meetings were included in the book.

(a) *Meeting on 20 January 2004*

(44) 每逢佳節倍思親。
Each time a fete day comes, I yearn doubly for my family.

[My Translation]
Alone in a strange land, feeling myself a stranger.
Each time a fete day comes, I yearn doubly for my family.

(b) *Meeting on 16 February 2007*

(36) 憂民之憂者，民亦憂其憂。
When a ruler grieves at the sorrow of his people, they also grieve at his sorrow.

[Translation by D.C. Lau][10]
(The people) will worry over the troubles of him who worries over their troubles.

(c) *Meeting on 24 January 2009*

(39) 民為邦本，本固邦寧。
People are the basis of a nation, and only when this basis is stable can the nation enjoy peace.

---

[10] Lau, *Mencius*, 33, 35.

[Translation by Luo Zhiye][11]
The people are the root of the nation.
If the root is tight,
The nation will be peaceful.

Another major festival in China is the Teachers' Day. In this book, quotations by Wen Jiabao were made in 2004, 2005, and 2008.

(a) *5 September 2004*

(57) 言之不足，故嗟歎之。(《詩經》)
If words are not sufficient, sighing can be better. (*The Book of Poetry*)

[My Translation]
The motion is moved in the heart and takes shape in words; *if words are not sufficient, sighing can be better.*

(56) 詩言志，歌詠聲，舞動容。
Poetry expresses one's thoughts, singing speaks one's voice, and dancing shows one's colour.

[My Translation]
Poetry gives expression to people's thoughts; singing prolongs the notes of people's voice; dancing shows people's sentimental colour.

(60) 言有物，行有格
Speak with substance and act by rules.

[My Translation]
The Master said, "*Speak with substance and act by rules;*"

(b) *9 September 2005*

(52) 不憤不啟，不悱不發。(《論語》)
I do not open up the truth to one who is not eager to get knowledge, nor help out anyone who is not anxious to explain himself. (*The Analects of Confucius*)

---

[11] Luo Zhiye, comp. and trans., *Sun Tsu's The Art of War.* (Beijing: China Translation and Publishing Corporation and the Commercial Press, 2007), 311-13.

[Translation by D.C. Lau][12]
The Master said, "*I never enlighten anyone who has not been driven to distraction by trying to understand a difficulty or who has got into a frenzy trying to put his ideas into words.*"

(53) 千教萬教，教人求真。(陶行知)
Whatever we teach is all about the pursuit of truths. (Tao Xingzhi)

[Translation by Barry Steben]
The duty of a teacher is: "*whatever we teach is all about the pursuit of truths.*"

(c) *9 September 2008*

(68) 學為人師，行為世範。(《舊唐書》)
Learn, so as to teach others; act, so as to serve as an example to all. (*The Old History of the Tang Dynasty*)

Yet another festival that is celebrated annually is the May-Fourth Youth Festival. Wen met students of Peking University in 2005, Beijing Normal University in 2006, and students in Beijing in 2007.

(a) *4 May 2005*

(66) 教是為了不教。(葉聖陶)
Teaching is in order not to teach. (Ye Shengtao)

[Translation of Barry Steben]
I have recently often said the following to people: "*The purpose of all teaching is to render the taught no longer in need of being taught.*"

(b) *4 May 2006*

(65) 大學不在於有大樓。(梅貽琦)
It's not buildings that make a university. (Mei Yiqi)

[Translation of Barry Steben]
I can say that "*a university is called a university not because it has a lot big buildings*, but because it has great teachers."

---

[12] D.C. Lau, trans., *The Analects of Confucius* (Lun yu) (Hong Kong: T[ ] University Press, 1983), 57.

(c) *4 May 2007*

(16) 非知之難，行之惟難；非行之難，終之斯難。(《貞觀政要》)
The difficult thing is not just to know something, but to do something; the difficult thing is not even to do something, but to be persistent in doing something. (*Notes on the Political Governance of Zhenguan*)

[My Translation]
There is an ancient saying which runs: "*The difficult thing is not just to know something, but to do something; the difficult thing is not even to do something, but to be persistent in doing something.*"

(2) **Speeches at Chinese Embassies**

When Wen Jiabao visits foreign countries, his usual practice is to meet overseas Chinese and staff of the Chinese Embassies. Included in this book are his visits to Chinese Embassies in Mexico, London, Slovakia, New Zealand, Finland, New York, and Spain.

(a) *15 December 2003* (Mexico)

(61) 明於識，練於事，忠於國。(梁啟超)
Clarity of knowledge, proficiency in affairs, and loyalty to the nation. (Liang Qichao)

anslation by Barry Steben]
With *his clarity of knowledge, his proficiency in affairs, and his to the nation*, if he had just had the chance to play some part in ing government policy, the effectiveness of his measures would unlimited.

(London)

，勿施於人。(《論語》)
others what you yourself do not desire. (*The Analects of*

of   au][13]
erhaps the word *shu* (forgiveness)! *Do not impose lf do not desire.*"

e Chinese

(48) 上下同心者勝。(《孫子兵法》)

The side that has superiors and subordinates united in heart will take the victory. (*The Art of War*)

[Translation by Roger Ames][14]
The side that has superiors and subordinates united in heart will take the victory.

(c) *7 December 2005* (Slovakia)

(32) 夕惕若厲。(《周易》)

In the evening, we are still careful and apprehensive. (The *Book of Changes*)

[Translation by Rudolf Ritsema and Stephen Karcher][15]
In the evening, he is still careful, apprehensive, and faultless.

(d) *6 April 2006* (New Zealand)

(10) 天行健，君子以自強不息。(《周易》)

As Heaven's movement is ever vigorous, a gentleman must ceaselessly strive along. (*The Book of Changes*)

[My Translation]
As Heaven's movement is ever vigorous, a gentleman must ceaselessly strive along.

(8) 先天下之憂而憂，後天下之樂而樂。(范仲淹)

To worry before the whole world worries, and to rejoice after the whole world rejoices. (Fan Zhongyan)

[My Translation]
No doubt they are worried before the whole world worries and they rejoice after the whole world rejoices.

---

[14] Roger T. Ames, trans., *Sun-Tzu: The Art of War* (New York: Ballantine Books, 1993), 113.

[15] Rudolf Ritsema and Stephen Karcher, trans., *I Ching: The Classic Chinese Oracle of Change: The First Complete Translation with Concordance* (Michigan: Element, 1994), 100.

(e) *11 September 2006* (Finland)

(108) 德不孤，必有鄰。(《論語》)
Virtue never stands alone. It is bound to have neighbours. (*The Analects of Confucius*)

[Translation by D.C. Lau][16]
The Master said, "*Virtue never stands alone. It is bound to have neighbours.*"

(f) *23 September 2008* (New York)
(34) 居官者當事不避難。(《國語》)
Those who are in official positions should be courageous to shoulder responsibilities and should not avoid difficulties. (*Discourses of the States*)

[My Translation]
Those who are in official positions should be courageous to shoulder responsibilities and should not avoid difficulties.

(g) *30 January 2009* (Spain)
(50) 悠悠天宇曠，切切故鄉情。(張九齡)
Long-lasting is the spacious heaven, deep are my home feelings. (Zhang Jiuling)

[My Translation]
Long-lasting is the spacious heaven,
Deep are my home feelings.

(3) Meeting Overseas Chinese in China

Wen Jiabao frequently meets overseas Chinese at major meetings, such as the Boao Forum, and he uses Chinese sayings to convey his feelings on these meetings. Two examples can be cited.

(a) *Mid-April 2008*: Wen met with Xiao Wanchang at the Boao Forum.

(95) 大道之行也，天下為公。(《禮記》)
When the Great Way prevails, the world is for the public. (*The Book of Rites*)

---

[16] Lau, *The Analects*.

[My Translation]
When the Great Way prevails, the world is for the public.

(b) *18 April 2009*: Meeting Qian Fu at the Boao Forum

(94) 利在一身勿謀也，利在天下必謀之。(胡宏)
I will not seek personal gains. But if the gains benefit the world, I will
certainly seek them. (Hu Hong)

[My Translation]
*I will not seek personal gains. But if the gains benefit the world, I will
certainly seek them.*

(4) Meeting Overseas Chinese in Foreign Countries

Wen Jiabao often meets overseas Chinese when he visits foreign
countries. When he met overseas Chinese in Canberra in Australia on 3
April 2006, he made the following quotation.

(7) 誰言寸草心，報得三春暉。(孟郊)
Who can say that the heart of inch-long grass will repay the sunshine of
spring. (Meng Jiao)

[My Translation]
She sets the stitches firmly and closely before he departs,
For fear that he will be slow to return.
Who can say that the heart of inch-long grass,
Will repay the sunshine of spring.

(5) Meeting Participants in Major Meetings

Wen Jiabao often exchanges views or seeks advice from members of
the National People's Congress and the Chinese People's Political
Consultative Conference. In this book, six quotations were cited by Wen
Jiabao in the meetings held in 2005, 2006, 2007.

(a) *5 March 2005*: Meeting with members at the Third Plenary Session of
the Tenth National People's Congress

(24) 居安思危，思則有備，有備無患。(《左傳》)
When living in peace, we have to think of danger. If we think, then we will
be prepared. If we are prepared, then we will have no worries. (*Zuo's
Commentary on the Spring and Autumn Annals*)

[Translation by Hu Zhihui][17]
The *Book of Changes* says, "*Reside in temperance and think of the dangers. If you think, then you will be prepared. If you are prepared, then you will have no worries.*"

(28) 事者，生於慮，成於務，失於傲。(《管子》)
Things are born out of planning, completed in practice, but lost in arrogance. (*Guanzi*)

[Translation by Allyn W. Rickett][18]
Now production materializes through planning, succeeds through diligent attention, but fails through negligence.

(80) 嚶其鳴矣，求其友聲。
Long, long, the bird will sing, expecting its mates to echo.

[Translation by Xu Yuanzhong][19]
From the deep vale below
To lofty trees are heard.
Long, long, the bird will sing
And for an echo wait.

(b) *23 May 2006*: Report in the Plenary Meeting of the Seventh National Congress of China Association for Science and Technology

(55) 十年磨一劍。(賈島)
It takes ten years to make a sword. (Jia Dao)

[My Translation]
It has taken me ten years to make a sword,
I do not know if it will pierce.

(c) *4 March 2007*: Meeting the Economy and Agriculture Groups in the Chinese People's Political Consultative Conference in Beijing

(76) 賢路當廣而不當狹，言路當開而不當塞。(《宋史》)

[17] Hu Zhihui, trans., *Zuo Zhuan: Zuo's Commentary* (Changsha: Hunan People's Publishing House, 1996), 753.
[18] Allyn W. Rickett, *Guanzi: Political, Economic, and Philosophical Essays from Early China: A Study and Translation* (Princeton: Princeton University Press, 1985), 118.
[19] Xu Yuanzhong, trans., *The Book of Poetry* (Changsha: The Hunan Publishing House, 1993), 311.

The chances for worthy people to advance should be wide but not narrow; the channel of communication with leaders should be open but not blocked. (*History of the Song Dynasty*)

(d) *13 November 2006*: Meeting with representatives of the China Federation of Literary and Art Circles at the Eighth National Congress. (2)

(38) 德惟善政，政在養民。(《尚書》)
The virtue of the ruler is seen in his good government, which is in the nourishing of the people. (*The Book of History*)

[Translation by Hu Zhihui][20]
An emperor's virtue should make governmental affairs good, the aim of the administration of government is to nourish the people.

(59) 今人乍見孺子將入於井。(《孟子》)
If a man were, all of a sudden, to see a young child on the verge of falling into a well. (*Mencius*)

[Translation by D.C. Lau][21]
Suppose a man were all of a sudden, to see a young child on the verge of falling into a well.

(6) Speeches at Major Meetings

Wen Jiabao often makes speeches at major meetings. The following two quotations were made in Hong Kong and China.

(a) *29 June 2003*: Speech upon the signing of CEPA in Hong Kong

(2) 杜鵑再拜憂天淚，精衞無窮填海心。(黃遵憲)
The fabled cuckoo weeping blood at China's woe, and the Jingwei bird filling the sea with pebbles untold. (Huang Zuxian)

[My Translation]
The fabled cuckoo weeping blood at China's woe,
And the Jingwei bird filling the sea with pebbles untold.

---

[20] Hu, *Zuo Zhuan*, 297, 299.

[21] Lau, *Mencius*, 73.

(b) *23 November 2006*: Speech at the Twelfth National Conference on Civil Affairs

(37) 去民之患，如除腹心之疾。(蘇轍)
To remove the calamities of the people is like taking away an illness of the heart. (Su Zhe)

[My Translation]
If you also seriously observe their performance, then *removing the calamities of the people is like taking away an illness of the heart.*

(7) Meeting with People on His Visits

There are all sorts of people Wen Jiabao meets in his work as the Premier of the State Council. Three quotations relating to his visits are included in the book. These are on medical works in Hong Kong, flood victims in Sichuan, and drug addicts in Yunnan.

(a) *30 June 2003*: Meeting with anti-SARS medical workers in Hong Kong (2)

(83) 上不怨天，下不尤人。(《中庸》)
One does not complain against heaven, nor does one blame the people. (*Doctrine of the Mean*)

[My Translation]
One does not complain against heaven, nor does he blame the people.

(84) 疾風知勁草。(《後漢書》)
Strong winds test the strength of the grass. (*History of the Later Han*)

[My Translation]
Work hard. *Strong winds test the strength of the grass.*

(b) *1 October 2003*: Visit to flood victims of the Wei River

(35) 心中為念農桑苦，耳裏如聞飢凍聲。(白居易)
My mind is on the hardship and suffering of the people, and my ears seem to hear the sighs of the people in hunger and cold. (Bai Juyi)

(c) *5 July 2005*: Meeting with drug addicts in Yunnan

(26) 逆水行舟，不進則退。(《增廣賢文》)
A boat sailing against the stream must forge ahead or it will be driven back. (*Ancient Chinese Proverbs*)

[My Translation]
Learning is like rowing a boat against the current: you must forge ahead or you will be driven back.

(8) Meeting with Experts

As the Premier of the State Council, Wen Jiabao often seeks advice from professionals on certain key issues. In the book, a quotation was made when he met health experts on 11-15 April 2008 to discuss healthcare reform.

(72) 啟進善之門。(柳宗元)
Open the door for the fine words. (Liu Zongyuan)

[My Translation]
Broaden the routes by which opinions are conveyed to the authorities and *open the door for the fine words*, and then the moral integrity of the ruler will exceed that of the sage kings at the dawn of civilization.

(9) Expressing Expectations on the Appointment of Officials

A typical example is Wen's messages to Donald Tsang at the two Swearing-in Ceremonies on 24 June 2005 and 9 April 2007.

(a) *24 June 2005*: Words to Donald Tsang at the Swearing-in Ceremony

(87) 士不可以不弘毅。(《論語》)
A gentleman must be strong and resolute. (*The Analects of Confucius*)

[Translation by D.C. Lau][22]
Zengzi said, "A gentleman must be strong and resolute, for his burden is heavy and the road is long."

(b) *9 April 2007*: Words to Donald Tsang at the Swearing-in Ceremony

(88) 死而後已，不亦遠乎。(《論語》)
Only with death does the road come to an end. Is that not long? (*The Analects of Confucius*)

---

[22] Lau, *The Analects*, 71.

[Translation by D.C. Lau][23]
Only with death does the road come to an end. Is that not long?

(10) Visits to Personalities

Wen Jiabao sometimes pays visits to renowned scholars and personalities. His visit to Ji Xianlin on 6 August 2007 can be taken as an example. During the visit, Wen quoted the following saying:

(62) 和合故能諧。(《管子》)
If there is concord and unity, there is harmony. (*Guanzi*)

[Translation by Allyn W. Rickett][24]
If you rear with the "Way," the people will be harmonized.

(11) Visits to Institutions in China

The two institutions that Wen Jiabao visited and mentioned in the book are the Counsellors' Office of the State and the Central Research Institute of Culture and History.

(a) *24 September 2007*: Visit to Counsellors' Office of the State and the Central Research Institute of Culture and History.

(73) 言能聽，道乃進。(《史記》)
When words can be heard, the Way will move forward. (*Records of the Grand Historian*)

[My Translation]
Yi Yin said, "How wise! *When words can be heard, the Way will move forward.*"

(b) *16 January 2009*: Talking with Counsellors of the State Council and Fellows of the Central Research Institute of Culture and History

(67) 文所以載道也。(周敦頤)
Literature is a vehicle of the Way. (Zhou Dunyi)

[My Translation]
Literature is a vehicle to convey the Way.

---

23 Lau, *The Analects*, 71.
24 Rickett, *Guanzi*, 275.

(12) Online Chatting with Netizens

Chatting online is now a very popular way of communication. In recent years, Wen Jiabao has engaged in online chats with Chinese and overseas netizens. During such a chat on 28 February 2009, four quotations were made.

(30) 其興也勃，其亡也忽。(《左傳》)
Its rise is quick; its fall is sudden. (*Zuo's Commentary on the Spring and Autumn Annals*)

[Translation by Hu Zhihui (1996: 115)][25]
Zhuang Wenzhong said, "Songs must be about to flourish. For Yu and Tang took the blame on themselves, *they prospered greatly.* Jie and Zhou threw the blame onto others, and *their fates were sealed in consequence.*"

(109) 凡交，近則必相靡以信，遠則必忠之以言。(《莊子》)
In all intercourse between states, if they are near to each other, there should be mutual friendliness, verified by deeds; if they are far apart, there must be sincere adherence to truth in their messages. (*Zhuangzi*)

[Translation by Burton Watson][26]
In all human relations, if the two parties are living close to each other, they may form a bond through personal trust. But if they are far apart, they must use words to communicate their loyalty.

(18) 鞠躬盡瘁，死而後已。(諸葛亮)
I have devoted my life to serving the people and will always do my best in the service. (Zhuge Liang)

[My Translation]
I have devoted my life to serving the people and will always do my best in the service.

(19) 春蠶到死絲方盡，蠟炬成灰淚始乾。(李商隱)
A spring silkworm keeps producing silk until it dies; a candle keeps giving light until it burns into ashes. (Li Shangyin)

---

[25] Hu, *Zuo Zhuan*, 115.
[26] Burton Watson, trans., *The Complete Works of Chuang Tzu* (New York: Columbia University Press, 1968), 60.

[My Translation]
The silkworm spins silk until its death.
The candle dries its tears until it turns to ashes.

(46) 城門失火，殃及池魚。(杜弼)
A fire on the city gate brings disaster to the fish in the moat. (Du Bi)

[My Translation]
And a fire on the city gate in the State of Song would bring disaster to the fish in the moat.

(13) Offering Words of Encouragement

On 22 May 2008, Wen visited Beichuan Secondary School in Sichuan. He wrote four characters on its blackboard to encourage students who survived the earthquake.

(33) 多難興邦。(《左傳》)
Difficulties rejuvenate a nation. (*Zuo's Commentary on the Spring and Autumn Annals*)

[Translation by Hu Zhihui][27]
It may happen that *their very difficulties result in strengthening their state power* and the enlarging their boundaries.

(14) Messages to Institutions in China

The last category of quotations that have no official translations are Wen's messages to institutions in China, such as his letter to the China Central Television (CCTV), the national TV station of the People's Republic of China and one of China's most influential media outlets, dated 8 April 2004.

(75) 知屋漏者在宇下，知政失者在草野。(王充)
He who knows the leakage of a house lives under its roof, and he who knows the mismanagement of a state stays on its land. (Wang Chong)

[My Translation]
Standing under the eaves, one knows that the house is leaking; in the community one knows that the administration is deficient.

---

[27] Hu, *Zuo Zhuan*, 1059.

[V] Translation of Sources

One of the most difficult tasks of translating the Chinese book into English is the translation of the sources of the quotations. Basically, all the sources can be divided into poems and lines from classics or popular works. 34 quotations, amounting to 27.41 percent, are lines from poems, while the rest are from lines from other types of work, such as essays or philosophical treatises. There are several ways of dealing with these sources, which are more difficult to translate than translating the quotations.

(1) Adopting the Existing Translations

Research is involved when searching existing translations of the source texts. Sometimes, translations of certain works are rather limited. It is therefore not difficult to use an existing translation to render the source text. Take *Guanzi* as an example. There are four quotations from this classical work which has been translated in full by W. Allyn Rickett (1985). The translation of the source of Article 62: "和合故能諧 (If there is concord and unity, there is harmony)" is therefore simple and direct.

(62) 和合故能諧
[出處及釋義]
畜之以道，則民和；養之以德，則民合。和合故能諧，諧故能輯，諧
輯以悉，莫之能傷。
—管仲《管子・兵法第十七》

If you rear with the "Way," the people will be harmonized. If nurture with the Virtue, the people will be united. Since they are harmonious and united, they can be brought in agreement. Since they are in agreement, they can live on intimate terms. Since they live in complete agreement and on such intimate terms no one is able to harm them.
— Guan Zhong, *Guanzi*, "Method of Warfare"

Yet some of the sources, such as *The Analects of Confucius* and *Mencius*, have been amply translated and the decision about what translation to use is a matter that deserves serious consideration. That is related firstly to the availability of the translations in the University Library System of The Chinese University of Hong Kong and other libraries in Hong Kong in general. And it is also related to the quality of translation of the original work. If a quality translation of a specific work mentioned in the book is available at The Chinese University or in private possession, then the translation of the source text would not be problematic.

Take *The Art of War*《孫子兵法》by Sun Wu 孫武 as an example. According to a study conducted by Ms Chen Huanhui 陳煥輝, between 1905 and 2003, there are over forty translations of the work. Her list is far from complete but it serves to illustrate the magnitude of the work of settling on a translation of the source text in the Chinese version of the book. The following is a list of translations made by different hands in different years.

Calthrop, Everard Ferguson, trans., *Sonshi*. Tokyo: Sanseido, 1905.

The Book of War: The Military Classic of the Far East. London: John Murray, 1908

Giles, Lionel, trans., *Sun Tzu on The Art of War: The Oldest Military Treaties in the World*. London: Luzac, 1910.

Machell-cox, E., trans., *Principles of War Sun Tzu*. Colombo, Ceylon: Royal Air Force Warfare Publication, 1943.

Sadler, A. L., trans., *The Military Classics of China*. Sydney, 1944.

Cheng, Lin, trans., *Suen Wuu, The Art of War*. Taipei: The World Book Co. Ltd., 1953.

Griffith, Samuel B., trans., *The Art of War*. Oxford: Clarendon Press, 1963.

Ko, Chen-sien 葛振先, trans., *The Art of War by Sun-Tzu*. Taipei: Chen Chung Book Co. Ltd., 1963.

Tang, Zi-chang 唐子長, trans., *Principles of Conflict: Recompilation and New English Translation with Annotation on Sun Tzu's Art of War*. San Rafael: T. C. Press, 1969.

Clavell, James, ed., *The Art of War by Sun Tzu*. trans. Lionel Giles, London: Hodder and Stoughton.

Yuan, Shibing 袁士檳, ed., *Sun Tzu's Art of War: The Modern Chinese Interpretation by Tao Hanzhang* 陶漢章. New York: Sterling Publishing Co. Inc., 1987.

Cleary, Thomas. *The Art of War*. Boston: Shanmbhala Publications, 1988.

Wing, R. L., trans., *The Art of Strategy*. Seatle, Washington: Main Street Books, 1988.

Luo, Shunde 羅順德, trans.,《孫子兵法》英譯本 (*English Translation of* The Art of War). Taiwan, 1991.

Pu, Yuanming 蒲元明, trans., *Sunzi's Art of War*. Chongqing: Chongqing Publishing House, 1992.

Ames, Roger. *Sun-Tzu: The Art of Warfare*. New York: Ballantine Books, 1993.

Huang, J.H., trans., *The Art of War: The New Translation*. New York: Quill William Morrow, 1993.

Pan, Jiafen 潘嘉玢 and Liu Ruixiang 劉瑞祥, trans., *A Chinese-English Bilingual Reader the Art of War*. Beijing: Military Sciences Publishing House, 1993.

Sawyer, Ralph D., trans., *The Art of War*. Boulder: Westview Press, 1994.

Krause, Donald G., trans., *The Art of War for Executives*. Berkley Publishing Group, 1995.

Zhang, Huimin, trans., *Sunzi: The Art of War with Commentaries*. Beijing: Panda Books, 1995.

Low, C. C. and Associates, trans., *Sun Zi's Art of War*, Singapore: Canfonian, 1995.

Kaufman, Stephen F., trans., *The Art of War: The Definitive Interpretation of Sun Tzu's Classic Book of Strategy*. Tuttle Publishing, 1996.

Luo, Zhiye 羅志野, trans., *100 Sun Tzu's The Art of War*. Beijing: China Translation and Publishing Corporation, 1996.

Yuan, Shibing 袁士檳, trans., *The Art of War*. Beijing: Foreign Language Teaching and Research Publishing House, 1997 / 1999.

Li, David H 李祥甫. *The Art of Leadership: A New-Millennium Bilingual Edition of Sun Tzu's Art of War*. Bethesda, MD: Premier Publishing, 2000.

Lin, Wusun 林戊蓀, trans., *Sunzi: The Art of War, Sun Bin: The Art of War*. Beijing: Foreign Language Press, 2001.

Denma Translation Group, trans., *The Art of War*. Shambhala Classics, 2001.

Minford, John, trans., *The Art of War*. New York: Penguin Group, 2002.

Han, Hiong Tan, trans., *Sunzi's The Art of War*. HH Tan Medical, 2002.

Tarver, D.E., trans., *The Art of War-Sun Tzu's Classic in Plain English with Sun Pin's The Art of Warfare*. Writers Club Press, 2002.

Gagliardi, Gary, trans., *The Art of War: An Illustrated Translation with Asian Perspectives and Insights*. Clearbridge Publishing, 2003.

Wee, Chow-Hou, trans., *Sun Zi Art of War: An Illustrated Translation with Asian Perspectives and Insights*. Prentice-Hall, Pearson Education, 2003.

Cleary, Thomas, trans., *The Art of War: Complete Text and Commentaries*. Shambhala, 2003.

Cantrell, Robert, trans., *Understanding Sun Tzu on The Art of War*. Center For Advantage, 2004.

Sawyer, Ralph D., trans., *The Essential Art of War*. New York: Basic Books, 2005.

Brennan, Paul, trans., *The Art of War for Martial Artists*. Odos Books, 2007.

Mair, Victor H., trans., *The Art of War: Sun Zi's Military Methods*. New York: Columbia University Press, 2007.

Huynh, Thomas, trans., *The Art of War: Spirituality for Conflict*. Skylight Paths Publishing, 2008.

When translating Article 120, Ames's translation of *The Art of War* is reproduced.

[Source Text]
故善用兵者，譬如率然。率然者，常山之蛇也。擊其首則尾至，擊其尾則首至，擊其中則首尾俱至。敢問：兵可使如率然乎？曰：可。夫吳人與越人相惡也，當其同舟而濟，遇風，其相救也如左右手。
－孫子兵法・九地》

[Source Text in Modern Chinese]
善於用兵的人，他指揮的部隊就如「率然」一樣。「率然」，是常山的一種蛇。擊它的頭部，它的尾部彈過來救應；擊它的尾部，它的頭部彈過來救應；擊它的腰部，它的頭尾一齊彈過來救應。或問：軍隊可指揮得像率然一樣嗎？回答是：可以。吳人與越人是相互仇視的，當他們同船過渡突遇大風時，他們相互救助起來如同左右手。

[English Translation by Roger Ames][28]
Therefore, those who are expert at employing the military are like the "sudden striker." The "sudden striker" is a snake indigenous to Mount Heng. If you strike its tail, its head comes to its aid; if you strike its middle, both head and tail come to its aid. Suppose I am asked: can troops be trained to be like this "sudden striker" snake? I would reply: they can: The men of Wu and Yueh hate each other. Yet if they were crossing the river in the same boat and were caught by gale winds, they would go to each other's aid like the right hand helping the left.
—*The Art of War*, Chapter 2, "The Nine Kinds of Terrain."

---

[28] Ames, *Sun-Tzu: The Art of War*, 158.

It is worth noting that in rendering Article 82, the translation of the poem by Yu Youren 于右任 could actually be found on the website in which a full translation of the press conference of Wen Jiabao on 18 March 2003 was provided.

Taiwan: Since the beginning of this year, the Taiwan side has come up with new suggestions and measures to improve the relations across the Taiwan straits. For instance, they have put forward the idea of setting up a mechanism to ensure peace and stability in the cross-strait relationship. They have also done something positive towards the three direct links including the direct shipping and air services. We hope to bring about sound interaction between the two sides of the Taiwan straits. In the past, we have not heard much directly from you on your perspective on the question of Taiwan. We would like to know what is your perspective and what is your knowledge about Taiwan? What will be the major items on the agenda of the new government concerning the work of Taiwan affairs? What expectations do you have on the question of Taiwan?
A: Through you, I would like to extend my best regards to our Taiwan compatriots. The achievement of complete reunification is the common aspiration of all Chinese people, including our Taiwan compatriots. When Taiwan is mentioned, lots of feelings well up. I cannot help thinking of the late *Mr. Yu Youren, a founding member of Kuomintang and participant in the Revolution of 1911. He wrote a poem to express his grief over national division. He wrote such a poem: Burying me on the highest mountaintop so that I can get a sight of my mainland. Mainland I see none, tears of sorrow cascade. Burying me on the highest mountaintop so that I can get a glimpse of my hometown. Hometown I see none, but [it] lives forever in my mind. The lofty sky is deeply blue, the vast wildness not seen through. Oh, boundless universe, would you hear me and this elegy of the nation.* What a touching poem he has written, which strikes a cord on the sentiment of all the Chinese people. The Chinese government will continue to unswervingly pursue the policy of peaceful reunification on the basis of "One Country, Two Systems." We will seek an early resumption of dialogue and negotiation between the two sides on the basis of the "One China-principle. We are against "Taiwan independence." We will continue to support more economic and cultural exchanges between the two sides. We want to bring about the early achievement of three direct links. We hope to make bigger progress in the process towards peaceful reunification.

The source of Article 82 is as follows:

葬我於高山之上兮，
望我大陸。
大陸不可見兮，只有痛哭！

葬我於高山之上兮，
望我故鄉。
故鄉不可見兮，永不能忘。
天蒼蒼，野茫茫，
山之上，國有殤。
－于右任〈望大陸〉

Bury me on the highest mountaintop
so that I can get a sight of the Mainland.
Mainland I see none, tears of sorrow cascade.
Bury me on the highest mountaintop
so that I can get a glimpse of my hometown.
Hometown I see none, but [it] lives forever in my mind.
The lofty sky is deeply blue, the vast wildness not seen through.
Oh, boundless universe, would you hear me and this elegy of the nation.
－ Yu Youren, "Getting a Sight of the Mainland."

(2) Providing New Translations

Another major method of putting the source text into English is by producing a new translation of the source text. Take Article 1 as an example. After searching and re-searching in the libraries of the Chinese University, it was found that the line quoted by Wen Jiabao: "苟利國家生死以，豈因禍福避趨之," which comes from the poem 〈赴戍登程口占示家人〉("For My Family on My Journey to Yili"), has not been translated. A new translation was produced based on the source text and its modern version provided in the book:

力微任重久神疲，再竭衰庸定不支。
苟利國家生死以，豈因禍福避趨之。
謫居正是君恩厚，養拙剛於戍卒宜。
戲與山妻談故事，試吟斷送老頭皮。
我憑微薄力量擔當重任，早已感到疲憊。體弱才庸，無法繼續支撐。
但若對國家有利，我定會生死以之，決不因個人禍福而避之。
只把我流放到邊疆是皇恩浩蕩，對我來說，做一個戍卒正是養拙之道。
我開玩笑地對妻子說，你也嘗試做首「斷送老頭皮」那樣的詩送我吧！

[My Translation]

I'm an incapable man with heavy responsibilities,
So I feel exhausted long time ago.
Weak and mediocre, I can't hold out any longer.

I'll do whatever is in the interests of my country even at the cost of my own life;
I would never shrink back because of personal weal and woe.

To live in banishment is a great favour from the emperor.
To be a garrison soldier at the frontier is a way of hiding my poor ability.
I joked with my wife and said
"Why don't you try writing a poem entitled 'My Old Man Has Lost His Life.'"
—Lin Zexu, "For My Family on My Journey to Yili."

(3) Adapting Existing Translations

Another way of translating the source text is to adapt slightly, sometimes maybe drastically, the existing translations of some popular poems or writings. Take〈遊子吟〉(The Song of a Travelling Son) by Meng Jiao 孟郊 as an example. This is a very popular poem which praises the love of one's mother. It has been translated by many hands. To fit the context of Wen's speech he gave in Australia, a new English version was produced, again based on the modern version provided in the book.

[Source Text]
慈母手中線，遊子身上衣。
臨行密密縫，意恐遲遲歸。
誰言寸草心，報得三春暉？
－孟郊〈遊子吟〉

慈母手中拿着針線，正給準備外出的兒子縫製衣服，母親擔心兒子走後遲遲回不來，就把衣服的針腳縫得密密的，使它更結實更耐穿一些。正像小草難以報答春天的陽光一樣，兒子怎能報答母親那深重的恩情呢？

[My Translation]
Needle in the hands of a loving mother,
Works into the clothes on the travelling son.
She sets the stitches firmly and closely before he departs,
For fear that he will be slow to return.
Who can say that the heart of inch-long grass,
Will repay the sunshine of spring.
—Meng Jiao, "Song of a Travelling Son."

In the speech he gave in Australia on 3 April 2006, Wen Jiabao said, "Everyone has two mothers: one is our birth mother, the other is mother country. Sometimes he started to miss mother country after a seven- or eight-day visit, he said. The long one stays in a foreign country, the more one misses one's mother country."

All the representatives applauded loudly in response to Premier Wen, and softly recited with Premier Wen "The Song of a Traveling Son": "Needle in the hands of a loving mother / works into the clothes on the traveling son / She sets the stitches firmly and closely before he departs / For fear that he will be slow to return / Who can say that the heart of inch-long grass / will repay the sunshine of spring."

(4) Revising Existing Translations

Sometimes a revised translation was produced based on an existing translation, such as the quotation of Article 15: "衙齋臥聽蕭蕭竹，疑是民間疾苦聲 (Lying in bed in my den, I heard the rustling of bamboos outside, and it just sounded like the moaning of the needy)," written by Zheng Xie (1693-1765).

[Source Text]
衙齋臥聽蕭蕭竹，疑是民間疾苦聲。
些小吾曹州縣吏，一枝一葉總關情。
－鄭板橋〈濰縣署中畫竹呈年伯包大中丞括〉

[Modern Text Translation]
臥在衙門的書齋裏靜聽竹葉沙沙響動，總感覺是民間百姓呼飢號苦的喊聲。在州縣裏像我們這些地位卑下的小官吏，民間每一件小事如同畫上每一條枝葉，總牽動着自己的感情。

[Translation by Anthony Cheung and Paul Gurofsky]²⁹
In my office study, resting, I listen to bamboos
    Mournful in the wind.
Is it the suffering of the oppressed people,
    I wonder?
We minor officials, what can we do
    But bestow all our concern on just this single
    Branch and leaf?
－Cheng Pan-ch'iao: "In the Magistrate's Office at Wei Hsien I Paint a Bamboo to Present to My Senior, Governor Pao K'uo."

---

²⁹ Anthony Cheung and Paul Gurofsky, eds. and trans., *Cheng Pan-Ch'iao: Selected Poems, Calligraphy, Paintings and Seal Engravings* (Hong Kong: Joint Publishing Co. (H.K.), 1987), 39.

[My Translation]

Lying in bed in my den, I heard the rustling of bamboos outside,
And it just sounded like the moaning of the needy.
We minor officials,
Though it may be as trivial as this single branch and leaf,
I will always bestow all our concern only if it is among people.
— Zheng Banqiao, "In the Magistrate's Office at Weixian I Paint a
Bamboo to Present to My Senior, Governor Bao Kuo."

[VI] Conclusion

There is much to be learned from this translation exercise. To translate
anything by a prominent statesman is a tall order for any translator. The
translation must be politically correct, factually accurate, officially
acceptable, stylistically appropriate, terminologically consistent, and
textually faultless. To achieve these criteria, searching and researching
must be considered as a proper method of translation. Searching refers in
general to efforts to find translations which are officially provided by the
websites such as "gov.cn," "xinhua.net," "people.cn," or Chinese Embassies.
Researching, in the context of this particular exercise, can be hyphenated
as re-searching to refer to the multiple levels of search that have to be
conducted before an equivalent can be found for a specific quotation or
source text. Researching can also be interpreted as a single word to refer to
the research efforts that are needed to locate the optimal translation out of
the potentially usable translations.

Perhaps a more detailed explanation of the above criteria may be in
order as a way of concluding this paper.

Politically Correct

The first criterion, to be politically correct, is of paramount importance
for political leaders of China, or indeed of any country. This can be seen in
the translation of Article 43: "察其言，觀其行 (Hear what they say and
then watch what they do)," which records an interview of Wen Jiabao by
Leonard Downie, an executive editor of the *Washington Post*, on 21
November 2003.

Downie asked Wen Jiao: "Dalai Lama has declared that he is not
seeking independence for Tibet. Do you foresee face-to-face meetings with
Dalai Lama and representatives of China?" Wen Jiabao replied by saying,
"Regrettably, Dalai Lama has not genuinely given up his position of Tibet
independence and has not given up the separatist activities aimed at

splitting the motherland. He also has not recognized that Taiwan is an inalienable part of Chinese territory. We have taken note of the recent remarks by the Dalai Lama but we still need to watch very carefully what he really does." Any mistranslation of the above remarks by Wen Jiabao would be of serious consequence.

Factually Accurate

To be factually accurate is also of great importance. Take Article 32 as an example. The Chinese text is as follows:

[Source Text]
2005 年，對於中國煤礦業來說是黑色的一年。據國家安全生產監督管理總局統計，全年煤礦共發生死亡事故 3341 起，5986 人失去生命。
2 月 14 日，遼寧省阜新孫家灣煤礦發生瓦斯爆炸，214 人死亡。
3 月 19 日，山西省朔州市平魯區細水煤礦發生重大瓦斯爆炸事故，72 人遇難。
7 月 11 日，新疆阜康神龍煤礦發生瓦斯爆炸事故，83 人死亡。
8 月 7 日，廣東梅州興寧市大興煤礦發生透水事故，121 人死亡。
11 月 27 日，黑龍江七台河礦難，171 人死亡。
12 月 7 日，河北唐山劉官屯煤礦發生重大瓦斯爆炸，108 名礦工遇難。

[My Translation]
The year 2005 was a black year to the coal mining industry. According to the statistics of the State Administration of Work Safety of the People's Republic of China, a total of 3,341 fatal incidents occurred in coal mines in the entire year, and 5,986 persons lost their lives.

On 14 February, there was a gas explosion at the Sunjiawan Coal Mine in Fuxin in Liaoning Province, involving 214 deaths.

On 19 March, there was a huge gas explosion at the Xishui Coal Mine in the Pinglu District of Shuozhou City in Shanxi Province, involving 71 deaths.

On 11 July, a blast at the Shenlong Coal Mine in Fukang in Xianjiang Uyghur Autonomous Region killed 83 persons.

On 7 August, flooding at the Daxing Coal Mine in Xingning Country in Meizhou City drowned 121 miners.

On 27 November, a mining disaster at Qitai River in Heilongjiang killed 171 people.

On 7 December, a huge explosion at the Liuguantun Coal Mine in the Kiping District of Tangshan City in Hebei Province claimed 171 lives.

Officially Acceptable

The translation of works by a political figure should also be officially acceptable. To achieve this, the use of official websites is very important. Article 90: "今年花兒紅了，明年花更好 (The red bauhinia is beautiful this year, and it will be even more beautiful next year)" may be cited as an example. As Wen Jiabao changed the wording of the original prose-poem by Ouyang Xiu, it would not be easy to come up with a translation of this recast line. By searching the Internet and finding the relevant website, an officially acceptable translation could be readily produced.

We begin by searching for the original Chinese text and its English translation provided by the website of the Ministry of Foreign Affairs of the People's Republic of China.

[Chinese Text of the Press Conference]
[香港經濟日報記者]：「今年是香港回歸祖國十週年，請問總理，對香港回歸十年以來的表現，您有什麼樣的評價？我們也知道總理一直非常關心香港的情況，您對香港未來的發展有什麼樣的希望？在今天剛剛通過的政府工作報告裏提到要加快金融體制改革。請問總理，香港作為一個國際金融中心，在我們國家未來的金融體制改革方面可以扮演什麼樣的角色？謝謝總理！」
[溫家寶]：「香港回歸十年了，確實走過了一條不平凡的道路。這十年來，中央政府堅定不移地貫徹執行『一國兩制』、『港人治港』、高度自治的方針，堅決按基本法辦事，沒有干涉屬於香港特別行政區內部的事務。
香港特別行政區政府團結香港市民，戰勝了亞洲金融風波等一系列的困難，經濟得到穩定、恢復和發展，民生得以改善。
香港目前處在一個重要的發展時期。我一直認為，香港背靠祖國、面

對世界，有著特殊的區位優勢。香港有著世界最自由的經濟、國際上
廣泛的聯繫，有著較為完備的法制和經濟管理人才的優勢。
香港的金融中心地位以至航運中心地位、貿易中心地位，是其他地區
不可替代的。值此香港回歸十年之際，我請你轉達對香港同胞的問候，
我衷心希望香港更加繁榮，更加開放，更加包容，更加和諧！紫荊花
盛開了，今年花兒紅了，明年花更好！」

[Official Translation of the Press Conference]
Hong Kong Economic Times: This year marks the 10th anniversary of
Hong Kong's return. What is your assessment of Hong Kong's performance
in the past 10 years since its return? We know that you care a lot about
Hong Kong. What are your expectations of Hong Kong's future growth? In
the Report on the Work of the Government just adopted today, you talked
about the need to accelerate the reform of the financial system. Hong Kong
is an international financial center. What role do you expect Hong Kong to
play in the reform of China's financial system?
Premier: In the past 10 years since its return, Hong Kong has made
significant strides on the road of advancement. Over the past 10 years, the
Central Government has faithfully observed the principles of "one country,
two systems" and "Hong Kong people administering Hong Kong with a
high degree of autonomy", and acted in strict accordance with the Basic
Law. It has not intervened in the administration of the Hong Kong SAR
Government. The Hong Kong SAR Government has united the Hong Kong
people in overcoming a number of difficulties, including the Asian
financial turmoil. As a result, Hong Kong has maintained economic
stability, recovery and growth and improved the well-being of its people.
Hong Kong is now at a crucial stage of development. It has always been
my view that backed by the mainland and facing the world, Hong Kong
has a unique geographical advantage. It has the freest economy in the
world, extensive links with the rest of the world, a full-fledged legal
system and a rich pool of managerial expertise. Hong Kong's position as a
financial center, shipping center and trade center is irreplaceable. On the
occasion of the 10th anniversary of Hong Kong's return, I would like to ask
you to convey my warm greetings to our Hong Kong compatriots. I
sincerely hope that Hong Kong will become more prosperous, open,
inclusive and harmonious. The bauhinia flower is in full bloom. The red
bauhinia is beautiful this year, and it will be even more beautiful next year.

The following are the source text in the Chinese book and its
translation, based on the official translation provided by the Ministry of
Foreign Affairs.

[引句背景]

2007 年 3 月 16 日上午，十屆全國人大五次會議閉幕會結束後，溫家寶在人民大會堂舉行的記者招待會上接受採訪。

香港《經濟日報》記者問：「今年是香港回歸祖國十週年。請問總理，對香港回歸十年來的表現，您有什麼樣的評價？我們知道總理一直非常關心香港的情況。請問總理，對香港未來的發展有什麼樣的希望？」溫家寶首先肯定了香港 10 年間取得的成就，並表示相信香港的地位不會被取代。他最後借媒體轉達了對香港同胞的問候，說：「值此香港回歸十年之際，我請你轉達對香港同胞的問候，我衷心希望香港更加繁榮，更加開放，更加包容，更加和諧！紫荊花盛開了，今年花兒紅了，明年花更好！」

[My Translation]
[Background to the Quotation]

On the morning of 16 March 2007, at the conclusion of the Fifth Session of the Tenth National People's Congress (NPC) Wen Jiabao met the Chinese and foreign press and answered their questions at a press conference held at the Great Hall of the People.

A reporter of the *Hong Kong Economic Times* asked: "This year marks the Tenth anniversary of Hong Kong's return. What is your assessment of Hong Kong's performance in the past ten years since its return? We know that you care a lot about Hong Kong. What are your expectations of Hong Kong's future growth?"

Wen Jiabao first affirmed the recent achievements of Hong Kong, and was confident that its position in the region would not change. Lastly, he conveyed through the media his greetings to the people of Hong Kong: "On the occasion of the 10th anniversary of Hong Kong's return, I would like to ask you to convey my warm greetings to our Hong Kong compatriots. I sincerely hope that Hong Kong will become more prosperous, open, inclusive and harmonious. The bauhinia flower is in full bloom. The red bauhinia is beautiful this year, and it will be even more beautiful next year."

Stylistically Appropriate

This criterion is extremely relevant in the case of translating this book in which sayings and lines from different genres are given. A number of examples can be cited to illustrate the importance of producing the original style.

(1) Couplet
身無半畝，心憂天下。
手釋萬卷，神交古人。
－左宗棠對聯

[My Translation]
I don't have half an acre of land to myself,
    But I care about my people across the land.
I read over ten thousand books
    And am spiritually attracted to the ancient.
－Couplet of Zuo Zongtang

Sometimes, it is necessary to produce a new translation based on an old one, such as the translation of the source text of Article 122: "萬物並育而不相害，道並行而不相悖 (All living creatures grow together without harming one another, ways run parallel without interfering with one another)."

[Chinese Source Text]
仲尼祖述堯舜，憲章文武；上律天時，下襲水土。辟如天地之無不持載，無不覆幬，辟如四時之錯行，如日月之代明。萬物並育而不相害，道並行而不相悖。小德川流，大德敦化。此天地之所以為大也。
－子思《中庸》

[Modern Version]
孔子繼承堯舜的傳統，以文王、武王為典範，上遵循天時，下符合地理。就像天地那樣沒有什麼不承載，沒有什麼不覆蓋。又好像四季的交錯運行，日月的交替光明。萬物一起生長而互不妨害，道路同時並行而互不衝突。小的德行如河水一樣川流不息，大的德行敦厚純樸、化育萬物。這就是天地的偉大之處啊！

[My Translation, Based on James Legge][30]
Zhongni handed down the doctrines of Yao and Shun, as if they had been his ancestors, and elegantly displayed the regulations of Wen and Wu, taking them as his model. Above, he harmonized with the times of heaven, and below, he was conformed to the water and land. He may be compared to Heaven and Earth, in their supporting and containing, their overshadowing and curtaining, all things. He may be compared to the four seasons in the alternating progress, and to the sun and moon in their successive shining. All living creatures grow together without harming one another; ways run parallel without interfering with one another. The

---

[30] James Legge, trans., *The Four Books* (Changsha: Hunan Publishing House, reprint 1996), 57.

smaller energies are like river currents; the greater energies are seen in mighty transformations. It is this which makes Heaven and Earth so great.
— Zisi, *Doctrine of the Mean*

Terminologically Consistent

In translating "About the Author" 作者簡介 or "About the Work" 作品簡介 in each article, one of the main difficulties is the rendition of proper names and official titles. In proper name translation, Hanyu pinyin Romanization has been used. As regards the translation of official titles, terminological consistency has been achieved by following the designations given in Charles O. Hucker's book *A Dictionary of Official Titles in Imperial China.*[31] An example is given below.

[作者簡介]
林則徐 (1785-1850)，清代愛國政治家、思想家、詩人。福建省福州市人。嘉慶十六年 (1811) 進士，授翰林院編修，先後擔任過江南道監察御史、東河河道總督、江蘇巡撫、湖廣總督等職。

[My Translation]
Lin Zexu (1785-1850), a patriotic politician of the Qing Dynasty, thinker and poet, was a native of Fuzhou in Fujian Province. He received the *jinshi* degree, the highest in the imperial examinations, in 1811, and served as Compiler at the Hanlin Academy. He also served as Censor of the Jiangnan Circuit, Director General of Conservation for the Eastern Stretches of the Yellow River, Governor of Jiangsu, and Governor-general of Hunan and Hubei.

Textually Faultless

Meticulous proofing is mandatory for translated works involving prominent leaders in China. Due to time constraints, this book is not free of typographical errors. And to meet the deadline of publication for the Frankfurt Book Fair, some of the errors spotted remained uncorrected in the final version. It is hoped that a corrected version will be available if the book has a second edition or printing.

Translations can never be perfect. There are always holes to be filled, errors to be corrected, and styles to be polished. Perhaps imperfections should be accepted as allowances for us to improve ourselves.

---

[31] Charles O. Hucker, *A Dictionary of Offical Titles in Imperial China.* (Stanford: Stanford University Press, 1985).

YU HUA'S FICTION HEADS WEST...
OR DOES IT?

ALLAN H. BARR
DEPARTMENT OF ASIAN LANGUAGES AND LITERATURES
POMONA COLLEGE

The work of Yu Hua 余華 (1960-), one of China's best-known contemporary authors, has been translated into over twenty languages, and in some European countries, notably France, it has been greeted with enthusiasm. In the United States, however, where all the book-length English translations of his work have been done, reception has generally been more muted. There are many reasons why Yu Hua's work, like that of other Chinese authors, has had difficulty making an impact in the United States, and it is questionable whether any English translation of his work, however outstanding, would succeed in altering that basic state of affairs; problems of translation, indeed, may be the least significant of the issues that have a bearing on the reception of Yu Hua's work. It may be instructive, nonetheless, to review the history of Yu Hua's work in English translation, for its twists and turns offer insights into the challenges facing contemporary Chinese literature as it reaches out to a Western audience.

Yu Hua's fiction to date has been rendered into English by quite a range of translators, with little continuity from one work to the next. Eight separate individuals have tried their hand at translating one or more of his early short stories, and five different pairs of hands have been involved in translating his four novels into English. With each new translator adapting in his or her own fashion to Yu Hua's narrative world, his fiction in English is perhaps a somewhat less coherent body of work than the original set of Chinese titles, but the active involvement of multiple translators has also meant that the bulk of Yu Hua's work has now appeared in English, most of it under the imprint of a major publishing house.

Yu Hua began to write in his early twenties, when he was employed as a dentist in his native province of Zhejiang, although it was not until 1987 that he hit his stride; his story "On the Road at Eighteen," published that year in *Beijing wenxue*, marks the true launch of his career as an author. Yu Hua's early stories, it is generally agreed, are perverse and disconcerting works of fiction; Liu Kang has characterized them as "couched in fragmented narrative sequences, twisted syntax, and grotesque images and metaphors."[1] One might think it would be a considerable challenge to translate such pieces successfully. In practice, however, their literary effects come over quite well in English. As an example of Yu Hua's early writing, let us consider the opening paragraph of his story "Summer Typhoon":

白樹走出了最北端的小屋，置身於一九七六年初夏陰沉的天空下。他在出門的那一刻，陰沉的天空突然向他呈現，使他措手不及地面臨一片嘹亮的灰白。於是記憶的山谷裏開始回蕩起昔日的陽光，山崖上生長的青苔顯露了陽光迅速往返的情景。[2]

Bai Shu emerged from the most northerly of the little houses to find himself under the somber summer sky of 1976. The sky appeared before him suddenly when he came out the door, and its resonant grey expanse took him by surprise. The valley of memory then began to reverberate with the glimmer of days gone by, although the moss that grew on its stony sides marked how swiftly that light had passed.

Here, as often in Yu Hua's early work, sentences are fairly short, with a clear grammatical structure; language is quite refined, with some unconventional, if mannered, turns of phrase that find natural counterparts in English.

Eight of Yu Hua's best early stories, originally published in China between the years 1987 and 1993, were translated by Andrew F. Jones and published in 1996 under the title *The Past and the Punishments*, a collection that is generally regarded as a fine piece of work. *Publishers Weekly* described the translation as "stately," with "passages of exquisite grace,"[3] and the *New York Times*, in one of its relatively rare reviews of contemporary Chinese fiction, also gave the translation its seal of approval.[4] Let us consider the opening lines of the title story:

---

[1] Liu Kang, *Globalization and Cultural Trends in China* (Honolulu: University of Hawaii Press, 2004), 106.

[2] "Xiaji taifeng" 〈夏季颱風〉, *Yu Hua zuopin ji* 《余華作品集》 (Beijing: Zhongguo shehui kexueyuan, 1995), 1:221. This story was first published in 1991. The translation that follows is mine.

[3] *Publishers Weekly*, 24 June 1996.

[4] *New York Times*, 27 October 1996.

一九九零年的某個夏日之夜，陌生人在他潮濕的寓所拆閱了一份來歷
不明的電報。然後，陌生人陷入了沉思的重圍。電文祇有「速回」兩
字，沒有發報人住址姓名。陌生人重溫了幾十年如煙般往事之後，在
錯綜複雜呈現的千萬條道路中，向其中一條露出了一絲微笑。翌日清
晨，陌生人漆黑的影子開始滑上了這條蚯蚓般的道路。[5]

On a summer night in 1990 in his humid apartment, the stranger opened
and read a telegram of unknown origins. Then he sank into a deep reverie.
The telegram consisted of just two words – "return quickly" – and
indicated neither the name nor the address of the sender. The stranger,
filing through the mists of several decades of memory, saw an intricate
network of roads begin to unfold before him. And of this intricate network,
only one road could bring the slightest of smiles to the stranger's lips.
Early the next morning, the lacquer-black shadow of the stranger began to
slide down that serpentine road like an earthworm.[6]

Although one could query one or two of the translator's choices in the last
couple of sentences—the repetition of "intricate network," for example, or
the handling of the earthworm simile—for the most part this passage reads
well and reflects the meaning and spirit of the original quite accurately; a
high standard of translation is sustained throughout the book. However,
despite a certain degree of critical success, *The Past and the Punishments*,
published by a university press, appears to have had little commercial
appeal and its readership is largely confined to students of Chinese
literature.

After the publication of *The Past and the Punishments* in 1996, a full
seven years followed before another book by Yu Hua appeared in
English—reflecting, perhaps, both the relative dearth of literary translators
and American publishers' lack of confidence in the profitability of Chinese
fiction in the U.S. market.[7] An even longer delay ensued before the
publication in English of Yu Hua's debut novel, *Zai xiyu zhong huhan*
《在細雨中呼喊》(1991), my translation of which was released in 2007
by Anchor Books under the title *Cries in the Drizzle*. Described by one

---

[5] "Wangshi yu xingfa" 〈往事與刑法〉, *Yu Hua zuopin ji*, 1:32.

[6] *The Past and the Punishments*, trans. Andrew F. Jones (Honolulu: University of
Hawaii Press, 1996), 114.

[7] By comparison, other European languages have been much quicker off the mark.
The French translation of *To Live* was published as early as 1994, nine years
before the English edition; the French translation of *Xu Sanguan mai xue ji* was
released in 1997, six years before the English edition; the Italian translation of *Zai
xiyu zhong huhan* came out in 1998, nine years before the English edition.

critic as Yu Hua's "first and last avant-garde novel," [8] *Cries in the Drizzle* bears some similarities to Yu Hua's later full-length works, but in its structure—"a serpentine, episodic collection of anecdotes forming a kind of Maoist-era kinderscenen," as *Kirkus Reviews* put it—and in its literary language it is more closely affiliated with his early short fiction. Its first-person account of childhood trauma and family dysfunction is told through the eyes of Sun Guanglin, a sensitive observer who leaves his small hometown in south China to pursue a university education and an unspecified but presumably intellectual career in the capital. The novel is dominated by Sun's mournful, sardonic voice and his graceful, evocative language, which is equally at home with references to Western literary classics as with quintessentially Chinese four-character phrases. With the strong architecture of its sentences and its rich lexicon, *Cries in the Drizzle* lends itself well to translation, as we can see in the following example from the second-half of the book:

> 正如樂極生悲一樣，我祖父在那個雨水飛揚的上午，對着天空發出極其勇敢的吼叫以後，立刻掉進膽怯的深淵，讓我看到了他不知所措後的目瞪口呆。孫有元在張嘴吼叫的那一刻，吃驚地感到體內有一樣什麼東西脫口而出，那東西似乎像鳥一樣有着美妙的翅膀的拍動。[9]

> "Joy at its fullest gives way to sorrow," they say, and no sooner had my grandfather delivered his fearless challenge to the heavens on that rain-swept morning than he was cast back into an abyss of misgivings, dumbstruck and lost. At the moment when he opened his mouth to yell, he felt to his astonishment that there was something inside him desperate to find an outlet, something that took wing with sublime, birdlike ease.[10]

Arguably the bleakest of Yu Hua's novels—"A grainy montage of suffering and survival, by turns morbid and mordant," according to one reviewer[11]— *Cries in the Drizzle* has found one or two admirers among its American reviewers, but rather few readers. It is certainly much less well-known than Yu Hua's second novel *Huozhe* 《活著》 (1992) and third novel *Xu Sanguan mai xue ji* 《許三觀賣血記》 (1995), English translations of which were both released in 2003 under the titles *To Live* and *Chronicle of a Blood Merchant*. These two books are written in a very different style from his early short stories and from *Cries in the Drizzle*:

---

[8] Liu, *Globalization and Cultural Trends in China*, 113.
[9] *Zai xiyu zhong huhan* (Haikou: Nanhai, 1999), 183-84.
[10] *Cries in the Drizzle*, trans. Allan H. Barr (New York: Anchor, 2007), 191.
[11] *Kirkus Reviews*, 15 August 2007.

they are works of "plain realism,"[12] written, as Richard King puts it, in "straightforward, colorful, and highly readable prose," using "short clauses and easy colloquial style."[13] Both novels use a relatively simple and limited vocabulary of fewer than two thousand characters.[14]

One might think that these books would be excellent candidates for translation into English, and indeed the translations have won plaudits from readers on Amazon.com and have been accorded high praise by at least one specialist in modern Chinese literature, who has hailed them as "admirable renditions," "masterful translations which are faithful to the voice of the original and work well as novels in English."[15] At the same time, both translations have come in for a fair amount of criticism. *Kirkus Reviews*, for example, delivered a rather damning verdict on the English rendition of *To Live*, faulting it for "infelicitous phrasing, shapeless sentences, vacuous rhetorical questions and fragments of American-inflected slang." "Yu Hua is an internationally celebrated author," the reviewer concluded, "but this English version of his work doesn't tell us why."[16]

Though it garnered a number of favorable reviews, Yu Hua's third novel, published under the title *Chronicle of a Blood Merchant*, has also failed to impress some of its English readers, and its sales have been disappointing. A reviewer for one American newspaper wrote: "The translated English of *Chronicle* is not beautiful, and at times can be slightly difficult to follow because it is a rigid, technical style."[17] A reader's review posted on Amazon.com under the title "Lost in Translation" is more explicit: "Something about this book is uncomfortable. The English is awkward; the language is choppy and void of emotion; it is hard to relate to the characters."[18] To anyone who has read this novel in the original Chinese, which is extremely fluid and idiomatic, brimming with emotion and full of characters with whom it is easy to empathize, this seems an astonishing thing to say.

---

[12] On "Plain Realism," see Liu Kang, 123-25.

[13] See Richard King's review of the English translations on the *Modern Chinese Literature and Culture* webpage, http://mclc.osu.edu/rc/pubs/reviews/king.htm.

[14] See "Yu Hua fun fact," http://paper-republic.org/authors/yu-hua/.

[15] See Richard King's review.

[16] *Kirkus Reviews*, 15 July 2003.

[17] *The Tennessean* (Nashville), 25 January 2004.

[18] See review by H. Huggins at http://www.amazon.com/Chronicle-Blood-Merchant-Yu-Hua/dp/1400031850/ref=sr_1_4?s=books&ie=UTF8&qid=132086 3389&sr=1-4.

Oddly, then, the translations of Yu Hua's more difficult early works tend to win positive reviews, while the translations of the seemingly easier, more accessible works—one of them by the gifted translator of *The Past and the Punishments*—are not always viewed so favorably. How do we account for this paradox? Perhaps we need to take a closer look at Yu Hua's "plain realism."

Let us consider first the opening lines of Yu Hua's 1995 short story "Victory":

一個名叫林紅的女人，在整理一個名叫李漢林的男人的抽屜時，發現一個陳舊的信封疊得十分整齊，她就將信封打開，從裏面取去了另一個疊得同樣整齊的信封，她再次打開信封，又看到一個疊起來的信封，然後她看到了一把鑰匙。[19]

Lin Hong, tidying Li Hanlin's drawer, came upon an old envelope, neatly folded, and when she opened it she found another envelope inside, folded just as neatly. Inside it she found a third envelope, and in that she found a key.

The vocabulary here is simple and straightforward, concrete and down-to-earth, with none of the literary flourishes that we encounter in Yu Hua's early stories and his debut novel. But for the translator there is a question lurking: should one try to respect Yu Hua's sentence units and render them intact in English, or should one feel free to break up a long sentence wherever convenient, given that there is often not a great deal of connective tissue bonding one clause to the next?

In this particular case, there is perhaps not very much at stake—although one may feel something has been lost by disengaging Lin Hong's discovery of the key from the rest of Yu Hua's original sentence. In other situations, however, the rearrangement of a Yu Hua sentence into multiple English sentences may have more serious repercussions. Let us consider an example from Chapter 20 of *Xu Sanguan mai xue ji*. Here, as so often in this book, Xu Sanguan—Yu Hua's everyman hero—has something he wants to get off his chest, and the impression is of a flood of words pouring effortlessly from his mouth. Depending on how we understand the ellipsis points in this passage, it consists of only one sentence, or at most two:

---

[19] "Nüren de shengli" 〈女人的勝利〉, *Huanghunli de nanhai* 《黃昏裏的男孩》 (Beijing: Xin shijie, 1999), 48. The translation is from my unpublished manuscript, "Boy in the Twilight."

你聽我說，我今天賣了血以後，沒有喝二両黃酒，也沒有吃一盤炒豬
肝，所以我現在沒有力氣……不是我捨不得吃，我去了勝利飯店，飯
店裏是什麼都沒有，祇有陽春麵，飯店也是鬧災荒，從前的陽春麵用
的是肉湯，現在就是一碗清水，放一點醬油，連蔥花都沒有了，就是
這樣，還要一元七角錢一碗，從前一碗面祇要九分錢。[20]

Listen to me. After I sold blood today, I didn't drink two shots of yellow
rice wine or eat a plate of fried pork livers. That's why I don't have any
energy left. It's not that I didn't want to eat some. I went over to the
Victory Restaurant, but all they have is plain soup noodles. They're in the
same boat as everyone else, what with the famine. Used to be they'd make
their soup noodles with meat broth, but now they use boiled water and
throw in a little soy sauce. They don't even have any spring onions. That's
the way it is. And they're asking one *yuan* seventy *fen* a bowl. Before it
was nine *fen* a bowl.[21]

In the English translation, the words used are generally well chosen and
true to the spirit of the original book. But what are the consequences when
one or two Yu Hua sentences are converted into no fewer than eleven
English sentences? Not only does the passage lose cohesion, it seems to
me, but the pace slackens and the protagonist's voice is muffled by the
succession of full stops. It no longer comes across as a spontaneous
outpouring of words, but is halting, even perhaps a little pedantic. Xu
Sanguan is in danger of becoming a bit of a bore, something he never is in
the Chinese original.

In order to replicate more fully the rhythm and cadence of Xu
Sanguan's speech, it might have been more effective to render it in no
more than two or three English sentences, such as:

Listen, after I sold blood today, I didn't drink my jug of rice wine and eat
my plate of pig livers, and that's why I've got no energy now. It's not that I
didn't want to spend money, and I went over to the Victory Restaurant all
right, but you can't get anything there except plain soup noodles—they're
in the same boat as everyone else, what with the famine. It used to be
they'd make their noodles with meat broth, but now it's just boiled water
with a squirt of soy sauce—forget about the scallions—and they're asking
one-seventy for that, when it used to be nine *fen*!

---

[20] *Xu Sanguan mai xue ji* (Nanjing: Jiangsu wenyi, 1996), 123.
[21] *Chronicle of a Blood Merchant*, trans. Andrew F. Jones (New York: Pantheon, 2003), 127.

Here is another example of a single continuous utterance, this time from the last chapter of the book, where Xu Sanguan's wife Yulan takes their eldest son to task for his perceived disrespect to his father:

一樂，你今天這樣說你爹，你讓我傷心，你爹對你是最好的，說起來他還不是你的親爹，可他對你是最好的，你當初到上海去治病，家裏沒有錢，你爹就一個地方一個地方去賣血，賣一次血要歇三個月，你爹為了救你命，自己的命都不要了，隔三、五天就去賣一次，在松林差一點自己賣死了，一樂你也忘了這事。[22]

And Yile, what you just said hurts the most of all. How could you, of all people, talk to your dad that way? You've always been his favorite son. And he's not even your real dad. Even so, he's always been so good to you. When you had to go to the hospital in Shanghai, he sold blood everywhere he could along the way, because we didn't have any money for the hospital bill. You're supposed to wait at least three months each time you sell blood, but to save *your* life, your dad put his own life in danger. He sold blood after three days, then sold it again five days later. And he almost died in Pine Grove because of it. But you seem to have forgotten about that.[23]

Again, although there is little fault to find with the translator's choice of words, the division of the passage—all one sentence in Yu Hua's Chinese—into shorter units seems to have a slight deadening effect, and one begins to wonder whether more effort should have been made to enhance the flow of Yulan's speech, perhaps rather along these lines:

Yile, it really upsets me to see you talking this way to your dad, when he loves you most of all. Why, he's not even your real dad, but he's always gone the extra mile for you, like that time you had to go to Shanghai for treatment and we didn't have enough money to pay the hospital bill, so he went off selling his blood in one place after another. They say you need three months' rest after selling blood, but to save your life your dad was all ready to lose *his*, selling blood once every four or five days until he practically sold his life away in Pine Grove—Yile, how could you forget that?

In the English translation of *Huozhe*, questions of narrative flow are also an issue, but they tend to be overshadowed by a more fundamental problem—the translator's handling of Yu Hua's language, the simplicity of which can make him both easy and difficult to translate. On the one

---

[22] *Xu Sanguan mai xue ji*, 251-52.
[23] *Chronicle of a Blood Merchant*, 250-51.

hand, the meaning of Yu Hua's words is usually perfectly transparent, and without very much thought one can readily give an intelligible rendering in English. However, when working with such spare and economical language, the stakes become higher: because the translator has so few Chinese words to work with, the English words chosen have to be just right, or the effect will be blunted. *Jingque* 精確 ("exact," "precise") is the term often used by Chinese critics to describe Yu Hua's language, and this is the quality that the translator needs to capture to convey Yu Hua's work to best effect. It is an issue that comes to the fore when we consider the English translation of *Huozhe*.

Let's consider an example from the opening pages of *To Live*:

> 我年輕時吃喝嫖賭，什麼浪蕩的事都幹過。[24]

> "When I was young, I ate, drank, whored and gambled—I took part in every disreputable thing there was." [25]

This is a typical remark by the book's main character, Xu Fugui, as he looks back wryly on his misspent youth. At first glance, the English translation seems a faithful enough transcription of the original: each word in the Chinese is given some kind of equivalent in English. The difference is that whereas the Chinese is completely idiomatic, the English is not. Although "吃" is a natural component of such Chinese phrases as "吃喝玩樂" or "吃喝嫖賭," in English we see nothing very problematic about eating—unless it is to excess—nor do we talk about "taking part" in "disreputable things." A more idiomatic rendering of Fugui's remark might be something like: "In my youth I just wallowed in dissipation: boozing, whoring, gambling—you name it."

Further into the novel, Fugui recalls a landmark event during the period when he and his wife were living separately after his squandering of the Xu family fortune:

> 家珍走後兩個多月，托人捎來了一個口信，說是生啦，生了個兒子出來，我丈人給取了個名字叫有慶。[26]

> Two months after Jiazhen left, a messenger came with an oral message. He said Jiazhen had given birth to a boy. My father-in-law had named him Youqing.[27]

---

[24] *Huozhe* (Shanghai: Shanghai wenyi, 2004), 10.

[25] *To Live*, trans. Michael Berry (New York: Anchor, 2003), 13.

[26] *Huozhe*, 45.

Again the English version does not compare well with the original Chinese. If one looks up *kouxin* "口信" in a standard Chinese-English dictionary, one will find it translated as "oral message," sure enough, but who actually would say this in English, and what self-respecting author would place "messenger" and "message" so close together? The limp rendering presents only information—and less information than Yu Hua's original, failing to make clear who sent the messenger. The Chinese text, on the other hand, does not simply report developments, for it is rich in feeling as well, conveying both Jiazhen's pride and Fugui's happiness at the birth of a son. Possibly the translator felt that "生啦" was redundant, given its overlap with "生了個兒子出來," but in the Chinese context, of course, the difference between the two expressions is crucial, and the combination has an important role to play in evoking the parents' sense of achievement. A more effective translation might have been:

> A couple of months after Jiazhen left, she sent word back that she'd had the baby—and it was a boy this time! My father-in-law had given him the name Youqing.

The question of voice is, I think, critical to the success of translations of Yu Hua. Yu Hua has often recalled that when writing *Cries in the Drizzle* he discovered—to his astonishment and delight—that characters have their own voices, and ever since he has emphasized that an author needs constantly to be listening to his characters as they speak. To catch the full flavour of the spoken word in Yu Hua's novels, a translator must strive to reach that same level of engagement with his characters.

In a review of the French translation (by Nadine Perront) of *Xu Sanguan mai xue ji*, Nicolas Zufferey has argued that in places her translation is too refined, failing to reflect the vocabulary and the cultural level of the narrator and using turns of phrase that are too elegant for the situation at hand.[28] A similar problem crops up at times in the English translation of *Huozhe*. Let's consider Fugui's recollections of Youqing's tragic death in the aftermath of the Great Leap Forward, a harrowing sequence that culminates in what is surely one of the most powerful lines in the whole book:

---

[27] *To Live*, 53.

[28] Nicolas Zufferey, *"Les Lumières de Hong Kong* and the mist of translation," *China Perspectives* 46 (March-April 2003), http://chinaperspectives.revues.org/document262.html.

我看着那條彎曲着向城裏的小路，聽不到我兒子赤腳跑來的聲音，月光照在路上，像是撒滿了鹽。[29]

I gazed at that narrow, twisting trail that led to town and heard the sound of my son running barefoot. The moonlight was shining on the trail, giving the illusion that a layer of salt had been sprinkled along it.[30]

It is a mystery why "聽不到" is here translated as "heard," but of more immediate concern is the rendering of the last twelve characters in Yu Hua's sentence—which evoke, through two beautifully compressed clauses, an arresting image that rings true on both a visual and an emotional level. While the simple, unpretentious language of the original is in keeping with the voice of an uneducated farmer like Fugui, in the translation the phrase "giving the illusion that" introduces a fussy editorial note that is absent from the Chinese text, and the wordiness of "a layer of salt had been sprinkled along it" weakens the force of the original comparison. A more accurate translation might read something like this:

> I gazed at the little path that wound its way toward town; no more would I hear the pounding of my son's bare feet as he came running home. The path gleamed in the moonlight, as though coated with salt.

So far we have been examining passages from the portions of *To Live* narrated by Xu Fugui. Let us consider now a sentence from the very first paragraph of the book, where the action is recounted by the narrator of the frame story, an educated young man from the city who stumbles upon Fugui and his ox when conducting ethnographic research in the countryside.

我喜歡喝農民那種帶有苦味的茶水，他們的茶桶就放在田埂的樹下，我毫無顧忌地拿起積滿茶垢的茶碗舀水喝，還把自己的水壺灌滿，我與田裏幹活的男人說上幾句廢話，在姑娘因我而起的竊竊私笑裏揚長而去。[31]

I had a special affection for that bitter tea that farmers brew. There would always be a bucket of just that kind of tea under a tree by the ridge between the fields, and without a second thought I would ladle out enough to fill my tea-stained bowl. Once I'd filled it to the brim, I'd start bullshitting with

---

[29] *Huozhe*, 133.

[30] *To Live*, 161.

[31] *Huozhe*, 2.

some of the male workers. The girls would whisper among themselves and then stifle their chuckles as I'd swagger off.[32]

In the published translation, the young urbanite's portion of the narrative is italicized, so as to distinguish it immediately from Fugui's reminiscences, which nestle inside the young man's narrative frame. But in Chinese a change of typeface is quite unnecessary; because the distinction between the two narrative voices is clearly embedded in the language itself, and no Chinese reader is likely to confuse the two. The elevated literary language of the urbanite narrator—represented here by such phrases as "毫無顧忌," "因我而起," "竊竊私笑," and "揚長而去"—regularly causes problems for the translator and leads to some peculiar renderings in the English edition.[33] In this particular example, the decision to translate "說上幾句廢話" as "start bullshitting" produces an incongruous effect, for the phrase is flanked by polished literary diction and clearly calls for less vulgar language. Unlike the French edition of *Xu Sanguan mai xue ji*, where the language was too refined, here the language is too crude.

In the English translation of *To Live*, problems of this kind are all too common. Here is a snatch of dialogue from early in the book, a passer-by's greeting to Fugui when he emerges from his disastrous last night of gambling:

早啊，徐家少爺。...瞧你這樣子，都成藥渣了。[34]

Good morning, Mr. Xu! ... Look at you! You look like shit![35]

Faced with the challenge of translating "都成藥渣了" (literally, "you've become the dregs of a herbal medicine," or, more colloquially, perhaps "You look like something the cat brought in"), the translator has simply taken the easy way out, despite its inconsistency with the respectful salutation a few words earlier.

---

[32] *To Live*, 3.

[33] Consider the following: 四周的人離開後的田野，呈現了舒展的姿態，看上去是那麼的廣闊，無邊無際，在夕陽之中如同水一樣泛出片片光芒。(*Huozhe*, 176): "After everyone around us left the fields, an atmosphere of unfolding emerged, which seemed so broad, so vast, so boundless. The setting sun was like a pool of water giving off ray after ray of light" (*To Live*, 213).

[34] *Huozhe*, 21-22.

[35] *To Live*, 27.

The English translation of *To Live*, in short, is an opportunity missed. *Huozhe* has to rank as something of a classic of Chinese literature in the post-Mao era, and Western readers' interest in the book has been significantly boosted by the success of Zhang Yimou's 1994 film adaptation. Through that cinema connection, *To Live* has gained higher visibility than Yu Hua's other novels and is used quite commonly in American high school and college courses on modern East Asia, but the English translation lacks the finesse that could have endowed the book with broader appeal, and it has never been picked up by a publisher in the United Kingdom.

Yu Hua's long-awaited fourth novel, *Xiongdi* 《兄弟》, was published in two volumes in China, in August 2005 and March 2006. Although it sold many hundreds of thousands of copies in China, *Xiongdi* was seen as a disappointment by many Chinese readers and critics and suffered some scathing criticism. In the West, it has been greeted much more warmly, particularly in France, where it enjoyed excellent sales and was awarded a literary prize. Prior to its release in the United States, it was speculated that *Brothers* might prove to be "China's first successful export of literary fiction"[36] and, although it failed to become a best-seller, the English translation by the wife-and-husband team of Eileen Cheng-yin Chow and Carlos Rojas did receive much more press attention than Yu Hua's previous novels. Reviews, however, have been somewhat mixed. At one end of the spectrum, it was hailed by Maureen Corrigan of National Public Radio as a "terrific literary achievement" —"a tremendous novel in tone and historical scope and narrative technique;"[37] the *New Yorker* described it as "impressive," a "relentlessly entertaining epic;" and in *Financial Times* Margaret Hillenbrand rated it "a tour-de-force."[38] Some reviewers were more equivocal: *Kirkus Reviews* found *Brothers* "insistently declarative and overemphatic," "a deeply flawed great novel,"[39] and Jess Row, in the *New York Times Review of Books*, found reading *Brothers* in English "a daunting, sometimes vexing and deeply confusing experience."[40] In a more forthrightly negative vein, Julia Lovell offered the following evaluation: "In the interests of achieving a faithful likeness, [Yu Hua] has discarded the cool, sparing voice that made his name as a serious novelist

---

[36] Pankaj Mishra, "The Bonfire of China's Vanities," *New York Times Magazine*, 23 January 2009.
[37] http://www.npr.org/templates/story/story.php?storyId=100423108.
[38] *Financial Times*, 23 May 2009.
[39] *Kirkus Reviews*, 15 December 2008.
[40] *The New York Times Book Review*, 8 March 2009.

between the 1980s and 1990s, and opted for crudeness in almost every respect."[41]

While crudeness is certainly a feature of *Xiongdi* in its original Chinese edition, it is further accentuated in the English translation. In Yu Hua's novel, the speech of the main character, Li Guangtou, is liberally laced with the expression *tamade*, which—though to my mind a rather mild expletive[42]—is almost invariably translated in *Brothers* as "fuck," and sometimes even as "motherfucker".[43] Frequent repetition of this uncouth phrase runs the risk of growing tiresome to the English reader, and it may detract from one of the most memorable scenes in the book. In Chapter 17, following the beating to death of Song Fanping (father of Song Gang, stepfather of Li Guangtou) by Red Guards in the previous chapter, a bystander (a man named Tao Qing, we learn later) is prevailed upon to take Song Fanping's body home in a cart. Tao Qing, naturally enough, does not relish this assignment, and he remains in a state of high dudgeon during much of the journey back to the boys' house, but he is basically portrayed as a decent and sympathetic man—one of the most positive figures in the book, in fact. He is far from insensitive to the grief of the two boys, and his impatience with them is always expressed within clear limits; the aggressiveness of the English expletives used to render his speech seems to me foreign to the scene in the Chinese original:

那人拉起板車又對着李光頭和宋鋼吼叫起來：「說！家在哪裏？」
　　宋鋼使勁搖頭，他哀求道：「去醫院。」
　　他媽的，」那人扔下板車說，「人都死啦，還去個屁醫院。」[44]

Hoisting the end of the cart, the man barked at them, "Quick! Where's home?"
　　Song Gang furiously shook his head. He pleaded, "Take him to the hospital."
　　"Fuck." The man threw down the cart. "He's already dead. What fucking hospital would we go to?"[45]

---

[41] *The Guardian*, 18 April 2009.

[42] As Lu Xun pointed out long ago, *tamade*—which he dubbed China's "national oath"—can actually be used in quite amiable contexts. See his essay "Lun 'tamade'" 〈論「他媽的」〉, *Fen* 《墳》 (rpt.; Beijing: Renmin wenxue, 1980), 228.

[43] *Brothers*, trans. Eileen Cheng-yin Chow and Carlos Rojas (New York: Pantheon, 2009), 104, 259.

[44] *Xiongdi* (Shanghai: Shanghai wenyi, 2005), I: 157.

[45] *Brothers*, trans. Chow and Rojas, 131.

Here not only is *tamade* rendered as "fuck," but *pi* becomes "fucking," erasing the difference between these two expressions in favor of a one-size-fits-all swearword. Tao Qing's exasperation at his predicament might have been better conveyed with a rendering such as this:

> The man grabbed the handles of the cart. "All right then, where's your house?" he yelled.
> Song Gang shook his head desperately. "Let's go to the hospital," he begged.
> "The hell with that!" The man flung down the cart. "He's dead, can't you see? What would be the point, for heaven's sake?"

The sometimes excessive use of obscenity, unfortunately, is symptomatic of a larger tendency to overlook distinctions in the original and use a single rendering in English where multiple words are used in Chinese. Expressions which differ slightly but significantly in their weight and meaning in the original novel such as "喜氣洋洋地問" (*Xiongdi* II: 5), "驚喜萬分地…說" (II: 8), "揮舞着手欣喜地說" (II: 11), "驚喜地…跳了起來" (II: 27), "興奮地叫着" (II: 28), "高興地哇哇大叫"(II: 116), "激動地說" (II: 192), and "興致勃勃地問" (II: 234) become respectively "asked excitedly" (*Brothers*, p. 217), "gestured excitedly" (p. 219), "waved excitedly and added" (p. 222), "excitedly jumped up" (p. 237), "excitedly cried out" (p. 237), "cried out excitedly" (p. 312), "said excitedly" (p. 377), and "excitedly asked" (p. 416). Repetition of this kind leads, perhaps, to a certain flattening effect in the English edition.

It has been twenty years since W.J.F. Jenner cautioned that "the craft of literary translation from modern Chinese into English needs far more thought than it usually gets,"[46] and a reading of Yu Hua's work in English suggests that this advice is still worth heeding. At the same time, although *Brothers* has not pleased all reviewers, for most readers the translation does the job perfectly well, judging from its many favorable on-line ratings. And, interestingly, the positive reception that the novel has received abroad—as compared with the storm of criticism it had to endure in China—may have been a factor in Yu Hua's decision to prepare his next book for release first in translation. *China in Ten Words* (original title: *Shige cihuili de Zhongguo* 《十個詞彙裏的中國》), a collection of essays that combine social commentary with personal reminiscence, was

---

[46] See Jenner's "Insuperable Barriers? Some Thoughts on the Reception of Chinese Writing in English Translation," in *Worlds Apart: Recent Chinese Writing and its Audiences*, ed. Howard Goldblatt (Armonk, N.Y.: M.E. Sharpe, 1990).

first published in September 2010 in a French edition, with English, German, Italian, Korean, and other versions to follow—but no mainland Chinese edition. To a certain degree, given the political sensitivity of some of the topics covered, [47] the decision to go straight to a foreign-language edition is unavoidable, but it also reflects the author's confidence that his work in translation can find an appreciative audience abroad. Despite the checkered history of Yu Hua's fiction in English translation, it has succeeded gradually in getting noticed and—in one form or another—his work seems assured of further exposure to the Western reading public.

---

[47] Excerpts from the opening chapter, recalling popular resistance to martial law in May 1989, were published in Yu Hua, "China's Forgotten Revolution," trans. Allan Barr, *New York Times*, 30 May 2009.

SUBJECTIVITY, TRADITION, AND TRANSLATION OF TAIWAN LITERATURE

KUO-CH'ING TU
DEPARTMENT OF EAST ASIAN LANGUAGES AND CULTURAL STUDIES
UNIVERSITY OF CALIFORNIA, SANTA BARBARA

In 1544 the first documentation of Taiwan appeared in world history records: When the first Portuguese ship passed by the island on the way to Japan, the sailors on board saw the green and luxuriant mountains and, amazed at their beauty, exclaimed, "*Ilha Formosa*" (the Beautiful Island). An accurate depiction of the island appeared for the first time in 1625 in a navigation map published in the Netherlands.

The modern history of Taiwan has spanned about four hundred years, beginning in the mid-sixteenth century from the late Ming and early Qing (Manchu) Dynasties, through various political phases, namely, occupation by Spanish and later Dutch (1624-1662) colonists, followed by the short-lived Dynasty (1661-1683) of Zheng Chenggong, who expelled the Dutch and fought the Qing to restore the Ming, only to be conquered by the Manchus in 1683. Taiwan was under the rule of the Qing Dynasty until 1895, when the Manchu government was defeated in the first Sino-Japanese War; according to the resulting Shimonoseki Treaty, Taiwan and the Pescadores (Penghu) were ceded to Japan as a colony, which lasted for fifty years (1895–1945). After World War II, the Nationalist government took over administrative control of the island and imposed martial law for almost forty years (1949-1987), and finally, after repeal of martial law, Taiwan became the democratic society that it is today.

As far as the modern history of Taiwan is concerned, there are two epoch-making events that have had a great influence on the society and culture of this island: the end of Japanese colonial rule in 1945 and the lifting of martial law under the Nationalist government in 1987. With the end of colonial rule, all political measures and the developments resulting from them changed completely from a Japan-centred to a China-centred orientation. The repeal of martial law permitted a Taiwanese consciousness to gain ground, and a Nativist movement rose to confront the China-oriented leitmotiv which had previously dominated all social, political, and cultural fields. In other words, from the end of World War II until the onset of the 1970s, literature in Taiwan claimed to be Chinese literature; but after the debate on regional literature in the 1970s, Taiwanese awareness became ever stronger and, in the light of the social reality in Taiwan at the time, people started to reexamine Taiwan's native culture, which heretofore had been neglected.

In fact, before the 1980s, for political and historical reasons, Taiwan literature, and even Taiwan-related studies as a whole, were not a common subject of academic research. At the end of the 1970s, mainland China adopted an open-door policy and began to encourage its scholars to undertake the study of Taiwan literature—which has since become a practical and prominent field of study in China. However, in Taiwan one had to wait until 1987, when martial law was lifted and the consequent freedom engendered fundamental changes in the social and political realities of Taiwan. Then scholars in Taiwan became energetically engaged in research on Taiwan literature and its native culture. Thus, after the 1980s, a new concept of Taiwan literature emerged, which diverges from the perspective that it is Chinese literature. By the 1990s, these studies had become an international phenomenon, attracting scholarly attention and research interest from Japan, Germany, France, and the United States.

In the historical development of Taiwan literature, Taiwan's subjectivity has become more and more conspicuous, as reflected in English and Japanese translations since the 1980s. The images of Taiwan's subjectivity, represented at different times in various anthologies, can be summarized as follows:

> During the period of anti-Communism of the 1950s, under the particular political circumstances, Taiwan, representing Free China, was distinguished from the Communist Mainland. Taiwan as represented in the anthologies of the 1960s was influenced by Western modernism and demonstrated originality in artistic expression, but thematically the works appeared indistinct and showed no individuality, and therefore incurred the criticism of modernist poetry and provoked the debate on regional literature during the 1970s. Before then, some literary anthologies from Taiwan had attempted to "represent" literature from China, or hoped to "replace" mainland China with Taiwan literature, to "fill" the vacuum in literature during the Cultural Revolution period. Following the regional literature debate, Taiwanese consciousness emerged, and many writers concerned with the social realities began to embrace Taiwan, so that realistic images of Taiwan reflected in the literary works became more and

more pronounced. After the repeal of martial law in the 1980s, Taiwanese consciousness became even more conspicuous. This trend has been reflected to some extent in the anthologies pertaining to those periods. Since editors of English anthologies to date do not have a strong sense of Taiwanese consciousness, Taiwan literature has been categorized as part of the grand tradition of China's new literature, indicating that, although Taiwan literature has its originality, it is still inseparable from the Chinese literary tradition. This is seen, for example, in *The Unbroken Tradition: An Anthology of Taiwan Fiction Since 1926*, edited by Joseph S. M. Lau (1983), or *The Columbia Anthology of Modern Chinese Literature*, edited by Joseph S. M. Lau and Howard Goldblatt (1995), in which literature from Taiwan is classed with literature from China and Hong Kong as a component of Chinese literature or literatures in Chinese worldwide. (See "Taiwan wenxue xingxiang jiqi guoji yanjiu kongjian: cong Ying-Ri fanyi de quxiang tanqi" [The Image of Taiwan Literature and Its International Studies: The Case of Different Orientations in English and Japanese Translations], *Proceedings of the International Conference on Postwar Taiwan Literature: Culture, Identity, Social Change*. Taipei: The Council for Cultural Affairs, June 2000.)

However, what is Taiwan literature? What characterizes Taiwan literature? In what way is Taiwan literature distinguished from the literature of China? Those questions epitomize the exploration of the subjectivity of Taiwan literature.

The development of literature cannot be separated from the works created within the context of time and space, and the time and space described in the literary works of Taiwan must be closely tied to Taiwan and its people. Therefore we can take land and people as the two fundamental factors of literature, and define Taiwan literature as follows: Works that, through the artistic technique of literature, express concerns with Taiwan and the life and destiny of its people; that is, an example of Taiwan literature is a written work expressing its aesthetic value and conscious identity with the land of Taiwan and the Taiwanese people, their society, history, and culture.

With respect to the four fundamental components of a literary work—author, reader, the language used for expression, and the world described in a work—the author, reader, and language do not necessarily bear an absolute relation to Taiwan. However, the literary world expressed in a work is most important as the place where subjectivity exists. The subjectivity of Taiwan literature exists in all the features and visages of living beings described in the works, which are intertwined with the land and destiny of the Taiwanese people, their society, history, and culture in the past, present, and future. This subjectivity is the spiritual backbone with which to build up the tradition of Taiwan literature, which can be observed from the perspectives of land, people, and history. These three angles can also be used to observe and study the literature in any region of the world. Taiwan literature is bound to have the aroma of the earth of Taiwan; it expresses the joys and grief of the Taiwanese people, and reflects the paths and vestiges of Taiwanese history. In other words, land, people, and history constitute a prism with which to examine the subjectivity of Taiwan literature. The subjectivity of Taiwan literature is constituted by Taiwan's unique geographical location, its people and society, and its historical development, and the literature produced from this uniqueness has a path of development different from that of the new literature developed in China.

In Taiwan the development of the new literature began during the Japanese occupation period, with the publication of the magazine *Taiwan Seinen* (*Taiwanese Youth*) in 1920, and Lai Ho's first prose "Wu-ti" ("Without Title") in 1925; his first story "*Dounaore*" ("Festival High Jinks") in 1926 marked the first writing in vernacular Chinese in Taiwan. Lai Ho is thus recognized as the father of Taiwan's new literature, and other major writers appeared and matured during the 1930s, with writings in both Chinese and Japanese.

It was a common belief in the pre-1980s Taiwan literary world that the development of Taiwan literature was kindled by the new literature of the May Fourth movement in China, brought to Taiwan by mainland writers in 1949. However, that was rectified at the end of 1970 by the poet Ch'en Ch'ien-wu, who asserted that modern poetry in Taiwan developed from twin rootstocks. He said, "We may consider the roots of this poetry as having two sources. People generally consider the source of the root that directly stimulated the bloom was the Modern School advocated by Dai Wangshu and Li Jinfa which Chi Hsien and Ch'in Tzu-hao brought from China. The second source was *l'esprit nouveau* of Modernism received during the Japanese colonial period, through the practice by Yano Hōjin and Nishikawa Mitsuru under the influence of the literary world in Japan." ("*Taiwan xiandaishi de lishi he shirenmen*" ["The History of Modern Poetry and Poets in Taiwan"], *Li* [*Bamboo Hat*] poetry magazine No. 40, December 1970).

This view is particularly significant in correcting the historical view on the history of Taiwan literature. Concerning the development of Taiwan literature, in addition to the fact that it has progressed in one continuous line originating with the new literature of the May Fourth movement in China, one has to accept the other long-neglected rootstock as a source— modernism, as practiced by Taiwanese writers during the Japanese occupation period via the literary circles in Japan. One cannot deny the fact that Taiwanese writers during the Japanese occupation period availed themselves of the Japanese language and followed the literary world of Japan to observe the trends of world literatures, and that Yang Ch'ih-ch'ang was directly influenced by Japanese surrealism advocated by Nishikawa Junzaburō; as a result, in 1933 there appeared an avant-garde magazine *Fūsha* (Le Moulin) advocating surrealism. Although its duration was short-lived, it sufficed to prove that this kind of surrealistic poetry style appeared in Taiwan as an avant-garde art form in the 1930s, but did not happen in the poetic circles of China at that time.

Taiwan's literary tradition must be established in the context of Taiwan's history. Tradition should not merely connote adherence to conventions or following in the footsteps of one's predecessors; as T. S. Eliot remarked, tradition involves the historical sense. The sense of history is a consciousness of lasting value that transcends time. In this sense, a masterpiece is a work that transcends the passage of time, remains fresh and new virtually forever, and thus becomes a classic. A nation's literary tradition is comprised of the classical works created by its writers in every generation. A creative work that has wrung out a writer's heart, as Ezra Pound observed, must "be new and stay new" in order to become a classic and merge into the eternal tradition. A classic with a historical sense has the value of the timeless and the temporal and, as Eliot has pointed out, these qualities together are what makes a writer traditional. In accordance with this viewpoint, Taiwan literature's tradition must be established on the classical works produced by Taiwanese writers from one generation to another.

The judgment and recognition of classical works in Taiwan literature certainly will reflect the different opinions of different people. In addition to the above-mentioned land, people, and history as three perspectives to examine the subjectivity of Taiwan literature, the intrinsic aesthetic value of the works and the extrinsic social and cultural values and influences also deserve consideration. Since the classical value lies in the timeless and universal values, the test of time and appreciation by readers of different languages through translations are also a touchstone for determining the classical value of a work. Taiwan literature under Japanese rule was excluded from Japanese literature as "*gaichi bungaku*" (literature of an outlying region), and, as seen by the China-centred, it has been discussed in terms of "*bianjiang wenxue*" (literature of the border area) as a tributary of Chinese literature. Therefore the appeal of Nativist literature in Taiwan implies the significance of root-searching, root-striking, and self-identification.

As explained above, Taiwan's subjectivity is closely bound up with the social and historical development in Taiwan. Subjectivity should be considered the touchstone for a work to become a classic in the history of Taiwan literature. Classical works of Taiwan literature will inevitably have the spirit and consciousness of Taiwanese subjectivity and, as a creative art, must display the common experience of true human nature and life experience, that is, both the particularity of Taiwan's subjectivity and the universality of art dealing with common human nature. This precisely is the justification for the appreciation and translation of Taiwan literature into foreign languages.

Since the nineties Taiwan literature has become a subject of study that has attracted international scholars' attention, and the scholarly research can be divided into the categories of studies on writers, studies on works, cultural criticism, textual research, historical investigation, and translation into foreign languages. The research thus achieved, includes the exploration of the originality and characteristics of Taiwan literature, its lineage of tradition, its main streams in development, and its historical authenticity, all of which factors will be conducive to defining the canons of Taiwan literature. The definition and characteristics of Taiwan literature thus constructed will provide the justification for the selection of representative works to be translated into English or other foreign languages as well as the criteria for selecting writers and their works for translation.

Since 1996, as a joint project between UCSB and the Council for Cultural Affairs in Taiwan, we have been publishing *Taiwan Literature: English Translation Series*, to introduce English readers to the voices of Taiwan from recent publications in Taiwan, namely, Taiwanese writers' and scholars' viewpoints on their own literature, and to enhance the study of Taiwan literature from international perspectives. The biannual journal has a focus for each issue and the contents of each issue comprise critiques, fiction, essays, poems, and studies. We have published twenty-six issues to date in thirteen years, and the themes include the following: "Taiwan Literature as a Subject of Study," "The Study of Taiwan Literature: An International Perspective," "Aboriginal Literature in Taiwan," "The Nativist Voice of Taiwan Literature," "Literature and Social Concerns," "Urban Literature and the Fin de Siècle in Taiwan," "Travel and Visiting One's Homeland," "Taiwan Literature, Nature, and Environment," "Taiwanese Folk Literature," "Children's literature in Taiwan," "Women's Literature in Taiwan," "Taiwan Literature and History," "Taiwan Literature and Folklore," "Lai Ho, Wu Cho-liu and Taiwan Literature," "Taiwan Literature and Hakka Culture," " Taiwan

Literature and the Ocean," "Mountains, Forests and Taiwan Literature," "Taiwan Literature during the Period of Japanese Rule," "Taiwan Literature and Home-Longing," "Taiwan Literature and Childhood," "Taiwan Literature and the February 28 Incident," "Myths and Legends of Indigenous Peoples in Taiwan," "Special Issue on Yeh Shih-t'ao," and "Special Issue on Yang Ch'ih-ch'ang."

Building on the foundation of the journal, the Center for Taiwan Studies at UCSB takes one step further to launch a second long-term publication project: *Taiwanese Writers Translation Series*. Different from the journal, this series aims at English translation of masterpieces or selected representative works of Taiwanese writers and at bilingual publication of anthologies. While the journal develops a theme for each issue, exposing various aspects of Taiwan literature and exploring its horizontal breadth, the *Taiwanese Writers Translation Series* will focus instead on the writer, with the objective of demonstrating the vertical lines of development and to display the historical positions of major writers and the lineages of literary traditions in Taiwan. This series targets scholars of contemporary Chinese literature and cultural studies as its readership, on the assumption that Taiwan literature will be taken as an important emphasis for those who teach contemporary Chinese literature, comparative literature, and world literatures in Chinese at the university level. With continuing effort and development, this series will ultimately serve as a guide for understanding the historical development of Taiwan literature and, by making the works accessible to a broader readership through translation and bilingual publication, will help deepen the research in Taiwan literature among international scholars as well as understanding for readers in general.

The development of Taiwan literature reflects Taiwan's unique historical sense, social realities, and life experiences, and thus differs from works seen in the contemporary literature of China. The differences have nothing to do with being better or worse, but demonstrate different contextual backgrounds—in time and space, cultural concerns, and literary worlds. Since both are primarily written in the Chinese language, it is unquestionable that both will become important components of world literatures in Chinese.

Taiwan literature should be like a flower of art rooted in the soil of Taiwan. Facing the opposing views between the China-centric and the Taiwan-oriented, we would rather hope that Taiwanese writers could transcend the intertwining ideology of political powers and set their sights beyond Taiwan and China with the whole world in view to create more artistic works with classical values that transcend time and space, which will compel translators to introduce Taiwan literature to the world. Thus Taiwan literature can not only contend in beauty and fascination with literature from China, it will become a particularly thriving branch in the garden of world literatures in Chinese, emitting Taiwan's unique fragrance, and become a part of the enduring classical literature appreciated worldwide. If Taiwan could produce these kinds of masterpieces, I believe the translators of the world would vie with each other to translate Taiwan!

CONTRIBUTORS

Allan H. Barr, Professor of Chinese at Pomona College, received his doctorate from University of Oxford. His dissertation concerned Pu Songling (1640-1715) and *Liaozhai zhiyi*, and literature of the late Ming and early Qing continues to be his main research interest; he is currently writing a book on the *Ming History* Inquisition of 1663. In recent years he has published several translations of contemporary Chinese literature, including Yu Hua's debut novel, *Cries in the Drizzle*, and a volume of essays by the same author, *China in Ten Words*.

Chan Sin-wai 陳善偉, Professor in the Department of Translation at The Chinese University of Hong Kong, is Chairman of the Department and Director of the Centre for Translation Technology. His research interests are computer translation and bilingual lexicography. His recent publications include *Longman Dictionary of English Language and Culture* (Bilingual Edition) (2003), *A Dictionary of Translation Technology* (2004), *A Topical Bibliography of Computer(-aided) Translation* (2008), *A Chronology of Translation in China and the West: From the Legendary Period to 2004* (2009), and *Famous Chinese Sayings Quoted by Wen Jiabao* (2009).

Mark Elvin is Emeritus Professor and Visiting Fellow, School of Culture, History and Language, College of Asia and The Pacific, Australian National University. After his B.A. in history at Cambridge (1959), he wrote his doctoral thesis (1969) on local democracy in Shanghai. In 1969 and 1970 he translated two books by Japanese scholars, the first being Hoshi Ayao's on the Ming tribute grain system, and the second Shiba Yoshinobu's on commerce during the Song Dynasty. Next came an analytical history of China's economy (1973), and an historical atlas of China with Caroline Blunden (1983). He then edited *Sediments of Time. Environment and Society in Chinese History* with Liu Ts'ui-jung (1998), and wrote *The Retreat of the Elephants. An Environmental History of China* (2004). Most recently he has contributed an overview, an introduction, and a chapter on premodern probabilistic thinking in China, for *Concepts of Nature in China and Europe*, edited by Günter Dux and Hans-Ulrich Vogel (Brill, 2010).

Fan Shengyu 范聖宇 is Lecturer in Chinese Studies in the School of Culture, History and Language, College of Asia and the Pacific, at the Australian National University. He received his Ph.D. from Beijing Normal University in 2003. His thesis title was "A Comparative Study of Two English Translation of *Hongloumeng*—Versions by David Hawkes and Yang Xianyi," which was published as《紅樓夢管窺》by China Social Science Press in 2004. He is at present the editor for the bilingual edition of the Penguin Classics *The Story of the Stone*, which will be published by Shanghai Foreign Language Education Press soon.

Tao Tao Liu 劉陶陶 is an Emeritus Fellow of Wadham College, University of Oxford, formerly University Lecturer in Modern Chinese in the Faculty of Oriental Studies. Born in Tianjin, China, and educated in London and Oxford University, she obtained her doctorate on early Chinese literature. She taught Chinese literature at the University of Oxford, working largely on Chinese literature of the early Republican era. She has translated Chinese literature from all eras, such as the poetry of Wen Yiduo, contemporary Chinese poetry, and the fiction of Li Qiao, a Taiwanese writer.

John Minford is Professor of Chinese Studies in the School of Culture, History and Language, College of Asia and the Pacific, at the Australian National University. He was previously Acting Dean of the School of Arts and Social Sciences at the Open University of Hong Kong. His translations include the last 40 chapters of *The Story of the Stone*《紅樓夢》, *The Art of War*《孫子兵法》, and *Strange Tales from a Chinese Studio*《聊齋誌異》, all with Penguin Classics. He has also edited, with Joseph S. M. Lau, *Classical Chinese Literature: An Anthology of Translations* (Vol. 1: From Antiquity to the Tang Dynasty), published by The Chinese University Press of Hong Kong and Columbia University Press. He is currently on leave as Professor in the Department of Translation, The Chinese University of Hong Kong.

Chloë Starr is Assistant Professor of Asian Christianity and Theology at Yale University Divinity School. From 2005-08 she taught modern and classical Chinese literature at Oxford, and prior to that was Senior Tutor of St John's College, Durham University. Her publications include works on both literature and theology; recent volumes include *Red-light Novels of the late Qing* (Brill, 2007), a co-edited volume *The Quest for Gentility in China* (Routledge, 2007) and an edited volume *Reading Christian Scriptures in China* (Continuum, 2008). She is currently editing and translating a Reader in Chinese Christian Theology and working on a volume on Chinese Intellectual Christianity.

Kuo-ch'ing Tu 杜國清 is Lai Ho and Wu Cho-liu Endowed Chair in Taiwan Studies and Director of the Center for Taiwan Studies at the University of California, Santa Barbara (USCB). He was born in Taichung, Taiwan, and graduated from National Taiwan University in 1963 with a major in English Literature. He received his M.A. in Japanese literature from Kwansei Gakuin University in 1970 and his Ph.D. in Chinese Literature from Stanford in 1974. His research interests include Chinese literature, Chinese poetics and literary theories, Taiwan Literature, comparative literature East and West, and worldwide literatures in Chinese. He is the author of numerous books of creative poems in Chinese, as well as translator of English, Japanese, and French works into Chinese and of contemporary works of Chinese into English. He is the co-editor of *Taiwan Literature: English Translation Series*, published by the Forum for the Study of World Literatures in Chinese at UCSB since 1996. His recent poetry collections include *Shanhe lueying* (A Sweeping View of the Mountains and Rivers of China) and *Yuyanji: Jinse wuduan wushi xian* (Jade Smoke Collection: Fifty Variations on Li Shangyin's Songs of the Ornamented Zither), both published by National Taiwan University Press in 2009.

John Wang 王靖宇 is Emeritus Edward Clark Crossett Professor of Humanistic Studies in the Department of East Asian Languages and Cultures at Stanford University. He also at various times held a Distinguished Professorship at Academia Sinica's Institute of Chinese Literature and Philosophy in Taipei, served as Head of the Division of Humanities at Hong Kong University of Science and Technology, and taught as Visiting Professor at University of Hong Kong, The Chinese University of Hong Kong, and National University of Singapore. His major publications cover fields ranging from early Chinese historical narratives to traditional Chinese fiction and drama, Chinese literary criticism, and Chinese language studies.

Laurence K. P. Wong 黃國彬 is Research Professor in the Department of Translation at The Chinese University of Hong Kong and Fellow of the Hong Kong Academy of the Humanities. At The Chinese University of Hong Kong, he was also Professor of Translation from 2006 to 2011, Associate Dean (Research) of the Faculty of Arts from 2007 to 2011, and Director of the Research Institute for the Humanities in 2011. He has published more than 30 books and numerous journal articles, covering such research areas as literary translation, translation studies, classical and modern Chinese literature, European literature, and comparative literature. His translations (between Chinese and European languages) include a 3-volume Chinese *terza rima* version of Dante's *La Divina Commedia*.